Prisoners of the Japanese in World War II

Prisoners of the Japanese in World War II

Statistical History, Personal Narratives and Memorials Concerning POWs in Camps and on Hellships, Civilian Internees, Asian Slave Laborers and Others Captured in the Pacific Theater

by Van Waterford

McFarland & Company, Inc., Publishers
Jefferson, North Carolina, and London

Van Waterford is the penname of Willem F. Wanrooy, born in 1925 in the former Dutch East Indies (now Indonesia), a POW at age 16, incarcerated for 3½ years. Wanrooy became a U.S. citizen in 1966.

British Library Cataloguing-in-Publication data are available

Library of Congress Cataloguing-in-Publication Data

Waterford, Van.
 Prisoners of the Japanese in World War II : statistical history, personal narratives and memorials concerning POWs in camps and on hellships, civilian internees, Asian slave laborers and others captured in the Pacific Theater / by Van Waterford.
  p. cm.
 Includes bibliographical references and index.
 ISBN 0-89950-893-6 (lib. bdg. : 50# alk. paper) ∞
 1. World War, 1939–1945—Prisoners and prisons, Japanese.
I. Title.
D805.J3W38   1994
940.54'7252—dc20   92-51097
                                                                 CIP

©1994 Van Waterford. All rights reserved

Manufactured in the United States of America

McFarland & Company, Inc., Publishers
  Box 611, Jefferson, North Carolina 28640

This work is dedicated to all who suffered
from enemy hands in the Pacific Theater of World War II.

It is especially dedicated to the more than 5,500
European, American, Australian and Indonesian comrades
who were with me on the *Junyo Maru*,
torpedoed on September 18, 1944,
and who disappeared in the depths of the Indian Ocean

Contents

Preface ix
Introduction 1
Chronology of Events 7

I. The Prisoners

1. Prelude to War: Aspects of the Japanese Relating to Their Treatment of Prisoners — 15
2. Occupation and Internment — 31
3. The World of the Camp Prisoner — 53
4. After the War: The World of the Ex-Prisoner — 81
5. War Crimes — 113
6. Conscript Asian Labor: Native Prisoners — 127
7. The POW Medal — 131
8. Andersonville National Historic Site and POW Museum — 135
9. Statistics — 141

II. Reference to Individual Prison Ships and Camps

10. The Prison Ships: The Overseas Transports — 149
11. Prison Camps — 171
    - Japan — 187
    - Formosa (Taiwan) — 214
    - Korea — 217
    - Manchuria — 218
    - China and Hong Kong — 221

French Indochina	234
Burma-Siam Railroad	236
Burma	244
Siam (Thailand)	249
Philippines	250
Malaya and Singapore	265
Sumatra (Dutch East Indies)	269
Java (Dutch East Indies)	296
Borneo	323
Other Islands and Territories	331

Appendices

A. The 1929 Geneva Convention Relating to the Treatment of Prisoners of War	345
B. Japanese Army Regulations for Handling Prisoners of War	353
C. United States Armed Forces Code of Conduct	359
D. Prisoner of War Resistance: U.S. Army Field Manual No. 21-78	361
E. Glossary of Terms Used by POWs	363
F. Special Literary Sources	367
G. Additional Sources of Information	369

Index 371

Preface

The testimonies of tens of thousands of men, women, and children who took part in inhumane incarcerations and hellish movements from one island to another, from one prison camp to another, have, over the years, been assembled in numerous books and reports published in England, the Netherlands, Australia, New Zealand, Canada, and the United States.

The testimonies of prisoners of war and civilian internees about their camp and prison experiences have been expressed to the world in basically two forms: personal, oral accounts to investigators shortly after the war, and notes and diaries written during incarceration.

This last method was not without danger, since the Japanese (for fear that conditions in the camps might become known) did not allow prisoners to write such accounts, and meted out severe punishment when prisoners were discovered to possess any paper or pens or pencils. The notes and diaries were guarded and hidden with the assistance of loyal friends in palm-leaf roofs, in the bottoms of cans and bamboo containers, under the ground, in the bamboo framework of beds, and inside bandages strapped around tropical ulcers on the legs.

This reference book is based on many of these diaries, memoirs, books, letters, documents, historical reconstructions and evaluations, military and personal accounts, bibliographies, and other resources in the United States, England, the Netherlands, and Australia concerning prisoners of the Japanese. It is a systematic, factual compilation from a large volume of this published material—nearly 100,000 pages read by this author.

The images, stories, and experiences of prisoners of the Japanese cannot be expressed solely in the form of lists, data, names, sources, and bibliographies. Therefore, to add the kind of realism needed to provide the researcher with an incentive to delve more deeply into this horrendous part of history, direct quotes from the descriptions of the almost unbelievable experiences endured by prisoners who chose to relate them have been included. Their accounts, from which the history of Japanese prisoners in World War II has been culled, cannot but be subjectively colored. However, the differences expressed in these documents make for the objectivity required in historiography. The Japanese destroyed most of their accounts and documents just before the war's end.

Although not definitive, this volume is the first comprehensive scholarly work on all the types of prisoners of the Japanese: POWs, civilian internees, Asian slave laborers, and prisoners in jails.

A truly exhaustive reference work on prisoners of the Japanese in World War II is impossible because the number of documents, books, personal accounts and diaries, reports, articles, and testimonies dealing with the subject is so great that even a list of them would fill several volumes. These works defy comprehensive description; quite apart from their great number they are written in all of the major languages of the world and in many other tongues as well.

The book is specifically organized to provide the widest range of historical data and factual representation and interpretation.

It is intended for use by scholars, researchers, and librarians who are looking for basic information on the subject in one volume. Although the book is designed primarily to be used in an integrated manner, each of the major sections also stands alone as a specialized reference.

Chapter 1 presents detailed information on the Japanese treatment of POWs and civilian internees.

Chapter 2 discusses all the aspects of being a POW and an internee in Japanese hands.

Being incarcerated is like living in a different world. Chapter 3 presents a wide range of topics related to this world. Chapter 4 provides references to the numerous psychological and physical effects of captivity.

Chapter 5 deals with Japanese-inflicted atrocities on captured prisoners.

Chapters 6 through 9 deal with various aspects of captives and captivity: "Conscript Asian Labor: Native Prisoners," "The POW Medal," the Andersonville POW Museum, and "The Numbers Game."

In Chapter 10, 57 prison ships—"hellships," as they were called—are listed and, when data are available, described.

Chapter 11, the most extensive one, discusses the POW camps and civilian internment centers that the Japanese set up, or established, at one time or another, to house their captives. A total of 378 POW camps and 358 civilian internment centers are referred to.

Escapes are the topic of Chapter 12.

A Chronology begins the volume. Just before the Index may be found the armed forces field manual, *Prisoner of War Resistance*.

Each chapter contains its own list of sources. The book also includes a list of names and addresses of research institutions around the world.

Preface

This work was researched and written as a fulfillment of a promise to more than 5,500 men who perished with the torpedoed *Junyo Maru* hellship in the Indian Ocean on September 18, 1944. With about 800 others, this author survived that disaster.

The book is also a testimony to the hundreds of thousands of men, women, and children—Dutch, British, Australian, New Zealander, American, Chinese, French, Filipino, Indonesian, Malaysian, Tamil, Thai, and Burmese—who died as captives of the Japanese or whose physical and psychological conditions today constantly remind them of this ghastly period in history.

Finally, it is hoped that the unusual experiences of so many POWs and internees may well be of interest to others—that their mental and physical tortures and struggles and their triumphs can be of some help to those who find themselves plunged suddenly into a "sea of troubles."

I am deeply indebted to my wife Mary, who for so many years, every day, had to consider and accept all the idiosyncrasies of an ex–POW and had to endure my many hours of frustration in putting this book together.

My important obligation is to an organization called Ex-Prisoners of War, Inc., especially to Helen Smith, the historian, and Sue Langseth, the editor, of the *Ex-POW Bulletin,* as well as to Philip Cockrill and Ken MacGuire in England and to Professor Gavan Daws in Honolulu.

I should like to express my appreciation to all who have shared their camp experiences by mailing me their diaries, personal accounts, books, and other documents.

"Meminisse anam oblivisci facilior":
It is easier to remember than to forget

Introduction

The world recalls vividly, through a stream of books, movies, and television programs, the atrocities of Dachau and Belsen, Buchenwald and Auschwitz. However, it recalls only dimly some of the atrocities that occurred in the Pacific during World War II—the Bataan Death March, for example, or the events at Sandakan, North Borneo, where hundreds of British Commonwealth prisoners were herded off to a camp and only six survived the march.

And who was responsible for the death of more than a million Southeast Asian slave laborers or the reigns of terror unleashed against Western civilian and military prisoners of war (POWs) in Japanese-occupied areas?

The arc of occupation and horror in Asia, Southeast Asia, and the Pacific extended from Manchuria in the north to the Dutch East Indies in the south and from Burma in the west to the Pacific Islands in the east.

The charges against the Japanese brought forward in the Tokyo War Crimes Trials were chilling. The list of atrocities that surfaced shook all those who were present; the spectators, mostly Japanese men and women, were grim faced and silent.

Current Japanese history books treat the war in the Pacific as if it barely existed (few of them have been published in English). The most valuable documents pertaining to the war were destroyed by the Japanese at the end of the war.[1] In contrast, in the Western countries that were most directly involved in the war against Japan in the Pacific—the United States, Great Britain, Australia, New Zealand, and the Netherlands—voluminous scholarly books, diaries, and personal accounts have been published on the Japanese POW and civilian internment camps in Asia during the occupation years of 1942 to 1945. Some of these works were printed shortly after the war—at a time when emotional reactions on the years of incarceration were still strongly felt—whereas others were put on paper years after the events of imprisonment, which made it often impossible to recapture actual thoughts and impressions of the moment. Most of the authors who wrote much later indicate, however, that the very nature of the events during captivity was such that they were imprinted indelibly on their memories and many details remained clear.

Herein lie the difficulties for the historian: to present a true picture of the Japanese atrocities inflicted on POWs and internees when only a Western viewpoint on these occurrences exists and personal accounts of these atrocities are either biased by speedy presentation or scattered by selective memory because of the time that had passed.

There is also another consideration. Like the pictures and films of the concentration camps, which showed almost unbelievably barbaric cruelties to Jewish and other men, women, and children, the accounts of Japanese atrocities were hardly accepted as truth by Americans and other Westerners. Today, a half century after the events they describe occurred, it is no surprise if the following accounts are taken as fiction by most readers.

A civilian woman internee writing in her diary:

> 26 May, 1945. My remuneration for services rendered—plucking some skinny chickens—is one head and a handful of intestines which I take home and clean in the creek, then make the most tasty chicken broth. The only bits we can't eat are the eyes and the beak. Chicken's eyebrows are a delicacy, and as for the brain! It is a bit small, but very sweet!
> 26 July, 1945. Another thing that worries us is that we are running out of coconut fibre. We use it for tooth brushes, with ash from the kitchen fireplace for toothpaste. Our mouths never feel clean now![2]

The following is from the account of a male POW in Burma:

> For your information, snake tastes like gritty chicken mixed with fish; dog tastes like rather coarse beef; cat like rabbit, only better; and lizards like something cut off a tire by Messrs. Dunlop.[3]

A U.S. Army nurse, interned in the Santo Tomas internment camp in the Philippines, gave the following statement during a postwar inquiry:

> Until you've tried to live out of half a suitcase year in, year out, parking all you own on the bed by day, and under the bed when you're asleep, you have no conception of the priceless value of liberty.
> Looking back, it is incredible how important little things seemed in Santo Tomas. I never had a knife or fork, and lived in perpetual fear of losing my spoon. I grew so accustomed to eating with a spoon that even after I came home, a month after our release I would catch myself picking up my spoon when I should be using a fork. My most vivid memories of the Santo Tomas world will be the little insignificant things that we take for granted at home. The longing for salt in granulated form instead of lumps that made us choke.[4]

Today, we don't eat chicken heads or cats. And we don't brush our teeth with a coconut brush using ash, or crave granulated salt. It was not long ago, however, that Americans experienced these conditions on their own soil—in 1864 at Andersonville, or Camp Sumter, Georgia, the largest Confederate military prison camp during the Civil War. As one prisoner, Michigan cavalryman John Ransom, confided in his diary: "There is so much filth about the camp that it is terrible to live here. With sunken eyes, blackened countenances from pitch pine smoke, rags and disease, the men look sickening. The air reeks with nastiness."

The following images of men deprived of food and medicine for months and years are graphically described in the books of two POWs on the infamous Burma–Siam Death Railroad, built under the savage control of the Japanese:

> That such skeletons could still retain a spark of life: staring eyes; beak-like noses; retracted lips; a green-grey skin; shoulder blades like knife-edges cutting through the skin; knee joints twice as thick as thighs; biceps thinner than wrists; and ribs almost devoid of covering. Yet, their ankles and stomachs were bloated horribly and these were the men not ill enough to go to the hospital.[5]

And

> These survivors of the Burma railway in 1943 did not look like men—on the other hand they were not quite animals. They had feet torn by bamboo thorns, working for months without any footwear. Their skins had no spare flesh at all on the calf and looked as if bullets had exploded inside them, bursting the meat outwards and blackening it. These were their ulcers of which they had dozens. Their thigh bones and pelvis stood out sharply and on the point of each thighbone was that red raw patch like a saddle sore or monkey's behind. All their ribs showed clearly, the chest sloping backwards to the hollows of the throat and collar bone. Arms hung down, stick-like, with huge hands, and the skin wrinkled where muscle had vanished like old men. Heads were shrunken on the skulls with large teeth and faintly glowing eyes sat in black wells—hair was matted and lifeless. The whole body was draped with a loose-fitting envelope of thin, purple-brown parchment which wrinkled horizontally over the stomach and chest, and vertically on sagging fleshless bottoms.[6]

Many of the books, diaries, and accounts dealing with the incarceration of Westerners and the use of Asian slave laborers by the Japanese armed forces carry some kind of statement such as, "Please, believe me, this is all true!" As Mabel Waln Smith, an American woman married to an Englishman and interned in Pootung, China, said: "There are some aspects of internment one cannot make understandable to an outsider."[7]

Colonel William C. Braly said in the Preface to his book, *The Hard Way Home:*

> The events I have set down here depicting life as we lived it day after day in the many Japanese prison camps are *not* exaggerated. If anything, they are an understatement. However, they do tell the truth about the Japanese army and how it conducted its prison camps.[8]

And as John Toland, a historian, wrote:

> Their ordeal was so horrendous that even today few Americans know what their countrymen went through, and some readers may perhaps find it difficult to believe that anyone could have survived. My research over the past twenty-five years confirms that what you are about to read is not an exaggeration but the grim truth.[9]

Wrote John McGregor in *Blood on the Rising Sun:*

> I submit the names of my co-prisoners in Outram Road Gaol [the Kempeitai, Military Police, prison in Singapore] for the reader's perusal adding sufficient information to establish authenticity should anyone be concerned, and to provide proof to any reader who may be harbouring a tendency to be sceptical regarding the truth of any of the many revelations which this story discloses.[10]

And, finally, said Preston John Hubbard, an ex–POW:

> The sense of internal conflict between the horror of war and the love of country is common among soldiers, especially POWs, who have seen and experienced the indescribable agonies that live on in unending nightmares. The most common symptom of that internal conflict is silence. Refusal to speak of experienced atrocities is not simply avoidance of painful memory. It is often the only response to the overwhelming questions I, and others like me, hear inside our private selves: *"How can they hope to know? How can I begin to make them understand?"*[11]

There may be some who say, "Why make us understand?" and who believe that personal accounts of prison experiences under the Japanese should be destroyed and their contents forgotten. "The war was a long time ago, and wounds have healed" (so they say who were not there). "Why read about human suffering?" they contend.

These people may someday want to visit Andersonville's Prisoner of War Museum, the only one of its kind in the United States. For the living, during the Civil War, Andersonville was a place of horror, where 45,000 prisoners lived in squalor and where 12,912 soldiers and sailors were buried side by side, shoulder to shoulder. A haunting sculpture stands in front of the headstones at Andersonville, honoring all American prisoners involved in all the nation's wars, and carrying the words of Zechariah: "Turn you to the stronghold, ye prisoners of hope."

According to Major Lewis F. Easterlin, grandson of William Easterlin, a confederate drummer boy at Andersonville prison, feelings continue to run deep about Andersonville and about the Civil War. "It's good to research history and research it right, good to remember history and remember it right."[12]

This author's need as a historian and ex–POW is to leave a historical record, a *reference book* on prisoners of the Japanese in World War II, to those on whom the future depends.

This book is for the generations who have not experienced a *world* war (and God willing, never will), and for future generations and researchers who may want to learn about the price to be paid for freedom.

There may be value in their knowing that death marches, the living hell of sealed boxcars, the stench of death, the green hell of the jungle, the mental rot of a jail, and the unspeakable holds of rusty transport ships can happen—and that people survived them. There may be value in knowing how men, women, and children can endure even the most desperate conditions and, in their will to retain their humanity, triumph over appalling adversity.

There may be value in knowing how men and women gave up their lives for their "brothers and sisters." How they helped each other to live. How where there had been darkness, there had come forces of light—where despair, hope—where fear, faith—where hate, love.

Said Virgil: *"Forsan et haec olim meminisse juvabit"* (Perhaps this, too, will be a pleasure to look back on one day). And perhaps it will someday be a pleasure to remember even this suffering.

In an overall sense, the following words by Cicero may serve as the basic theme for this volume: *"Acriones autem mortus sunt intermissal libertatis quam retentae"* (freedom suppressed and again regained bites with keener fangs than freedom never endangered).

NOTES

1. IMTFE, record p. 49759 and exhibits 2001, 2011: Instructions by the Ministry of War and the chief of the Kempeitai to destroy all dossiers and documents.
2. Betty Jeffrey (an Australian nurse interned in a civilian camp in Sumatra, Dutch East Indies [now Indonesia]), *White Coolies,* Sydney, 1954, pp. 167 and 178.
3. Russell Braddon, *The Naked Island,* London, 1952, 1982, p. 465.
4. Colonel Eunice F. Young, U.S. Army Nurse Corps, *American Ex-Prisoners of War,* Paducah, 1988, p. 69.
5. Roy Bulcock, *Of Death but Once,* Melbourne, 1947, p. 167.
6. Braddon, *The Naked Island,* pp. 360–361.
7. Mabel Waln Smith, *Springtime in Shanghai,* London, 1957, p. 145.

8. Colonel William C. Braly, *The Hard Way Home*, Washington, DC, 1947.

9. John Toland, Introduction, in Manny Lawton, *Some Survived*, Chapel Hill, NC, 1984.

10. John McGregor, Introduction, in McGregor, *Blood on the Rising Sun*, Perth, 1978.

11. Preston John Hubbard, *Apocalypse Undone*, Nashville, 1990, p. 253.

12. Quoted in Charles Hillinger, "Andersonville, GA, Museum Honors the Nation's POWs," *Los Angeles Times*, January 8, 1989.

Chronology of Events

1941

Dec. 7	Japan attacks Pearl Harbor. The Japanese land at Kota Baru, East Malaya.
Dec. 8	United States declares war on Japan. The Netherlands declares war on Japan. Japanese forces enter Hong Kong.
Dec. 10	The Japanese land in the Philippines.
Dec. 19	The Japanese occupy Penang, West Malaya.
Dec. 22	The Japanese land in North Borneo.
Dec. 24	Wake Island falls to the Japanese.
Dec. 25	Hong Kong falls to the Japanese.
Dec. 29	The Japanese land in the Tambelan Islands.

1942

Jan. 1	Guam captives are transported to Japan.
Jan. 2	The Japanese occupy Manila, the Philippines.
Jan. 11	The Japanese land in Menado, North Celebes.
Jan. 12	Tarakan oil fields, East Borneo, and Menado, North Celebes, are all in Japanese hands.
Jan. 23	The Japanese occupy Rabaul, New Guinea.
Jan. 29	Pontianak, West Borneo, is in Japanese hands.
Jan. 30	The Japanese land in Ambon and Boeton, the Moluccas.
Feb. 1	Ambon Island is in Japanese hands.
Feb. 13	The Japanese land in Bangka Islands, east of Sumatra.
Feb. 15	The fall of Singapore.
Feb. 16	The fall of Palembang and Djambi, South Sumatra.
Feb. 19	The fall of Kieta, Bougainville Islands.
Feb. 20	The fall of Bali.
Feb. 27	Battle of the Java Sea.
Feb. 28	The Japanese land in West and Central Java.
Mar. 8	Capitulation of the Dutch East Indies.
Mar. 8	The Japanese land in West New Guinea.
Mar. 9	Rangoon falls to the Japanese.
Mar. 13	The Japanese occupy Medan, East Sumatra. Women in South Celebes are interned.
Mar. 17	The Japanese occupy Padang, West Sumatra.
April	The Japanese occupy Burma. Westerners in Sumatra are interned. British and American civilians in Java are interned.

April 1	Key cities in West New Guinea are occupied.
April 3	British troops that pulled out of North Borneo are interned in South Borneo.
April 6	Civilians in South Sumatra are interned. The Japanese establish a military tribunal in Singapore, overseeing Malaya and Sumatra.
April 11	Registration begins of all Western civilians in Java over age 17.
May 6	Corregidor surrenders.
May 16	British and Dutch POWs are transported from East Sumatra to South Burma.
May 25	Massive roundups begin of Western men in Batavia and other cities in Java.
June	The Japanese consolidate their forces on Wake, Marshall, Gilbert and Bismarck islands; Iwo Jima; New Guinea; and the Dutch East Indies. POWs are transported from Camp O'Donnell to Cabanatuan, both in the Philippines. General Tojo announces, "No work, no food!" Japanese POW camp chiefs meet in Tokyo.
June 5	The hospital ship *Op ten Noort* is taken by the Japanese.
June 14	The start of internment of Westerners in Java.
June 17	Civilian internees transported from West Borneo to Kuching, North Borneo.
June 25	All nonworking Western males in Java, except young boys and the elderly, are to be interned; women, old men, and children are to be assigned to city blocks—"protective centers" (thereafter called "protective city blocks"). Internment begins in Batavia.
July	800 POWs die at Cabanatuan, the Philippines. Japanese forces are now pushed into a "defensive posture" overall.
July 12	The Day of Beating in Ambon camp, the Moluccas.
August	High-ranking Allied officers—colonels and up—and civilian personnel are shipped from Java to Formosa.
Aug. 8	The first group of POWs from Sumatra arrive at Thanbyuzayat, Burma, to work on the railroad.
Aug. 15	A Bureau of POWs in Tokyo assumes control of all prisoners in Java.
Aug. 26	Western male civilians who have evaded capture in East Borneo are murdered by the Japanese. Later, the women and children are also massacred.
Sept.	Koreans are assigned guard duties in most POW internment camps; they are hated more than are their Japanese counterparts. The requirement that POWs and internees sign the "No Escape" document creates disturbances among captives.
Sept. 9	Registration begins of all women, children, and older men for assignment in protective city blocks in Java.
October	1,930 POWs leave the Philippines by *Totturi Maru* for Manchuria and Japan to be used as slave laborers. 890 POWs are transported from Java to Burma, Malaya, and Japan. Work starts on the Burma–Siam railroad. The War Ministry in Japan announces basic food allowances for POWs.
Oct. 2	Protective city blocks are occupied by women and children in Batavia, Malang, Semarang, and Bandoeng, West Java.
Oct. 7	The United Nations Commission for the Investigation of War Crimes is established.

Chronology of Events

Oct. 13	The mass internment of civilians begins in Bandoeng, West Java.
Oct. 15	The transportation of POWs from Java to Singapore begins. Others follow.
Oct. 17	The internment of civilians in Tjideng camp, Batavia, to be completed this month.
Nov.	1,000 POWs move from Luzon Island to Davao Penal Colony (both in the Philippines). 1,500 POWs are transported on *Nagato Maru* from the Philippines to Osaka, Japan. 1,800 POWs are assigned to perform slave labor at Nichols, Clark, Nielson, and Palawan airfields, the Philippines.
Nov. 18	More internments and roundups of civilians take place all over Java.
Dec.	Red Cross supplies and mail reach POWs at Bilibid and Cabanatuan, the Philippines, and Japan, and Shanghai, China. The total mortality through this month at Cabanatuan: 2,545 POWs. The first *romushas* (Javanese slave laborers) are sent outside the Indies.
Dec. 27	The first of the *Ambarawa* camps (Central Java) are put to use.

1943

January	POW transports continue to leave Java.
Jan. 2	High-ranking Allied military and civilian personnel are transported from Changi, Singapore, to Karenko, Formosa.
Jan. 15	*Nitimei Maru*, with 1,000 POWs on board, is attacked enroute from Penang, West Malaya, to Moulmein, Burma. Most of the POWs are saved. The Japanese urge the Dutch Eurasians to work together with the Japanese and assimilate with the Indonesian people.
Feb.	Baron Hideo Kodama travels through the Japanese-occupied territories. His report—a compilation of complaints by POWs and internees of how they are being treated—does not result in positive changes by Japan.
March	Most Western civilians in Japanese-occupied territories are now behind barbed wire.
Mar. 17	Civilian internees are transported from Ambon, the Moluccas, to Makassar, South Celebes.
April	Massive movements of internees take place from camp to camp throughout the Dutch East Indies. McCoy, Mellink, Dyess, and other American POWs escape from Davao Penal Colony, the Philippines.
Apr. 12	All internees from Tjihapit camp in Bandoeng, West Java, are locked out from the outside world.
Apr. 18	POWs are transported to Flores and Ambon islands, East Dutch East Indies, to work on airfields.
May	Tjideng camp in Batavia is locked out from the outside world.
May 11	Second Washington Conference: Dutch East Indies will not be reconquered through military actions.
May 23	Executions are carried out of Europeans in East Java who were suspected of anti–Japanese actions.
May 29	Executions take place of some Dutch Eurasians who refused to become members of Japanese-supported native forces.
July	More roundups occur of Javanese *romushas* (conscript laborers).

July 15	The Japanese make a POW propaganda movie using Australian POWs.
August	500 American POWs are transported to Kyushu, Japan.
Sept.	No Westerners, except Eurasians, walk around free in Japanese-held territories.
Sept. 19	More roundups take place of Eurasians and others suspected of anti-Japanese activities. Many are put in prison and then executed.
October	96 American civilians are executed on Wake Island. 800 American POWs are shipped from the Philippines to Japan.
Oct. 17	The Burma–Siam railroad is completed.
Nov. 29	The *Suez Maru*, with POWs on board, is torpedoed by USS *Bonefish*, east of Java.
Dec.	A second shipment of Red Cross parcels reaches some camps in Luzon, the Philippines, and China and Japan.
Dec. 17	The decision is made in Tokyo to consider civilian internees in all territories, except Java, Sumatra, and Malaya, as POWs and to treat them accordingly.
Dec. 25	A distribution of Red Cross parcels to internees takes place in many camps.

1944

January	Boys 10 and over are removed from their mothers and placed in civilian camps for men. [Dutch East Indies]
Jan. 19	Dutch communications experts and their families are transported from Java to Japan to continue their work in Japanese factories.
March	The Japanese decide to move most American POWs from the Philippines to Japan. Two shipments, totaling 500 men, leave for Japan. The new Japanese command in Singapore is the Seventh Army of Malaya, Sumatra, and Java.
Mar. 8	POWs in North Sumatra are put to work on a railroad (work lasts until October).
Mar. 13	Colonel Masayuki Nakata is appointed chief of all POW and internment camps in Java.
April 1	All civilian internees in Java, Sumatra, and Malaya are now considered POWs and are treated accordingly.
May	A distribution of Red Cross parcels takes place throughout the Japanese-occupied territories.
May 14	The first transport of POWs begins from Batavia to Padang, West Sumatra, to work on the railroad.
June	1,200 POWs are moved from Davao, the Philippines, to Luzon, the Philippines. Transportation begins of POWs from Burma and Siam to Japan.
June 19	The first American-Japanese sea battle in the Philippines takes place.
June 26	*Harukiku Maru*, en route from Medan, East Sumatra, to Singapore, is torpedoed by HMS *Truculent*. Hundreds of POWs perish.
July	More than 2,500 POWs leave the Philippines on *Matti-Matti Maru* and *Nissyo Maru* for Japan. POWs from Flores, Lesser Sunda Islands (Dutch East Indies), return to Java.
July 12	(Also the 17th and 23rd.) Groups of POWs are transported from Java to Pakanbaroe, Sumatra, to work on the railroad.

August	985 POWs leave the Philippines for Japan on board the *Noto Maru*. POWs return from Ambon, the Moluccas, to Java.
Sept.	A U.S. submarine sinks the *Shinyo Maru* carrying the last POWs from Mindanao, the Philippines. Many men perish; 82 survivors are rescued by guerrillas and returned to Australia.
Sept. 18	The *Junyo Maru*, with more than 6,000 prisoners en route from Batavia to Padang, West Sumatra, is torpedoed by HMS *Tradewind*. Only about 900 men survive.
October	High-ranking military and civilian personnel are shipped from Formosa via Japan to Manchuria. About 1,100 POWs are shipped from the Philippines to Formosa on the *Haru Maru*. About 1,800 POWs being shipped on *Arisan Maru* from the Philippines to Japan are torpedoed by U.S. submarine. Five men reach China and freedom. Four are recaptured. The rest perish. [Nine of 1,800 survived.]
Oct. 20	U.S. forces land on Leyte, the Philippines.
Nov.	Japanese army headquarters is moved from Manila to Saigon, French Indochina.
Nov. 26	Hundreds of women internees walk out of Brastagi camp, North Sumatra, in protest of bad treatment. Severe punishments follow.
Dec.	U.S. carrier planes sink the *Oryoku Maru*, with 1,619 POWs on board. Nearly 900 die. Survivors continue on to Japan on the *Enoura Maru* and *Brazil Maru*.
Dec. 13	American forces land on Mindoro, the Philippines. Burma is recaptured by British forces.

1945

January	The *Enoura Maru* is bombed at Takao, Formosa; more than 219 POWs are killed. The *Brazil Maru* reaches Japan with about 500 survivors on board of the original 1,619 men from the *Oryoku Maru*. An organization called Relief of Allied Prisoners of War and Internees (RAPWI) is established.
Jan. 10	U.S. forces land on Luzon.
Feb.	U.S. Rangers liberate 516 POWs at Cabanatuan. The U.S. Sixth Army frees 828 POWs at Bilibid Prison.
March	The Japanese order POWs moved from areas threatened by Allied attacks.
April	A U.S. submarine sinks the *Awa Maru* Red Cross ship after U.S. guarantees its safe passage.
May	Shanghai POWs are moved to a camp near Peking.
May 1	Allies land in Tarakan oil fields, East Borneo.
May 4	Americans recapture Davao Island.
June 5	In Tjideng camp, Batavia, commandant Kenichi Sonei orders all food thrown away—and for two days no food is supplied—as punishment for a minor infraction by the women in the camp.
June 10	One of the largest camps—Tjihapit camp, Bandoeng, West Java—is practically closed, and the internees are moved to Batavia.
July 5	The Philippines are completely liberated.
July 26	Potsdam declaration.

Aug. 6	The first atomic bomb is dropped on Hiroshima.
Aug. 8	The second atomic bomb is dropped on Nagasaki.
Aug. 10	The Japanese ask for peace.
Aug. 14	President Truman announces that Japan has unconditionally surrendered. The war is over.
Sept. 2	A ceremony marking the official signing of surrender documents by the Japanese takes place on board the USS *Missouri*.

I
THE PRISONERS

THE RECONCILER

Chapter 1

Prelude to War: Aspects of the Japanese Relating to Their Treatment of Prisoners

Many works have been devoted to the preliminaries of the Pacific War. It is the intent of this chapter to discuss certain facets of Japanese culture and history that are related to the taking and incarceration of POWs and civilian internees and their subsequent treatment.

Japanese Militarism

Japan, a nation of 3,900 islands, lived in feudal secrecy for centuries until Portuguese traders made the first Western contact with it in A.D. 1534. Japanese rulers soon sealed off the country again for another 250 years until the arrival of U.S. Commodore Matthew Perry in 1852 opened up Japan for whaling and other trade.

During its seclusion from foreign influences, a tribe, called the Yamato, unified Japan through a common belief that the Japanese race was superior to all others because it gave expression to the most natural, moral, and spiritual culture on Earth.

To strengthen this philosophy and to prevent Western influences from penetrating its empire after 1852, the ruling elite initiated the Meiji Restoration of 1867, bringing the emperor out of obscurity in Kyoto to the new capital of Edo, later called Tokyo.

The ruling elite was also responsible for a more fervent revival of the Shinto religion. Shinto, or "the way of the gods," was in the beginning essentially nature worship, in which the spirits of natural forces or objects, *kami,* inhabited such universally respected phenomena as the sun, the stars, the moon, storms, and certain trees and peculiarly eroded rocks.

In the myths concerning the islands' origin, the land itself was divinely created by the mating of gods whose human offspring—the emperor—was charged with the divine injunction to rule the sacred land. To carry out this injunction, the emperor was given three sacred treasures: a mirror, a necklace, and a sword.

The Shinto philosophy is filial devotion and loyalty. The emperor is the father of the people, who respond to him as dutiful sons and daughters sharing in the divinity he reflects.

Shinto's insistence upon loyalty, devotion, and service was conveniently exploited by the militarists in the mid-19th century to get the people to accept warfare as a part of life. Succeeding generations of the two-sworded samurai—the professional warriors—united in their belief in conquest and their craving for world rule. They followed a consistent pattern in a drive for power, which culminated in Japan's defeat of Russia in the Russo-Japanese War of 1904–05.

The Japanese ruling class used this military success and subsequent self-confidence to transform Japan into a modern country under the slogan *fukoku-kyohei*—rich country, strong army. The aim of this revolution was to prevent Japan from becoming like her neighbor China, the helpless victim of colonialism.

Japan's self-confidence was combined with a burning rage at her position as a "have-not" power. Japan, in the early 20th century, had only 142,270 square miles and 75 million people to feed, whereas Australia and Canada, with 6.5 million people each, had 3 million and 3.5 million square miles of land, respectively. The United States had another 3 million square miles. France had a colonial empire of 3.8 million square miles, Britain had over 2 million square miles in Africa alone, Belgium had 900,000 square miles, and Portugal had 800,000 square miles, while the Dutch ruled a territory of over 13,000 islands of which only a few thousand were inhabited.

Japan could not feed her people—by 1940 she was short 65 million bushels of rice a year. To pay her rice imports, Japan had to export manufactured goods, but these were increasingly denied entry by Western tariff barriers. Furthermore, other countries' anti-Japanese immigration policies prevented Japan from relieving her population pressures. As a result, Japan saw only one way to solve her problems: the conquest of other territories.

In 1931, the so-called Kwantung army, which had been guarding Japanese interests in Manchuria since the defeat of Russia in 1905, seized control. It dubbed the acquired territory "Manchuko," the state of Manchu—a new area for Japanese to emigrate to. On July 7, 1937, a skirmish between patrolling Japanese troops and a Chinese unit led to a major Japanese attack and full-scale war.

The militarists intensified the philosophy of the emperor's divinity and the glory of dying for him, emphasizing the heroism and exploits of the early samurai, who were glorified in the philosophy of the *bushido*—the warrior who believed in honor, obedience, and valor.

The people, both young and old, were trained to believe that loyalty to the emperor, in all its sacrificial manifestations, was the greatest expression of the human spirit. The racialist cult of the emperor (which implied that the Japanese emperor system should be applied to the whole world and that in the emperor was expressed the wholeness of the Japanese people) became the wellspring for the commonly held notion of uniqueness. It reached the level of an article of faith that Japanese culture, Japanese language, Japanese people, Japanese customs, Japanese emotions—yes even the design of Japanese brains and intestines—were unique in more ways than all other cultures and peoples of the world. *Nihonjiron*, the principle of what it meant to be Japanese, expanded rapidly.

The people's nationalistic feelings were fostered and encouraged by the military-dominated political regime which exerted its influence through state-controlled schools and communication media. These politicians had a strong foundation upon which to build: racial superiority, military invincibility, and the belief that it was Japan's destiny to rule East Asia.

Whereas in most other cultures, an inward-looking propensity might encourage pacifist isolationism, in Japan these notions were harnessed to military aggression.

In a speech by Foreign Minister Arita on June 29, 1940, Japan reiterated its mission to establish a New Order in East Asia and to expand that area from Burma and the eastern part of India to Australia and New Zealand.

None of the Western nations with interests in the Pacific was able to challenge this Japanese program. The Netherlands, which owned the Dutch East Indies, had been overrun by the Germans; France, which colonized Indochina, had surrendered to Germany; Great Britain, with colonies in Burma, Malaya, and Singapore, was involved in a battle of survival with Germany; and the United States, with interests in the Philippines, Guam, and Wake, was isolationist.

In September 1940 the Japanese pressured the French shadow government in Vichy to allow Japanese troops to be stationed in French Indochina. The French gave in, and Japanese armed forces poured into the area.

In July 1941, when Japanese troops landed at Cam Ranh Bay and occupied Saigon and Danang, the United States announced a complete oil embargo of Japan. Britain and the Netherlands followed suit.

The Japanese were deeply disturbed by these measures. A flurry of diplomatic efforts followed, with demands and counterdemands from each side. It then became clear to the Western nations that Japan had serious intentions of dominating East Asia by establishing a Greater Asia Co-Prosperity Sphere.

Within the framework of their ideology, the Japanese entertained two contradictory ideas at once: They prepared for war while sincerely searching for peace. The United States wasn't ready to fight a war with Germany, let alone a second war with Japan. President Roosevelt opted for a resumption of economic relations with Japan—a plan that might have provided a basis for further diplomatic talks. The Japanese never saw it.

U.S. Army Intelligence became aware in late 1941 of massive Japanese convoys of battleships and troop transports moving southward from Japan. The United States sent one last document, with 10 stern conditions known as "The Ten Points." The Japanese decided to "strike now," rather than sit quietly and be economically strangled. They were under no illusion about the ultimate military and economic odds against them if they took on the West.

Irrational or not, the Japanese frustration and desperation in 1941 was expressed by General Hideki Tojo as follows: "There are times when we must have the courage to do extraordinary things, like jumping with eyes closed off the veranda of the Kiyomizu Temple."

On December 7, 1941, at 7:49 A.M., Captain Mitsuo Fuchida, commander of a Japanese air strike force, ordered his radioman to send to his fleet of planes and Tokyo the fateful message, "Tora! Tora! Tora!"— Tiger! Tiger! Tiger!—thus launching the attack on Pearl Harbor.

At the same time, Japanese forces invaded Hong Kong, and for all practical purposes World War II had started.

Ten days later the Japanese army swarmed south via Siam 600 miles through the Malay Peninsula and attacked Singapore from the rear. After three weeks of heroic resistance by the British Third Army, General Arthur Ernest Percival, governor of Singapore, was compelled to sign an unconditional surrender on February 15, 1942, and was taken prisoner, together with 70,000 men.

The Japanese advanced south and east through the Dutch East Indies, and three weeks after the fall of Singapore, on March 8, Tokyo announced the fall of Java and the total surrender of the Dutch.

In the meantime fierce battles in the Philippines continued. After four months of heavy fighting, Bataan fell on April 9, 1942. A month later, on May 6, the desperate resistance put up by the heroes of Corregidor for five months came to an end.

In the Pacific, Japanese forces attacked Wake Island on December 8, 1941. For two weeks, they unmercifully bombed the island. The American commander, Major James Devereux, surrendered on December 23, 1941.

On March 8, 1942, Burma and the Andaman Islands in the Bay of Bengal fell. In March and April Japanese forces conquered the Admiralty

Islands and the Bismarck Archipelago, with the New Britain, New Ireland, and Solomon Islands. That was as far east as they could get; Midway, New Caledonia, Fiji, and Samoa were never conquered.

The battles in the Coral Sea in May 1942 and at Midway in June 1942 proved the turning point in Japan's offensive stance. And to the west, they were never able to conquer and occupy Ceylon and India.

Racial Bias

The confrontation between Japan and the Western nations in the 1920s and 1930s also involved the issue of racial bias. In 1907, for example, the San Francisco school board voted to exclude Orientals from attending city schools, a ruling that the Japanese government indignantly protested. The school board rescinded the order, but only after President Theodore Roosevelt interceded and promised to reduce the influx of Japanese laborers into the United States.

A few years later, the racial issue flared up again over the California growers' resentment of the low-cost competition by Japanese farmers in their state. Previous federal legislation had already curtailed the immigration of Chinese laborers and now the Californians began to influence Congress to pass the Exclusion Act of 1924: to ban all further immigration by Orientals, notably the Japanese. Repercussions by Japan were immediate and vehement. The American ambassador to Japan resigned, and upon his return to the United States, he denounced this act. In Japan the government declared the act's effective date to be observed as "Humiliation Day."

Thousands of miles away, Australia similarly excluded Japanese immigrants by racial bans and quotas.

American concerns and negative feelings about the Japanese continued. Wallace Irwin, a San Francisco newspaperman, for example, created a character named Hashimura Togo, a Japanese who spoke pidgin English and worked as a houseboy for an American family. Togo was pictured as a buck-toothed, ever-smiling, ultrapolite, but crafty little man. Through magazines and newspapers, and later in books, this stereotypical Japanese image reached millions of American households. The Japanese were not pleased. As national relations worsened, many stories of Japanese ineptness—their poor eyesight, their mechanical ineptitude, and more—circulated.

Noted American journalist Mona Gardner wrote the following in her memoirs of her travel through Asia and Southeast Asia:

> The young Japanese came in slowly. He was almost unrecognizable in his new [military] uniform. His great broad country man's torso was bunched

into inadequate khaki, which strained about his massive shoulders and billowed too generously over his hips. His long supple arms, which we had many times seen him use like legs to climb out over the second-story veranda and along the eaves as he mended the bath-stove pipe, were six inches too long for his new sleeves. Somehow the bulges of his trousers and the clumsy wrapping of his puttees seemed to have telescoped his legs so as to make them appear even shorter than they were. Instead of seeing the full-muscled, infectiously healthy son of the soil we were accustomed to seeing, the tinsmith was now a cartoon of a soldier.[1]

In *War Without Mercy,* John Dower explained how stereotyped and often blatantly racist thinking contributed to poor military planning, atrocious behavior, and the adoption of exterminatory policies by the West. Distorted perceptions and unrestrained violence occurred on all sides in the Pacific War.[2]

The Allies explained that a defect in the inner ear made the Japanese incompetent pilots and that Japanese in general resembled "photographic prints of the same negative." Propaganda literature warned that the enemy was not merely a "buck-toothed, near-sighted, pint-sized monkey, but a robotlike creature"; that the Japanese were children, savages, near-lunatics; that their anal-retentive character was a function of their toilet training; and that their inferiority complex was well justified.

Other comments mentioned that Japanese skulls were some 2,000 years less developed than Western skulls and that the Japanese people were a kind of freak survival in the modern world.

The wartime press stated that "the Japs were invariably subhuman," likened them to vermin, to rats, and particularly to apes. Of Japanese Americans who were about to be interned, the *Los Angeles Times* wrote: "A viper is nonetheless a viper wherever the egg is hatched."

The Japanese, on the other hand, believed that by waging war, they were protecting themselves from the white race that had turned Asia into a colony. They argued, for example, that the Yamatoist Japanese had to colonize the Korean Peninsula out of an obligation to rescue "inferior races."

The Japanese also lived with biases against what they called the "soft and inferior Westerners." They considered combing "dandruff" from the hair, for example, as extravagance. Selfishness, hedonism, liberalism, materialism, money worship, and individualism were Anglo-American ideas.

Japanese cartoonists depicted President Roosevelt and Prime Minister Churchill as half-horse, half-badger, dressed in a costume combining the Almighty Dollar and the piratical skull and crossbones. As John Dower noted:

> During the war, the Japanese routinely referred to themselves as the leading race [shidō minzoku] of the world. Like their American and

Commonwealth adversaries, they called on a variety of metaphors, images, code phrases, and concepts to affirm their superiority—ranging from expressions that demeaned non-Japanese to elaborate affirmations of their own unique qualities. And as also happened to their enemies, their prejudices affected their war conduct; the way they evaluated, and frequently misjudged Allied capabilities; the attitudes and policies they adopted toward other Asians within the Co-Prosperity Sphere; and how they fought and died.[3]

Throughout the war, racial propaganda continued unabated.[3] In the *Osaka Mainichi* of August 15, 1944, the following statement appeared:

Difficulty grows: Americans are epicurean wild beasts. No nation on earth lives as much on meat as the Americans. This has deprived them of what should be the adequate quota of human decency. They have degenerated to such a depth that the resentment one would usually feel against a human being would be a luxury when applied to Americans. Since indignation towards the Americans would be sheer waste of sentiment, mankind owes it to itself to exterminate them with the same positive zeal as a civilized community would manifest in eradicating obnoxious insects.[4]

Japanese soldiers looked upon the Americans as pleasure seeking, soft, and materialistic. They were convinced that in battle the Imperial Japanese Army and Navy would prevail: Japan had never lost a war.

Who and what were these Japanese soldiers?

The Japanese Soldier

Drilled to have no fear of death, to sacrifice himself for the progress of the race, the Japanese soldier showed again and again, in China, Malaya, Burma, and the Philippines, that he was well trained, disciplined, tenacious.

He was trained to believe that loyalty, in all its sacrificial manifestations, was the greatest expression of military spirit. Inflexible duty was its corollary, with a fatalistic bind to a life of service.

His own outstanding military behavior, even in a life-and-death battle, would be publicized only briefly while he was alive. Lavish praise and great honors came after death. This twofold policy prevented the creation of national heroes, while further underlining the glory of death on the battlefield.

The devotion of the individual was marshaled into group action in a way that has been maintained for centuries. Group control has always been important. On his own the Japanese soldier could be highly individualistic;

each man had his own ideas on the proper way of doing the job. Thus, commanders in the field frequently disregarded orders from the Tokyo War Ministry because more direct action suited their own desires or those of the cliques to which they were highly loyal. The explanation generally was that they were acting in the emperor's best interests—that there were as many ways to serve the emperor as there were Japanese.

Regulations prevailed, however, in the army and navy. The Imperial Rescript to soldiers and sailors, for example, consisted of several precepts that the serviceman had to follow: (1) he should consider loyalty his essential duty; (2) he should think of duty as weightier than a mountain and death as lighter than a feather; (3) he should never fall into disgrace and bring dishonor to his name; (4) he should always obey orders; (5) he should be brave; and (6) he should avoid frivolity and extravagance.

In essence this Imperial Rescript embodied the code of bushido: honor, obedience, and valor.

The Allied soldier went to war believing that the best way he could show his love and devotion to his country and his family was to win the war as quickly as possible and then to return whole to share with his wife and children a new life in a better world. In contrast, the Japanese soldier went into battle with the conviction that his loyalty and devotion could be shown effectively by dying in his emperor's service and bringing honor to his name and family.

The relatives of a captured Allied soldier took comfort in the fact that he was still alive and that he might survive to return to them. The relatives of a captured Japanese serviceman were never notified. If they suspected that he was imprisoned, they were obliged to show that he had brought everlasting dishonor to his family and himself and that it would be better if he were dead because he was marked as a traitor to the imperial cause.

Most of the Japanese soldiers were conscripted peasants, toughened by strenuous military training and deprivation. They were insular—had never left the areas they were brought up in—and were ignorant about peoples and places in other parts of the world. To these soldiers the possibility was grim and real that Great Britain and the United States would attack and invade their islands and that they would be tortured heartlessly. According to Mona Gardner:

> Men, who never saw the men and customs of other nations, told each other and their sons how infinitely superior *they*, the Japanese, were to all other peoples. And lacking any comparisons, the tendrils of this faith were nurtured in the hothouse of isolation until they matured into a gigantic forest which throws its shadows over all of Japan. Japanese officers, who are appallingly ignorant of international affairs, of economics, of geography, continue to dictate the textbooks from which the farmers [and future soldiers] learn their lessons. It isn't that there is

so much factual misinformation about other countries in these textbooks, it is that other countries simply aren't mentioned. The sun is made to shine only on Japan and the deeds of the Japanese people.[5]

There are a few other points to take into account. First, an important facet of the Japanese attitude was the keeping up of appearances, or face-saving. Second, living not only geographically, but psychologically on top of volcanoes, the Japanese are a highly emotional people, and it is essential for them to give vent to their emotions. Yet, these fits of rage are subject to sudden checks at will. Third, during World War II, tenderness of heart by a Japanese soldier was scorned, except with respect to children. Fourth, the Japanese soldier had no capacity for keeping himself occupied in off-duty hours. No reading material—except newspapers—was provided and he was allowed to write only a few postcards home. There was endless conversation, but seldom laughter. Fifth, to keep up its rigid manly standards, the Japanese army left little room for extensive medical care.

Although not all Japanese servicemen shared the same characteristics, the degree of conformity to a national pattern was remarkable.

Captor-Captive Relationships

It is important at this point to discuss how the American and Japanese sociological, cultural, historical, and political facets just described were responsible for certain actions and reactions by both the Japanese captors and their Allied captives.

These facets may be summarized as (1) the economic strangulation of the Japanese by the West, (2) stereotyping and racist thinking by the West, (3) continued colonialism by the West, (4) the Yamato belief in the superiority of the Japanese (*shidō minzoku*), (5) the cult of bushido, (6) the individualism of the Japanese soldier within the framework of group action, (7) the dishonor of a captured Japanese soldier, (8) the insularity of the Japanese soldier, (9) the emotionality of the Japanese soldier, and (10) the tough training of the Japanese soldier. All these elements of Japanese and American "thinking," in a variety of combinations, greatly influenced the way the Japanese treated their prisoners and the way the prisoners reacted, and their behavior toward Japanese and Korean guards.

Other factors that influenced Japanese behavior toward their captives were the actions of the A-B-C-D (American, British, Chinese, and Dutch) bloc, such as the Dutch action to join the United States in the oil embargo against Japan. There was also the Japanese fury against the United States for placing Japanese Americans in concentration camps shortly after the attack on Pearl Harbor.

The following excerpt of a speech by Consul-General Y. Ishizawa, broadcast via the Dutch East Indies radio network, and subsequent publication of this speech in newspapers, had an enormous influence on the treatment of Dutch and American prisoners by the Japanese in the occupation years that followed:

> Dear listeners: Immediately after the start of the Pacific war on December 8, I was interned together with other consular officials and for three months I suffered physically under the hands of my captors. The treatment of other Japanese citizens, old men seventy years of age, and women and children, many weak and feeble, was inhumane and unpardonable. Since November 1940, under the leadership of his Excellency Kenkichi Yoshizawa, I negotiated with Dr. H. J. van Mook and Mr. J. E. van Hoogstraten, both of the Department of Economic Affairs, about an amicable solution concerning our trade situation. I had discussions with your Governor General about the negative attitude of England and the United States against Japan, but that we had no quarrels with the Dutch East Indies. On the contrary: our desire had always been to find a peaceful solution to our differences and that the Indies should not blindly follow England's and America's lead. Mr. E. N. van Kleffens, Minister of Foreign Affairs in Holland, refused to even receive me in audience during his visit to the Indies. And so did many other officials of your government.
>
> Let me repeat again: Japan has always attempted to strike a bargain with the Indies in a peaceful manner in accordance with the ideal of a common welfare in East Asia. Unfortunately, your leaders, influenced by England and America, decided otherwise. In the meantime, the economic pressure on Japan by the British and Americans became unbearable and to release some of that pressure we decided to send our troops into South French Indo China. We informed your government that this action was not meant to expand to the Indies. However, your leaders considered our occupation of Indo China a direct threat and announced an economic blockade—trade between Japan and the Indies was halted. Of the 7,000 Japanese people in your country, 6,000 had to abandon their profitable businesses and were sent back to Japan.
>
> This total economic blockade could be qualified as more than a military action on your part and that of your allies. Your provocative attitude notwithstanding, we kept our patience, and when hostilities broke out, our declaration of war was aimed at England and America only—not the Indies. But, dear listeners, the Indies, not realizing their own military weakness, decided to declare war on Japan, at the same time as England and America did. It is only now that you realize the real power of the Japanese Empire. You will also begin to know how little the authorities of the Indies knew about Japan and how wrong their policies against our country were. Your politicians and bureaucrats attained the attitude of "policing" instead of really trying to understand Japan's position.
>
> Dear listeners, the situation has now radically changed. Your three hundred year rule over your colonies has come to a tragic end as a result of the misguided policies of the leading figures in your government. It is your task now to really grasp this new situation and to change your conceited attitude accordingly and to cooperate with the Japanese command.

It is not my intention at all to plead for your cooperation, because we will take appropriate measures against those who rebel against us. I repeat, it is your attitude that determines our actions.[6]

The incarceration of Japanese Americans in the United States greatly incensed the Japanese. It was one of the factors responsible for the harsh treatment of Allied POWs and civilian internees by the Japanese.

> More U.S. Brutality Bared by Internee: Kiyoshi Miyazaki, former manager of the New York branch of the Mitsui Bussan Kaisha, revealed how the Americans mistreated the Japanese internees. Meals were not only very bad, but were meager.... We were placed in miserable tents, five persons to a tent ... forced to cook our own meals and wash toilets ... when boarding exchange ship were called back and compelled to pay 1942 income tax.[7]

In another statement published in the Dutch East Indies, called the "American Atrocities," which expresses the Japanese anger over the internment of Japanese Americans, the Japanese occupation forces made it indirectly clear that Western prisoners should not be surprised if they received the same kind of treatment from the Japanese, which, as a matter of fact, they did.

If from the following statement by Domei about the concentration camps for Japanese Americans the phrase "native born American citizens as well as alien immigrants" is eliminated; "the white race" is substituted for "the Japanese race"; "racetrack stables at places like Santa Anita and Tanforan" are changed to, for example, "Ambarawa women's camp and Santo Tomas camp"; and the word "desert" is eliminated, we would get a statement of the Japanese treatment of Western women and children in internment camps in Asia:

> The mass evacuation of more than a hundred thousand innocent civilians—women and children as well as men, native born American citizens as well as alien immigrants, for no other reason than the fact that they happened to be of the Japanese race, was an act of persecution without parallel in history. Conditions attendant of this wholesale forced exile have been beyond description. Harmless people forced to abandon their homes and their businesses, forced to throw away their life's work, herded by the thousands into racetrack stables at places like Santa Anita and Tanforan to be penned up without any adequate housing facilities and in some cases without proper food and with insufficient medical care, only to be moved to even worse permanent camps in bleak desert areas, where under military guard they have been set to work to eke out a miserable existence on land which had never been considered cultivable before.[8]

When Mrs. Agnes Newton Keith and other women and children were interned in an abandoned quarantine station at Berhala in North Borneo, she made the following comment:

> That leaking, rotting, unventilated, unlighted, wooden-windowed building was retribution on us Europeans for allowing such a place to exist for the housing of anyone. It has once been used for quarantine of Asiatic arrivals, and in this same building we had imprisoned some of the Japanese internees five months before, when North Borneo was still British. When I entered the building that night I wished that we had never initiated the idea of any human being occupying it.[9]

One reason for the Japanese behavior toward Western prisoners and internees that was often overlooked by the captives was that most Japanese soldiers came from small overcrowded villages and lived a simple life. These soldiers had never been in contact with foreigners and had no concept of Western-style living with such amenities as natural gas, electricity, and plumbing, which they considered luxuries. Their lack of knowledge of other cultures, and belief in their uniqueness and in the impossibility of foreigners' understanding *them,* often served as an explanation in the face of criticism of Japanese behavior toward Western captives.

Through a variety of announcements and statements in the media, the Japanese attempted to educate the Western citizens in the "occupied" territories. The propagandistic tone of these announcements and the fact that they were expounded in a period of fear and uncertainty, chaos and confusion, contributed to the hate and anger of the Westerners toward the Japanese. The following are some of these "educational announcements":

> The people of Nippon are convinced of their responsibilities towards world peace. Nippon is the sun: protector of the land and provider of light and warmth to all beings on earth. The Nippon Empire will increase in power and importance, like the sun rising higher in the sky—this is eternal and it is also the meaning of the name Nippon.
> In the creation of the world, land was the first. And the first land was Nippon, Land of the Rising Sun. No one can challenge the sun—to do so is like the snow melting in the heat of the sun. This is the iron-clad law on earth. Therefore, those opposing Nippon will undergo the same experience as the snow. All people of Nippon believe in this law.[10]

> "Hakko ichiu" is the eight corners of the world under one roof: the Japanese roof. All countries form an organic system, with Japan as the brains, and continuously developing under the leadership of Tenno, His Majesty the Emperor. Says Tenno: "People of Japan cultivate within you the National Ideal, so that Japan becomes the example for all the countries in the world."[11]

Even POWs, especially those with an objective viewpoint, were aware that the treatments they received from their Japanese captors were often based on retributions for either prewar embargoes or other Allied actions. The following statement from an Australian POW is an example:

> The Jap had not forgotten the high-handed Dutch behavior at the economic conference in Java in 1940. They had remembered that their "duck-legged" spokesman had been sneered down at by a specially selected parade of the tallest men in the Dutch army; that the Dutch representative who had called a meeting for eleven o'clcok had refused to wait five minutes for the tardy Nip. Who can say that such small things as these did not influence the subsequent Japanese attitude. It seems more than likely that face-saving has an excellent memory for details.[12]

Of all the works listed in the Sources to this chapter, John W. Dower's book is one of the most important. It is a complex and nuanced study that was reviewed in *Newsweek* by Peter S. Prescott under the headline "The 'Japs' vs. the 'Roundeyes'." As Prescott wrote:

> The American strain of racism works by lumping other people into groups of spurious homogeneity and then denigrating them, occasionally to some crude comic effect. Japanese racism derives from the country's isolation and mythology; it seeks the elevation of the Japanese by stressing the purity of the Yamato race, the superiority of its destiny. Low road or high road, the route is inadequate to the destination.[13]

The tragic and unfortunate victims of these existing racial prejudices between the Japanese and the Europeans and Americans were the POWs and civilian internees. As John Power noted:

> In this milieu of historical forgetfulness, selective reporting, centralized propaganda, and a truly savage war, atrocities and war crimes played a major role in the propagation of racial and cultural stereotypes. The stereotypes preceded the atrocities, however, and had an independent existence apart from any specific event. General Blanny's reference to the infinite superiority of his men, and his call to exterminate the inhuman Japanese, the apes, the vermin; or Japanese references to their purity, and their call to chastise the fiendish foe, or kill the Anglo-American devils — such expressions, in actuality, were not at all random. They belonged to webs of perception that had existed for centuries in western and Japanese culture, and the atrocities were taken as simply confirming their validity.[14]

It is important to note Mr. Dower's statement that "the stereotypes preceded the atrocities." Although the Japanese atrocities against their POWs and civilian internees cannot be condoned or justified, Dower's research and the other bibliographical sources provide a well-balanced view of the relationships between Japanese captor and Western captive and a better understanding of the cause and effects of this complex, explosive, and controversial subject.

NOTES

1. Mona Gardner, *The Menacing Sun*, New York, 1939.
2. John W. Dower, *War Without Mercy: Race and Power in the Pacific War*, New York, 1986.
3. *Ibid.*, p. 203.
4. Colonel William C. Braly, *The Hard Way Home*, Washington, DC, 1947.
5. Gardner, *The Menacing Sun*, p. xviii.
6. Rijksinstituut voor Oorlogsdocumentatie; Amsterdam, Indonesian Collection 6868 (hereafter RvO IC), Netherlands State Institute for War Documentation (hereafter NSIWD).
7. Reported by Domei, Japan; quoted in Braly, *Hard Way Home*, p. 89.
8. RvO IC 9818, NSIWD.
9. Agnes Newton Keith, *Three Came Home*, London, 1948, p. 42.
10. RvO IC 6260, NSIWD.
11. RvO IC 6262, NSIWD and International Military Tribunal of the Far East (hereafter IMTFE) 675A.
12. Roy Bulcock, *Of Death but Once*, Melbourne, 1947, p. 12.
13. Peter S. Prescott, "The Japs vs. the Roundeyes," *Newsweek*, June 30, 1986.
14. Dower, *War Without Mercy*, p. 73.

SOURCES

Argall, Phyllis. *My Life with the Enemy*. New York, 1944.
Allen, Louis. "Japanese Literature of the Second World War," *Proceedings of the British Association for Japanese Studies* 2:1 (1977), 117–156.
———. "A Footnote to Ienaga on Malaya," *Proceedings of the British Association for Japanese Studies* 5:1 (1980), 113–126.
Argyle, C. J. *Japan at War*. London, 1976.
Ashihara, Yoshinobu. *The Hidden Order: Tokyo Through the 20th Century*. New York, 1989.
Ballard, J. C. *Het Keizerrijk van de Zon*. Vianen, the Netherlands, 1985.
Benedict, Ruth. *The Chrysanthemum and the Sword: Patterns of Japanese Culture*. Boston, 1946.
Bergamini, David. *Japan's Imperial Conspiracy*. New York, 1971.
Braly, Colonel William C. *The Hard Way Home*. Washington, DC, 1947.
Brines, Russell. *Until They Eat Stones*. New York, 1944.
Brown, Courtney. *Tojo: The Last Banzai*. London, 1967.
Bulcock, Roy. *Of Death but Once*. Melbourne, 1947.
Butow, Robert J. C. *Tojo and the Coming of War*. Princeton, NJ, 1961.
Costello, John. *The Pacific War*. New York, 1981.
Deacon, Richard. *Kempeitai: A History of the Japanese Secret Police*. New York, 1983.

Dower, John W. *War Without Mercy: Race and Power in the Pacific War.* New York, 1986.
Embree, John. *The Japanese.* Washington, DC, 1943.
———. *The Japanese Nation.* New York, 1945.
Feis, Herbert. *The Road to Pearl Harbor: The Coming of the War Between the United States and Japan.* Princeton, NJ, 1950.
Fletcher, William H. *The Search for a New Order: Intellectuals and Fascism in Prewar Japan.* Chapel Hill, NC, 1982.
Foreign Morale Analysis Division, Bureau of Overseas Intelligence, Office of War Information, Record Group No. 208, National Archives. "Japanese Behavior Patterns," Report No. 25. Washington, DC, September 15, 1945.
———. "The Japanese Emperor," Report No. 27. Washington, DC, October 31, 1945.
———. "Japanese Personalities and Reactions as Seen in Soldiers' Diaries," Report No. 30. Washington, DC, December 19, 1945.
Friend, Theodore. *The Blue-Eyed Enemy: Japan Against the West in Java and Luzon.* Princeton, NJ, 1988.
Gardner, Mona. *The Menacing Sun.* New York, 1939.
Gibson, Michael. *The Samurai of Japan.* London, 1969.
Goethe, John. *Japan Fights for Asia.* Boston, 1943.
Grew, Joseph C. *Ten Years in Japan by a U.S. Ambassador.* New York, 1944.
Havens, Thomas P. H. *Valley of Darkness: The Japanese People and World War II.* New York, 1978.
Holton, D. C. *The National Faith of Japan: A Study in Modern Shinto.* New York, 1938, 1965.
Hoogenband, C. van den, et al. *Nederlands Indie Contra Japan,* 7 vols. Bandoeng, Indonesia, 1949.
Hoyt, Edwin P. *Japan's War: The Great Pacific Conflict, 1853–1952.* New York, 1986.
Ienega, Saburo. *The Pacific War, 1939–1945.* New York, 1978.
———. *Japan's Last War: World War II and the Japanese.* Canberra, Australia, 1979.
Ike, Nobutaka. *Japan's Decision for War: Records of the 1941 Policy Conference.* Stanford, CA, 1967.
Iriye, Akira. *Power and Culture: The Japanese-American War, 1941–1945.* Cambridge, England, 1981.
Ishii, Ryosuke, ed. *Japanese Legislation in the Meiji Era.* Tokyo, 1958.
Jansen, Marius B., and Gilbert Rozman, eds. *Japan in Transition: From Tokugawa to Meiji.* Princeton, NJ, 1986.
Johnson, Sheila K. *American Attitudes Toward Japan, 1941–1975.* Stanford, CA, 1975.
Jones, F. C. *Japan's New Order in East Asia: Its Rise and Fall, 1937–1945.* Oxford, 1954.
Kato, Masuo. *The Lost War.* New York, 1946.
Keith, Agnes Newton. *Three Came Home.* New York, 1946.
Kim, Jai-Hyup. *The Garrison State in Prewar Japan and Postwar Korea.* Washington, DC, 1978.
Kodama, Yoshio. *Sugamo Diary.* Tokyo, 1960.
Kuno, Yoshi Saburo. *Japanese Expansion on the Asiatic Continent: China, Russia, Korea,* 2 vols. Port Washington, NY, 1967.
Lebra, Joyce C., et al. *Japan's Greater East Asia Co-Prosperity Sphere in World War II: Selected Readings and Documents.* Oxford, 1975.

Lebra, Takie Sugiyama. *Japanese Patterns of Behavior.* Honolulu, 1976.
Lindbergh, Charles. *The Wartime Journals.* New York, 1970.
Lorry, Hillis. *Japan's Military Masters: The Army in Japanese Life.* New York, 1943.
McCoy, Alfred W. *Southeast Asia Under Japanese Rule* (Monograph Southeast Asia Studies, Series No. 22). New Haven, CT, 1980.
Maki, John M. *Japanese Militarism: Its Causes and Cure.* New York, 1945.
Mayer, S. L. *De Japanse Oorlogsmachine.* Amsterdam, 1978.
———, ed. *The Rise and Fall of Imperial Japan, 1894–1945.* London, 1976.
Mishima, Yukio. *The Way of the Samurai: Hagakure in Modern Life.* New York, 1977.
Morley, James W., ed. *The Fateful Choice: Japan's Advance into Asia, 1939–1941.* New York, 1980.
Morris, Ivan, ed. *Japan, 1931–1945.* Lexington, MA, 1968.
Mosley, Leonard. *Hirohito: Emperor of Japan.* Englewood Cliffs, NJ, 1966.
Myers, Ramon H., and Mark R. Peattie, eds. *The Japanese Colonial Empire, 1895–1945.* Princeton, NJ, 1984.
Nakamura, Hajime. *The Ways of Thinking of Eastern Peoples.* Tokyo, 1960.
Nitobe, Inazo Ota. *Bushido, the Soul of Japan.* Tokyo, 1909, 1969.
Onodo, Hiroo. *Mijn Dertigjarige Oorlog.* Amsterdam, 1975.
Peattie, Mark R. *Isiwara Kanji and Japan's Confrontation with the West.* Princeton, NJ, 1966.
Reischauer, Edwin O. *Japan, Past and Present.* New York, 1946.
Sakai, Saburo. *Samurai.* London, 1959.
Shigemitsu, Mamoru. *Japan and Her Destiny.* New York, 1958.
Silberman, Bernard S., ed. *Japanese Character and Culture.* Tucson, AZ, 1962.
Singer, Kurt. *Mirror, Sword and Jewel: A Study of Japanese Characteristics.* New York, 1973.
Smethurst, Richard J. *A Social Basis for Prewar Japanese Militarism, the Army and the Rural Community.* Berkeley, CA, 1976.
Staal, M. van der. *Het Masker van Nippon.* Amsterdam, 1936.
Storry, Richard. *The Way of the Samurai.* New York, 1978.
Takeuchi, Tatsuji. *War and Diplomacy in the Japanese Empire.* New York, 1935.
Tanaka, Chikagu. *What Is Nippon Kokutai? Introduction to Nipponese National Principles.* Tokyo, 1935.
Toland, John. *The Rising Sun: The Decline and Fall of the Japanese Empire, 1936–1945.* New York, 1970.
Tsurumi, Kazuko. *Social Change and the Individual: Japan Before and After Defeat in World War II.* Princeton, NJ, 1966.
Tsurumi, Shumsuke. *An Intellectual History of Wartime Japan, 1931–1945.* London, 1986.
Tulischus, Otto D. *Tokyo Record.* New York, 1943.
Turnbull, Stephen R. *The Samurai: A Military History.* London, 1979.
———. *The Book of the Samurai: The Warrior Class of Japan.* New York, 1982.
Varley, H. Paul. *The Samurai.* London, 1970.
———. *Japanese Culture: A Short History.* New York, 1973.
Ward, Robert S. *Asia for the Asiatics?* Chicago, 1945.
Wilson, William Scott. *Ideals of the Samurai: Writings of Japanese Warriors.* Burbank, CA, 1982.
Yamamoto, Tsunetomo. *Hagakure: The Book of the Samurai.* Tokyo, 1979.
———. *Hagakure: A Code to the Way of the Samurai.* Tokyo, 1980.
Yumoto, John M. *The Samurai Sword: A Handbook.* Tokyo, 1958.
Zich, Arthur, et al. *The Rising Sun.* Alexandria, VA, 1977.

Chapter 2
Occupation and Internment

Japanese Conquest of Asia

In fewer than six months, Japan had seized what the Dutch, English, and French colonial powers had taken 300 years and more to acquire. More than 3 million square miles of land in Southeast Asia and practically the entire western half of the Pacific had become the domain of the Japanese emperor. About 350 million indigenous people had been added to the emperor's subjects, and about 350,000 European and American prisoners were in Japanese hands.

In conquering Southeast Asia, the Japanese had created an empire that they would dominate not only militarily, but politically, economically, and culturally. In their scheme of ruling Asia, there was no room for conquered Westerners to live freely in the occupied territories. There were to be no bonds, no contacts, between the "freed Asian peoples" and their ex-colonial rulers.

Under Japanese leadership the evidence of the decadence of European domination had to be eliminated and the divine mission of a new Asian economic community, to be known as "The Greater East Asia Co-Prosperity Sphere," would be established with Japan as its center.

The Japanese were exultant that they now had the opportunity to humiliate the Americans, British, Dutch, and Australians, who for so long had looked down on the Japanese as inferior beings. They relished the fact that the Westerners, who had lost so many battles against the Japanese in such a short time, could now be locked up behind barbed wire and be treated at will.

Prisoners of Japan

The places of imprisonment and internment were as varied as the localities and the circumstances in which soldiers and civilians became captives. There was no typical POW or civilian-internee experience. The conditions of incarceration were, on the whole, better for civilians than for POWs. For the latter, a broad policy of brutality appeared to have been imposed by the various Japanese army commanders—the will of local commanders seemed to have been the dominating factor—but some surprisingly humane conditions were offered to small groups in favored localities. Generally, both POWs and internees were badly fed by Japanese standards, and atrociously by Western standards.

The rights and obligations of POWs are defined in the Geneva Convention, but the Japanese paid only lip service to the convention's rules and regulations. They violated the letter and spirit of the convention in almost every prison and internment camp because of their cynical disregard of every humane consideration and their desire first to humiliate and then to destroy their captives.

POWs

The hours following capture are always the most anxious for a POW. He has no guarantee that his surrender will be accepted.

The Japanese did not interrogate all their POWs. When they did, they often used violence before, during, and after the interviews, to enforce their demands for accurate information.

Captivity usually began with a long march, during which the POWs carried all their baggage. Those captured in small groups often had their valuables taken from them, whereas those who surrendered in larger units were better able to retain them.

Although the POWs did not realize it at the time, the clothes they carried with them into captivity were likely to have to last them the three or more years of their imprisonment. Therefore, prudence in selecting the proper kit to take into prison camp paid heavy dividends.

The housing quarters allotted to newly captured POWs were usually the worst of their captivity, partly because of the exigencies of war, and partly because of the unpreparedness of the Japanese to accept the surrender of large numbers of POWs. In addition, POWs frequently were given no food during the first two or three days of captivity. As POW Hugh V. Clarke noted:

> Being a POW of the Japanese was to become an involuntary subscriber to an extraordinary lottery. You could remain hungry and bored in Changi [Singapore] but relatively undisturbed by the Japanese captors; you could work on the wharves and food dumps and grow fat, if prepared to risk the inevitable bashings or worse if caught scrounging; you could journey to Japan in the early years of the war [Allied submarines permitting] and live in conditions not much worse than a Japanese miner or factory worker; or you could crack the bad-luck jackpot and end up on the Burma-Siam railway.[1]

One of the more interesting, if literary, definitions of a POW came from England's Winston Churchill:

> A Prisoner of War: it is a melancholy state. You are in the power of the enemy. You owe your life to his humanity, your daily bread to his compassion. You must obey his orders, await his pleasure, possess your soul in patience. The days are very long; hours crawl by like paralytic centipedes. Moreover, the whole atmosphere of prison is odious. Companions quarrel about trifles and get the least possible enjoyment from each other's society. You feel a constant humiliation in being fenced in by railings and wire, watched by armed guards and webbed about with a tangle of regulations and restrictions.[2]

Churchill wrote these words before World War II, not knowing then what it would mean to be a POW of the Japanese. Mr. Churchill's statement that "it is a melancholy state" stands in sharp contrast to the words of an unknown POW at Andersonville during the Civil War—described by Major Pat Reid and Maurice Michael as one of "a wretched crowd of 33,000 sick, starving, dirty human beings existing in filth and squalor in thousands of huts, lean-to's, and dugouts, all massed together within a stockaded area of 26 acres"—who wrote:

> I am dying, comrade, dying
> Far away from friends and home
> In this rebel den I'm lying
> Suffering, starving, all alone.

"The prisoner of war is not a criminal, not a transgressor but merely an unfortunate who has been defeated in an armed struggle," Reid and Michael concluded.[3]

Historical reference. It is not known when those captured in war first became the property of their captors, but the practice is believed to have been established by 2000 B.C. The captured soldier was either ransomed for money or property or became a surplus captive treated with callous cruelty. In 352 B.C. Alexander the Great drowned 3,000 men he had captured at Krokos.

As time went on, the system changed; along with the ransoming of prisoners, a system of bartering developed—an exchange of warrior for warrior. On the whole, however, killing POWs was the common practice when cities were captured during the Middle Ages and even later.

Then, captors realized that it would be logical to feed and house POWs and make use of their labor in one way or another. According to Reid and Michael:

After the seventeenth century it was generally agreed that the POW was in the power of the state that captured him, not of the individual captor, so that responsibility for his treatment rested with the state, thus paving the way for the international conventions of the nineteenth and twentieth centuries.[4]

"However," as the *Encyclopaedia Britannica* (11th edition), stated: "Too much confidence must not be placed in regulations concerning the conduct of war. Military necessity, the heat of action, the violence of the feelings which come into play will always at times defeat the most skillfully combined rules diplomacy can devise."

It was not until October 18, 1907, that POWs acquired a status in international law, when the Hague Convention laid down extensive rules regarding POWs that remained in operation during World War I. Among the provisions of the convention were these:

- That after every battle, the combatant shall take steps to look for the shipwrecked, sick and wounded, and protect them from pillage and ill-treatment. When they become prisoners of war, the detaining power shall send a list of names to the country of origin of the POW and shall treat the sick and wounded and bury the dead.

- That hospital ships shall be respected and cannot be captured. That these ships shall not be used for military purposes and shall be distinguished by markings and flags.

However, these rules proved inadequate and were revised in 1929 under the Geneva Convention. World War II showed clearly that still more was needed, and further amendments were made in 1949.

The Geneva Convention. Signed at Geneva on July 27, 1929, by 47 nations, the Geneva Convention was ratified or adhered to by 34 countries. Since Japan had not formally ratified this convention before the outbreak of World War II, the Allied powers sought an assurance from Japan in early 1942 that she would adhere to the convention. Japan replied that she was not formally bound to the convention, but would apply it *mutatis mutandis* ("with changes applied") toward Allied prisoners of war.[5]

The Geneva Convention basically provides "complete codes of the laws of war" and contains a provision that it shall remain in force between the belligerents who are parties to it even though one of them is not a contracting power.

The provisions that had the most influence on the lives and ultimate treatment and fate of the POWs of the Japanese were Articles 2, 7, 9, 11, 12, 13, 18 (General); 30, 31, 32 (Labor); 40, 42 (External Relations); 45, 46, 47, 51, 54, 56 (Disciplinary Punishment); 60, 65, 66 (Judicial Punishment); and 77 (Information).[6] The text of these provisions is presented in Appendix A.

Contact between Japan and the United States. In spite of the suddenness with which hostilities broke out on December 7, 1941, Japan and the United States remained in diplomatic contact through the neutral countries of Argentina, Sweden, and Switzerland. Shortly after the formal declaration of war, the U.S. Department of State took on the issue of the proper treatment of American nationals in Japanese hands, contacting the Japanese government through the Swiss minister in Tokyo. The Japanese assured the United States that the provisions of the Geneva Convention of 1929 would be applied to American POWs, although Japan had not as yet ratified the convention treaty. This information was received at the American Legation in Bern, Switzerland, on February 4, 1942, and was the first specific communication between the two belligerents concerning POWs.

Japan and the United States then sent each other assurances that each would apply the Geneva Convention regulations. However, on February 24, 1942, the Swiss minister in Tokyo received information that the Japanese would "apply on condition of reciprocity the Geneva Convention for treatment of prisoners of war and civilian internees insofar as the Convention's regulations shall be applicable." Japan made the point (for all practical purposes to all the Allies) that she was not obligated to comply with this treaty because she had not ratified it, but that she was complying with it in part, anyway, and thus was assuming the role of an obliging benefactor.

POW Information Bureau. In compliance with Article 7 of the Geneva Convention, Japan created the Prisoner of War Information Bureau (PWIB).[7] The PWIB, enacted by Imperial Ordinance No. 1246, dated December 27, 1941, was a bureau outside the cabinet but under the supervision of the premier.[8] Because the premier delegated all matters pertaining to POWs to the minister of the army and since the portfolios of the premier and minister of the army were both held by Tojo, he was actually in sole charge of the PWIB.

Imperial Ordinance No. 1246 set forth the following articles:

- The purpose of the PWIB, namely, that its prime concern would be communication, correspondence, and information on prisoners.

- The location of the PWIB (in Tokyo).

- The manner in which the PWIB would be staffed.

- The chain of command, from the premier to the minister of the army to the director of the PWIB.

Although the PWIB was supposedly under the direct supervision of the minister of the army, it was actually the all-powerful Military Affairs Bureau, the most important bureau in the Ministry of the Army, that acted as the supervisory organ, handling all POW matters until the War Prisoner Control Bureau (also referred to as Prisoner of War Management Bureau) was created.[9]

Even after this new bureau was created, the important Military Affairs Bureau not only acted as a clearinghouse for all orders from the minister of the army, but was in reality the direct supervisory organ, the power having been delegated to it by Premier Tojo. Thus, Major General Muto, head of the Military Affairs Bureau at the time the PWIB was created, was actually in charge of both the PWIB and the War Prisoner Control Bureau. This arrangement was in conflict with the Geneva Convention, which states that the "Prisoner of War Information Bureau shall be a separate, impartial organ outside of control by the various war departments."

This was the situation, then, when the Japanese forces began their move southward, capturing great numbers of Allied prisoners. Japanese unit commanders in the field would take any prisoners captured to a divisional compound after a hasty interrogation. From the various compounds the prisoners would be sent to prison areas designated by the army commanders (not by Tokyo).

Meeting in Tokyo on the treatment of POWs. The overall policies on the treatment of POWs were decided at meetings of the bureau chiefs of the Ministry of the Army. At such a meeting in late April 1942, the treatment of POWs captured in the southern areas was discussed. Those present at this meeting were Premier Tojo; Kimura, vice minister of the army; Tominago, chief of the Personnel Bureau; Sato, chief of the Military Affairs Bureau; Tanaka, chief of the Military Service Bureau; Kan, chief of the Ordinance Bureau; Kurihashi, chief of the Intelligence Bureau; Miki, chief of the Surgeon General's Bureau; Oyama, chief of the Legal Affairs Bureau; Nakamura, chief of the Gendarmerie; Hoda, chief of the Armed Forces Bureau; Matsumura, chief of the Army Press Bureau; and private secretaries. The decision that this imposing array of Japanese bureaucrats made was that prisoners were to be treated in accordance with Ministry of Army Notification No. 22, dated December 14, 1904, to be modified as the need arose.[10] These Japanese army regulations for handling POWs are presented in Appendix B.

From this point on, the actual treatment accorded POWs and the policy sent down from the Ministry of the Army decidedly conflict. For example, in the Philippines, Japanese troops, under the command of Lieutenant General Homma, violated not only the Geneva Convention of 1929, but the spirit of the Japanese regulations concerning POWs. They forced American POWs to march for miles without food or water, placed them in unsheltered areas without proper sanitation, allowed them to die by the thousands without medical assistance, and informed them that this treatment was a planned attempt to eliminate unwanted POWs. Nowhere, however, are there indications that such treatment was directly ordered by the Ministry of the Army in Tokyo. Tojo, as minister of the army, assumed responsibility for such actions but denied having ordered them.[11]

General Homma, commander of the Philippine area, also denied having ordered such treatment. A comment by Kunji Suzuki, chief of the Tokyo War Camps, is interesting, in that it sums up the attitude of high-ranking Japanese toward POWs: "Although prisoners of war in Europe are regarded as honorable war prisoners, in Japanese eyes they are considered as pitiful war prisoners. Pitiful because they are, according to Japanese opinion, under the greatest disgrace possible."

POW labor forces. During a meeting of the various prison camp commanders in September 1942 in Tokyo, Lieutenant General Mikio, then chief of the Prisoner of War Control Bureau, stated that "war prisoners should not pass a single day eating the bread of idleness."[12] Mikio stated that the intent was to use POW labor to the utmost to increase production in Japan. He also stated that the Japanese should try to make a reasonable and efficient use of POWs, refraining from force and impatience.

General Uyemura mentioned that the "no work, no food" program, to be applied to *all* POWs, would be in violation of the Geneva Convention because officers were not liable for common labor. However, Tojo decided to utilize the officers as laborers even though it was the sworn intent of the Japanese to respect the spirit of the Geneva Convention.

> Rather than having tens of thousands of POWs to just feed and guard them, the Japanese thought it a brilliant solution to put these men to work. It would enable the Japanese to build railways, airfields, and huge equipment shelters, and to have these men as labor gangs work on docks, in the mines and factories. In the jungles of Burma and Sumatra and on the Japanese home islands themselves, the POWs could not easily escape or cause any trouble.[13]

In many ways, however, the Japanese underestimated the ingenuity of the POWs, who sabotaged anything and everything they could. As Burma POW Roy Bulcock described:

> At dawn the working parties assembled, swallowed a plate of pap and perhaps a mug of lukewarm, sugarless tea made the night before, and off we went to the docks, the aerodrome, the oil refinery, petrol and bomb dumps, and the numerous other slave-gangs, where we sweated and suffered and bled. "Bled" is no exaggeration, for men worked barefooted on bomb-scarred ground covered with broken glass, handled jagged metal

plates and had their scalps split open because they didn't "speedo" (go fast enough) sufficiently to please the bad temper of the guards.

In spite of the danger of discovery, prisoners became adept at bending the lugs on bombs, making petrol drums leak, and loading railway trucks so that the doors would jam shut and couldn't be opened. Perhaps the most strenuous job was moving forty-foot lengths of fifteen-inch piping from a destroyed oil refinery, for the Nips would never allow sufficient men for the weight involved, and frequently the pipe would be dropped on someone's foot. A task would be set for the day and had to be completed, no matter how long we went without food.[14]

POWs as propaganda tools. It was at these "policy" meetings in Tokyo that the decision was made to use the POWs as a means of enhancing the trust, confidence, and respect of the peoples of Asia for Japan. Thus, in direct contradiction to previous dictates from the ministry, POWs were humiliated in public in Seoul, Korea; Chosen, Manchuria; Manila, the Philippines; and Singapore, Malaya.

Japan was ready to step forward as the Champion of the East, to carve an empire out of the Orient, and to free the Asians from the curse of the "white peril." Hence, Japan had another use for the POWs—propaganda —for nothing would so add to the prestige of the Japanese as the sight of white men humbly sweeping dung from the streets under the bayonets of Nipponese troops.[15]

Japanese treatment of POWs was importantly affected by the ignorance of ordinary Japanese soldiers, junior-grade officers and below, of the western concept of being an honorable POW. They generally had no place on their social scale for any POW, who was considered lower than any animal, not entitled to the same treatment as even a dog. Only strict restraints from above could keep the ordinary Japanese soldier, indoctrinated to fight to the death, from despising and abusing prisoners (those who would not fight to the death).

Contempt for captives. A contempt for POWs was the natural outcome of the code of bushido, inculcated into the Japanese soldier as part of his basic training. According to bushido, it was cowardly to show one's back to the enemy and to surrender to him; it brought dishonor to one's name and family. When the first American POWs surrendered in large numbers in Bataan, the Japanese were astounded to receive requests that their names be reported to the U.S. government so their families would know they were alive.

Japanese soldiers did not distinguish between those who fought honorably and courageously until surrender was inevitable and those who gave up without a fight. All POWs were the same; they were not entitled to respect because they had lost their honor.[16] Men who should have been dead could have no rights.

In their own armed services and even to some extent in civilian life, the Japanese practiced the active brutality of which POWs were so often the victims. The noncommissioned officer, himself struck by his superiors, passed on the blows to the private on any occasion of displeasure, and the humble private slapped or clubbed the POW. Among the POWs the consensus of opinion seemed to be that the Japanese were brutal, rather than sadistic, and largely unaware of their own brutality, which found its target in an animal as readily as in a helpless POW.

The Japanese were arrogant in victory and obsessed with a desire to take revenge on individuals for the white race's galling pretensions to superiority over the colored. This obsession led to their calculated humiliations of prisoners.

In the camps the conditions were appalling. Accommodations were inadequate, sanitation nonexistent. The prisoners were systematically beaten and subjected to a variety of tortures; those who were recaptured after escaping were shot or beheaded by sword, the usual Japanese method.

The extent of ill treatment can be appreciated by the following comparison: In the European theater of war, of the 235,470 British and American POWs who were captured by the Germans and Italians, 9,350, or 4 percent, died in captivity. In contrast, 31.4 percent of the POWs in the Pacific theater of war died in captivity (see Chapter 9).

The degree to which the prescribed POW regulations were followed depended on the commanding officer of each prison camp. In camps where atrocities such as deadly beatings, deliberate starvation, and extreme torture were committed, the camp staff was directly at fault. That the high command did not investigate the camps showed their lack of concern.[17]

In 1943 the Japanese War Ministry published the following regulation: "In case a prisoner of war is guilty of an act of insubordination, he shall be subject to imprisonment or arrest, and ANY OTHER MEASURES DEEMED NECESSARY FOR THE PURPOSE OF DISCIPLINE MAY BE ADDED." It was the common practice to inflict corporal punishment for the slightest offense. In its mildest form such punishment consisted of slapping, beating, and kicking. Thousands died of this form of punishment alone, for many were already diminished by disease and starvation.

Food and health. The staple diet was rice and vegetables. The rice would be served with traces of sugar, with pickles or vegetables, and occasionally with shreds of meat or fish. Vegetable soup was also commonly served.

The deficiency in vitamins was felt after six months. Although many men caught such tropical diseases as malaria, dengue, or dysentery, it was malnutrition from slow starvation that immeasurably increased the deadliness of all the diseases. To a large extent, it was calculated malnutrition.

The amount of food that the prisoners bought with their own funds or they received as gifts was taken into account by the Japanese. It was apparently the Japanese policy to keep their captives below normal—below Japanese standards, that is—so they would be less likely to give trouble.

The following are some specifics concerning food items.

- Food was never adequate: 8 ounces of poor-grade rice made into a thin gruel (called *lugao* in the Philippines) twice a day. The rice contained much foreign matter, such as insects, fine gravel, weevils.

- The quantity of rice in grams ranged from 238 in Changi, Singapore; to 280 in Java, Sumatra; to 350 in Mukaishima, Japan; to 360 in Manchuria. Throughout the camps in Japan the daily ration was 750 grams for those on full work in mines and in factories, 500 grams for those doing light and administrative work, and 300 grams for hospital patients.

- The basic staple was rice in the Philippines, Dutch East Indies, French Indochina, Burma, Siam, China, Formosa, and Japan. In China, there were some supplies of barley and wheat. In Japan there were some camp reports of barley, millet, soybeans, corn, and wheat. In Manchuria the staples were kafir corn and beans, with some wheat flour.

- Vegetables consisted of greens, vegetable tops, camote (sweet potato) and camote tops, vines, and roots; carrots, radishes, seaweed, field weeds, okra, lily roots, watercress, and cabbage. Vegetables were boiled into soup, and small amounts of meat were sometimes added.

- Meat was issued in minute portions—a quarter ounce per man per week, usually rotten. Meat issues came from *carabao* (beef), horse, pig, rabbit, octopus, snake, duck, fish, dog, and cat. If it was *carabao*, it was usually bones, stomach, or other edible offal. On one occasion in Karenko, Formosa, after vultures circled the camp for days, they suddenly disappeared. The next day the Japanese announced "duck soup"; the POWs called it "buzzard broth."

- Additional nutrients furnished in some places were banana buds, papaya, mango, and beans. Sugar was either available in fair amounts or was rare. Salt was often mentioned as deficient.

- Canteens or commissaries were allowed in a number of camps, depending upon the possibility of purchases from outside the camps. Fresh fruits, canned goods, jams, jelly, coffee, tea, cocoa, and mung beans were available in limited amounts.

- Food "supplements" for daily survival encompassed any dog, cat, grasshopper, lizard, crow, worm, rat—any obtainable animal or insect. An

American colonel who was a POW in Formosa bragged about his fine rat trap. After liberation, he caught a rat at his home. As he threw it in the trash, his eyes filled with tears and he quietly said, "It was such a big fat one."

Escapes. During the war the Japanese POW regulations were amended to permit an escaping prisoner to be punished in the same way as a deserter from the Japanese army. Under this regulation the death penalty was imposed in nearly every case in which a POW attempted to escape or had escaped and been recaptured. Escapes are dealt with in more detail in Chapter 11.

Destruction of documents. From Japan's initiation of war until her unconditional surrender, the murder, torture, ill treatment, and willful neglect of POWs continued unceasingly. Those who committed these crimes never expected that retribution would follow, for as one of them said, "we shall be victors and will not have to answer questions." When it finally became apparent that Japan would have to surrender, there was an organized attempt to destroy all documentary and other evidence of the ill treatment of POWs and civilian internees.[18]

On August 20, 1945, the chief of the Prisoner of War Camps sent a signal to all commands in which POW camps were located, and the following two extracts are striking testimony of the Japanese guilt regarding the treatment of prisoners, military and civilian:

• Documents that would be unbearable in the hands of the enemy are to be treated in the same way as secret documents and destroyed.

• Personnel who ill treated POWs and internees or who are held in extremely bad favor by them are permitted to take care of the situation by immediately transferring or fleeing without a trace.

Red Cross food parcels. Red Cross food parcels are mentioned in almost every Military Tribunal report or other war documentation. In some camps Japanese officials refused them, and in others they stashed the parcels away and never gave them out. Many camps delayed issuing the food and then gave out only small amounts at a time. When canned goods were issued, the Japanese punctured them to force their immediate consumption. In all reports concerning Red Cross food, these supplies were credited with saving lives just in time or providing that little extra to extend survival. Almost all parcels were opened and ransacked by the Japanese before they reached the prisoners.

The following are examples of multinational and American Red Cross parcels, their destinations and contents. The first multinational Red Cross food, medicine, clothing and other items reached the Philippines in November 1942:

> 22,160 eleven-pound parcels from the United States and Canada
> 271 cases of drugs from the United States and Canada
> 210 cases bulk foodstuffs from South Africa
> 2,220 articles of clothing from the United States
> 640 pairs of shoes from the United States
> 3,360 toilet kits from the United States
> 3,588 toilet articles from the United States
> 6,120 cakes of soap from the United States
> 25,000 packs of cigarettes from the United States
> 4,896 tins of tobacco from the United States

The second shipment, from Great Britain alone, reached Manila in December:

> 13,750 eleven-pound food parcels
> 8,725 cases of bulk food
> 87 bales of clothing

A standard American Red Cross parcel contained the following items (Canadian and British parcels contained similar but not identical items):

> Evaporated milk, irradiated—one 14½-ounce can
> Lunch biscuit (hardtack)—one 8-ounce package
> Cheese—one 8-ounce package
> Instant cocoa—one 8-ounce tin
> Sardines—one 15-ounce tin
> Oleomargarine (Vitamin A)—one 1-pound tin
> Corned beef—one 12-ounce tin
> Sweet chocolate—two 5½-ounce bars
> Sugar, granulated—one 2-ounce package
> Powdered orange concentrate—two 3½-ounce packages
> Soup (dehydrated)—two 2½-ounce packages
> Prunes—one 16-ounce package
> Instant coffee—4-ounce tin
> Cigarettes—one pack of 10
> Smoking tobacco—one 2¼-ounce package[19]

Aid to prisoners in the Far East. The *Prisoners of War Bulletin* was published monthly by the American Red Cross (starting sometime in 1943) to inform Americans at home about the POWs and internees held by the Japanese, Germans, and Italians. In the October 1944 issue, the American Red Cross expressed its concern about a number of aid programs to the prisoners in the Pacific theater. For example, it was stated that there was no positive assurance that the 80,000 multivitamins shipped weekly were reaching their intended destinations.

The Red Cross was also concerned that the Japanese had not yet approved the appointment of a delegate of the International Committee of the Red Cross in the Philippines. (A similar situation existed in Siam, Burma, Malaya, and the Dutch East Indies.) The Red Cross deplored the lack of vital information about the many camps in these regions and stated that until the Japanese permitted neutral representatives to make inspections, most of the questions about the treatment of the prisoners, camp locations, and other important details would remain unanswered.

"There is no wish to exaggerate the importance of the steps recently taken to get aid, relief and encouragement to the prisoners in the Far East," the bulletin stated. "Much more needs to be accomplished before there can be any feeling of satisfaction at what has been done."[20]

> The exchange of American and Japanese nationals at Marmagoa, in Portuguese India, was set for October 15, 1943. The diplomatic exchange ship *Gripsholm* is carrying relief supplies for American prisoners of war and civilian internees in the Far East, valued at over US $1,500,000, as well as next of kin packages. The American Red Cross has confirmed that the relief supplies shipped a year ago for prisoners in the Philippines were received and distributed last January (1943), and that their arrival was most timely.[21]

The question arises: How much did the Red Cross know about the distribution of parcels? There was no one in the camps to tell them how much was really given to each prisoner and when. Similarly, the prisoners had no idea how much the Red Cross had shipped and how many parcels the Japanese had distributed in all the camps. After the war a huge number of parcels were found stored in warehouses all over the Pacific.[22]

Liquidation/disposal of POWs. One question was always on the minds of the prisoners: What are the Japanese plans in case the Allies land near camps in which POWs are incarcerated? Early in 1942 the Japanese already had contingency plans; these plans were modified as the war progressed.[23]

The prisoners were convinced that POWs in camps in the larger towns would not be the victims of mass murder because of the stir such a massacre would create. Others, in smaller camps located in the interior, were seriously worried about the consequences of possible Allied landings and advances into the areas near the camps.[24]

The following is from the monthly report on POWs by the Japanese vice-minister of war:

> As the war situation has become very critical, I have been ordered to notify you not to make any blunders in the treatment of prisoners of war based upon the attached Outline for the Disposal of Prisoners of War according to the change of situation, when the havocs of war make themselves felt in our Imperial Homeland and in Manchuko.[25]

As the war progressed in favor of the Allies, the Japanese had second thoughts about the "disposal" of POWs to avoid an unfavorable bargaining position during peace negotiations.[26]

Release/liberation. In most of the Japanese-controlled areas, there was a time lag between the capitulation and the rescue of prisoners in Japanese hands. In many areas prisoners knew, from their secret radio sets or from the admission of their guards, exactly when the war had ended. However, a week or so passed in many cases before the Japanese could bring themselves to make a formal announcement.

In many camps this interval was used to flood the camp with food, medicines, and hoarded Red Cross parcels. The Japanese intention of fattening up the prisoners and internees before they were released was often childishly obvious. However, it was impossible to remedy years of malnutrition in a week or two, especially because starved men, women, and children could not immediately adjust their digestions to a fuller and richer diet.

In Japan itself, Allied aircraft soon identified the camps and began dropping food, cigarettes, medicines, and clothing, as well as two-way radios, by which the prisoners could make known their condition and their specific wishes for help.

The Repatriation of Allied Prisoners of War and Internees (RAPWI) was in action soon after Japan's capitulation, although the delay in arranging for the surrender of Malaya and Singapore entailed a wait that was trying to most prisoners in those areas.

Prisoners and internees were evacuated as rapidly as possible; by air, mostly, if they were fit enough. The prisoners and internees in China were liberated by the British fleet. Prisoners and internees in the Dutch East Indies had a much harder time because of the announcement of independence by the Indonesians and many subsequent attacks on Westerners.

The capitulation of Japan took most prisoners and internees by surprise. The POWs and internees knew that the war had been going badly for Japan, but they feared that the Japanese would fight on, as they had so often declared they would. So many heartening rumors had proved groundless in the past that liberation was a mental jolt to most prisoners. The emotion was almost unbearable. The transition from misery to happiness had been too abrupt.

Civilian Internees

Introduction. The civilian internees were, on the whole, better treated by the Japanese than were the POWs. Civilians were interned because the Japanese were determined to wipe out all Western colonial "influences"; they felt threatened by "enemy" Westerners walking about freely with antagonistic attitudes toward the occupying forces.

In a subtler form of torment, the Japanese simply dumped men, women, and children behind guarded gates of small, and sometimes large, city blocks fenced in by bamboo matting and barbed wire, where the internees were left to fend for themselves. Every humiliation was imposed upon the captives to degrade them in the eyes of the local Asian populations. For political, military, and psychological reasons, the Japanese decided on either immediate or gradual internment of the civilians, depending upon the area in which the Westerners were living.

In general, the Ministry of Foreign Affairs made up the rules for the internment of civilians. In 1943, the Ministry of War decided to apply the "Regulations for the Treatment of Prisoners of War" to all civilian internees in the territories supervised by the army: Hong Kong, the Philippines, Burma, Malaya, Sumatra and Java (Dutch East Indies), and North Borneo.[27] This notification and its amendment allowed the Japanese to treat the civilian internees as POWs of noncommissioned officer rank. A regulation on the management of army internment camps was issued in January 1944 by Field Marshal Terauchi in Saigon.[28] From these regulations, regional ones were designed for Java, Sumatra, and Borneo.[29]

General treatment. Although the treatment of civilian captives was, on the whole, less harsh than that of the POWs, the internees suffered the same ill treatment in relation to food and medicine. The only difference was that internees were rarely used as slave labor and only occasionally used to work on military-oriented projects. Since civilian internment centers were, in general, much larger than POW camps, the civilians mainly had to maintain their camps or "protective centers" (city blocks).

The men and women were not excluded from being slapped or beaten or from receiving other punishments. However, children were not harmed, although they suffered from malnutrition in the same manner as did the adults.

Reports concerning the overall treatment of civilians were compiled in the same way as those of the POWs: interviews and inquiries. Some of the internees saw fit to stress the more favorable features of their experience, while others emphasized the more unfortunate facets.

Treatment in the various areas of Asia. The civilians interned in Malaya were gradually concentrated in Changi peninsula, first in the Changi prison—the civil jail built to accommodate 600 native prisoners but made to receive 3,000 or more internees—and later in Sime Road barracks; in both camps there were separate sections for men and for women and children. In these camps, conditions were more rigorous than in most other internment centers, and after October 1943 approximated closely those experienced by the POWs. The camps were governed internally by a complex and democratic organization that succeeded in checking, if not in eliminating, rackeetering, which was, of course, connected with obtaining extra food. Discipline, including bowing to the Japanese, was not so much a matter of severity as it was humiliating, and there were many indiscriminate bashings. Punishment for the men included beatings, kneeling in the sun for long periods, and other "subtle" methods. However, a library of 7,000 books was collected, and concerts, plays, and other community activities helped to make the time pass.

On October 10, 1943, known to Changi internees as "the double tenth," the scene changed abruptly. The *kempeitai*, the Japanese military police, descended on Changi, searched the buildings, and left carrying off 50 men and three secret radios they had found. The Japanese suspected that the internees were sending out radio signals and attributed a successful Allied attack on a Japanese convoy to these signals. How the internees were to collect the information they were supposed to have sent out was never given any consideration. Not all the 50 men who were interrogated returned, and most of those who did had been badly injured. Everyone endured a cut in food rations, and all forms of study and recreation were abolished except for a weekly concert.

The treatment of civilian internees was also severe at Kuching, North Borneo, where the food was poor and a man often received a beating for smiling through the barbed wire without permission at his wife and children.

In China, both in Shanghai and Hong Kong, conditions were less harsh. In Hong Kong, apart from the inevitable matter of food, the internees were not badly treated, and the Japanese even gave up attempts to teach them to bow. Parcels from friends outside the camps were allowed to be brought into the camps once a month.

In Bangkok, Siam, the civilian centers were inspected by the Japanese but not controlled by them. The conditions there were relatively mild.

Many of the internees in China and Japan were missionaries. The Japanese treated them with some respect, which was not the case with military chaplains captured with Allied forces. Many missionaries were not interned until months after Japan had entered the war. Japanese respect for old age showed itself, for example, in their treatment of a small group of nuns and Protestant missionaries interned in Japan. These internees were allowed to go shopping and for walks under guard. They were treated with kindness by their guards and exchanged language lessons with them.

A missionary who ran an orphanage in Hong Kong was allowed to remain in charge of it and was not interned. She was given access to the orphanage in a bank seized by the Japanese, had a pass to move about, and was not molested even when soldiers were quartered in part of the building. Instead, the Japanese, who cherish children, sent some of their own food to the orphans. Except for the increasing food shortages, she could hardly have been better treated. In contrast, a priest in the Philippines, although not interned until 1944, found that the 2,000 internees in Los Banos camp were being fed starvation rations, although the American troops who liberated them found nearby warehouses stuffed with rice.

Those interned in the Dutch East Indies experienced intermittently severe forms of discipline. On occasion, hundreds of men were lined up and forced to beat each other, in a form of collective punishment usually reserved for POWs. In spite of the acute shortage of food, the Japanese frowned on personal efforts to supplement rations; nearly everywhere they made trading "over the fence or wall" an offense. However, even harsh punishments failed to stop the internees. At Weishian, China, one man was caught getting eggs in over the wall and was imprisoned in a cow shed for two weeks. Since he was a Trappist monk, he rather enjoyed his solitary confinement, however.

Another world. The physical appearance of the men, women, and children internees resulting from the brutal treatment they had received from their captors was best described by a British officer who visited Java, the Dutch East Indies, shortly after the war. Lieutenant Colonel Reid-Collins was sent to Batavia, where he arrived on September 18, 1945, to organize emergency air supplies to POW camps and civilian internment centers in Java and Sumatra. In Batavia alone, he was responsible for feeding 65,000 prisoners and internees.

His first reaction on visiting the camps was "that he was in another world and talking to people who had already died."[30] The internees and POWs had indeed lived for years in another world, with its own rules and laws, its own social and political structure, inhabited by people with a set of attitudes and habits that could exist only in a prison camp environment, controlled by captors who had little regard for the well being of those they held captive. One observation by Reid-Collins leads naturally into the next chapter (The World of the Camp Prisoner):

> Another abnormality that Reid-Collins noticed was the urge to acquire and possess trivial things: a piece of string, an old cigarette packet, a piece of cellophane paper. He found that the women carried about with a collection of useless material, such as old tins and pieces of cloth. When the ex-internees travelled from Padang, Sumatra to Batavia, en route for Holland, they took with them these old tins and make-shift cooking utensils. On board the ship, the mothers brushed the crumbs off the tables

after each meal and took them away. All these scraps they kept in the tins, so ingrained was the habit of hoarding every morsel.[31]

NOTES

1. Hugh V. Clarks, *Last Stop Nagasaki*, Sydney, 1984.
2. Winston S. Churchill, *A Roving Commission*, New York, 1939, quoted in *The Hard Way Home*, Col. William C. Braly, Washington, DC, 1947, p. 152.
3. Major Pat Reid and Maurice Michael, *Prisoner of War: The Inside Story of the POW*, London, 1984.
4. *Ibid.*, p. 50.
5. IMTFE, exhibits 1468, 1494, 1956, 1679, 1958, 2027; record pp. 27140, 14558.
6. From "Multilateral Agreements, 1918–1930," U.S. Department of State, pp. 930–96. IMTFE record pp. 17191–92, 27124–27. Affidavit and testimony: 36415–17. Application of Geneva Convention to POWs and civilian internees—Great Britain–Japanese negotiations: IMTFE 14754–90, 14846–83. U.S.-Japanese negotiations: IMTFE 14728–32, 14734–53, 14792–822, 13826–36, 15001–17. Ratification—Japanese army reply: IMTFE 27181; Japanese navy reply: IMTFE 27178–80. Treaty conventions, international acts, protocols: U.S. Senate Document 134, IV (1923–1937), 5229. Note: The Geneva Convention of 1929, signed by 47 nations, has but one reference to civilians: "individuals who follow armed forces without directly belonging thereto, such as newspaper correspondents and reporters, suttlers, contractors"—and states that they shall be treated as military prisoners of war, leaving the application of terms of the convention to general noncombatant internees as a matter of national option.
7. Rapport du Comité International de la Croix Rouge: Vol. 1, pp. 324, 463; Vol. 2, pp. 167, 222: Japanese Bureau for Information on Prisoners. IMTFE, exhibits 1980C and 1980E and 1981A and 1981B: Statement by General Tojo that there was no need for the Allied Governments or Red Cross to complain about the treatment of prisoners; the Government in Tokyo had absolute confidence in their local commanders. IMTFE, record pp. 12872–73, 15506–53, 16085–90, 16097–101, and 34311–37: Handling of protests.
8. IMTFE, record pp. 14440–43, 17526–30, 27129–43, 35584.
9. IMTFE, record pp. 585, 16966, 32959–63, 33126–29, 33160–61: Military Affairs Bureau. IMTFE, record pp. 5653–65 and 5799–801: POW Affairs Central Investigation Committee. IMTFE, record pp. 33294–96, 33311–12, 33371–74, 33416, 33418–20, 33424–26, and 33504–22: General.
10. IMTFE, exhibits 1980B and 1960: Statement that no central order was issued to mistreat prisoners, but rather an order given to the military to adhere to strict discipline. War Ministry Notification No. 22, February 14, 1904, as amended by the War Ministry Notification Nos. 167, 1904–7, 1905–31, 1914–30 and 57, 1943: Japanese Regulations for the Treatment of POWs—General Provisions, Capture and Evacuation of POWs, Imprisonment and Administration of POWs. War Ministry Notification No. 29, April 21, 1943, as amended by Notification No. 58, 1943: IMTFE, exhibit 1965A.
11. IMTFE, record p. 442688: There was no proof that maltreatment of prisoners was ordered or instigated by Tokyo. IMTFE, record pp. 27655ff.; RvO IC 775; 779; 2365; 2366; 5279: On the contrary, Tokyo insisted that the commanders

were told to treat the prisoners humanely, and that this was recorded in specific Rules and Regulations for the Treatment of Prisoners.

12. IMTFE, record p. 14285; exhibits 1960, 1962; record p. 14361 and on; document No. 2688: Decision and principle of General Tojo that "no one eats who does not work." The forced labor was to be done on a "voluntary" basis.

13. Note by this author.

14. Roy Bulcock, *Of Death but Once*, Melbourne, 1947.

15. IMTFE, exhibit 1977: Picture stories of good treatment of POWs. IMTFE, record pp. 13707ff.: Propaganda movies on captured POWs.

16. IMTFE, record pp. 27117ff., p. 42618, and exhibit 3043: Military discipline of Japan much different from the rest of the world's armed forces.

17. IMTFE, record pp. 14747ff., exhibits 2017 and 2022: Statement by the Japanese that prisoners were treated well; there was sufficient recreation and medical treatment and that abuse never occurred, unless prisoners disobeyed certain rules. RvO IC 9735; IMTFE, exhibit 3051; record pp. 49676ff.: Orders to commanders in the field to improve treatment of prisoners to avoid negative Allied propaganda. IMTFE, record pp. 17752, 27147, 35667–69, and 35768–76: Japanese Foreign Ministry affidavit and testimony on treatment of POWs and civilian internees. IMTFE, record pp. 27282–309, 27315–48, 27354–85, 33294–96, 33311–12, 33371–74, 33416, 33418–22, 33424–26, and 33504–22: Japanese Navy Ministry affidavit and testimony on treatment of POWs and civilian internees. IMTFE, record pp. 5493–96, 5506–07, 5510–12, 14426–28, 14431–37, 14440–76, 14558–91, 14597–604, 27182–90, 27435–37, 35162–64, 35247, 35319–22, 35553, 35585–89, 3576876: General treatment of prisoners.

18. IMTFE, record p. 49759 and exhibits 2001, 2011: Instructions by the Ministry of War and the chief of the Kempeitai to destroy all dossiers and documents.

19. E. Bartlett Kerr, *Surrender and Survival*, New York, 1985, pp. 125–127.

20. *Prisoners of War Bulletin* (American Red Cross) 1:4 (August 1943).

21. *Prisoners of War Bulletin* 1:6 (November 1943).

22. *Prisoners of War Bulletin* 2:10 (October 1944). Rapport du Comité International de la Croix Rouge, Vol. 1, pp. 68A, 159, 461, 464a, 463, 500, 484: General Red Cross aid information. Vol. 1, pp. 479, 480, 512–517; and IMTFE, record p. 5392: Shipment of money and goods to prisoners. Rapport du Comité International de la Croix Rouge; Vol. 1, pp. 473ff.; RvO IC 9735; and IMTFE, exhibit 3051: Measures taken by the U.S. and Europe to aid POWs and civilian internees held by Japan. Dr. D. van Velden in "De Japanse Burgerkampen" [Japanese civilian internment camps], Franeker, the Netherlands, 1977, p. 130; IMTFE, exhibit 2016, record p. 27147; and RvO IC 9742: Help from the Red Cross and neutral countries to prisoners and internees. Van Velden, op. cit., p. 134; IMTFE, exhibit 2016, record p. 14728; and RvO IC 359, 6209, 10081, 3165, and 3633: Assistance and relief operations: Japan. Van Velden, op. cit., p. 135; IMTFE, exhibit 2016: Assistance and relief operations: Camps in China. Van Velden, op. cit., p. 144; RvO IC 3636: Financial support to prisoners in China. Van Velden, op. cit., pp. 158–162; RvO IC 567, 603, 604, 1782, 2416, 3474, 3630, 3638, 3717, 4120, 4265, 9703, 9741, 9760: Financial support to prisoners in the Dutch East Indies. Van Velden, op. cit., p. 175; IMTFE exhibits 2028 and 2033: Distribution of Red Cross parcels. Van Velden, op. cit., pp. 176–177; Rapport du Comité International de la Croix Rouge, Vol. 1, p. 477: Shipment of Red Cross parcels—Asama Maru: July 1942, 6,993 crates; Tatsatu Maru: September 1942, 48,818 crates; Kamakura Maru: October 1942, 47,210 crates; Teia Maru: October 1943, 140,000 parcels.

23. RvO IC 787; 4349.
24. War Ministry, Asia Conference Report No. 1456, May 6, 1942: Disposal of POWs. IMTFE exhibit 1965A: Disposal of enemy aliens in distress. IMTFE, exhibits 2015, 1978, record pp. 11442, 12781, 13420, 13495, 14911ff.; exhibits 1622, 1655–1658, 1668, and 1686: Outline and plans for the disposal of POWs and internees in case Allied forces would land in the various areas of the Dutch East Indies. RvO IC 4349.
25. IMTFE exhibit 1978; Notification Army—Asia Secret, No. 2257; March 17, 1945: Outline for the disposal of POWs.
26. Policy March 11. 1945: With the greatest efforts, prevent the POWs from falling into the hands of the enemy. Further, carry out a transfer to other places for those POWs for whom it is necessary.
27. IMTFE exhibit 1965A; also note 10. RvO IC 2158.
28. RvO IC 9901; 2158.
29. Dr. D. van Velden, op. cit., pp. 565–575; appendixes 8, 9, and 10. IMTFE, record p. 14361, document 2688.
30. Lord Russell of Liverpool, *The Knights of Bushido*, London, 1958, p. 209.
31. *Ibid.*, p. 210.

SOURCES

Prisoners of Japan

Allen, Louis. "To Be a Prisoner." *Journal of European Studies* 16 (1986), 233–248.
Bailey, Ronald. *Prisoner of War*. New York, 1982.
Barker, A. J. *Prisoner of War*. New York, 1975.
Beaumont, Jaon. "Rank, Privilege and POW." *War and Society* (Australia) 1:1 (1983), 67–94.
———. *Survival and Leadership in Captivity, 1941–1945*. Sydney, 1988.
———. "Victims of War: The Allies and the Transport of POWs by Sea, 1939–1945." *Journal of the Australian War Memorial* 2 (1983), 1–7.
Brugmans, I. J., et al. *Nederlands Indie Onder Japanese Bezetting* [Dutch East Indies under Japanese Occupation]. Franeker, the Netherlands, 1960.
Cohen, Elie A. *Human Behavior in the Concentration Camp*. New York, 1953.
Dull, Paul S., and Michael Takaaki. *The Tokyo Trials*. Ann Arbor, MI, 1957.
Flory, William E. B. *Prisoner of War: A Study in the Development of International Law*. Washington, DC, 1942.
Foreign Analysis Division, Bureau of Overseas Intelligence, Office of War Information, Record Group 208; National Archives. *The Attitudes of POWs*. Washington, DC.
Georgetown University. Institute of World Policy. *Prisoners of War*. Washington, DC, 1948.
Hall, David O. W. *Prisoners of Japan*. Wellington, New Zealand, 1949.
Hatch, Gardner, ed. *American Ex-Prisoners of War*. Paducah, KY, 1988.
Manes, Donald L. "Barbed Wire Command: The Legal Nature of the Command Responsibilities of the Senior Prisoner in a Prisoner of War Camp." *Military Law Review* 1 (1960), 3–4.
Myers, Hugh N. *Prisoners of World War II*. Portland, 1965.
Newman, Samuel A. *How to Survive as a Prisoner of War*. Philadelphia, 1970.

Reid, Pat, and Maurice Michael. *Prisoner of War: The Inside Story of the POW.* London, 1984.
Stenger, Charles. *American POWs in WWI, WWII, Korea and Vietnam.* Washington, DC, 1979.
United States. Army Forces in the Western Pacific. *American and Allied Personnel Recovered from Japanese Prisons.* Manila, 1945.
———. Congress. House Committee on Foreign Affairs. *Prisoners of War—Repatriation or Internment in Wartime: American and Allied Experiences, 1775 to Present.* Washington, DC, 1971.
———. National Personnel Records Center. Records pertaining to World War II American Ex-POWs, NPRC 1865-35, change 4. Washington, DC, 1970.
———. Naval War College. "Prisoners of War International Armed Conflict." *International Law Studies* (Howard S. Levie, ed.) vols. 59 and 60. Washington, DC.
———. Office of the Provost Marshal General. POW Operations Division. *History of POW Information Bureau, 19 December 1941–1 October 1945.* Washington, DC, 1945.
———. ———. *Supplement to History of POW Information Bureau, 14 August 1945–1 February 1946.* Washington, DC, 1946.
———. Veterans Administration. Office of Planning and Program Evaluation. *POW: Study of Former Prisoners of War.* Washington, DC, 1990.
———. War Department. "Procedure for Progressing, Return and Reassignment of Recovered Personnel." Washington, DC, April 21, 1945, rev. August 17, 1945.
———. ———. Publicity in connection with escaped, liberated or repatriated POWs, to include evaders of capture. Washington, DC, March 29, 1945.
Vaughan, Elizabeth Head. *Community Under Stress: An Internment Culture.* Princeton, NJ, 1949.
Velden, Dr. D. van. *De Japanse Burgerkampen* [The Japanese Civilian Camps]. Franeker, the Netherlands, 1977.

The Treatment of POWs

Adachi, Sumio. "Unprepared Regrettable Events: A Brief History of Japanese Practices on Treatment of Allied War Victims During World War II." *Studies Cultural and Social Science* (Yokosuka National Defense Academy, Tokyo), 1982.
Bartlett-Kerr, E. *Surrender and Survival.* New York, 1985.
Dull, Paul S., and Michael Takaaki. *The Tokyo Trials.* Ann Arbor, MI, 1957.
Ex-Prisoners of War, Inc. *Packet 10: The Japanese Story.*
International Red Cross. *Basic Rules of the Geneva Convention and Their Additional Protocols.* Geneva, 1983.
———. *Inter Arma Caritas: The Work of the International Committee During the Second World War.* Geneva, 1947.
———. *Report of the International Committee on Its Activities During the Second World War. Vol. 1: General Activities, Vol. 2: Central Agency for POWs, Vol. 3: Relief Activities.* Geneva, 1948.
———. *Report on the Interpretation, Revision and the Extension of the Geneva Convention of July 27, 1929.* Geneva, 1938.

Levie, Howard S. "The Employment of Prisoners of War." *American Journal of International Law* 57 (1963), 318–353.

———. "Penal Sanctions for Maltreatment of Prisoners of War." *American Journal of International Law* 56 (1962), 433–468.

———. "Prisoners of War and the Protecting Power." *American Journal of International Law* 55 (1961), 374–397.

Mowery, E., et al. *The Historical Management of POWs: A Synopsis of the 1968 U.S. Army Provost Marshall General's Study Entitled: A Review of the U.S. Policy on Treatment of POWs*. San Diego, CA: Naval Health Research Center, 1968.

Summers, Stephen. "Japanese Treatment of Allied POWs 1941–1945." Unpublished BA thesis, Bundoora, Victoria, Australia, 1983.

United States. Office of Strategic Services. Research and Analysis Branch. *Factors Underlying Japanese Treatment of Prisoners*. Washington, DC, 1944.

———. War Department. Bureau of Public Relations. *Japanese Atrocities to Prisoners of War* (Joint press release of the War and Navy departments containing stories of Japanese atrocities and brutalities to the American and Philippine armed forces who were prisoners of war in the Philippine Islands). House Document 393, 78th Cong. 2nd Sess. Washington, DC.

———. ———. Military Intelligence Division. *Prisoner of War Camp Conditions in Japan*. Washington, DC, 1944, 1949.

van Velden, Dr. D. *De Japanse Burgerkampen* [Japanese Civilian Camps]. Franeker, the Netherlands, 1977.

IMTFE. Exhibits 1468, 1494, 1622, 1655, 1668, 1679, 1958, 1960, 1965A, 1977, 1978, 1980B, 1980C, 1980E, 1981A, 1981B, 2001, 2011, 2015, 2016, 2017, 2022, 2027, 2028, 2033, 2688, 3043, 3051.

IMTFE. Record pp. 585, 594–96, 5392, 5493–96, 5506–07, 5510–12, 5653–65, 5799–801, 12781, 12872–73, 13420, 13495, 13707, 14285, 14361, 14426–28, 14431–37, 14440–76, 14558–91, 14597–604, 14728–32, 14734–53, 14747, 14754–90, 14792–822, 14846–83, 14911, 14826–36, 15001–17, 15506–53, 16085–90, 16097–101, 16966, 17191–92, 17526–30, 17752, 26412–20, 26555, 27117, 27124–27, 27229–43, 27140, 27147, 27278, 27181, 27182–90, 27282–309, 27315–48, 27354–85, 27433, 27693–722, 27435–37, 27863, 31687–98, 32959–63, 33126–29, 33160–61, 33294–96, 33311–37, 33371–74, 33416, 33418–22, 33424–26, 35162–64, 35247, 35319–22, 33504–22, 35553, 35584–89, 35667–69, 35768–76, 36415–17, 36825–34, 36837–39, 42618, 42688, 49676, 49759.

RvO IC: 359, 604, 775, 779, 787, 1782, 2158, 2365, 2366, 2416, 3165, 3474, 3580, 3630, 3633, 3636, 3638, 3669, 4120, 4265, 4349, 5279, 5717, 6209, 9703, 9735, 9741, 9742, 9760, 9813, 9901, 9989, 10081.

Chapter 3
The World of the Camp Prisoner

Introduction

When the invading Japanese forces in World War II occupied huge landmasses in Asia, Southeast Asia, and the Pacific, hundreds of thousands of Europeans, Chinese, Americans, British, Australians, New Zealanders, and Dutch were subsequently interned in hundreds of prison camps. Many more of the indigenous people of the various areas were rounded up and transported throughout Asia to work camps.

Internees and POWs of the Japanese knew that their lives after the war would be different from others because they had experienced being captives of an enemy, an occupying force of the land in which they had lived. They knew that the effects of these experiences would be long lasting.

Being a captive was a trauma from which many did not recover in spite of their repatriation or restoration. Remnants of their trauma can be found in little things, fifty years after. Many keep surplus food in the house, will not drive foreign cars, and hold attitudes of gratitude, acceptance, and deep patriotism.

As a group, and individually, they survived conditions for which there is no training and for which none was prepared. They suffered numerous stresses daily in the presence of their enemy and heard commands in a foreign language that brought immediate physical punishment if not obeyed. Often their daily situation, for more than three years, was an emotionally charged experience full of hatred, anger, fear, and frustration. In the eyes of their captors they were not worth saving. Stricken with dysentery and other diseases and skeletal in appearance, they were held in contempt by the Japanese.

As wars are different, so are prisoners' experiences of them; the ultimate tests in one war are seldom the same as the ultimate tests in the next. But in all the many circumstances in which men, women, and children have found themselves after capture, there has nevertheless been a common set of traits that have been indispensable to survival. Among these are moral integrity, a love of God and country or the equivalent, an aptitude for "reading" the captor's culture to establish a tactical defense or a posture that best thwarts him.

In their struggles for survival, the captives inevitably engaged in selfishness, racketeering, meanness, and injustice. Yet these negative behaviors were, in most POW camps and civilian centers, few, compared with the courage, optimism, and loyalty to their fellows with which the vast majority faced starvation, disease, and persecution. Everyone lived nakedly; after the first few weeks every person came to know the frailties and follies of his or her neighbor.

In this chapter, the author has made liberal use of *Community Under Stress: An Internment Culture*, by Elizabeth Head Vaughan, published by Princeton University Press in 1949, and now in the public domain. In his extensive research, this author has found that Vaughan's book covers the subject of the prison culture in a Japanese camp in greater detail than does any other work. Some parts of the Vaughan book are directly quoted in the present volume, while others have been paraphrased to cover both POW camps and civilian internee centers (her book deals with the civilian internment camp in Bacolod, the Philippines, whereas most works on imprisonment by the Japanese have been written by men and have been concerned mostly with the conditions of POWs, rather than of civilians). Interspersed through the text of the present work are accounts from other authors, either to corroborate or to dispute Vaughan's observations.

The 148 internees in Bacolod camp ranged in age from 3 months to 80 years and were of American, British, Dutch, Filipino, Spanish, and Italian nationality. The important questions raised by Vaughan's account of the experiences of this conglomerate of people are these:

• What are the acculturation processes of a group that must suddenly substitute for or do without some of the necessities of daily living?

• What is the effect on the individual and the group of the lack of solitude and privacy?

• Who finds adjustment behind barbed wire most difficult: men, women, or children?

Camp Organization

Food

William H. McDougall, a civilian internee, wrote:

> Hunger throws into bold relief a man's true self. It strips away the false front behind which hypocrites masquerade. From others it removes the mediocrity which disguised them as only ordinary men and reveals the hidden rock of noble character.
>
> Hunger, in my opinion, does not change the intrinsic things that make one good and another bad. It only accentuates the stuff of which a man is made. His reaction depends on the kind of man he is. He may quit trying and lie back on his mat in a state of apathy, or he may work still harder to live. If he is a quitter and does not try he also usually is a chronic bellyacher. Loudly he denounces as incompetent or dishonest his leaders and all workers. But he himself will not lift a finger to help anyone. If he is a worker he redoubles his efforts to earn money or acquire food by handicrafts, trading or black marketing. The entrepreneur falls into two classes; he who works solely for the purpose of keeping himself alive and he who works for profits he can bank after the war.
>
> The man who works for post-war profits operates openly as a loan shark or racketeer trading on the cupidity or hunger of his fellows. Such men are not peculiar only to internment camps. The honest worker will stay honest, no matter how desperate or fanatic to obtain food.[1]

There are two distinct aspects of social control in Bacolod camp: Japanese regulations and internees' policies. Because the Japanese indicated there were no provisions for feeding internees, camp policies on feeding the men, women, and children had to be drawn up. These policies concerned central cooking facilities, growing their own food in gardens, commandeering and collecting private funds to purchase food supplies, and commandeering and collecting all private food stock for collective use. Immediately, two antagonistic groups established themselves: for and against the use of individual "riches" for the benefit of the group.

A plan to curtail the use of available foods was bitterly denounced. To demand hunger and possible further ill health of internees while canned goods remained in their care was characterized by some as inexcusable and inhuman. The food situation was soon solved because internees were transported to Manila.

Observations made by Russell Braddon, a POW in Malaya, provide perhaps the "ultimate" answer:

> The distribution by turn of "leftover seconds" was an institution that remained with us through all the days that were to follow until the war ended in 1945. They are a striking example of civilized man's ability to resist even the animal gnawings of starvation in the interest of communal effort.[2]

It had become apparent to the men in Braddon's camp that the only way to survive as a group was for the individual to subordinate his desires to society's rules for that society (the prison camp) to survive.

Vaughan also observed that men, women, and children who had adopted island habits—who had lived in an integrated manner in the Philippine society—found internment less difficult than did those who had held themselves aloof from the island culture. Americans or Europeans who transplanted themselves and their family to the tropics and had them sent back to their homelands for all the accustomed foods and other amenities of life, found the conditions in the camp almost unbearable. To this group, the adoption of new food, living conditions, and habits was emotionally as well as gastronomically upsetting. Being faced with a bowl of *tinola*, a clear soup in which a fish head with wide eyes floated, caused some foreigners to become nauseous and to leave the dining room, whereas Philippinized men, women, and children consumed the *tinola* with relish. It was also difficult for nonacculturized persons to eat the Philippine dried *dilis* fish or *carabao* (water buffalo). To ease the acceptance of *carabao* by foreigners, it was introduced in a stew in which the other ingredients partially killed the real or imagined horsy taste. The POWs learned sooner than did the civilian internees that to survive they had to eat almost anything that was edible—cats, dogs, frogs, snakes, grubs, fungus, crude vegetable oil, green leaves from almost anything that grew, roots, and grass.

All captives, both POWs and civilian internees, were faced with two elements of "death": disease and starvation. For most of them, nothing was worse than starvation and the degrading aspects associated with it. As Kate Caffrey wrote about the men who labored on the Burma–Siam railway: "The worst part of being consistently hungry is the degradation at finding oneself so preoccupied with food that one becomes indifferent to the needs of others."[3] Yet, the captives did not always selfishly ignore their fellow prisoners or certain moral values to gain extra food. As Mary Thomas, an internee in Changi prison, Singapore, noted:

> The women who were cruelly hard, critical and grasping in competition with any, even the old or sick who interfered with their chances of survival, would not lift a finger to do the Japanese work which would have gained them extra food rations and other privileges.[4]

Ultimately, it was the discipline and organization of the camp leaders that were responsible for increased survival rates for the group of captives as a whole.

Work and Health

The labor policy in civilian internment centers depended for its success entirely upon its altruistic appeal and the internees' recognition of joint responsibility. Certain essential duties were assigned to the men, wrote

Elizabeth Head Vaughan, such as carpentry, toilet sanitation, and garbage disposal, whereas domestic duties and care of the sick became the responsibility of the women.

As a whole the internees worked hard. Only once was there open rebellion against camp duties, when a former executive defied any internee to make him work. When he was ignored by the others, he sheepishly returned to his assigned tasks.

As was true in many camps, medical care was atrocious; there was a lack of medicines and only one doctor was available. However, in an effort to prevent the spread of communicable diseases in the camp, the internees underwent a series of injections by a Filipino doctor against dysentery, typhoid, and cholera.

To maintain the health of 28 children in the camp, special dishes appeared on the camp menu: cassava pudding, eggs, and tender cuts of camp livestock.

Several adults objected to the special menus for children on the basis that adults should not have to jeopardize *their* health in favor of that of the youth. Resentment toward special treatment of children was complicated by racial issues: there were more mestizo (mix-blooded) children than white children in the camp. However, any plan to classify the children and babies who needed milk (the white children) and those who did not (the Filipino children, who, after breast feeding, ate a diet similar to that of adults: rice, fish, bananas, vegetables) would have been extremely difficult. Should the division be made on the basis of food habits? Racial heritage? Or skin color?

The issue was further complicated by the facts that some interned mestizos had been among the wealthiest residents of the islands before the war and that contributions of food for communal use had been accepted from both dark-skinned and white adults. Ultimately, the children "won."

Recreation, Religion, and Communications

Recreation, religion, and communications were important elements in the world of the camp prisoner. A former instructor in a Filipino boy's school exercised the greatest initiative in organizing recreation in the camp: baseball, horseshoe pitching, dramatics, bridge, and poker games. Few holidays passed without attempted celebrations.

Regular church services were held by various religious groups in the camp. Although only one-third of the population in Bacolod participated in the religious programs, the camp was quiet during the hours of all religious services out of respect for the faithful.

Communication with the outside world was severely limited; no use of the mails was granted nor contacts with other camps—and there were no attempts to escape from Bacolod. Knowing little about the outside world, interned men and women pieced together bits of facts with fancy to create war rumors. Both wishful thinking and anxieties gave direction to these rumors.

Adjustment to the Camp Culture

Introduction

Adjustment to the internment situation was an individual matter, influenced by such factors as age, sex, national origin, and previous socioeconomic status, but it followed certain general trends. Vaughan referred to the works of two British doctors: A. L. Fischer, who coined the expression "barbed wire disease," and Dr. P. H. Newman, who preferred the expression "barbed-wire attitude," to denote a new mental attitude by a POW or internee. This disease or attitude has four stages: (1) a time of acute mental stress that accompanies forcible adaptation to a lower plane of existence (the breaking-in period), (2) recovery of morale and the rearrangement of shattered values (the convalescence period), (3) boredom, and (4) the repatriation period.

Both stages 1 and 2 entail an adjustment to mental stress, social degradation and ultimately moral degradation. "We're seeing life as it really is, without the veneer and polish. I don't like it," wrote Freddy Bloom, a POW in Changi, Singapore.[5]

Although this state of existence has been described by many captives, others have emphasized that comradeship forced many prisoners and internees to develop their more virtuous qualities, such as loyalty and generosity. In an amusing but poignant way, one prisoner created a "recipe" for a positive barbed-wire attitude:

> Recipe: 3 cups of forgiveness
> 2 spoons of hope; 2 cups of loyalty; 4 cups of love; 1 barrel of laughter; 1 spoon of friendship; 4 quarts of faith.
> Take love and loyalty, mix thoroughly with faith. Blend with tenderness, kindness and understanding. Add friendship and hope. Sprinkle abundantly with laughter. Bake it with sunshine. Serve daily with generous helpings.[6]

Internment Values

After 11 months in a French internment camp, Ija Korner, a trained psychologist, wrote that *character* differences showed greater constancy than did the *emotional* differences of internees.[7] Korner pointed out that whereas character showed great resistance to mass influence by other internees, emotional responses followed a new camp clique pattern, rather than an individual pattern.

Vaughan observed that Bacolod internees, who felt compelled to action that was contrary to their prewar roles and their accompanying system of values and who could not develop new values in keeping with the changed situation, suffered acute emotional disturbance or spiritual bankruptcy. Civilian internee William H. McDougall commented that "when the spiritual reservoir of the soul is empty, one has only one companion: despair."[8]

Some adjusted themselves to internment values more easily than did others. According to Vaughan, women seemed to adapt themselves to camp life more readily than did male internees; although the situation was new to them, the domestic activities and role were not entirely so. Interned men, on the other hand, found their days filled with actions both unfamiliar and repulsive to them—cleaning toilets, burying garbage, cutting grass, and others. The easier adjustment of women was apparently due to the social and cultural characteristics of the two sexes, as well as to biological differences. The traditional self-sacrifice and resignation expected of women aided them in the internment situation.

Cultural and racial characteristics also accelerated or retarded adjustment to Bacolod camp life, said Vaughan. The tyranny of reality was too great for some, who engaged in daydreaming and fantasies as an escape route. Many internees abandoned themselves voluptuously to the current that led to the unknown.

To what extent should dreams be used not only as an escape but as life on a larger plane, freer even than life outside the camp? According to Vaughan's research and observations, the first necessary step in the adjustment to internment was to face the facts. As long as one avoided doing so, adjustment was impossible; once one did so, however, a major hurdle was overcome. But where should one stop facing facts and begin to make believe? How should one alternate between them? And when should either or both be used?

Stanley S. Pavillard, a POW medical doctor on the Burma–Siam railroad, described varying states of mind as follows:

> It was at these two camps that we volunteers and many others really learned to adapt ourselves to the fact of being prisoners. We had to reshape and redirect our whole outlook: life became a game of make believe and we acquired the knack of turning our attention entirely away from personal discomfort and deprivation. Together with a sense of humour this psychological technique saved morale and life as well.
>
> As a doctor I had many opportunities of studying the mental reactions of my fellow prisoners, and all too often I saw men failing to adapt them-

selves to this make believe game, this mental camouflage of reality, and then in consequence becoming morose and gloomy and, in the end, invariably dying.[9]

Robert S. Woodworth noted:

A person remains unadjusted to a state of affairs if he has not sensed it, or if the facts, though new, have left no impression on him, or if he dislikes the situation and is unwilling to take the appropriate action. His dislike and unwillingness may even prevent him from seeing the situation as it is and so lead to maladjustment.[10]

Vaughan concluded that more influential than anything in adjusting to internment were the prewar cultural patterns to which the individuals had adhered.

Community Under Stress

Threats to life and health, physical discomfort, deprivation of sexual satisfaction, impossibility of gaining a livelihood, enforced idleness, and the unpredictable behavior of the captors created stress-related problems for the internees (and the POWs).

Threats to Life and Health

The early fear of death from assault by camp guards was replaced in Bacolod camp with a fear of death from starvation or disease. The threats of life were at some stages more imagined than real, but the suffering was nonetheless acute, for a "feeling of threat can be in itself a dynamic stimulation to other reactions." Added to the basic desire to live was anxiety about the future well being of dependents in case of death. As William H. McDougall said, "The will to live was vital to survival. When the will is gone, the flood sweeps in, drowning the life too tired to fight."[11]

The threats to life and the associated "will to live" were strong in some and weak in others. The efforts associated with the will to live created stressful conditions, yet this will was the ultimate tool of survival. As a POW in the Philippines expressed it, "As long as you kept faith and the determination to live, you had the will power to keep on living, no matter what the circumstances."[12]

Those who could not handle the stress of willing to live, simply died. Prisoner of war Ernest Gordon described how he and others turned the fear of death into a reason for living, and what happened to those who did not.

Dying was easy. When our desires are thwarted and life becomes too much for us, it is easy to reject life and the pain it brings, easier to die than to live. It is an easy thing to adopt a philosophy of despair, to say, "I mean nothing; there is nothing; nothing matters; I live only to die."[13]

One factor that was mentioned over and over in the captives' personal accounts was *hope*. As Richard W. Peterson observed: "When I asked this ex–POW what character trait offered survival to him as a camp inmate, he immediately replied: 'Hope! . . . Hope!'"[14]

Stan Sommers, an ex–POW, stated:

> Medical studies have proven how hope sustains many human beings allowing them to endure incredible amounts of pain and punishment. The dictionary defines hope as "confident expectation." So it is not just wishful thinking or blind optimism, but a real gut level belief that the situation will get better and eventually pass into history. Survivors confidently expected to be released at some future time.[15]

Catherine Kenny, an Australian nurse and internee in Sumatra, the Dutch East Indies, noted: "If we had given up we wouldn't have come back; it's as simple as that. If we gave up hope, we'd have just died."[16] Similarly, Bessie Sneed, an internee in the Philippines wrote: "It was the spirit of the people that kept many alive. The theory of 'mind over body' was well proven. Invariably, when an internee gave up hope, he or she was dead within a few days."[17]

Physical Discomfort

Physical discomfort characterized the entire period of internment at Bacolod, wrote Elizabeth Head Vaughan. Poorly prepared and inadequate food, overcrowding, the absence of chairs and comfortable beds, and exposure to tropical sun and rain caused bodily pain and mental disturbance. The continual thwarting of the basic drive for comfort resulted in cumulative physical and mental fatigue and undue irritability. In many of the personal accounts "overcrowding" and the "lack of comfort" were mentioned as stress-causing factors, especially when the internees saw no prospect of an end to it.

Said one prisoner, "Living together, in so little space, day after day, week after week, month after month, we got to know each other too well. Each stood before the other, 'naked,' bare, stripped of all veneer. It was often terrifying."

Wrote Singapore internee Freddy Bloom: "There's the clank of dishes. Two women are trying to build a chair and there's the hammering. And of course, there's the constant chatter . . . chatter . . . chatter!"[18]

Hilda Corpe, internee in a camp in Rangoon, Burma, wrote: "One was forced to live side by side, face to face with those one instinctively disliked. Many times during the day one longed for the privacy and solitude which only the night could confer."[19]

Concerning the issue of privacy, Vaughan referred to philosopher Irwin Edman, who summarized his belief in the importance of privacy as follows:

> Just as man can be satiated with too much eating, and irritated by too much activity, so men become "fed up" with companionship. The demand for solitude and privacy is thus fundamentally a physiological demand, like the demand for rest. Companionship, even the most desirable kind, exhausts nervous energy, and may become positively fatiguing and painful. A normal life demands a certain proportion of solitude just as much as it demands the companionship of others.[20]

Loss of the Means of Subsistence

Added to the actual suffering that internees experienced from the loss of essential foods and clothing was anxiety as to how these and other material losses might affect their postwar status and security. Often culturally determined, anxieties concerning the future crowded out more veritable threats in the present.

Deprivation of Sexual Satisfaction

The type of casual, nonsexual association that the Japanese permitted husbands and wives who were interned together in Bacolod was unsatisfying. Yet husbands and wives who were separated by the war suffered far greater sexual deprivation, in the broader implications of a lack of affection. The sexual anxieties that loomed large in the minds of the POWs were also present in the civilians who were separated by internment from their spouses. A fear of the infidelity of spouses and sweethearts is a widespread anxiety among people brought up in Western culture.

Restricted Movement and Isolation from Prewar Associates

Though there were no periods of enforced idleness in the Bacolod camp, the camp activities were not satisfying. The goal of day-by-day subsistence failed to call forth the efforts and enthusiasm of prewar long-range incentives.

The restrictions of movement and communication resulted in restrictions of thought and speech. Internees tended to talk mainly about the past. The monotony of internment encouraged this as an effort to satisfy the thwarted desires for new experiences.

Bacolod internees were isolated from their own groups of prewar voluntary associates, but there was no isolation of individual from individual within the camp.

Threats to Family Members and Friends

Internees who were separated from family members and friends were afflicted with particular anxieties. However, the wartime cessation of income caused acute distress to all internee heads of families who had adults or children who were dependent upon them and for whom they could no longer provide. These men were unable not only to continue to support their families financially but to protect them physically.

Ridicule and Rejection by Fellow Prisoners

Ridicule will bring almost any individual to terms, while the most stubborn rebel will bow before ostracism or the threat of expulsion from his group. These tactics were used by the larger group of internees to make would-be noncomformists adhere to camp policies.

Capricious and Unpredictable Behavior by Guards

Throughout the administration of one Japanese commandant, the guards were out of control; complaints about them from the internees were futile. Guards amused themselves by sitting in their second-story windows across the road from the camp with field glasses focused on the internees' bedrooms. Since the sparse camp furnishings brought by internees did not include shades or curtains and the rooms were too hot to close the solid windows each time a modest internee wished to dress, the only recourse for privacy was to duck beneath the window sills. The guards also peeked into toilets, showers, and bedroom windows as they walked about the grounds and entered living quarters unannounced. These trespasses upon personal privacy were ultimately, however, no more vexing than were the guards' other activities.

Colonel Ota's successor as commander in the Philippines, for example, was an enigma. After consistently refusing to act upon the internees' requests for food, the new colonel arranged for the delivery of produce and cash while preparing to close up the camp. Despite these last-minute arrangements, internees were puzzled by the colonel's announcement that they were to be "charged" for water and electricity used during their internment.

Subjection to Enemy Propaganda

Internees in Bacolod were subjected to a persistent Japanese propaganda program. General facts about the progress of the war were not only withheld from internees, but they were forbidden to discuss the war in their private conversations. The only reading materials provided by the Japanese were cartoons and anecdotes about the misdeeds and inefficiency of the white man in the Far East. Typical of such material was the statement in the Japanese-controlled *Hong Kong News* of January 14, 1942: "The vaunted supermen of the white race have melted like butter." Such statements were part of a scheme to convince Asians to cooperate with the Japanese, and the widespread acceptance by Asians of such statements accelerated the degradation of internees started by the conditions of internment.

Awareness of Personal Degradation

In the Bacolod camp, men and women ate with their fingers and with spoons because there were not enough knives and forks; they did not bathe often because of the uncertainty and inadequacy of the water supply; and they screamed at children and at each other because they were too tired to move near enough for normal conversational tones. Mary Thomas, an internee in China, wrote:

> Internment was a revelation of humanity when it is stripped of pretense and of all the decorations and supports with which ordinary civilian life demands that we shall try to conceal our essential selves. I came to believe that it would be an ideal society in which one could obliterate the purely artificial and accidental values which make one person more "respected" than another.[21]

Daphne Jackson, interned in Java, had a far more emotional response toward the actions of some other women in her camp:

> In the camp very few people retained good manners and the speed with which some degenerated into little more than animals was horrifying. Thieving, lying, telling tales to curry favor with guards or staff went on all the time. As far as I could see, the old saying that "trouble brought out the best in one" was very much a half-truth. The good people in camp got better, but the bad ones got far, far worse.[22]

This observation concurs with Vaughan's that "pre-war cultural patterns to which internees had adhered were the most influential in the adjustments to internment."

Jackson thought that the behavior of some of the other internees was "horrifying," which agrees with P. A. Sorokin's statement that "calamity on a personal basis or on a nationwide scale is disturbing to the emotions and thoughts of those within its range of influence."[23]

Many POWs and internees rose above the degradation factor and decided that "self-respect was one of the essentials of survival. Once a man (or a woman) lost the last remnants of self-respect, he/she had virtually lost everything, including the will to survive."[24]

Rumors

One factor within the Bacolod camp contributing to disorientation was the existence of rumors, which could not be stopped. However, the situation changed for the better when the group was transferred to Santo Tomas camp, where a secret radio provided "real" news instead of rumors.

Children and Young People

Children and young people in the Bacolod camp had their own special problems. Camp life affected the mental as well as the social life of young people. With a paucity of playthings, small children tended to hoard the few toys they could find or create. *Things* became all-important. What was "mine" to one child, such as stones, bottles, and empty tin cans, was frequently the basis of dispute with another child or his or her parents. Each child attempted to mark every piece of glass, wood, string, or stone that he or she wished to add to his or her collection.

The children's continued stay with their mothers during captivity prevented the maladjustments that might otherwise have occurred. Furthermore, since what the children believed about conditions under which they lived was more important than the actual conditions, their parents deliberately patterned their values and attitudes for them.

Respect and consideration for the authority of the Japanese were instilled into children by the parents (who nevertheless feared, hated, and distrusted their captors). The parents also discouraged their children from developing prejudices against the Japanese because they were members of a different race. The parents realized that by teaching hatred of the racially different Japanese, the groundwork could be laid inadvertently for the cultivation of prejudice against all groups who were physically or culturally unlike the children.

Parents guarded their speech in the presence of their children because they sensed that adult hatreds and fears might permanently affect the character of their children by leading to frustration and vindictive behavior.

Camp discipline was severe. Unbroken silence was demanded of children during the daily two-hour siesta. Children stood at attention through long roll calls and inspections. However, unless they became overtired by the physical demands made upon them, the disciplinary regulations were not in themselves harmful.

Communal Concerns versus Individuality

The urge for mere survival, normally subordinated amid the complexities of civilized society, assumed primacy in the Bacolod camp. In this situation individual desires and fears were identified with the survival of the group. A new group economic ideology emerged in which the group's welfare superseded, for the time being, individual rights of ownership. The group became the unit for survival or annihilation.

Severed from outside sources of aid, deprived of all assets except those at hand, individuals sought a modicum of personal security in group unification. But after several months of sharing and evidence that the crisis was to be of a longer duration than was at first expected, the fervor for group solidarity waned and individualism began to reassert itself.

Internees began to question the validity of one's right to make demands on the property and the time of another individual. At this stage prewar concepts of unselfishness, human rights, and honesty and fair play underwent scrutiny and redefinition. Nonetheless the voluntary social order that had fostered the communal ownership plan was not abolished. The internees' general recognition of their interdependence went deeper than the sharing of canned goods.

Conclusions

The experiences of the captives support the following conclusions:

• A difficult adjustment accompanied the adoption of new culture traits, but women seemed to adapt themselves to the internment situation more readily than did men. Filipino men, women and children, and others who lived with Filipinos and had adopted island habits, also found internment less difficult than did those who had held themselves aloof from the island culture.

• Asian internees found adjustment easier with regard to camp food, the absence of privacy, and cultural anxieties about the future. Among the Westerners, the missionaries and men under age 50 experienced fewer anxieties about what would happen after the war than did lay groups and men over age 50.

- Young children did not experience the feeling of frustration that adults typically did. Because they were housed with their mothers, the children's sense of security was relatively unshaken. In periods of extreme peril, such as the shelling of Santo Tomas camp by the Japanese, it was officially recognized that there was less hysteria and disorder in the quarters in which children were present than in those occupied only by adults.

- The drive for security resulted in an internment ideology that approved the equal distribution of property. Leadership in the communal, cooperative camp society cut across national, racial, and cultural lines. Confinement caused internees to exercise capabilities never demanded of them in a technological, highly stratified social order outside the camp.

Art, Artifacts, and Literature

Introduction

Mrs. Vaughan devoted one chapter of her book to the development of artifacts, stating that there was general evidence that the internment camp brought forth certain practical skills and often ingenious capabilities that were latent in men and women in their prewar society.

The world of the camp forced prisoners to create such necessary items as cookware and utensils, which were not readily available or had worn out. Likewise because of the destructive qualities of heat and rain on leather, shoes wore out rapidly and the need for them became acute.

Children needed toys. Smokers needed a substitute for the rapidly dwindling supplies of tobacco and cigarettes. Others needed purely creative endeavors through which they could vent their anger and frustration or provide fellow prisoners with a sardonic, sarcastic or humorous look at themselves and camp life; they wrote poems and drew cartoons or more serious, realistic pictures. These "artists" have provided the world with an additional look into the world of the camp prisoner, apart from direct accounts.

Artifacts

The preparation and consumption of food required the creation of more implements than did any other single endeavor. Internees devised a variety of ingenious solutions to the lack of everyday items.

For cups and mugs, a can was encircled with a stiff wire near the top and bottom. Twisted wire was then formed into a firm handle. But after a while the cans started to rust. Then bottles were tried. The most effective method of removing the necks was to fill the bottles with water to the desired break point and then pour a few drops of oil or melted fat into them. A lighted splinter dropped inside caused a clean break. Wire bands and handles were adjusted to fit the glass mugs.

In fashioning plates, bowls, and utensils, coconut shells were opened near the end containing the eyes. Outer and inner surfaces of the shell were polished clean. To the coconut shells were attached wire or stick handles.

Wooden *bakias* were made to replace worn leather shoes. Wood found in the camp was cut and whittled by hand to form the soles and heels. Some were rounded on the bottom to allow a rolling motion in walking. Strips from automobile tires provided a single strap on the front part of the bakia. Children as well as adults learned to curl their toes to hold the bakias on their feet.

Toys, including small rakes and shovels, dolls, blocks, and balls, were handmade from tin cans, wood, wrapping string, and animal bones.

Buttons and belt buckles were made from carved coconut shells; similarly, knitting needles and crochet hooks were made from cut and shaped bamboo. Toothpaste was made from wood ash.

Since laundry soap was unavailable, clothes were cleaned by an American Indian method. Soiled clothes were rubbed together in clear water, then rinsed; the wet garments were spread flat on the grass in sunlight and were sprinkled with water every half hour or hour during the day as they became dry. During a full moon, clothes were left out overnight, flat upon the grass, to benefit from the bleaching and cleansing efforts of moonlight and dew.

To replace cigarettes, sun-dried papaya leaves and dried grass were rolled in notebook paper.

A small charcoal stove could be made from two cans, one small, one large. A letter H was cut an inch above the bottom of the large can and the flaps were bent inward. A letter H was cut horizontally on the side and at the bottom of the small can, and the flaps were bent outward. The large can was then filled with earth up to the bottom of the figure H. Holes were punched on the side of the small can just above the H. Short pieces of wire were inserted across the inside to form a grate. The small can was placed inside the larger one with the new openings lined up. The space between the two cans was filled with damp earth, packed tightly. The burning charcoal and packed earth retained the heat once it got hot.

Art

After the war a number of illustrated works were published containing art and poetry done by POWs and internees during their captivity. A few prisoners had access—one way or another—to oil paint and watercolors with which to make small paintings. One such prisoner was Iris Parfitt, a Singaporean internee whose black-and-white and color illustrations were accompanied not by poetry, but by prose narratives.

As entertainment chairwoman in her camp, Parfitt helped organize impromptu talks, recitals, variety concerts, Shakespeare and slapstick performances, classical music and jazz, burlesque and comedy, and even a circus to "help for a few brief moments, to forget."

In the foreword of Parfitt's book, H. R. Chessman, director of the Education Malayan Union in Kuala Lumpur, wrote:

> In her "Jailbird Jottings" Miss Iris Parfitt gives us glimpses of the life that the women led and gives us some idea of the attitude and outlook that enabled them to come triumphant through all trials and tribulations.[25]

Miss Parfitt herself wrote the following preface:

> It must, I think, be granted that the way in which the camp [Changi Jail and Sime Road Camp, Malaya] and its entertainers have fought against odds which the outside world can never understand, has been magnificent. We may not have kept fit, but we have laughed and kept sane; we have kept beauty alive in the midst of grimness and sordidness and pleasured in spite of our pain.[26]

Some prison artists were so affected by what they observed and experienced in the world of the camp prisoner that they captured occurrences in raw detail. These artists included Charles Burki (a Dutchman), Benjamin Charles Steele (an American), Leo Rawlings (an Englishman), and Ronald Searle (an Englishman). Others expressed themselves in subtler form or by way of cartoons.

Poetry

In the introduction to his book *Bars from Bilibid Prison*, Charles Brown succinctly explained why prison camp poetry flourished:

> If you lock a man up, he will eventually write something. If he has no paper, or other suitable writing material, he will write it on the walls of his cell, or possibly even on his shirt. Most prisoners don't own shirts. Those who are so fortunate as to own one usually have a poem or two scribbled on the tail of it. Why prisoners try to write poetry is still one of the unfathomable mysteries of literature; however, nearly all of them tamper with the muse long-suffering.
>
> Some of the verses . . . were scribbled during the siege of Bataan on the backs of labels removed from corned beef cans. The others were written on odd scraps of paper while I was a prisoner of the Japanese in old Bilibid

Prison. Paper in Bilibid was a very precious commodity, and as there was a decided shortage of corned beef on Bataan, my friends have no doubt been spared a great deal. The little sheaf of writing is the survivor of many shakedowns and searches at the hands of my captors. Had it been found, I would most assuredly have been executed. The Japanese with all their faults, at least have a love for good literature, and in any case, the punishment would for once have fitted the crime.

As I have intimated, a great deal of poetry has been written by prisoners. Suffice it to say that most of it is bad; however, as long as men persist in locking up their neighbors, as they have been doing since the beginning of time, the poetic effusion is a natural consequence. As for my own verse, I have no illusions. However, I do believe that whether it be good or bad, the lines will bear a special significance to the thousands of Americans who lived under the sword of the "Samurai" as prisoners of the Japanese for three long years. They were written solely for the amusement of my fellow prisoners, when the days were long, and the nights even longer. Winston Churchill once said, referring to his own imprisonment by the Boers, that the "days passed by like paralytic centipedes." Truly, ours passed in the same manner. I must say, however, that if the centipedes referred to by Mr. Churchill were paralyzed, then ours in comparison were not only similarly afflicted, but were in addition burdened with hundred-pound sacks of buckshot. Thus passed the days in old Bilibid Prison.

I trust that what I have written will remind my old cellmates of those other days.

> When our lives were there to sacrifice
> In prison ship, or lack of rice

I also trust that they will not be reminded too well.[27]

Combination of Art and Poetry

A number of prison camp authors illustrated their own poetry. Others collaborated with a poet or an illustrator.

None accomplished their feats with fame and fortune in mind; they simply wanted to express what they saw and how they reacted to it.

The following is poet Alfred Stahl's explanation:

This little volume [illustrated by John L. Jay] was not written with the intention of gathering laurels as a poet, nor does it claim to have any literary merit nor will it ever provide material wealth. No, it was created in an effort to bridge the long weary and futile hours from 9 A.M. to 5 P.M., when we were hungrily waiting for the next scanty meal, and also to preserve my sanity in this maelstrom of human deficiencies, and yes, mean viciousness.

What first happened to be merely a "pass-time" proved with its progress to be a stimulant, and finally, with the encouragement and good counsel of my fellow jail-birds, the thought matured to make it available to all and sundry. I am quite certain it will provide an interesting and (in retrospect) amusing hour, and will give you, in years to come, a good survey of the human side of our enforced vacation and "How We Took It."[28]

The writing often reflected deep despair:

80 Centimeters

Here we live on 80 centimeters—the space to eat, sleep and write. Perhaps the next stage would be better: stiff on 50 centimeters, and carried away, hidden in a coffin. And then the whole world to roam around in and to float like a cloud into heaven. Clouds and birds playing sonatas—without baggage, guards, spies. An oil lamp, dark shadows—but a thousand moons and ten thousand suns.[29]

Children, however, often served as a source of hope for the adults.

"Mama, may I have your bakias for a moment—it makes me feel so tall." In all the hunger and misery, our little children teach us a lesson in satisfaction—to continue on in a pleasant mood.

Jannie, born in camp, doesn't know "father" and "home." In all her life she has never seen a city and words like "cupboard" and "carpet" are only sounds. Also, she has never worn any socks or shoes. But on mama's bakias she is to us a striking example: even though moving forward is difficult, she remains courageous, cheerful.[30]

Sometimes a note of bitterness was hard to conceal:

The mattress athlete: I refuse to work outdoors—that means working for the Nip and that is treason. I cannot work in the hospital: that's not for me. I cannot contribute to the camp community: how can I? I do not receive sufficient fat, protein and vitamins and barely 1200 calories.

I wait for the Americans to come.... But, oh my God why does that take a long time to happen?

For these "athletes" freedom often came too late.[31]

The latter writer drew a picture parodying Winston Churchill's famous words, "Never in the field of human conflict was so much owed by so many to so few." The artist's words, "Never in the history of mankind has so much been bowed by so many to so few," referred to the obligatory bowing by the prisoners to any Japanese they encountered.[32]

Humor

The power of humor to relieve stress is widely acknowledged. Laughter made the POWs and internees feel good and has been attributed with helping them to get better when they were ill. As the following two accounts show, confinement did not deaden a sense of humor in the prisons and camps.

In a POW camp, a young Japanese guard asked with curiosity: "How do I address a British officer?"

"Stand at attention," was the answer, "salute and say 'Good morning Sir, my name is mud, sir. It looks like rain today.'"

A young British army doctor, Captain Stanley Pavillard, devised a form of "occupational" therapy for his fellow inmates. As he later described it: "We devoted much time and effort to the pursuit and capture of bugs and lice, which we then slipped in vast quantities into the Japanese soldiers' huts."[33]

The camp prisoner suffered a lack of food, medical treatment, and freedom, among other deprivations, but there was an unfortunate abundance of one element: insects. Ants, fleas, lice, and bedbugs were all present in great numbers. No insect was loathed more than the bedbug. It has been pictured in most cartoons and drawings and described vividly in parodies.

The bedbug seemed to be an unconquerable pest. He multiplied rapidly and traveled and fed only at night. During the day he crawled back into the woodwork and slept on a full stomach of human blood. He was noiseless and his bites did not sting enough to awaken the victim. The bites caused enough itching, however, to make the victim scratch and break out in sores.

There were no insecticides or sprays to fight insects, but someone finally came up with the idea of scalding them to death. Thereafter it became standard procedure to take all bedding and clothing out of the squad area and douse the wooden bunks and floor with boiling water from the kitchen. Another method was to spread the bedding and clothes in the hot tropical sun and watch them squirm in the heat, and then smashing them with a swatter.[34]

There was even at least one ode to the bedbug in poetry:

Look, I see a bedbug crawling around. He is big. He came crawling out of that hole. Squash him to death. However, we should not forget, if we notice these little beasts, that they may have come from our husband's body—perhaps. But whatever, if you have one on you, it feels as if there are ten.[35]

Music

Although music was played in a number of POW camps and civilian internment centers, few original compositions came out of these prison camps. A Lieutenant Saunders, an American POW at Davao camp in the Philippines, composed the well-known song "The Yanks Are Comin'."[36]

Before the war Saunders had been pianist and arranger with the Jan

Garber orchestra. He headed up the shows in camp and, according to many accounts, "Yanks" was a tremendous hit sung by a trio consisting of Saunders, Robie Roberson, and Shavey Peoples. Saunders did not survive the war; the other two did.

Two other original "camp compositions" were published in Annie Ofeigsen-Takes's book, *Wel en Wee* [Weal and Woe], but the composer is not known. The first composition is called "Tangerang," an ode to the camp in which Annie was held captive, and the other is entitled "War." Lyrics are in Dutch.[37]

POW Lingo

In her book *Out in the Midday Sun*, Kate Caffrey devoted an entire chapter to "The Question of Language." She aptly posed two questions: (1) When you are a Japanese in charge of a group of prisoners and you must give them orders, and you cannot speak English, where do *you* begin? and (2) When you are an Allied prisoner, you need to have some idea what your captors are saying to you, but you do not speak Japanese, so where do *you* begin? "Out of this necessity," wrote Ms. Caffrey, "one of the strangest examples of lingua franca ever developed between these two utterly different peoples."[38]

A whole new vocabulary was formed, often consisting of a combination of pidgin English, Malay, and Japanese. An interesting aspect of this new lingo was that since there is no real profanity in Japanese, the guards would incorporate some English swear words into their speech. A closely knit group, the prisoners developed a jargon of their own, much of it incorporating general World War II slang.

As John Coast, a POW working on the Burma–Siam railroad, pointed out:

> While we were in such close daily contact with the Nips, and while we lived so on top of each other, and saw each other's faults and weaknesses so clearly, it may be of interest to consider the peculiar slang in which we used to express our opinions of the Nips and ourselves.[39]

In the POW camps the development of the new lingua franca (which was not so well developed in civilian internment camps) was influenced by the mixture of men from different branches of military service and different nations with locals. There grew a remarkable fusion of army, navy, and air force slang from servicemen from Australia, England, the United States, and the Dutch East Indies in such locales as Malaya, Siam, the Indies, the Philippines, China, Korea, Manchuria, and Japan—all of which were under Japanese control. The glossary listed in Appendix E was culled primarily from Rohan Rivitt's book *Behind Bamboo*, although terms have been added from other works as well.

Camp Recipes

Introduction. With the world of the camp prisoners centered on food—or, to be more specific, the lack of it—the prisoners had to be creative in finding ways to enhance the taste of their food and to introduce new dishes.

In the research for this book, the author found only one title dealing primarily with camp recipes: *Recipes from Bilibid*.[40] In the extensive literature on prisoners of the Japanese, however, a number of authors did include some recipes.

In Fred Stevens's book, *Santo Tomas*, one internee, Mrs. Jessie Bell Hanson, devoted a chapter to the ingenuity of prisoners in inventing dishes that could exist only in a prison camp. Some of these dishes offered the nutritional virtues of little fat or cholesterol. Mrs. Hanson wrote:

> It was amazing how new recipes would spring up. Girls with degrees in home economics would compare ideas with Filipino girls who remembered how their mothers baked with a banana leaf on the bottom of the pan to keep the bread from sticking. Soon they would have a new recipe worked out which would be improved on by other women until it just seemed right.[41]

The following are recipes from Hanson's chapter:

> *Jam*: a combination of pineapple, small native limes, and brown sugar.
> *Strawberry jam*: finely chopped eggplant, small native limes, and brown sugar.
> *Bread and hotcakes*: one cup rice mush (rice boiled slowly and gently into a thick gruel), two cups rice flour, one level tablespoon starch, one-third cup yeast, two teaspoonfuls soda, a little salt, margarine, and sugar (or mashed bananas). Add enough water to make a thick batter when bread is intended; add more water for hotcakes.
> *Bomber bread* (emergency biscuits that do not spoil over time): 2 cups rice flour, 1 teaspoon salt, 2 tablespoons shortening, 1 teaspoon soda, 1 teaspoon vinegar, and water to mix. Make a stiff batter. Roll on a board. Dust with flour and cut out biscuits with the removed top of a corned beef can. Place in a greased pan and bake until well browned.[42]

Mary Thomas, an internee in Changi, Singapore, had some interesting hints:

> • Do not throw away *prune pits* without first cracking them for the kernels. The kernels are good alone or make a palatable addition to fried rice.

- Do not throw away *papaya seeds*. They taste like mustard and are wholesome and make an excellent flavoring for soup or fried rice.
- Do not throw away *cheese rinds*. Fry them; they are palatable and contain all the nourishment of the cheese.[43]

Some recipes from Betty Jeffrey, Australian nurse internee in Sumatra:

> *Potato chips*: finely cut cucumber skins and banana skins. Fry in a little oil until crisp. Sprinkle with salt.
> *Anchovy paste*: gather leftover fish bones and wash and dry them. Dry-bake them on a piece of tin; pound them while still hot; add salt, pepper, and lime juice and stir in a little palm oil to make a paste.[44]

Improvisations and creativity in camp cooking were not solely the domain of the women. The POWs and male internees showed as much inventiveness and feverish energy in their cooking as did the women.

The cooks in the central kitchen often created masterful dishes, especially during holidays. The following is a "mass" recipe of a Christmas pudding, described by Ronald Hastain, a POW on the Siam–Burma railroad:

> The cookhouse possessed among its utensils two eight-gallon, galvanized iron baths. Into each of these was placed about four gallons of cooked steamed rice that had been minced. To this was added a small quantity of ground soya bean, a gallon of ground rice, palm sugar, pork oil, peanuts, tamarinds, grated ginger root and candied peel. The peel was made from strips of pomelo rind boiled in palm sugar and had been prepared, together with the jams, a few days before Christmas. The mixture was well-stirred by all and sundry with the traditional ritual of making a wish, and then a portion was placed in the now empty, but still greased margarine tins, each of which held fifty-four ounces. The puddings were then carefully steamed for two and a half hours. They turned out of the tins with a cake appearance, and when cold were cut into twelve slices. The puddings were kept together, although sliced and decorated on top with cream made from whipped margarine and white sugar. They were served with a hot sweet sauce made from ground rice, white sugar, margarine, milk, tamarind and lime.[45]

The Secret Wireless Set

"Despite starvation and abuse, the soldiers had one thing that we did not have [in the women's camp] to keep up their morale—they had authentic news of the outside world. Throughout their imprisonment a homemade radio was concealed and functioned in the British soldiers' camp," wrote Agnes Newton Keith, an internee in North Borneo.[46]

The Japanese suspected that in virtually all POW and civilian men's camps secret radio receivers were used to receive the latest information on the progress of the war and other news from the outside world. Knowing that the Japanese guards' discovery of a hidden receiver in camp would mean an almost certain death for the owner or owners, the men nevertheless stubbornly built and used these radios.

To minimize discovery or betrayal by informers, the owner or owners informed only three or four highly trusted men about the existence of a hidden receiver. Code names (such as "Birdie," "Dicky-Bird," and "Canary") were used when talking about the set, and lingo (such as "Doings," "Doovah," "Dope," "Good Guts," "Griff," and "Swen") indicated that there was news from the radio.

As Michael P. O'Connor, a civilian internee in North Borneo, described the set used in his camp:

> Mrs. Harris was a small camp-made wireless receiving set made of bits and pieces from all over the camp area, including some stolen from the Japanese area. It was kept somewhere in the officers' camp, and listening was done at night with the most elaborate precautions. The deprivation of news which would follow its discovery by the Japanese would be a minor disaster compared with the almost certain torture of its operators by the Kempeitai, with execution to follow; and this although it was not a transmitting set. It was built into an army dixie, and when not in use was generally kept hidden in a cavity under the ashes of a fireplace in the kitchen, the bricks having been replaced over it. One day, while the set was being repaired on a table in the middle of the hut, and no watchers had been posted, a Japanese officer suddenly strolled into the hut. An officer, turning his back on the table, went towards the Japanese. An old blanket was hastily thrown over the pieces of the set. The Japanese officer strode past the table and out of the hut without a glance.[47]

These hidden radio sets were enormous morale builders, enabling the men to keep in touch with the living world. And the men laughed and laughed, for in many camps the Japanese never found a radio. The hiding places were as varied as the imagination of the men could make them—a recess in a kitchen wall, a false-bottom table, a mess kit, a field flask, an underground cache.

Equipment and parts to build the sets were collected from a great number of sources. Some were smuggled into the camps from outside. Most receivers were of the regenerative, oscillating detector type, utilizing one stage of radio frequency amplification and one stage of audio amplification.

NOTES

1. William H. McDougall, *By Eastern Windows*, New York, 1949, p. 186.
2. Russell Braddon, *The Naked Island*, London, 1982, pp. 209–210.
3. Kate Caffrey, *Out in the Midday Sun*, Sydney, 1973, p. 187.
4. Mary Thomas, *In the Shadow of the Rising Sun*, Singapore, 1983, p. 189.
5. Freddy Bloom, *Dear Philip: A Diary of Captivity, Changi, 1942–1945*, London, 1980.
6. *Far East POW Newsletter* (London) (85 January–February), 1984, p. 1.
7. Ija Korner, "Psychological Needs of the Individual Dissolving in the Mass, and the Possibility of Clinical Help," *Journal of Social Psychology* 16 (1942), 143–150.
8. McDougall, *By Eastern Windows*, p. 243.
9. Stanley S. Pavillard, *Bamboo Doctor*, New York, 1960.
10. Robert S. Woodworth, *Adjustment and Mastery*, Baltimore, 1933, p. 55.
11. McDougall, *By Eastern Windows*, p. 235.
12. Ben Waldron and Emily Burneson, *Corregidor: From Paradise to Hell*, San Francisco, 1988, pp. 164, 205.
13. Ernest Gordon, *Through the Valley of the Kwai*, New York, 1962, pp. 72–73.
14. Richard W. Peterson, "Strengths Found in Former Prisoners of War," *Ex-POW Bulletin* (April 1990).
15. Stan Sommers, "Coping with Captivity," *Ex-POW Bulletin* (October 1985).
16. Catherine Kenny, *Captives*, St. Lucia, 1986, p. 128.
17. Bessie Sneed, *Captured by the Japanese*, Denver, 1946, p. 92.
18. Bloom, *Dear Philip*, p. 43.
19. Hilda C. Corpe, *Prisoner Beyond the Chindwin*, London, 1955, p. 120.
20. Irwin Edman, *Human Traits and Their Social Significance*, Boston, 1920, p. 138.
21. Thomas, *In the Shadow of the Rising Sun*, p. 47.
22. Daphne Jackson, *Java Nightmare*, Padstow, England, 1979, p. 77.
23. P. A. Sorokin, *Man and Society in Calamity*, New York, 1942, p. 10.
24. Peter Hartley, *Escape to Captivity*, London, 1952, p. 164.
25. Iris G. J. Parfitt, *Jail-Bird Jottings: The Impressions of a Singapore Internee*, Kuala Lumpur, 1947.
26. *Ibid.*, Preface.
27. Charles Thomas Brown, *Bars from Bilibid Prison*, San Antonio, 1947.
28. Alfred J. Stahl, *How We Took It*, New York, 1945.
29. Willem Brandt, *Indonesische Nachten* [Indonesian Nights], The Hague, pp. 14–15.
30. Annie Ofeigssen-Takes, *Wel En Wee* [Weal and Woe], Epe, the Netherlands, 1955, pp. 98–99.
31. M. G. Hartley, *Mijn Kamp, Niet Door Hitler* [Mein Kampf, Not by Hitler], Amsterdam, 1946, p. 76.
32. *Ibid.*, p. 35.
33. Arthur Zich and the Editors of Time-Life Books, *World War II: The Rising Sun*, New York, 1977.
34. Manny Lawton, *Some Survived*, Chapel Hill, NC, 1984, pp. 62–63.
35. Ofeigssen-Takes, *Wel En Wee*, pp. 56–57.
36. The song appears in *Ex-POW Bulletin* (July 1983).

78   Prisoners of the Japanese in World War II

37. Both songs can be found in Ofeigssen-Takes, *Wel En Wee*, pp. 8, 48.
38. Caffrey, *Out in the Midday Sun*, p. 236.
39. John Coast, *Railroad of Death*, London, 1946.
40. Halstead Fowler and Dorothy Wagner, *Recipes from Bilibid*, New York, 1946.
41. Jessie Bell Hanson, "You Take a Little Garlic." Fred Stevens, *Santo Tomas*, New York, 1946, p. 247.
42. *Ibid.*, pp. 247–249.
43. Thomas, pp. 214–215.
44. Betty Jeffrey, *White Coolies*, Sydney, 1954, p. 131.
45. Ronald Hastain, *White Coolie*, London, 1947, p. 168.
46. Agnes Newton Keith, *Three Came Home*, Boston, 1947, p. 269.
47. Michael O'Connor, *The More Fool I*, Dublin, 1954, pp. 177–178.

SOURCES

Selected Sources Used by Elizabeth Vaughan in *Community Under Stress: An Internment Camp Culture*:

Allport, G. W., and Postman, Leo. *The Psychology of Rumor*. New York: Henry Holt, 1947.
de Terente, Violette. "I Was Interned Forty-Six Months." *Christian Science Monitor* (December 9, 1944).
Edman, Irwin. *Human Traits and Their Social Significance*. Boston: Houghton Mifflin, 1920.
Elliott, Mabel, and Merrill, Francis. *Social Disorganization*. New York: Harper & Bros., 1941.
Embree, John F. *Causes of Unrest at Relocation Centers*. Washington, DC: United States Department of the Interior, 1943.
Ford, Carey, and MacBain, Alastair. *The Last Time I Saw Them*. New York: Scribner's, 1946.
Freud, Anna, and Burlingame, Dorothy. *War and Children*. New York: Medical War Books, 1943.
Harrison, Earl H. "Civilian Internment—American Way." *Survey Graphic* 33 (May 1944), 229–233.
Helion, Jean. *They Shall Not Have Me*. New York: E. P. Dutton, 1943.
"History of Santo Tomas." *Prisoner of War Bulletin* (American National Red Cross) (April 1944).
Jacobi, Johan. *The Psychology of Jung*. New Haven, CT: Yale University Press, 1943.
Koestler, Arthur. *Scum of the Earth*. New York: Macmillan, 1941.
Korner, Ija. "The Psychological Needs of the Individual Dissolving in the Mass and the Possibilities of Clinical Help." *Journal of Social Psychology* 16 (1942), 143–150.
Leighton, A. H. *The Governing of Men*. Princeton, NJ: Princeton University Press, 1946.
Linton, Ralph. *The Cultural Background of Personality*. New York: Appleton-Century, 1945.

_____. *The Study of Man.* New York: Appleton-Century, 1936.
McCall, J. E. *Santo Tomas Internment Camp—Woodruff.* Lincoln, NE, 1945.
McCoy, M. H., et al. *Ten Escape from Tojo.* New York: Farrar & Reinhart, 1944.
Maslow, A. H. "Conflict, Frustration and the Theory of Threat." *Journal of Abnormal and Social Psychology* 38 (1943), 81–86.
Nerac, Eleanore. "Refuge in Internment." *Independent Woman* 21 (April 1942), 113–114.
Newman, P. H. "The Prisoner of War Mentality." *British Medical Journal* 1 (January 1944), 8.
Prichard, Rosemary, and Rosenzweig, Saul. "The Effects of War Stress Upon Childhood and Youth." *Journal of Abnormal and Social Psychology* 38 (1942), 329–344.
Shaffer, Laurance F. *The Psychology of Adjustment.* Boston: Houghton-Mifflin, 1936.
Sheridan, R. E. *Recollections of Four Years, 1941–1945.* Manila: La Salle College, 1946.
Smith, William A. "In Weisien Prison Camp." *Asia and the Americas* 46 (July 1946), 318–323.
Sneed, Bessie. *Captured by the Japanese.* Denver: Bradford-Robinson, 1946.
Sorokin, P. A. *Man and Society in Calamity.* New York: E. P. Dutton, 1942.
Stevens, Fred H. *Santo Tomas.* New York: Stratford House, 1946.
Terry, Carol. *Kept.* Philadelphia: Ramabai Mukti, 1945.
Woodworth, R. S. *Adjustment and Mastery.* Baltimore, MD: Williams & Wilkins, 1933.

SOURCES

Beaumont, Joan. *Survival and Leadership in Captivity, 1941–1945.* Sydney, 1988.
Brandt, Willem. *Indonesische Nachten* [Indonesian Nights]. Amsterdam, 1946.
Brougher, Brigadier General William E. *Baggy Pants and Other Stories.* New York, 1965.
_____. *The Long Dark Road: Poems.* Atlanta, GA, privately printed, 1946.
Brown, C. C. *Mural Ditties and Sime Road Soliloquies: Prose and Illustrations.* Singapore, 1948.
Brown, Charles Thomas. *Bars from Bilibid Prison: Poems.* San Antonio, TX, 1947.
Burki, Charles. *Achter de Kawat* [Behind Barbed Wire: Prose and Illustrations]. Amsterdam, 1978.
Cohen, Elie A. *Human Behavior in the Concentration Camp.* New York, 1953.
de Ruyter, Gwendolyn, and Tuckerman, Ingeborg. *Tjideng-Zwart op Wit: Poems and Illustrations* [Tjideng Camp: Black on White]. Amsterdam, 1977.
Downer, Sidney F. *Raggle-Taggle: A Collection of Stories, Poems, Articles, Sketches and Drawings: POW Camp Shirakawa, Formosa, during 1944.* Aldershot, England, 1947.
Fortier, Malcolm Vaughn. *The Life of a POW Under the Japanese: In Caricature as Sketched by Col. Malcolm Vaughn Fortier.* Spokane, WA, 1946.
Fowler, Halstead, and Wagner, Dorothy. *Recipes from Bilibid.* New York, 1946.
Hartley, M. G. *Mijn Kamp; Niet Door Hitler* [Mein Kampf: Not by Hitler]. Amsterdam, 1947.
Harvey, Eleanor T. M. *Sonnets from Captivity and Other Poems.* Philadelphia, 1949.
Jacobs, Eugene C. *Blood Brothers: A Medic's Sketch Book.* New York, 1984.

Lee, First Lieutenant Henry G. *Nothing But Praise: Poems*. Pasadena, CA, 1984.
McCall, J. *Santo Tomas Internment Camp in Verse and Reverse*. Lincoln, NE, 1945.
Newsberg, Alan, ed. *Benjamin Charles Steele: POW Drawings*. Billings, MT, 1986.
Newman, Samuel A. *How to Survive as a Prisoner of War*. Philadelphia, 1970.
Ofeigssen-Takes, Annie. *Wel en Wee* [Weal and Woe]. Epe, the Netherlands, 1955.
Parfitt, Iris G. J. *Jail-Bird Jottings*. Kuala Lumpur, 1947.
Rawlings, Leo. *And the Dawn Came Up Like Thunder: Illustrations and Drawings*. London, 1972.
Reid, A., ed. *Railroad to Hell: Being a Selection of Paintings by Leo Rawlings*. London, 1950.
Searle, Ronald. *Forty Drawings*. London, 1945.
Skvorzov, A. V. *Chinese Ink and Brush Sketches of POW Camp Life in Hong Kong*. Hong Kong, 1948.
Sprod, George. *Life on a Squared-Wheel Bike: The Saga of a Cartoonist*. Sydney, 1983.
Stahl, Alfred J. *How We Took It: The Lost Tribe of the Philippines: Poems and Cartoons*. New York, 1945.
Tullipan, Ray, and de Grey, Shin. *Changi Souvenir Songbook: A Selection of Musical Numbers*. Narrowmine, Australia, 1946.
Wijngaard, Maria. *De Niet Verloren Jaren: Gedichten* [The Years Not Lost: Poems]. 1972.

Chapter 4

After the War: The World of the Ex-Prisoner

Introduction

However future researchers may analyze the bases of Japanese behavior and attitudes toward their captives, being a prisoner of the Japanese was a traumatic experience from which many never recovered in spite of their successful readjustment.

Some POWs and internees came home permanently disabled or prematurely aged. None emerged unscathed from the experience. One finds remnants of the trauma in little things: for example, many keep surplus food in the house; refuse to drive foreign automobiles; and hold attitudes of gratitude, acceptance, and deep patriotism.

Living in a prison camp affected all men, women, and children who experienced it, regardless of age, nationality, where or when they were captured, or how long they were held in captivity. The aftereffects of their imprisonment have been multifaceted and enormously complex because the human mind and body are extremely complex mechanisms. The internees and POWs were affected, or impaired, both psychologically and physically by the incarceration—each in a different manner, in a different intensity, and at a different time.

The literature and documentation on the aftereffects of camp imprisonment are voluminous. This chapter brings together a large part of the published documentation of these effects.

Vindictiveness and Anger

No subject has been so hotly debated among camp prisoners as their feelings of hate and revenge toward their former captors. Many former POWs and internees show little apparent vindictiveness in reaction to their captivity; their feeling is rather one of contempt. Only a few express outright hatred.

In a lengthy article in the *Ex-POW Bulletin*, Guy Kelnhofer, an ex–POW who was captured on Wake Island, wrote:

> Very few mental health professionals realize that we are angry and that we have just cause for the anger we carry inside ourselves. To be effective counselors of ex–POWs and internees they must put aside the simplistic notion that we have to forgive our enemies and find peace by renouncing our anger. Would that it were that simple.[1]

The personal accounts of ex–POWs reveal their ambivalent feelings. They often state that they have no feelings of hostility toward their captors, but that they do not wish to extend the hand of friendship. They deny feeling hatred, calling it a poison, but they do clearly loathe their ex-captors. Some say that they will talk to the older Japanese generation, but that distrust and hatred have not disappeared.

One of the themes of ex–POWs' and ex-internees' attitudes is hating not the Japanese, but the general concepts of violence, greed, sadism, intolerance, arrogance, and ruthlessness. Perhaps the most profound statement on this topic came from Father Francis Herlihy, a Roman Catholic priest, who was interned in Rabaul, New Britain:

> No one should be asked to sympathise with sadism and barbarity. No one can deny Japan's appalling record of these things in China, Malaya, Burma, the Indies, and the Philippines. No one should wonder at the cold, white rage of men whose comrades have been degraded, tortured and brutally murdered. Yet, although this rage may be just, it tends, like all rage, to be blind, even as blind as the hatred of the Japanese for us.
>
> There is something more profitable for us than return of hatred; more noble in us than mere anger; more vital to us than vengeance. It is the recognition of cold, objective truth. That the entire Japanese race committed these crimes, or shared in their guilt, is not true. That these crimes have proved the Japanese to be a "sub-human" race, incapable of ever winning the world's respect, is not true. The Japanese who committed these acts of cruelty, the people on our side who gloated over the results of the atomic bomb, are all fellow beings of our own: they are not products of differing philosophies.[2]

Positive Aspects of Internment

At the opposite emotional extreme is a feeling that the imprisonment was actually a positive experience. As ex–POW Kenneth Harrison expressed it, "It was an experience that money could not buy, and now that's all over, I wouldn't have missed it for quids."[3] Although many POWs and internees may feel they gained an education that no books or university could have taught them, not many have expressed it openly.

Some of the women internees acknowledged having gained certain values from their captivity, as Jessie Elizabeth Simons noted:

> Looking back over those years I find that in many ways I do not regret the experience. I learned the meaning of comradeship. This is an indefinable bond among those who have lived and suffered together. I realize the depth and meaning of comradeship among those who have been through it together. Even now, though surrounded by friends and relatives, I still long for my old pals. It is not what happens to you that matters, it is your Reaction.[4]

Through discussions and treatment after the war, many camp prisoners became aware that in the hard school of incarceration they learned lessons that have influenced and assisted them for the rest of their lives. They learned patience, thrift, self-sufficiency, the essence of loyalty, duty, fairness, the deeper meaning of commitment, solid covenant relationships, the value of freedom.

They also learned that courage and tenacity and indomitable fortitude are more than a match for life's most difficult challenges. They learned to function successfully in situations that would crush anyone lacking these qualities. Thus, the strength of ex–POWs and internees is their ability to look back to their survival during trying times and gather the will to move forward and to find the courage to face the vicissitudes of their present lives.

History of U.S.-POW Medical Research (MedSearch)

Since POW MedSearch is today part of the organization American Ex-Prisoners of War (Ex-POWs), Inc., a brief history of this group is warranted. American Ex-POWs grew out of the Bataan Relief Organization, which was formed in New Mexico by two mothers whose sons were POWs in the Philippines.

The group grew, was incorporated in 1943, and changed its name in 1946 to Bataan Veterans' Organization. In 1949, the name was changed again to American Ex-Prisoners of War to include all former POWs of any war.

An Ex-POW emblem was designed by former POW Bryan I. Doughty of Denver, Colorado. Heraldic symbols representing justice are balanced on swords. Curves at the top of the shield portray the two massive military defeats suffered by the United States—at Bataan and the Belgian Bulge. The motto, *Non Solum Armis*, is Latin for "Not by Arms Alone."

Shortly after the war it became apparent to governmental officials, medical doctors, psychologists and psychiatrists and social workers that the aftereffects of captivity were so widespread that in whatever fashion possible—organized or nonorganized—something had to be done to assist the ex-captives.

The great dream of American POWs to establish a hospital for former POWs could not be realized. The organization concentrated on the goal of obtaining more and better treatment for all ex–POWs.

The organization did so by supporting congressional bill HR 7711, which provided for a study of the mental and physical consequences of malnutrition and starvation of POWs and internees during World War II. That bill resulted in P.L. 744, dated February 3, 1954, stating that a study was necessary to determine the procedures and standards to be applied in the diagnosis of the mental and physical condition of former POWs, the life expectancy of former POWs, standards to be applied for the evaluation of claims, and the manner in which the conditions were service connected.

It took many years for the government to acknowledge that former POWs and internees had suffered grossly from their years in captivity and that they were entitled to some form of compensation, depending upon the severity of their aftereffects and to what degree the aftereffects were connected to the time spent in the camps.

In 1969, the then–national commander of the organization, John Lay, initiated a Medical Research, or MedSearch, Committee to research thoroughly and publish any information related to the aftereffects of incarceration.

Through the years this MedSearch Committee, especially under the leadership of Stan Sommers and his wife Peggy, has been responsible for a number of valuable accomplishments, including the publication of information packets containing booklets on a variety of medical topics and the realization of P.L. 97-37, the Former Prisoner of War Benefits Act. Without any medical background, members of the MedSearch Committee have, over the years, made the organization's motto, "We exist to help those who cannot help themselves," come true.

Physical and Psychological Aspects of Long-term Captivity

Many studies initiated after World War II were related to illnesses contracted during captivity by former POWs and internees. One of the classic examples of these illnesses was severe malnutrition, which spawned a range of nutritional and vitamin deficiency diseases.

The most striking disease was polyneuritis or Vitamin B deficiency, which was universal to all captives, especially in the Pacific. This disease caused a chain reaction of other physical deficiencies, or so-called presumptive diseases, that are accepted by the Veterans Administration (VA) as being related to "internment experiences: avitaminosis; beriberi, including beriberi heart disease; chronic dysentery; helminthiasis (intestinal parasites or worms); malnutrition; pellagra; any other nutritional deficiency; psychosis; any of the anxiety states; dysthymic disorder, or depressive neurosis; organic residuals of frostbite; posttraumatic osteoarthritis; peripheral neuropathy; irritable bowel syndrome; and peptic ulcer disease.

This list is not complete. Today, attempts are being made to expand this list and to define the diseases more clearly so they can be understood and recognized more easily by personnel in VA hospitals and others in the medical field. Diseases that need more study and analysis include posttraumatic arthritis and beriberi heart disease.

Most POWs and internees learned as captives that they could not help their situation by complaining. They made the best of what they had, and this attitude was carried over as a way of life after captivity ended. With this way of coping so deeply ingrained, it seems that most of them denied having any physical or psychological problems. As the years went on, however, their problems worsened, and at some point, they had to convince the VA that they had had illnesses and disabilities all along.

Many ex–POW medical experts believe that numerous factors cannot be measured scientifically in many cases and cannot be detected until they are in advanced stages, especially if they are not complained of. As Dr. William R. Shadish noted in a presentation to the American Ex-POWs in October 1990:

> We don't have time for long term studies to prove all the disability ratings. No Ex-POWs will be here if they have to wait for scientific proof such as the Department of Veterans Affairs says they need, but doesn't exist now.[5]

Disability-rating Problems

Despite the enactment of P.L. 97-37, which provides for disability payments to all American ex–POWs, disability ratings for ex–POWs and most recently for civilian internees remain a problem. The following extract from a paper by Dr. Guy J. Kelnhofer describes these problems:

> ...Very few have been awarded a high rating. This conclusion is at odds with the current medical understanding of the lifetime consequences of long periods of physical and psychological torture. The VA

rating pattern suggests that these men have largely *escaped* the types of disabilities that normally would be for those who survive such traumatic circumstances....

The ex–POW who comes to the VA today to explain the origin of his injuries caused by long-term imprisonment is likely to find it difficult to relate to those who are examining him. If the VA examiners he sees have never missed more than a few meals in their lives, what can they really understand about the effects on the former prisoner of years of semi-starvation? Words tend to lose their meaning when experiences differ so widely that common terms like "hunger" do not convey the same understandings of what is meant....

Few at the VA are trained to understand the strength of the constraints which govern a former inmate of a death camp. The ex-prisoner who managed to survive such an ordeal was able to do so only because he adapted him- or herself totally to those life-threatening conditions.... As a consequence, he tends to be hostile, suspicious, withdrawn and wary. He is, by training, secretive and he learned the hard way to hide his true feelings. He continues to conduct himself as though the world is still dangerous and uncertain....

Kelnhofer points out that the difficulties in fairly assessing former prisoners' and internees' disabilities stem not from a lack of concern within the Veterans Administration but rather from a lack of information. It is not universally realized, for example, that the prisoners of the Japanese were subjected to conditions of the kind that actually were prevalent. An understanding of the unique plight of these former prisoners and internees would, Kelnhofer argues, greatly aid in establishing appropriate disability ratings:

> If the VA personnel will learn to view these men [and women] as the survivors of suffering and of horrors that few can even imagine, then there is some small prospect that our few remaining ex–POWs (and civilian internees) will come to have the confidence in that system which too often now is lacking.[6]*

With the inclusion of extensive bibliographical references, medical and sociological researchers may be able to extract appropriate information on the physiological and psychological aftereffects of incarceration and thus, it is hoped, the problems of disability ratings of ex-captives that are occurring today will diminish.

Since POWs and civilian internees—men and women—have experienced the same sufferings and maltreatment in the Japanese prison camps, this author has added the "female" gender to the quote from Dr. Kelnhofer's paper. His paper and the seven that follow serve as an introduction to the complex and expansive issue of the disability ratings of the aftereffects of imprisonment in camps.

Impressions of Medical Officers in Prison Camps

Memory is always selective, especially as time increases the distance between the present and the happenings and experiences from the past. This effect makes it difficult for the historian to analyze reports from those who are retelling their stories and to filter out of the narratives the emotional baggage attached to them so as to extract basic, rational information for a true historical perspective. It becomes even more difficult when narratives on certain technical subjects are presented by laypersons.

The following two synopses of articles are exceptions because the technical information was written by ex–POW medical officers shortly after the war.

Impressions of a POW medical officer. Dr. Mack L. Gothier discussed a number of topics in his article: fabrication of medical supplies and devices; phases of malnutrition, acute and chronic; beriberi, polyneurotic and edematous; vitamin B-1 therapy; cardiovascular findings; hypertension; neuropathy; burning feet syndrome; and rheumatic fever.

His article may be summarized as follows: (1) Approximately 1,100 prisoners were treated between July 1943 and March 1945, with a mortality of only 66 patients. (2) The endocrinologic aspects of avitaminosis have been emphasized, especially the disturbance of the liver, thyroid, pituitary, and adrenal glands. (3) The difference between the acute and the chronic phase of malnutrition has been emphasized. (4) Beriberi appears to be a multivitamin deficiency disease, and further study is necessary to determine its pathogenesis, course, and treatment. (5) The vasomotor aspects of beriberi have been enumerated, with the possible relationship to the lack of hypertension among the rice-eating races. (6) The relationship of diarrhea to the edematous type of beriberi has been stressed. (7) Retinal degeneration caused by vitamin B-1 deficiency did not respond well to vitamin B-1 therapy, but xerophthalmia responded favorably to cod-liver oil treatment. (8) The average weight loss among POWs was approximately 40 pounds. (9) Intraperitoneal sulfanilamide was used extensively in abdominal surgery with favorable results. (10) The possible beneficial effects in cases of pulmonary tuberculosis of a low-calorie, low protein, fat-free diet have been suggested. (11) Poor results were obtained in the treatment of amebiasis. (12) Untoward reactions to the sulfa drugs were seldom observed among POWs. (13) A high incidence of acute infectious hepatitis occurred, but acute rheumatic fever was rare.[7]

Experiences of a medical officer in a Japanese prison. In his article, Dr. Emil P. Reed described the various conditions during the Bataan Death March and subsequent diseases and illnesses in the various camps: (1) rice belly, or inguinal hernia; (2) dysentery, malaria, and deficiency diseases; (3) nutritional amblyopia; (4) pellagra; (5) dengue fever; and (6) limber neck.[8]

Medical Facts on Long-term Captivity

The medical aftereffects of incarceration. The following is from a short article by Stanley G. Sommers, research chairman, POW Med-Search:

> Many of us lost from 40 to 60 percent of our bodyweight for a prolonged period of time. Medical experts agree this causes irreversible damage to all body systems and organs.
> We suffered from a multiplicity of deficiencies and infective diseases for a prolonged period of time without adequate medication—this also leads to many serious medical problems later in life.
> We lived under constant fear of torture or death, never knowing when they would behead us or shoot us.
> As a result of this we suffer from the KZ Syndrome (German for concentration camp). The KZ Syndrome consists of:
>
> * Failing memory and difficulty in concentration;
> * Nervousness, irritability, restlessness;
> * Fatigue;
> * Traumatic dreams;
> * Headaches;
> * Depression;
> * Moodiness;
> * Loss of initiative;
> * A feeling of insufficiency;
> * Shunning large crowds and social activities.
>
> Since repatriation morbidity studies have shown that POWs have a higher incidence rate of illness and disease in all body systems.[9]

Testimony on POWs' physical illness. The following is an abstract of Dr. Theodore Woodward's testimony before the Committee on Veterans' Affairs of the United States House of Representatives in 1985:

> The Veterans Administration should be permitted through congressional action to accept as sufficient evidence of service connection the findings and analysis of reliable epidemiologic and medical data including psychologic considerations involving former POWs and the *generally accepted medical literature* on conditions prevalent among former POWs.
> Additionally, *published medical evidence available* is more than sufficient for award of compensation relative to a number of disorders. The former POWs who have been demonstrably exposed to excessive and prolonged stress and deprivation should be presumed service-connected for the following diagnosed conditions:

- Cardiovascular conditions leading to arteriosclerotic heart disease, hypertension and cardiomyopathies with such consequences as arrhythmias and embolization.

- Neurological abnormalities, derived from malnutrition, avitaminosis, peripheral neuropathy, similar deficiency diseases, and optic atrophy.

- All psychiatric and psychological disabilities, including the symptoms of alcoholism resulting from often recognized chronic anxiety and depressive states.

- Altered susceptibility to illnesses, such as tuberculosis occurring at any time, chronic lung disease (e.g. for laboring in coal, copper or asbestos mines) and certain allergic disorders.

- Major hepatic disorders, such as hepatitis, chronic active hepatitis leading to cirrhosis and hepatoma; also organic intestinal diseases, such as colitis.

- Peripheral vascular disease, such as frozen feet syndrome.

- Arthritis, such as traumatic arthritis and certain connective tissue diseases.[10]

Aftereffects: The Mind

The central nervous system and the temporal lobes of the brain are the seat of our emotions. Because of its intricacy, this system is the most susceptible to abuse and privation, and it is incapable of replacing dead or damaged elements and thus can never be repaired. In the opinion of 48 medical experts, "These ailments and disabilities [the aftereffects of incarceration in *all* body systems] may appear long afterwards and no time limit can be set for their appearance."[11]

Approximately 85 percent of the POWs of the Japanese suffered from the anxiety states or psychoses. The primary differences between POWs and others were primarily psychiatric problems and malnutrition during imprisonment.[12]

Post–Traumatic Stress Disorder (PTSD)

One of the most distressing conditions of former POWs and internees is chronic PTSD. One physician and a group of psychologists conducted two separate evaluations of ex–POWs to determine certain aspects of symptoms associated with PTSD.

Dr. Norman S. White conducted psychiatric evaluations on 30 ex–POWs who were held captive in the Philippines. He noted:

> Recently I conducted psychiatric evaluations of 30 of these men, aged 57 to 67 years, 37 years after their repatriation from Japanese prison camps in the Philippine Islands, Japan and Manchuria. Twenty-six, or more than 85 percent, had sufficient symptomatology to support the diagnosis of chronic post-traumatic stress disorder of at least moderate severity. Based on a scale of intensity of symptomatology ranging from 1 to 5; 8 of the 26 men scored in the 1 to 3 range, and 18 scored in the 4 to 5 range, reflecting the presence of the disorder to a marked and often incapacitating degree.[13]

Dr. White also discussed sleep disorders, flashback phenomena, and associated phenomena.

> Treatment consisted of psychotherapy, and the administration of a tricyclic agent, doxepin, in doses ranging from 25 to 100 mg. before bedtime. Benzodiazepines are occasionally prescribed—chlordiazepoxide in doses of 10 mg. 1 to 3 times a day or adprazolam .5 mg. at the same frequency.[14]

Three psychologists from the VA Medical Center in Palo Alto conducted a study by means of mailed questionnaires. One hundred eighty-one ex-POWs returned questionnaires, which were distributed at state and regional POW meetings in the Midwest in the spring of 1984. The psychologists concluded that the findings were important but suggestive, rather than conclusive.[15]

PTSD in the older veteran. In an extensive article, Dr. Merrill Lipton and Dr. William Schaffer describe the results of group meetings with ex-POWs. They discuss in detail the recurrent memories of each individual; dissociativelike states; the reexperiencing of traumatic events either in nightmares or in daytime ruminations, or both; numbing of responses or emotional "anesthesia" and the inability to get close to others; and symptoms of excessive autonomic arousal.

When group members feel comfortable enough to talk about their imprisonment, they all express strong guilt feelings about their experiences. As the authors state:

> The guilts are handled in groups by discussions of the realities. These include reassurance that fear is "normal" in such circumstances, they did their best under the conditions [they were willing to fight, but were ordered to surrender and thus became POWs] and one must accept his best as good enough and not expect more of himself.
> Having been in similar circumstances, group members can reassure one another in these matters. This helps to leave the past behind.[16]

PTSD and the POW. Dr. Robert L. Obourn uses the definition of PTSD from the American Psychiatric Association's *Diagnostic and Statistical*

Manual of Mental Disorders (DSM-III) in which PTSD is categorized as an anxiety disorder brought on by an extraordinary and distressing event which the sufferer continues to experience long after the actual cessation of the event.[17]

Observations of PTSD among POWs. Clinical psychologists who work daily with ex–POWs in Veterans Administration Medical Centers (VAMCs), and whose impetus for working with these patients comes from their early associations with PTSD, often provide valuable information concerning the treatment of PTSD victims.

Two psychologists, Barbara F. Key and Robert G. Bobbitt, wrote an article describing (1) how to stimulate feedback from others afflicted with PTSD, (2) how to let POWs and their families know that there is help and understanding of their particular problems at every level, and (3) how to present a few basic observations about treating veterans and their loved ones.

These authors discuss such topics as hiding PTSD symptoms, guilt feelings, and the aftermath of trauma, as well as mechanisms of transformation and neutralizing the traumatic aftermath. They end by advocating a stronger system of dissemination of information among therapists working with ex–POWs and internees.[18]

Toward a rational pharmacotherapy for PTSD. The use of medication to ease the symptoms of Post-Traumatic Stress Disorder is discussed by Dr. Matthew J. Friedman of the VAMC in White River Junction, Vermont.

In his article, which is supported by 62 bibliographical references, Dr. Friedman describes the biological correlates of PTSD, clinical psychopharmacology, diagnostic considerations, and meshing treatment with symptoms. In his conclusions, he states that pharmacotherapy is useful primarily as an adjunct to the psychological (intrapsychic and or behavioral) treatment of PTSD. He hopes that a better understanding of the biological correlates of PTSD will lead to a rational pharmacotherapy for this disorder.[19]

PTSD: a conversation with Dr. Charles Figley. In October 1987, Dr. Charles R. Figley, noted scholar on PTSD, was interviewed by George Bittle, counseling psychologist with the Veterans Administration regional office in Indianapolis. In this interview, Dr. Figley addresses the important issues of PTSD and describes how these issues affect the population of veterans and other people who work with them.

Dr. Figley also defines the disorder; explains the differences between PTSD and other psychological disorders; presents the correct diagnosis; and discusses who is predisposed to the disorder, factors that make an individual more amenable to treatment, treatment modalities of choice, the guilt component, and vocational rehabilitation strategies.[20]

Psychological Effects of the POW Experience

The captivity experience and its psychological consequences. In a comprehensive paper, Dr. John F. Russell discusses the long-term psychological effects of captivity, particularly on former POWs and civilian internees, in widely different settings. What happens to an individual who is suddenly and unexpectedly transformed from the status of a person to that of an object? How does one endure and cope with such a catastrophic event? What are the long-term effects on health and adjustment? How does one adapt to the world after the camp? What are the liberation syndromes? The repatriate finds that the reality of being back home, free again, is not the same as the dream of freedom.[21]

Psychological effects of the POW experience. Although Dr. Gayle K. Lumry's article deals with the POW experience in the European theater, its contents apply to all POWs and internees. Dr. Lumry discusses the following topics: (1) the physical effects of psychological stress; (2) controlled experiments—loss of physical fitness, loss of sleep, isolation, effect of stress; (3) man's search for meaning, Musselman, the concentration camp syndrome, and Japanese versus German prison camps; and (4) Danish, French, German, and Norwegian studies of late symptoms, neurological findings, employability, decline in intellect, and psychiatric problems.[22]

Some observations of a VA POW psychiatrist. This article by Dr. Clarence E. Carnahan, a staff physician at the Loma Linda VA Hospital in 1984 (the time his observations were published) describes the multidisciplinary program at Loma Linda for the evaluation and treatment of American ex–POWs, with an emphasis on the psychiatric aspects of the program.

As of 1984, the program had worked with over 350 ex–POWs and was helpful to veterans and their families. Dr. Carnahan states that approximately one-third of the patients received psychiatric interviews.[23]

Depression in POWs. Dr. Nardini's article describes 28 essential stress factors, such as boredom and ennui, worry about family, physical disease, beatings and abuse, and forced marches under alien conditions. All of these factors were present in POW and internment camps.[24]

Long-term effects of a prolonged stress experience. The results of a Canadian study of ex–POWs in Hong Kong indicated that these men were in a chronic depressive state, masked by tension and anxiety. The researchers state that years of captivity led to impairment of emotional functioning, even in individuals who in daily life were able to function adequately.[25]

Diagnostic criteria for anxiety states. Packet 2, published by American Ex-POWs, contains a partial list of the anxiety states, or anxiety neuroses, from the *Diagnostic and Statistical Manual of Mental Disorders* of the American Psychiatric Association. It lists, for example, 12 diagnostic criteria for panic disorders; 7 diagnostic criteria for generalized anxiety disorder and obsessive compulsive disorder; and 13 diagnostic criteria for PTSD.[26]

General adaptation syndrome (GAS). In this article, Dr. Nealis describes GAS in terms of three stages that characterize an organism's response to stress: alarm, resistance, and exhaustion. He states that the GAS theory predicts that individuals who have been under constant stress may eventually become psychologically and behaviorally "helpless" in the face of stress that continues to emerge from memories of captivity.[27]

The Japanese POW syndrome: the short fuse. This article is a brief extract from Dr. Charles Brown's assessment of an anxiety reaction born out of the agony of Bataan and the despair of Corregidor, nurtured by 3½ years in the fertile soil of danger, misery, and starvation.[28]

A POW syndrome. This article concludes that apathy helps the ex-POW to maintain personality integration in the face of severe reality and psychological stresses.[29]

The concentration camp syndrome (KZ Syndrome). A descriptive bibliography of this syndrome, which was coined on the basis of 11 symptoms most often demonstrated in Norwegian ex-prisoners on psychiatric examination.

The syndrome has been validated for all who were "camp captives."[30]

Alcoholism. In this lengthy article Dr. William Paul Skelton discusses the general symptoms of alcoholism and the definite diagnosis of this disease, as well as the problem of alcoholism among patients who are veterans.[31]

Ex-POW group therapy from the group therapist's perspective. This article presents a brief discussion of a VA group therapy program using video documentaries of the POWs' experiences and their group activities as a therapy method.[32]

Adaptation and coping during captivity: the POW experience. Dr. Robert Joseph Ursano and Dr. James Jay Rundell discuss numerous issues connected with the POW experience. They contend that the POW is greatly influenced by the environmental and sociocultural factors of the captivity setting and that the most important coping mechanisms are communication, maintenance of military social structure, and a flexible personality.

They also briefly discuss the aftereffects of the POW experience, such as medical illness, PTSD, adjustment disorder, depression, anxiety disorders, substance disorders, and family problems.[33]

Aftereffects: The Body

Introduction

The brutal and inhumane treatment—beatings, torture, slave labor, and starvation—endured by many POWs and civilian internees of the Japanese has been well documented.

Many of the prisoners lost 40–60 percent of their body weight for a prolonged period.

Medical experts agree that the multiplicity of deficiencies and infectious diseases that these captives experienced caused irreversible damage to all body systems and organs.

This damage has also led to many serious medical problems later in these captives' lives.

The *Physician's Manual for Examination of Veterans* and a VA circular described the following:

Disorders Directly Related to the POW Experience
- Malnutrition, avitaminosis, beriberi and wet beriberi, and residuals of pellagra
- Neurological diseases
- Sensorineural deafness
- Chronic dysentery

Disorders Probably Related to the POW Experience
- Symptomatic osteoarthritis
- Spondylosis, spondylolisthesis
- Osteoporosis vertebral, post-traumatic arthritis in association with lumbar disc degeneration
- Radioculopathy
- Cardiovascular aging

Disorders Possibly Related to the POW Experience
- Arteriosclerotic cardiovascular disease
- Residuals of beriberi heart disease
- Stroke, cerebral atrophy
- Neoplastic diseases: skin, lung, bowel, prostate

Disorders Not Related to the POW Experience
- Diabetes, familial tremor, thyroid diseases, goiter and nongoitrous hyperthyroidism, or primary or secondary hypothyroidism
- Impotence and gonadal deficiency, gynecomastia

Commonest Syndromes of Neurological Diseases

In a short statement, Dr. Alvin C. Poweleit described the commonest syndromes of neurological diseases dating back to the days of captivity and long periods of malnutrition: peripheral neuropathy, optic neuritis, optic atrophy, and sensorineural hearing loss. He noted:

> POWs now are reaching an age when the degenerative changes of old age are likely to occur. These changes will be made more severe due to malnutrition since their neurological reserve may be less. Autopsy findings on POWs done soon after the war showed extensive degeneration and demyelination in areas such as the posterior columns or eighth cranial nerve generally correlating with deficits seen later in life.[35]

Peripheral neuropathy in former POWs. Following World War II, studies revealed that former POWs suffered nutritional neuropathy. More recent studies of this group report persistent nutritional neuropathy dating back to captivity. The Livermore VA Medical Center tested former POWs and found that in addition to nutritional deficiency, other factors contributing to peripheral neuropathy may be exhausting physical labor during imprisonment and injury to the feet and legs caused by cold temperatures.

Dr. Chang-Zern Hong at the VA Medical Center in Long Beach, California, examined 52 former POWs, 32 of whom were in Japanese camps. Two tables in his article reflect the results of these extensive examinations, including such characteristics as numbness, impaired vision, hearing disorder, and persistent impairment of sensory systems. Electrodiagnostic findings were also tabulated, reflecting, for example, neuropathy with both abnormal EMB and abnormal NCS or either abnormal EMB or NCS. Former POWs with a history of cold injury were also evaluated.[36]

Treatment of painful peripheral neuropathy. In this article Dr. William Paul Skelton discusses the use on 12 men of phenytoin (Dilantin) or carbamazepine (Tegretol) in an attempt to relieve the pain in their feet that they suffered for 45 years. He concluded: "I feel I have discovered two excellent medications for pain control in former POWs who had otherwise achieved no relief of foot or leg pain since captivity."[37]

Nutrition. In this seminar paper, Dr. Robert L. Obourn discusses the nutritional aspects of the POW experience, which show up in glossitis, cherlitis, stomatix, edema, diarrhea, gastroenteritis, pellagra, and beriberi. Acute nutritional deficiency illnesses and chronic aftereffects are described.[38]

Beriberi and the ex–POW. In a brief summary Dr. William Paul Skelton discusses the definition and symptoms of beriberi.[39]

Avitaminosis in ex–POWs. An extensive discussion and analysis of all the aspects of vitamin deficiencies and their aftereffects. Peripheral B5 neuritis; thiamine; vitamin B2, B3, B6, B7, B9, and B12; and vitamin A and vitamin C deficiencies are discussed.[40]

Scurvy. In this article, Dr. Skelton discusses the various aspects of scurvy, which results from a lack of vitamin C in the diet. Vitamin C is a water-soluble vitamin that is absorbed by the small intestine and is stored in tissues in direct proportion to its use. Since humans are unable to synthesize vitamin C, we are dependent on outside sources for its supply.

The treatment of scurvy is vitamin C replacement. With this treatment, the bleeding of the skin tissues stops within 24 hours, muscle and bone pains quickly subside, and the gums begin to heal within two to three days.[41]

A review of pellagra. In this article Dr. Skelton discusses the aspects of this disease that are the result of a deficiency of niacin in the diet. Pellagra is much more devastating than simply rough skin; it is the illness of the "three D's": dermatitis, diarrhea, and dementia, of which the latter is the most complex. In the early stages the patient may have insomnia, irritability, nervousness, anxiety, and depression. The treatment of pellagra is a niacin supplement in the diet, but the dementia often proves untreatable.[42]

Heart disease and the ex–POW. In this lengthy paper, Dr. G. M. Hargraves, a British physician, describes all the factors of heart disease applicable to the disability claims of British and other ex–POWs. This article is an excellent overview of the heart disease of POWs in the Far East that is related to their captivity.[43]

Hypertension. In this paper Dr. Skelton discusses all the aspects of high blood pressure and its various causes.[44]

Hypertension in the American ex–POW. Dr. Lawrence R. Moss discusses the illness of hypertension, a "disorder that has long been regarded as having a multifactional etiology." He addresses the question of whether there is a possible causal connection between the POW experience and the subsequent development of hypertension, even when this development is delayed for several years.[45]

Parkinson's Disease. This article presents a general discussion of this disease, its symptoms and treatment.[46]

Osteoarthritis. In this article a brief description and discussion of osteoarthritis is presented. Clinical symptomatology and treatment are listed.[47]

Joints: pathology of the captivity of the POW. In a brief paper some points of the osteoarticular pathology of the ex–POW are described, such as Bechtrew disease, Reither syndrome and Looser Milkmann syndrome.[48]

Back and joint disorders. This article notes that POWs experienced a chronic trauma of the back, hips, and knee joints from heavy labor and protracted overexertion. Hence a number of physical war injuries have proved permanently disabling and have resulted in reduced work capacity during the postwar period.[49]

Arthritis caused by intestinal amebiasis. This article is an extract from a larger paper discussing polyarthritis and amoebic arthritis.[50]

Eyes and ears. Numerous pathological changes in eyes and ears caused by incarceration are discussed in various brief papers and articles.[51]

Malaria. Malaria, an acute and sometimes chronic infectious disease caused by parasites introduced into the red blood cells by a mosquito bite, is discussed in various articles.[52] Of the several types of malaria, plasmodium falciparum and plasmodium vivax were the two that infected POWs and internees.

There are reports of malaria affecting the heart, lungs, brain, kidney, and liver. The complications and manifestations of malaria include cerebral malaria, conditions of the nervous system, cardiac malaria, rupture of the spleen, and ocular complications.

An article in the *Ex-POW Bulletin* also discusses a number of aspects of malaria.[53] It lists a number of sources and catalogs the complications of malaria, including cerebral malaria, blackwater fever, cardiac malaria, and ocular complications.

Impotence. Several aspects and symptoms of impotence are discussed in this brief article.[54]

Prison camp syndrome. This article reveals that the interrelated disorders of prison camp syndrome are widespread among ex-captives. It discusses somatic and psychological aftereffects, ranging from organic brain and arteriosclerotic damage to loss of memory and inability to function.[55]

Strongyloidiasis. This article describes all the facets of this intestinal condition caused by infestation by strongyloides, a worm that is especially prevalent in Burma-Siam. The infection was discovered and effective treatment was developed only recently.[56]

Cirrhosis of the liver in ex–POWs. Hepatomegaly (cirrhosis of the liver) in ex–POWs of the Japanese is a common finding. It is frequently associated with dyspepsia and general malaise and a tenderness of the enlarged liver, together with episodes of fever; particularly when diarrhea is involved, the condition is usually regarded as amoebic hepatitis and is treated as such. In the four cases described in this article, cirrhosis of the liver was suggested by the clinical and biochemical findings and confirmed by biopsies.[57]

Beriberi heart disease. Dr. John J. Robinson states that beriberi heart disease is common in the United States and that the diagnosis is confused with that of arteriosclerotic heart disease. He lists a number of combinations of symptoms that may indicate beriberi heart disease and concludes that a diagnosis is dependent on data, such as clinical history and therapeutic source.

Dr. Ralph E. Hibbs describes the various causes and symptoms of beriberi heart disease, its manifestations, and his conclusions concerning its treatment.

Dr. Gill, Dr. Henry, and Dr. Reid report on the case of an Englishman who suffered severe "wet" beriberi while a POW of the Japanese. Following his release he developed a congestive cardiomyopathy that increased in severity until his death 31 years after repatriation. Autopsy findings were consistent with chronic cardiac damage due to beriberi.[58]

Morbidity of POWs in Australia. In this article, four Australian experts discuss physical complaints uncovered in interviews with ex–POWs: conditions of the alimentary, cardiovascular, dermatological, genitourinary, ocular, and respiratory systems.[59]

Wives of Ex-POWs and Internees

A Wife's Approach to POW Problems

Phyllis Schroeder, RN, discusses the various steps an ex–POW or an internee should take to care for himself and to fill out his medical history forms. She concludes that the concern for buddies who supported each other during captivity should be continued.[60]

An Emotional Survival Kit

Elvera Hornung, MSW, LCSW, presents specific advice on how to prepare for life after the death of one's spouse and discusses such topics as a new identity, new tasks, and other aspects of widowhood.[61]

Wives of Ex-POWs and What They Should Know

In this article Dr. Maria Kelnhofer discusses at length all the aspects of being the wife of an ex–POW and how to cope with the associated problems. She also suggests six specific actions that a wife can take to cope more effectively with her ex–POW or internee husband.[62]

A Wife's View of Her Ex-POW Mate

In another article, Dr. Kelnhofer, herself the wife of an ex–POW, Dr. Guy Kelnhofer, talks about her experiences as the wife of an ex–POW. She discusses at length the anger wives have because of their husbands' conditions, such as PTSD; the right to be angry; and how to release this anger and to transfer it into positive actions.[63]

Living with an Ex-Prisoner of War

Psychologist Rachel E. Nelson discusses the development of her understanding of her husband's POW experiences, and attending ex–POW therapy groups. She also presents in her paper the primary characteristics of POW families, and how to recognize these characteristics.[64]

Themes Expressesd by POWs and Their Wives

In this article, Jane J. Firey, MSW, discusses her experiences with POW therapy groups and the various themes associated with them. She describes the demand for recognition by ex–POWs, issues of trust, suspicion of foreign powers, loyalty and patriotism, and the importance of bonding. She then discusses the various concerns that wives have expressed to her about their ex–POW husbands.[65]

A Letter from the Wife of an Ex-POW and a Professional Reply

These letters express the heartbreaking feelings of the wife of an ex–POW concerning her marriage and children and her struggle to keep her husband in a nursing home—the impact of imprisonment on the members of one family—and the reply by Dr. Maria Kelnhofer.[66]

Testimony of the Experiences of the Children of an Ex-POW

This article presents the profound and revealing testimony of the experiences of the son and daughter of an ex–POW with their father's sufferings.[67]

Letter from an Ex-POW's Wife

The following is from a letter written by the wife of an ex–POW. It represents perhaps one of the truest and most dramatic expressions of the feelings of a POW wife.

> To My Husband with Deep Love and Understanding: I don't know how you can say "You don't know what it was like unless you were there."

I was there, I live it and breathe it every day I am with you. It is in our living room, and it's in our bedroom too. I feel the death and mutilation of the war. With every remark you make, a little piece of me dies; my self-respect and self-esteem shrivel. The humiliation is there. Every time I look in the mirror I see the destruction.

I feel the silence and nothingness that death leaves when I am attacked by your silence. It is loud!

I have also felt the need to survive, to draw on every ounce of strength I have left to go on, no matter what. I have felt the darkness and the loneliness; the insanity of it all, in the POW camp of my mind. When I thought of ending it all during those dark minutes, I realized that I had to be there, I had to be strong for both of us. My life wasn't my own to end (I had to go on for my buddies). I've been scared, but I thank God I've never been afraid.

I was not a POW; it came to me. Can't you see that I went through that same experience, too? We go through it together; we survived. We're doing more than surviving now, we're living. We walk through hell together just like you did with your buddies.

Oh yes, I have felt the guilt you have felt, too. With every mistake I've made, and when I've hurt you. You can never be as hard on me as I am on myself. I'm a lot like you. That's why some things are lessons well learned. They teach us not to make the same mistakes again.

We must survive together, life and love have a meaning. There really is "a light at the end of the tunnel." In the darkness, take my hand.[68]

Widowhood: What an Ex-POW's Wife Should Know

Packet 5 of the American Ex-Prisoner of War, Inc., contains a number of articles for the wives and relatives of ex–POWs about all the aspects to consider when the men die. Articles deal with burial, autopsy, and a number of important issues of concern at the moment of widowhood.[69]

Forms

Record of Personal Affairs: A seven-page form in which to list personal data; POW information; the location of the military service personal file; the location of family records; the location of other important papers; bank accounts; charge accounts; U.S. savings bonds; safety deposit box; stocks, bonds, and securities; property ownership; life insurance; other insurance; employer; membership in private associations; VA information; funeral-burial arrangements; and other miscellaneous data.

Autopsy Request Form: addressed to a private physician or pathologist.

"What Are We Worth?" Form. A single sheet on which to list assets and debts.

Authorization for Release of Patient's Records: A one-sheet form.

Request Pertaining to Military Records: A two-page form related to information needed to locate military records.

Former POW Medical History: A four-page form used to fill in everything related to the time spent in imprisonment—camps, abuses experienced, diseases, illnesses, and so on.

NOTES

1. Guy J. Kelnhofer, Jr., Ph.D., "Anger and the Ex-POW," *Ex-POW Bulletin*, 1984.
2. Father Francis Herlihy, *Now Welcome Summer*, Dublin, 1948, pp. 232–233.
3. Kenneth Harrison, *The Brave Japanese*, Adelaide, Australia, 1966, pp. 279–280.
4. Jessie Elizabeth Simons, *While History Passed*, Melbourne, Australia, 1954.
5. William R. Shadish, "Detection of the Aftereffects of Captivity," *Ex-POW Bulletin* (January 1991), pp. 23–28.
6. Guy J. Kelnhofer, Jr., Ph.D., "Disability Rating Problems for Ex-POWs," *Ex-POW Bulletin* (September 1990), pp. 27–30.
7. Mack L. Gothier, "Impressions of a POW Medical Officer—Shinagawa Camp," *Ex-POW Bulletin* (1987).
8. Emil P. Reed, MD, "Experiences of a Medical Officer in a Japanese Prison," *Texas State Journal of Medicine* 42 (January 1947), 543–547.
9. Stanley G. Somers, "The Aftereffects of Incarceration, Medical Facts," *Ex-POW Bulletin* (November 1989), p. 23.
10. Theodore E. Woodward, MD, "Testimony June 19, 1985," *Ex-POW Bulletin* (August 1985), pp. 17–20.
11. *The International Conference of the World Veterans Federation—The Hague, November 20–25, 1961*; and *Ex-POW Bulletin* (May 1985).
12. Harold C. Morris, MD, "Disease Characteristics of and Ratable Under Public Law," *Ex-POW Bulletin* (March 1983).
13. Norman S. White, MD, "Post Traumatic Stress Disorder," *Hospital and Community Psychiatry* 34:11 (November 1983); and *Ex-POW Bulletin* (April 1984).
14. *Ibid.*
15. Harold R. Dickman, Ph.D., et al., "POWs and PTSD Symptoms: A Summary of Initial Findings," *Ex-POW Bulletin* (October 1985).
16. Merrill I. Lipton, MD, and William D. Schaffer, Ph.D., "Post Traumatic Stress Disorder in the Older Veteran," *Ex-POW Bulletin* (July 1988).
17. Robert L. Obourn, MD, "PTSD and the POW," *Ex-POW Bulletin* (June 1988), pp. 29–33.
18. Barbara F. Key, MA, and Robert G. Bobbitt, Ph.D., "Observations of PTSD Among POWs," *Ex-POW Bulletin* (September 1988).
19. Matthew J. Friedman, MD, Ph.D., "Toward Rational Pharmacotherapy for Post Traumatic Stress Disorder: An Interim Report," *American Journal of Psychiatry* 145 (1988), 281–285; and *Ex-POW Bulletin* (June 1989).
20. Charles R. Figley, MD, *Ex-POW Bulletin* (June 1989).
21. John F. Russell, "The Captivity Experience and Its Psychological Consequences," *Psychiatric Annals* 14(4) (1984), 250–254.
22. Gayle K. Lumry, "Psychological Effects of Prisoner of War Experience," *Ex-POW Bulletin*, August 1984.

23. Clarence Carnahan, MD, "Some Observations of a VA POW Psychiatrist," *Ex-POW Bulletin*, January 1985.

24. John E. Nardini, MD, "Depression in Prisoners of War," *Ex-POW Bulletin*, December 1988.

25. V. A. Kral, et al., "Long-term Effects of a Prolonged Stress Experience," *Canadian Psychiatric Association Journal* 12 (1967), 175–181.

26. *Stresses of Incarceration, Aftereffects of Extreme Stress, Residual Nervous Conditions*, Packet 2, Ex-POWs, Inc.

27. Perry M. Nealis, "General Adaptation Syndrome: Is the Ex-POW's Life a G.A.S.?" *Ex-POW Bulletin*, May 1990.

28. Colonel Charles T. Brown, MC, "The Short Fuse," *Diseases of the Nervous System* 10 (11) (November 1949); also in Packet 2, Ex-POWs, Inc.

29. Harvey D. Strassman, MD, et al., "A POW Syndrome: Apathy as a Reaction of Severe Stress," *American Journal of Psychiatry* 112 (1955), 998; and Packet 2, Ex-POWs, Inc.

30. *The Concentration Camp Syndrome*, Packet 2, Ex-POWs, Inc.

31. William Paul Skelton, III, MD, "Alcoholism," *Ex-POW Bulletin*, August 1989.

32. James E. Bailey, "Ex-POW Group Therapy from the Group Therapist's Perspective," *Ex-POW Bulletin*, April 1991.

33. Robert Joseph Ursano, and James Jay Rundell, MD, "Adapting and Coping During Captivity," *Ex-POW Bulletin*, May 1991.

34. *Physician's Manual for the Examination of Veterans*, chapter 17, and DVB Circular 21-8-3, rev. 12-6-1993 DVD, Veterans Administration, Washington, DC; and "Disorders Directly Related to the POW Experience," *Ex-POW Bulletin*, September 1984.

35. Alvin C. Poweleit, MD, "Commonest Syndromes of Neurological Diseases," *Ex-POW Bulletin*, September 1983.

36. Chang-Zern Hong, "Peripheral Neuropathy in Former Prisoners of War," *VA Practitioner* and *Ex-POW Bulletin* (both n.d.).

37. William Paul Skelton, III, MD, "Treatment of Painful Peripheral Neuropathy," *Ex-POW Bulletin*, June 1990.

38. Robert L. Obourn, MD, "Nutrition," *Ex-POW Bulletin*, June 1984.

39. William Paul Skelton, III, MD, "Beriberi and the Ex-POW," *Ex-POW Bulletin*, February 1988.

40. William Paul Skelton, III, MD, "Avitaminosis in POWs," *Ex-POW Bulletin*, October 1989.

41. William Paul Skelton, III, MD, "Scurvy," *Ex-POW Bulletin*, June 1988.

42. William Paul Skelton, III, MD, "A Review of Pellagra," *Ex-POW Bulletin*, September 1988.

43. G. M. Hargreaves, MD, "Heart Disease and the Ex-POW," *Ex-POW Bulletin*, November 1990.

44. William Paul Skelton, III, MD, "Hypertension," *Ex-POW Bulletin*, February 1987.

45. Lawrence R. Moss, "Hypertension as Related to the American Ex-POW," *Ex-POW Bulletin*, February 1990.

46. William Paul Skelton, III, MD, "Parkinson's Disease," *Ex-POW Bulletin*, December 1990.

47. William Paul Skelton, III, MD, "Osteoarthritis," *Ex-POW Bulletin*, 1988.

48. *Joints: Pathology of the Captivity of the POW*, International Medical Conference, Brussels, November 1962, in Packet No. 3, Ex-POWs, Inc.

49. A. Strom and E. Eitinger, *Norwegian Concentration Camp Survivors*, Oslo University Press, Oslo, 1968.
50. "Arthritis Due to Intestinal Amebiasis," *Annals of Internal Medicine* 34 (1951), 1129–1231.
51. Packet 2, Ex-POWs, Inc.
52. *Malaria*, Packet No. 3, Ex-POWs, Inc.
53. "Malaria," *Ex-POW Bulletin*, August 1991.
54. *Impotency*, Packet No. 3, Ex-POWs, Inc.
55. Dr. Ulrich Venzlaff, "Prison Camp Syndrome," *Medical World News* 6 (April 24, 1965), 52–53; and Packet 3, Ex-POWs, Inc.
56. Otto C. Schwartz, *Strongyloidiasis*, Packet No. 3, Ex-POWs, Inc.
57. E. G. McQueen, "Cirrhosis of the Liver in Ex-Prisoners of War, Japan: A Preliminary Communication," *Medical Journal of Australia* (July 28, 1951); and Packet No. 3, Ex-POWs, Inc.
58. John J. Robinson, MD, "Degenerative Heart Disease Resembling Beriberi," *Southern Medical Journal*, 1960; Ralph E. Hibbs, MD, "Beriberi (Heart Disease) in Japanese Prison Camps," *Annals of Internal Medicine* 25(2) (August 1946); and *Ex-POW Bulletin*, August and September 1975; and G. V. Gill, et al., "Chronic Cardiac Beriberi in a Former Prisoner of the Japanese," *British Journal of Nutrition* 44(3) (1980), 273–275; and Packet No. 4, Ex-POWs, Inc.
59. J. L. Duncan, et al., "Morbidity of POWs in Australia," *Ex-POW Bulletin*, April 1991.
60. Phyllis Schroeder, RN, "What Every POW's Wife Should Know," Packet No. 5, Ex-POWs, Inc.
61. Elvera Hornung, MSW, LCSW, "An Emotional Survival Kit," *Ex-POW Bulletin*, November 1988.
62. Maria I. Kelnhofer, MD, "Wives of Ex-POWs and What They Should Know," *Ex-POW Bulletin*, June 1986.
63. Maria I. Kelnhofer, MD, "A Wife's View of Her Ex-POW Mate," *Ex-POW Bulletin*, July 1987.
64. Rachel E. Nelson, MA, "Living with an Ex-Prisoner of War," *Ex-POW Bulletin*, February 1987.
65. Jane J. Firey, MSW, "Themes Expressed by POWs and Their Wives," *Ex-POW Bulletin*, November 1987.
66. "A Letter from the Wife of an Ex-POW and a Professional Reply," *Ex-POW Bulletin*, May 1988.
67. "Testimony of Experiences as a Child of an Ex-Prisoner of War," *Ex-POW Bulletin*, July 1987 and January 1990.
68. "Letter from an Ex-POW's Wife," *Ex-POW Bulletin*, February 1986; and Packet No. 5, Ex-POWs, Inc.
69. "Widowhood: What an Ex-POW's Wife Should Know," Packet No. 5, Ex-POWs, Inc.

SOURCES

Adams, B. D. "Diseases Characterized by Abnormalities of Posture and Movement," in *Principles of Neurology* (4th ed.), McGraw-Hill, New York, 1989, pp. 937–943.
Alleman, R. J., and G. H. Stollerman. "The Course of Beriberi Heart Disease in

American Prisoners of War in Japan," *Annals of Internal Medicine* 28 (1948), 949.
Archibald, H. C., and R. D. Tuddenham. "Persistent Stress Reaction After Combat: A 20-Year Follow-Up," *Archives of General Psychiatry* 12 (1965), 475–481.

_____ and _____. "Persistent Stress Reaction After Combat," *Archives of General Psychiatry* 12 (1965), 475–481.

_____ et al. "Gross Stress Reaction in Combat," *American Journal of Psychiatry* 119 (1962), 317–323.

Arnold, A. *Selected Bibliography, II; Post Traumatic Stress Disorder with Special Attention to Vietnam Veterans* (25th revision). Phoenix, AZ, VA Medical Center, 1986.

Arnold, Al. "Inpatient Treatment of Vietnam Veterans with PTSD," in Sonnenberg ed.

Bacharach, A. "L'Asthenie du deporte," Presse med. 63 (1955), 63–64.

Baird, J. T., and D. A. MacDonald. "Survey of Optic Atrophy in Hong Kong Prisoners of War After Ten Years," *Medical Services Journal* (Canada), November 1956.

Baker, S. "Traumatic War Injuries," in *Comprehensive Textbook of Psychiatry* (3rd ed.), Baltimore, MD, 1980.

Beebe, G. W. "Follow-up Studies of World War II and Korean War Prisoners," *American Journal of Epidemiology* 101(5) (1975), 400–422.

Bell, P. G., and J. C. O'Neill. "Optic Atrophy in Hong Kong Prisoners of War," *DVA Treatment Services Bulletin*, November 1947.

Bensheim, H. "Die KZ-Neurose Rassisch Verfolgter," *Nevenartz* 31 (1960), 10.

Bettelheim, Bruno. "Individual and Mass Behavior in Extreme Situations," *Journal of Abnormal and Social Psychology* 38 (1943), 417.

Birkhimer, L. J., et al. "Post Traumatic Stress Disorder: Characteristics and Pharmacological Response in the Veteran Population," *Comprehensive Psychiatry* 26 (1985), 304–310.

Blaha, F., et al. *Folgen des Drieges fur de menschliche Gesundheit* (Report 4), Congress Med. Della FIR, Bucharest, 1964, pp. 121–244.

Blake, D. J. "Treatment of Acute Post Traumatic Stress Disorder with Tricyclic Antidepressants," *South Medical Journal* 79 (1986), 201–204.

Blanchard, E. B., et al. "A Psychophysiological Study of Post Traumatic Stress Disorder in Vietnam Veterans," *Psychiatric Quarterly* 54 (1982), 220–229.

Blankenhorn, M. A. "The Diagnosis of Beriberi Heart Disease," *Annals of Internal Medicine* 23 (1945), 398–406.

_____ et al. "Deficiency Diseases in the Cincinnati General Hospital: A Ten-Year Study," *Journal of the American Medical Association* 140 (1949), 1315.

Blankenhorn, M. A., et al. "Occidental Beriberi Heart Disease," *Journal of the American Medical Association* 131 (1946), 717.

Bloom, Freddy. *Dear Philip: A Diary of Captivity*, London, 1980, p. 157.

Bondy, C. "Versagungstoleranz und Versagungssituation," *Psychische Spatschaden* (Basel) (1967), pp. 1–13.

Branchey, L., et al. "Alcoholism in Vietnam and Korea Veterans: A Long-term Follow-up," *Alcoholism: Clinical and Experimental Research* 8 (1984), 572–575.

Brende, J. O. "Electrodermal Responses in Post Traumatic Syndromes," *Journal of Nervous and Mental Disorders* 170 (1982), 352–361.

Brill, N. O. "Neuropsychiatric Examinations of Military Personnel Recovered from Japanese Prison Camps," *Bulletin of the U.S. Army Medical Department* 5 (1946), 429–438.
Brown, Charles T., MD. "Malaria," *Ex-POW Bulletin*, November 1967.
Brown, D. Denny. "Neurological Conditions Resulting from Prolonged and Severe Dietary Restriction," *Medicine* (Baltimore) 26 (41) (1947), 113.
Burgess, R. C. "Deficiency Diseases in Prisoners of War: Changi, Singapore," *Lancet* 2 (1946), 411–418.
Burstein, L. "Treatment of Post Traumatic Stress Disorder with Imipramine," *Psychosomatics* 25 (1982), 681–687.
Carroll, B. J., et al. "A Specific Laboratory Test for the Diagnosis of Melancholia: Standardization, Validation, and Clinical Utility," *Archives of General Psychiatry* 38 (1981), 15–22.
Cedarbaum, J. M. "Parkinsonism: Guidelines for Diagnosis," *Drug Therapy* (November 1985), 38–81.
Chodoff, P. "Late Effects of the Concentration Camp Syndrome," *Archives of General Psychiatry* 8 (1963), 323–333.
_____. "Late Effects of the Concentration Camps as a Psychological Stress," *Archives of General Psychiatry* 8 (1963), 323–333.
Clark, C. A., and I. B. Sneddon. "Nutritional Neuropathy in Prisoners of War and Internees from Hong Kong," *Lancet* 2 (1946), 734–737.
Clarke, Hugh V. *Last Stop Nagasaki*, Sydney, 1984, p. 65.
Cohen, B. M., and M. Z. Cooper. *A Follow-up Study of World War II Prisoners of War* (VA Medical Monograph), U. S. Government Printing Office, Washington, DC, 1954.
_____ et al. *A Follow-up Study of World War II Prisoners of War* (VA Medical Monograph), Veterans Administration, Washington, DC, 1954, pp. 1–75.
Conte, H. R., et al. "Combined Psychotherapy and Pharmacotherapy for Depression," *Archives of General Psychiatry* 43 (1986), 471–479.
Crawford, J. N., and J. A. G. Reid. "Nutritional Disease Affecting Canadian Troops Held Prisoner of War by the Japanese," *Canadian Journal of Research*, 25F (1947), 53–85.
Cruikshank, E. K. "Painful Feet in Prisoners of War in the Far East, Review of 500 Cases," *Lancet* 2 (1946), 369–372.
de Veen, W. "Rheumatism and Deportation," *World Veterans Federation*, November 1961.
Deller, Ltc. John J., Jr., MC. "Malaria Hepatitis," *Military Medicine* 132 (1967), 614–620.
Dobbs, D., and W. P. Wilson. "Observations on Persistence of War Neurosis," *Diseases of the Nervous System* 21 (1961), 40–46.
Eitinger, L. "Concentration Camp Survivors in Norway and Israel," Allen & Unwin, London, 1964.
_____. "Psykiatriske folgestilstander hos tidligere konsentras-jonsleirfang," *Norske Lawgeforen* 81 (1962), 805–808.
_____ and A. Strom. *Mortality and Morbidity After Excessive Stress*, Humanities Press, New York, 1973.
Factors Used to Increase the Susceptibility of Individuals to Forceful Indoctrination: Observations and Experiments. Symposium No. 3, Group for the Advancement of Psychiatry, December 1956.
Falcon, S., et al. "Tricyclics: Possible Treatment for Post Traumatic Stress Disorder," *Journal of Clinical Psychiatry* 46 (1985), 385–389.

Feighner, J. P., et al. "Comparison of Alprazolam, Imipramine and Placebo in the Treatment of Depression," *Journal of the American Medical Association* 249 (1983), 3057–3064.

Fernando, T. B., et al. "Cirrhosis of the Liver in Ceylon and Its Relation to Diet," *Lancet* 2, p. 205.

Fisher, M. "Residual Neuropathological Changes in Canadians Held Prisoners of War by the Japanese (Strachan's Disease)," *Canadian Service Medical Journal* 11 (1955), 157–199.

Folkow, B. "Physiological Aspects of Primary Hypertension," *Physiological Reviews* 62(2) (April 1982), 347–484.

Frankl, Victor. *Man's Search for Meaning.* Washington Square Press, New York, 1959.

Friedman, M. J. "Post-Vietnam Syndrome: Recognition and Management," *Psychosomatics* 22 (1981), 931–943.

Friedman, S. B., et al. "Urinary 17—Hydroxycorticosteroid Levels in Patients with Neoplastic Disease," *Psychosomatic Medicine* 25 (1963), 364–376.

Gibberd, F. B., and J. P. Simmonds. "Neurological Disease in Ex–Far East Prisoners of War," *Lancet* 2 (1980), 135–137.

Gill, G. V., and D. R. Bell. "Persisting Nutritional Neuropathy Amongst Former War Prisoners," *Journal of Neurology, Neurosurgery and Psychiatry* 45 (1982), 861–865.

_____ and _____. "Persisting Tropical Diseases Amongst Former Prisoners of War of the Japanese," *Practitioner* 224 (1980), 801–803.

_____ and _____. "Strongyloides Stercoralis Infection in Far East Prisoners of War," *British Medical Journal* (September 1979), 572–574.

_____ et al. "The Health of Former Prisoners of War of the Japanese," *Practitioner* 225 (1981), 531–538.

Gillespie, R. D. *Psychological Effects of War on Citizen and Soldier.* W. W. Norton, New York, 1942.

Gillman, J., and T. Gillman. "Structure of Liver in Pellagra," *Archives of Pathology* 40, p. 239.

Gostas, T. W. *Prisoner.* Western Publishing, New York, 1974.

Gottlieb, M. L. "Impressions of a POW Medical Officer in Japanese Concentration Camps," *Naval Medical Bulletin* 56 (5) (1946), 663–673.

Gould, S. E. *Beriberi Heart, Pathology of the Heart.* Charles C. Thomas, Springfield, IL, 1960.

Grad, B., and V. A. Krol. "The Effects of Senescence on Resistance to Stress," *International Journal of Gerontology* 12 (1957), 172–181.

Griffin, S. G., and M. J. Friedman. "Depressive Symptoms in Propranolol Users," *Journal of Clinical Psychiatry* 47 (1986), 453–457.

Gronvik, O., and A. Lonnum. "Neurologiske folgetilstander hos tidligere konsentrasjonsleirfanger," *Norske Laegeforan* 81 (1961), 808–810.

Hall, R., and P. Malone. *Psychiatric Residuals of Prolonged Concentration Camp Experience.* Naval Health Research Center, Report No. 74-70, 1973.

Hanifin, J. M., and A. C. Cuetter. "Inpatients with Immersion Foot Tape Cold Injury Diminished Conduction Velocity," *Electroencephalography and Clinical Neurophysiology* 14 (1974), 173–178.

Harvey, A. M. "Type of Neuritis Associated with Malaria Fever," *Bulletin of Johns Hopkins Hospital* 75 (October 1944), 225–231.

Hauri, P., et al. "Sleep in Agoraphobia with Panic Attacks," *Sleep Research* 14 (1985), 128.

Henderson, F. W. "Beriberi Heart Disease in Elderly Patients," *Geriatrics* 15 (1960), 398.
Henry, J. P. "Stress, Salt and Hypertension," *Social Science and Medicine* 26(3) (1988), 293–302.
Hibbs, O. R. "Beriberi in Japanese Prison Camps," *Annals of Internal Medicine* 25 (2) (1946), 270–282.
Higgitt, A. C., et al. "Clinical Management of Benzodiazepine Dependence," *British Medical Journal* 291 (1985) 688–690.
Hocking, F. "Human Reactions to Extreme Environmental Stress," *Medical Journal of Australia* 11 (12) (September 18, 1965), 477–483.
_____. *Starvation: Social and Psychological Aspects of a Basic Biological Stress*. Australian Medical Association, Archdal Medical Monograph 6 (1969), 1–20.
Hogben, G. L., and R. B. Cornfield. "Treatment of Traumatic War Neurosis with Phenelzine," *Archives of General Psychiatry* 38 (1981), 440–445.
Hong, C. Z. "Electrodiagnostic Findings of Persisting Polyneuropathies Due to Previous Nutritional Deficiency in Former Prisoners of War," *Electromyography and Clinical Neurophysiology* 26 (1986), 351–363.
Jacobs, E. C. "Effects of Starvation on Sex Hormones in the Male," *Journal of Clinical Endocrinology* 8 (1948), 227–232.
_____. "Gynecomastia Following Severe Starvations," *Annals of Internal Medicine* 28 (1948), 792–796.
_____. "Oculo-oro Genital Syndrome: A Deficiency Disease," *Annals of Internal Medicine* 35 (1951), 1049–1054.
Jervey, L. P. "Prolonged Myocardial Disease Due to Beriberi, with Necropsy After 18 Years," *American Heart Journal* 54 (1957), 621.
Jones, Thomas C. "Malaria," in *Textbook of Medicine*, 1975.
Katz, C. J. "Neuropathologic Manifestations Found in Japanese Prison Camps," *Journal of Nervous and Mental Disorders* 103 (1946), 456–465.
Katz, J., et al. "Stress, Distress and Ego Defenses: Psychoendocrine Responses to Impending Breast Tumor Biopsy," *Archives of General Psychiatry* 23 (1970), 131–142.
Keane, T. M., et al. "A Behavioral Formulation of Post Traumatic Stress Disorder in Vietnam Veterans," *Behavior Therapist* 8 (1985), 9–12.
Keehn, R. "Follow-up Studies of World War II and Korean Conflict Prisoners Mortality to January 1, 1976," *American Journal of Epidemiology* 3 (1980), 194–211.
_____. "Follow-up Studies of World War II and Korean War Prisoners, to January 1976," *American Journal of Epidemiology* 111(2) (1980), 194–211.
Keeler, M. H. "Adverse Reaction to Marihuana," *American Journal of Psychiatry* 124 (1967), 674–677.
Kenny, Catherine. *Captives*. St. Lucia, 1986, pp. 161–162.
Kerr, E. Bartlett. *Surrender and Survival*. New York, 1985.
Keystal, H. *Massive Psychic Trauma*. International Universities Press, New York, 1969.
Kinney, L., and M. Kramer. "Sleep and Sleep Responsivity in Disturbed Dreamers," *Sleep Research* 14 (1985), 140.
Kitchner, I., and R. Greenstein. "Low Dose Lithium Carbonate in the Treatment of Post Traumatic Stress Disorder: Brief Communication," *Military Medicine* 150 (1985), 378–381.
Klein, Hilel, et al. "Former Concentration Camp Inmates on a Psychiatric Ward," *Archives of General Psychiatry* 8 (1963).

Knight, R. B., et al. "Psychological Stress, Ego and Defenses in Children Hospitalized for Elective Surgery," *Psychosomatic Medicine* 41 (1979), 40–49.

Kolb, L. C. "The Place of Narcosynthesis in the Treatment of Chronic and Delayed Stress Reactions of War," edited by S. M. Sonnenberg et al., American Psychiatric Press, Washington, DC, 1985.

———— et al. "Propranolol and Clonidine in Treatment of the Chronic Post Traumatic Stress Disorders of War," in *Post Traumatic Stress Disorder: Psychological and Biological Sequelae*, edited by B. A. van der Kolk, American Psychiatric Press, Washington, DC, 1984.

Kraft, G. H., in *Practical Electromyography*, edited by E. W. Johnson, Baltimore, 1980, pp. 155–205.

Kral, V. A., et al. "Long-term Effects of Prolonged Stress Experience," *Canadian Psychiatric Association Journal* 12 (1967), 175–181.

Kramer, M. "Dream Disturbance," *Psychiatric Annals* 9 (1979), 50–60.

———— and L. Kinney. "Is Sleep a Marker of Vulnerability to Delayed Post Traumatic Stress Disorder?" *Sleep Research* 14 (1985), 181.

———— et al. "Sleep in Delayed Stress Victims," *Sleep Research* 11 (1982), 113.

Krol, V. A. "Masked Depressions in Middle-Aged Men," *Canadian Medical Association Journal* 79 (1958), 1–5.

Krystal, H., and W. G. Niederland. "Clinical Observations on the Survivor Syndrome," *American Psychiatric Association Journal* 121 (1965), 136–138.

Lahey, Q. J., et al. "Physiologic Observations on a Case of Beriberi Heart Disease, with a Note on the Acute Effects of Thiamin," *American Journal of Medicine* 14 (1953), 248.

Later Effects of Imprisonment and Deportation. International Conference of the World Veterans Federation, held at the Medical and General Reference Library, Veterans Administration, Washington, DC, November 20–25, 1961.

Lavie, P., et al. "Long-term Effects of Traumatic War-related Events on Sleep," *American Journal of Psychiatry* 135 (1979), 175–178.

Lawton, Manny. *Some Survived*. Chapel Hill, NC, 1984, pp. 235–236.

LeQuesne, P. M. "Persisting Neuropathy in Former War Prisoners," *British Medical Journal* 286 (1983), 917–918.

————. "Persisting Nutritional Neuropathy in Former War Prisoners," *British Medical Journal* 286 (1983), 917–918.

Letarte, F., and P. Simard. "Visual Complaints from Hong Kong Repatriates," *DVA Treatment Services Bulletin*, November 1947.

Levenson, H., et al. "Traumatic War Neurosis and Phenelzine," *Archives of General Psychiatry* 39 (1982), 1345.

Lifton, R. J. "Home by Ship: Reaction Patterns of American Prisoners of War Repatriated from North Korea," *American Journal of Psychiatry* 110 (1954), 732–739.

Lonnum, A. *An Analytical Survey of the Literature Published on Delayed Effects of Internment in Concentration Camps and Their Possible Relations to the Nervous System—Effects on Imprisonment*. World Veterans Federation, Paris, 1961.

————. *Neurological Disorders: Norwegian Concentration Camp Survivors*. Oslo University Press, Oslo, 1968, pp. 85–123.

McNamara, J. O., et al. "The Kindling Model of Epilepsy: A Critical Review," *CRC Critical Reviews in Clinical Neurobiology* 1 (1985), 341–391.

Mallory, P. F., et al. "Validation of a Multi-method Assessment of Post Traumatic Stress Disorders in Vietnam Veterans," *Journal of Consulting and Clinical Psychology* 51 (1983), 488–494.

Malseed, R. T., and F. J. Goldstein. "Enhancement of Morphine Analgesia by Tricyclic Antidepressants," *Neuropharmacology* 18 (1979), 827–829.

Mason, J., et al. "Elevated Urinary Norepinephrine/Cortisol Ratio in Post Traumatic Stress Disorders," *New Research Program and Abstracts, 138th Annual Meeting of the American Psychiatric Association*, Washington, DC, American Psychiatric Association, 1985.

Mason, J. W. "Clinical Psychophysiology: Psychoendocrine Mechanisms," in *American Handbook of Psychiatry* (vol. 4), ed. M. Reiser. Basic Books, New York, 1975.

_____ et al. "Urinary Freecortisol in Post Traumatic Disorder," *Journal of Nervous and Mental Disorders* 174 (1986), 145–149.

Medical Department, U. S. Army, "Communicable Diseases: Malaria," *Preventative Medicine in World War II* 6 (1963).

_____, "Infectious Diseases," *Internal Medicine in World War II* 2 (1963).

Meerlo, J. "Persecution Trauma and the Reconditioning of Emotional Life: A Brief Survey," *American Journal of Psychiatry* 125 (1969), 1187–1191.

Mellman, T. A., and G. C. Davis. "Combat-related Flashbacks in Post Traumatic Stress Disorder: Phenomenology and Similarity to Panic Attacks," *Journal of Clinical Psychiatry* 46 (1985), 379–382.

Mellnik, Brig. Gen. Steve. *Philippine Diary 1939–1945*. New York, 1969, p. 315.

Merkel, W. C. "Plasmodium Falciparum Malaria: The Coronary and Myocardial Lesions Observed at Autopsy in Two Cases of Acute Fulminating P. Falciparum Infection," *Archives of Pathology* 41 (March 1946), 290–298.

Milanes, F. J., et al. "Phenelzine Treatment of Post-Vietnam Stress Syndrome," *VA Practitioner* (June 1984), pp. 40–47.

Moran, C. "Depersonalization and Agoraphobia Associated with Marihuana Use," *British Journal of Medical Psychology* 59 (1986), 187–196.

Morgan, H. J., et al. "Health of Repatriated Prisoners of War from the Far East," *Journal of the American Medical Association* 130 (1946), 995–999.

Morita, K., et al. "Suppression of Amygdala-kindled Seizures in Cats by Enhanced GABAergic Transmission in the Substantia Innominata," *Experimental Neurology* 89 (1985), 225–236.

Nardini, J. "Vitamin Deficiency Diseases in Allied Prisoners of the Japanese," *Naval Medical Bulletin* 47 (2) (1947), 273–278.

Nefzger, M. D. "Follow-up Studies of World War II and Korean War Prisoners," *American Journal of Epidemiology* 91(2) (1970), 123–128.

Niederland, W. G. "The Problems of the Survivor," *Hospital* 10 (1961), 233–247.

Norquist, Ernest. *Our Paradise: A GI's War Diary*. Hancock, 1989, p. 345.

Noyes, R., Jr., et al. "A Withdrawal Syndrome After Abrupt Discontinuation of Alprazolam," *American Journal of Psychiatry* 142 (1985), 114–116.

Paul, H., and H. Herberg. "Psychische Spatschaden nach politischer Verfolgung," p. 396.

Pelletier, Lawrence L. *Chronic Strongyloidiasis in WW II Far East POWs*. Wichita VA Medical Center, January 4, 1983.

Pitts, F. N., and J. N. McClure. "Lactate Metabolism in Anxiety Neurosis," *New England Journal of Medicine* 277 (1967), 1329–1336.

Poe, R. O., et al. "Multiple Determinants of 17-Hydroxycorticosteroid Excretion in Recruits During Basic Training," *Psychosomatic Medicine* 32 (1970), 369–378.

Post, R. M., and R. T. Kopanda. "Cocaine, Kindling and Psychosis, *American Journal of Psychiatry* 133 (1976), 627–634.

Ravaris, C. L., et al. "Xanax and Inderal in Panic and Agorophobic Outpatients," *New Research Programs and Abstracts, 139th Annual Meeting of the American Psychiatric Association*, Washington, DC, American Psychiatric Association, 1986.

Redmond, D. E., Jr., and Y. H. Huang. "New Evidence for a Locus Coeruleus-norepinephrine Connection with Anxiety," *Life Sciences* 25 (1979), 2149–2162.

Reif, A. "Stigmata der vergangenheit: Psychiatrisch-psychologische Untersuchungen in Polen," *Arztl. Rraz.* 19 (1967), 2334.

Richards, J. G., et al. "Stress and Cardiovascular Disease: A Report from the National Heart Foundation of Australia," *Medical Journal of Australia* 148 (May 16, 1988), 510–513.

Ruff, George E. "Isolation and Sensory Deprivation," in *American Handbook of Psychiatry*, edited by S. Arieti, Basic Books, New York, 1966.

Russell, F. P. "Epidemiology of Malaria in the Philippines," *American Journal of Public Health* 26 (January 1936), 1–7.

———. "Malaria in the Philippine Islands," *American Journal of Tropical Medicine* 13 (March 1933), 167–178.

Saphir, O. *The Heart in Nutritional Diseases: A Text on Systemic Pathology* (Vol. 1). Grune & Stratton, New York, 1958.

Schlesinger, P., and A. B. Benchimol. "Beriberi Heart Disease," *American Heart Journal* 46 (1953), 245.

——— and ———. "Cardiac Disease Simulating Arteriosclerotic Heart Disease," *American Heart Journal* 42 (1951), 801.

Schmieder, R. E., et al. "Psychophysiologic Aspects of Essential Hypertension" *Journal of Human Hypertension* 1 (1987), 215–222.

Schoonenberg, Bernard. *De Poorten der Hel* [The Gates of Hell], Bussum, the Netherlands, 1978, p. 98.

Scolossberg, A., and M. Benjamin. "Sleep Patterns in Three Acute Combat Fatigue Cases," *Journal of Clinical Psychiatry* 39 (1978), 546–549.

Segal, H. A. "Initial Psychiatric Findings of Recently Repatriated Prisoners of War," *American Journal of Psychiatry* 111 (1954), 358–363.

Seyle, H. "Stress: It's a G.A.S.," *Psychology Today* (September 1969), 25–27.

———. *The Stress of Life*. McGraw-Hill, New York, 1976.

Sheehan, D. V. "Current Concepts in Psychiatry, Panic Attacks and Phobias," *New England Journal of Medicine* 307 (1982), 156–158.

———. "Current Perspectives in the Treatment of Panic and Phobic Disorders," *Drug Therapy* 7 (1982), 179–193.

Shen, W. W., and S. Park. "The Use of Monoamine Oxidase Inhibitors in the Treatment of Traumatic War Neurosis: Case Report," *Military Medicine* 148 (1983), 430–431.

Simons, R. "Nutritional Disorders of the Skin Among Prisoners of War in the Far East," *British Journal of Dermatology* 61 (1949), 210–215.

Skelton, William P. "Beriberi in Former POWs of the Japanese," *VA Practitioner* 5 (10) (1988), 89–95.

Spies, T. D., et al. "Pellagra, Beriberi, and Riboflavin Deficiency in Human Beings: Diagnosis and Treatment," *Journal of the American Medical Association* 113 (1939), 931.

Spillane, J. D., and G. I. Scott. "Obscure Neuropathy in the Middle East," *Lancet* 1 (1945), 261–264.

Sprague, H. B. "The Effect of Malaria on the Heart," *American Heart Journal* 31 (April 1946), 426–430.
Srichaikul, T. "A Study of Pigmentation and Other Changes in the Liver in Malaria," *American Journal of Tropical Medicine and Hygiene* 8 (1959), 110.
Stenger, C. *Life-Style Shock.* Veterans Administration, Washington, DC, October 1972.
Strachan, H. "On a Form of Multiple Neuritis Prevalent in the West Indies," *Practitioner* 59 (1987), 477.
Strassman, H., et al. "A Prisoner of War Syndrome: Apathy as a Reaction to Severe Stress," *American Journal of Psychiatry* 112 (1956), 998–1003.
Strom, A., et al. "Examination of Norwegian Ex–Concentration Camp Prisoners," *Journal of Neuropsychiatry* 4 (1962), 43.
Takahashi, K., and H. Nakamura. "Axonal Degeneration in Beriberi Neuropathy," *Archives of Neurology* 33 (1976), 836–841.
Theorell, T. "On Biochemical and Physiological Indicators of Stress Relevant to Cardiovascular Illness," *European Heart Journal* 9 (1988), 705–708.
Thomas, P. K., and B. Holdoff. *Peripheral Neuropathy* (vol. 2). W. B. Saunders, Philadelphia, 1984, pp. 1479–1511.
Thygeses, P. "K- Syndrome," *Medical Arv.* 11 (1968), 117–127.
Tietz, E. I., et al. "Amygdala Kindled Seizure State Is Related to Altered Benzodiazepine Binding Site Density," *Life Sciences* 36 (1985), 183–190.
"Trial Research Project: Programs for Evaluation and Research," *Evaluation and Change* (Special Issue). Minneapolis Medical Research Foundation, Minneapolis, 1980.
Trowell, H. C., and E. M. K. Muwazo. "Severe and Prolonged Underfeeding in African Children," *Archives of Diseases in Childhood* 22, p. 110.
van der Kolk, B. A. "Psychopharmacological Issues in Post Traumatic Stress Disorder," *Hospital and Community Psychiatry* 34 (1983), 683–691.
─────, et al. "Inescapable Shock, Neurotransmitters, and Addiction to Trauma: Toward a Psychobiology of Post Traumatic Stress," *Biological Psychiatry* 20 (1980), 314–325.
─────, et al. "Nightmares and Trauma: A Comparison of Nightmares After Combat with Lifelong Nightmares in Veterans," *American Journal of Psychiatry* 141 (1984), 187–190.
Vedder, E. B. "The Pathology of Beriberi," *Journal of the American Medical Association* 110 (1938), 893.
Veterans Administration Study of Former Prisoners of War. United States Government Printing Office, Washington, DC, May 1980.
Victor, M., in *Peripheral Neuropathy* (vol. 2), edited by P. J. Dyck et al. Philadelphia, 1984, pp. 1899–1940.
Vitale, J. J. "Nutritional Disease," in *Pathologic Basis of Disease* (2nd ed.), edited by S. L. Robbins et al. W. B. Saunders, Philadelphia, 1979, pp. 483–520.
Walker, J. I. "Chemotherapy of Traumatic War Stress," *Military Medicine* 147 (1982), 1029–1033.
Weiss, S., and R. W. Wilkins. "The Nature of Cardiovascular Disturbance in Vitamin Deficiency States," *American Physician* 51 (1949), 341.
Wilke, G. "Akute cerebrale Hungerschaden in Krigsgefengenschaft und ihre Neurologischen und Psychiatrischen Folgen," *Psychiatrie der Gegenwart* (Berline) (1961), pp. 792–806.
─────. "Über den Hirnbefund bei einem Heimkehrer mit schwerer Hungersystrophie," *Deutsche Nervenheilkunde* 171 (1954), 188–402.

———. "Zur Frage der Hirnodeme bei Unterernahrung," *Deutsche Med. Wschr* 75 (1950), 172–173.

Wilson, J. D. "Disorders of Vitamins: Deficiency, Excess, and Errors of Metabolism," in *Harrison's Principles of Internal Medicine* (10th Ed.). McGraw-Hill, New York, 1983, pp. 461–469.

Wolf, S., and H. S. Ripley. "Reactions Among Allied Prisoners of War Subjected to Three Years of Imprisonment and Torture by the Japanese," *American Journal of Psychiatry* 104 (1947), 180–193.

Wolff, C. T., et al. "Relationship Between Psychological Defenses and Mean Urinary 17-OHCS Excretion Rates, I: A Predictive Study of Fatally Ill Children," *Psychosomatic Medicine* 26 (1964), 576–592.

——— et al. "Relationship Between Psychological Defenses and Mean Urinary 17-OHCS Excretion Rates, II: Methodological and Theoretical Considerations," *Psychosomatic Medicine* 26 (1964), 592–609.

Yost, J. "The Psychopharmacologic Treatment of the Delayed Stress Syndrome in Vietnam Veterans," in *Post Traumatic Stress Disorders of the Vietnam Veteran*, edited by William T. Cincinnati. Disabled American Veterans, 1980.

Chapter 5
War Crimes

Introduction

The Tokyo War Crimes Trial, known as International Military Tribunal for the Far East (IMTFE), was the Pacific counterpart of the Nuremberg trials. The IMTFE, however, did not capture as much attention and publicity as did the Nuremberg trials; today, almost 50 years later, it is virtually unknown outside Japan.

The IMTFE had its origin in the Cairo Declaration of December 1, 1943, in which the United States, Great Britain, and China announced their intention to punish Japan for her aggression. The Potsdam Declaration of July 26, 1945, enlarged upon this determination, warning that stern justice was to be meted out to all war criminals, including those who mistreated POWs and internees. The basic policy for the trial of Japanese war criminals was set forth in this declaration, which was accepted by Japanese representatives on September 2, 1945, as part of the instrument of surrender.

General Order No. 20, General Headquarters, SCAP, April 25, 1946, outlined the tribunal's constitution, jurisdiction, functions, and procedures.

In the dock at Tokyo were 28 leaders of the Japanese state, both civilian and military. The following is a list of their names and the sentences they received:

- General Sadao Araki: life imprisonment; paroled 1955.
- General Kenji Doihara: sentenced to death.
- Colonel Kingoro Hashimoto: life imprisonment; paroled 1954.
- Field Marshal Shunroku Hata: life imprisonment; paroled 1954.
- Baron Kiichiro Hiranuma: life imprisonment; paroled 1955.
- Baron Koki Hirota: sentenced to death.

- Naoki Hoshino: life imprisonment; paroled 1955.
- General Seishiro Itagaka: sentenced to death.
- Okinori Kaya: life imprisonment; paroled 1955.
- Marquis Koichi Kido: life imprisonment; paroled 1955.
- General Heitaro Kimura: sentenced to death.
- General Kuniaki Koiso: life imprisonment.
- General Iwane Matsui: sentenced to death.
- Yosuke Matsuoka: died of tuberculosis during the trial.
- General Jiro Minami: life imprisonment; paroled 1954.
- General Akira Muto: sentenced to death.
- Admiral Osami Nagano: died of natural causes during the trial.
- Admiral Takasuni Oka: life imprisonment; paroled 1954.
- Shumei Okawa: freed in 1948, after spending some time in a psychiatric ward.
- General Hiroshi Oshima: life imprisonment; paroled 1955.
- General Kenryo Sato: life imprisonment; paroled 1956.
- Mamoru Shigemitsu: seven years' imprisonment; paroled 1950.
- Admiral Shigetaro Shimada: life imprisonment; paroled 1955.
- Toshio Shiratori: life imprisonment.
- General Teiichi Suzuki: life imprisonment; paroled 1955.
- Shigenori Togo: 20 years.
- General Hideki Tojo: sentenced to death.
- General Yoshijiro Umezu: life imprisonment.

On the bench were 11 representatives (judges) of the Allied powers: Sir Wiliam Webb, president (Australia); E. S. McDougall (Canada); Ju Ao Mei (China); Lord Patrick (England); H. Bernard (France); R. B. Pal (India); B. V. A. Röling (the Netherlands); E. H. Northcroft (New Zealand); D. Jaranilla (the Philippines); I. M. Zaryanov (Soviet Union); and M. C. Cramer (the United States).

The indictment at the Tokyo trial charged that the defendants were members of a criminal, militaristic clique that controlled events within the

Japanese government and within Japan proper between January 1, 1928, and September 2, 1945, and that the policies the defendants pursued were the cause of serious world troubles, aggressive wars, and great damage to the interests of peace-loving peoples, as well as to the Japanese people themselves. The majority judgment (there were also five separate opinions) found that this charge had been proved.[1]

The proceedings and judgment of the Tokyo trial were based on a charter, published on January 19, 1946, by General Douglas MacArthur, who also established the IMTFE to implement the Declaration of Potsdam and the Terms of Surrender, which called for "the meting out of stern justice to war criminals."[2]

There was general disagreement, stated professor Onuma, that historical evidence had demonstrated that there were a large number of cases of crimes against humanity: murder, extermination, enslavement, deportation, and other inhumane acts committed by the then-Japanese government or with the acquiesence of that government.[3]

"According to the Charter, a fair trial was to be held," wrote Professor Röling.

> The point is whether this may be possible after a war in which unbridled war propaganda has taken place and feelings of hatred and contempt have been systematically stimulated. It is certainly incorrect to maintain that this kind of post-war trial serves only to provide the victor with the possibility of proving his war propaganda. But the influence of cultivated feeling upon opinion is strong. Inevitably, on occasion, reality is strained. The more nations such an international court of justice represents, the smaller the risk thereof is; for distortion or camouflage of history is then more limited because certain distortions or disguises are mutually begrudged.[4]

The foregoing deals with judgment but does not address the question of how far criminal liability extends for permission to act and omission to stop and prevent. And why the atrocities? Why the crimes against POWs and internees? On June 25, 1943, General Tojo issued the following instructions to newly appointed chiefs of POW camps:

> In Japan we have our own ideology concerning prisoners of war, which should naturally make their treatment more or less different from that in Europe and America. In dealing with them, you should, of course, observe the various regulations concerned, aim at an adequate application of them. At the same time, you must not allow them to lie idle doing nothing but eating freely for even a single day. Their labor and technical skill should be fully utilized for the replenishment of production, and contribution rendered toward the prosecution of the Greater East Asiatic War for which no effort ought to be spared.[5]

The application of these instructions accounted, in part, for the atrocities committed against POWs and civilian internees. There were other reasons for the Japanese committing atrocities, as noted by Arnold C. Brackman:

> Several tidbits of information emerged that provided a fresh insight into Japan's mistreatment of POWs. The IPS—prosecution—tendered in evidence secret documents in which senior Japanese Army officers and civilian officials agreed on the need to parade Allied POWs in Korea publicly and to work POWs in Japan in degrading jobs to dampen pro–American and pro–British sympathies among the Korean and Japanese peoples. In one document, General Itagaki [later sentenced to death], then the commander in Korea, asked imperial headquarters in Tokyo to ship him 2000 Anglo-American POWs so that he could humiliate them and "make the Koreans realize positively the true weight of the might of our emperor," thereby stamping out pro–Anglo-American feeling. In Japan the governor of Kanagawa Prefecture secretly informed the War Ministry that the use of Allied prisoners as slave labor was necessary to weaken the "considerably pro–Anglo-American" attitude among the people in his region. Evidence was also tendered that Tokyo planned to execute all POWs—more than 30,000—in the event of an Allied invasion of Japan. Repeatedly during the trial camp survivors testified that POW camp commandants had told them that they would be killed if Japan was invaded. No documents were introduced to support these charges: the supposition was that the secret directives relating to the disposal of POWs had been destroyed in the pyres ignited after Japan's surrender. However, as the prosecution's case drew to a close, after months of investigations, the IPS produced a War Ministry directive dated March 17, 1945, and stamped "Army Secret No. 2257" in which the vice minister of war, sitting in Tokyo, notified field commanders, "As the war situation has become very critical, I have been ordered to notify you not to make any blunders in the treatment of prisoners of war based upon the attached "Outline for the Disposal of Prisoners of War According to the Change of Situation" when the havocs of war make themselves felt in our imperial homeland and Manchuria. The outline did not order the murder of prisoners, but it "recommended" that in the event of an Allied invasion of Japan, the prisoners "be set free." In light of Japanese treatment of Allied prisoners during the war, it is fair to interpret this suggestion to mean "free from earthly concerns."[6]

The facts and aspects of the Tokyo trial have been controversial. Laurens van der Post, author of numerous books on the time he spent as a POW, wrote:

> I myself was utterly opposed to any form of war trials. I refused to collaborate with the officers of the various war crimes tribunals that were set up in the Far East. [Besides the Tokyo war crimes trial, numerous local trials were initiated.] There seemed to be something unreal, if not utterly false, about a process that made men, like the War Crimes Investigators

from Europe, who had not suffered under the Japanese, more bitter and vengeful about our suffering than we were ourselves.

There seemed to be in this the seeds of the great, classic and fateful evasions in the human spirit which, I believe, both in the collective and in the individual sense, have been responsible for most of the major tragedies that confront us in the world today. I refer to the tendencies in men to blame their own misfortunes and those of their cultures on others; to exercise judgment they need for themselves on the lives of others; to search for a villain to explain everything that goes wrong in their private and collective courses. And, as I saw it we had no moral surplus in our own lives for the lives of others. We needed all our moral energies for ourselves and our own societies.[7]

With reference to the trial of General Yamashita and the Manila massacre, attorney Adolf Frank Reel wrote that with the insurmountable problems faced by the Japanese in the Philippines—the confusion of divided command, poor communication, the lack of food and oil, and the overwhelming power of the American army and navy—Japan had been ill equipped to fight a modern war against a first-rate military power. Just as Americans had underrated Japan before the attack on Pearl Harbor, so had they overrated her afterward.[8]

The Literature

The amount of documentation on the war crimes and atrocities committed by the Japanese is truly overwhelming. At least 27 books discuss the factors concerning the war crime trials in Tokyo. In addition, there are numerous indexes, inventories, transcripts, reviews, and surveys of the documents, including two bibliographies and one encyclopedia. To guide researchers through this mass of documents, a few of the important books are listed here with reference to their contents.

The Tokyo Judgment, by B. V. A. Röling and C. F. Ruter, two volumes, over 1,200 pages. Topics: Vol. 1. Majority Judgment, Contents, Judgment, Notes, Separate Opinion of the President, Dissenting Judgment of the Member from France, Concurring Opinion of Justice Jaranilla from the Philippines. Vol. 2. Judgment of Justice by Pal of India and Opinion of Justice Röling of the Netherlands.

The Knights of Bushido by Lord Russell of Liverpool is a comprehensive account of the atrocities the Japanese inflicted on POWs and civilian internees. The table of contents includes 1. The China Indicent, 2. The General Treatment of POWs, 3. Life and Death on the Burma-Siam Railway, 4. The Massacre of POWs (a) December 1941: Stanley Hospital, Hong Kong—170 nurses and wounded men. (b) December 1941: 200 prisoners in Hong Kong. (c) January 1942: Alexandria Hospital, Singapore

—doctors, nurses, patients. (d) January 1942: Soebang, Java—wounded soldiers, nurses, women, children. (e) February 12, 1942: Banka Island—65 Australian nurses, 200 women and children, elderly men, 25 British soldiers. (f) February 4, 1942: Rabaul, New Guinea—24 Australian soldiers. (g) March 1942: Kota Radja, Aceh—POWs. (h) October 1943: Wake Island—96 POWs. (i) December 1944: Palawan Island—POWs, 5. The Prison Hulks (Hellships), 6. The Death Marches, 7. The Prison Camps, and 8. The Civilian Internment Centers.

The Tokyo War Crimes Trial, edited by C. Hosoya, N. Ando, Y. Onuma, and R. Minear, reviews the trial more than 35 years after it happened. It is a compendium of papers and comments from a number of participants in a 1983 symposium. Both at that time and since, the Tokyo trial has raised a number of fundamental questions, from the perspectives of international law as well as from history. One major aspect of the symposium was to draw attention to the Eurocentrism of the legal ideas, personnel, and historical thinking of the Tokyo trial.

Many articles in the book discuss whether the trial was fair. The four major chapters in the book are (1) the Tokyo trial from the perspective of international law, (2) the Tokyo trial in historical perspective, (3) the Tokyo trial from the perspective of the quest for peace, and (4) the contemporary significance of the Tokyo trial.

The Case of General Yamashita, by attorney Adolf Frank Reel, is an extensive account of the trial, held in Manila, of General Yamashita, who was accused and indicted for the atrocities in Manila after the landing of American forces in Leyte in 1945.

The opening words are indicative of the tone and direction of the book:

> The significance of the issue facing the court today cannot be overemphasized. An American military commission has been established to try a fallen military commander of a conquered nation for an alleged war crime.[9]

With these words, Justice Murphy of the United States Supreme Court opened his opinion in the case of General Yamashita.

The military commission that tried the general was entirely American, the high court that ruled on the case was American, and the general who approved and executed the sentence was American. The United States made the decision, pronounced the law, and set the precedent, which will not be lost on the world. If the decision was right and just, contends the author, it will become a precedent for justice among nations. If the decision was wrong, it must turn into a curse upon justice among nations, unless the wrong is acknowledged to the world.

In this alone lies the importance of the case of General Yamashita. This alone is the reason why the book was written, Reel notes.

War Crimes, War Criminals, and War Crime Trials: An Annotated Bibliography and Source Book, by Norman E. Tutorow, with the special assistance of Karen Winnovich, is a complete annotated bibliography of the major publications on both the Nuremberg and Far East trials. The bibliography makes no claim to be exhaustive, but it can be considered representative.

This 600-page volume consists of the following sections:

- Reference
- General Works and Subsidiary Topics
- Early War Crimes, War Criminals and War Crime Trials
- World War II War Crimes
- World War II War Crimes: The Holocaust
- World War II War Crimes: Concentration Camps
- World War II War Criminals
- World War II War Crime Trials in Asia
- General and Reference Works
- Special Studies
- War Crime Trials—non–IMTFE
- War Crime Trials—IMTFE
- Nuremberg International Military Tribunal
- American Military Tribunals—non–IMTFE
- Allied Military Tribunals and National Trials
- Adolf Eichman Trial
- Vietnam War and War Crime Trials
- Miscellaneous
- 18 Appendices

Uncertain Judgment: A Bibliography of War Crime Trials, complied by John R. Lewis, is intended to be a comprehensive "working rather than definitive" bibliography on a relatively narrow theme within the spectrum of war-peace studies. With regard to the prisoners of the Japanese in World War II and the IMTFE, the listings are numbered as follows:

- Section 1: General reference: 1–61
- Section 2: Background issues: 67–531
- Section 3: Historical issues: 532–2560
  IMTFE: 1916–2147
  Literature: 2321–2324
- Section 4: Subsidiary issues: 2561–2861a
  Japanese militarism: 2947–3007
  Treatment of POWs: 3008–3091
  U.N. and war crimes: 3166–3198
  Occupation government: 3199–3226
  Japan: 3253–3258
  Allied administration of justice: 3259–3267

The Tokyo Trials, compiled by Paul S. Dull and Michael Takaaki, is a 94-page listing of the document numbers of the IMTFE. This research tool is an index to the nearly 50,000 pages of the proceedings of the IMTFE.

Methods of Torture

Although POWs and civilian internees were often punished by various methods of torture for infractions of the rules established by their guards or for not obeying general orders, it was the dreaded Kempeitai—the Japanese counterpart of the Gestapo—that handled the punishment for more serious offenses. The Kempeitai was administered by the Japanese War Ministry. It had full powers of arrest and investigation over both civilians and military personnel.

Kempeitai methods for the torture of captives were exercised in all areas under Japanese control and were implemented uniformly by camp guards, local police, and the other branches of the armed forces. The more common methods of torture used were as follows:

The Water Treatment. The victim was bound and secured in a prone position. Water from a hose was forced through the victim's nose and mouth into the lungs until the victim lost consciousness. Pressure was then applied to the body, often by jumping on the abdomen. When the victim was revived, the procedure was repeated. (5.1)

Burning. The victim was burned with cigarettes, lighted candles, hot irons, hot oil, or scalding water on sensitive parts of the body, such as the nostrils, ears, abdomen, sexual organs, and, in the case of women, the breasts.

Electric Shock. Open ends of wire, connected to an electrical source, were applied to the same sensitive parts as described under burning.

The Knee Spread. The victim, with hands tied behind the back, was forced to kneel with a pole—about 3 inches in diameter—inserted behind both knee joints, to spread the joints. Pressure was then applied to the thighs—by jumping on them, for example—and the knee joints were separated, causing excruciating pain.

Suspension. The victim's body was suspended from a tree or specially constructed pole by the wrists, arms, legs, or neck, causing separation of joints from their sockets. Often, the victim was beaten in this position. (5.2)

Kneeling on Sharp Instruments. The victim was forced to kneel on the sharp edge of a wooden block or other item, often holding a heavy item, such as a rock, in his hands. This method was also often combined with beatings. (5.3)

Removal of Fingernails. This method was known as the "Chinese torture." Fingernails were pulled out with a pair of pliers, or small bamboo chips were driven under the fingernails and sometimes lighted.

Denial of Food and Water. For minor infractions a victim was tied to a tree under the hot tropical sun for two to three days and nights, and refused water and food—a bucket of water, which the victim could never reach, was placed in front of him/her. (5.4)

Beatings. This was the most common form of torture. The most minute infraction of rules, disobedience, or anything could incite the guards or any Japanese around the prisoners to beat, kick, and slap a prisoner. Pieces of wood or bamboo were used for these beatings, resulting in broken bones, internal injuries, or lacerations. In many instances, the victims lost consciousness only to be revived and to suffer more beatings. On occasion prisoners were beaten to death.

Other Methods. If left to their own devices, individual noncommissioned officers and privates alike could come up with a variety of methods to punish and torture their captives. For example, while being refused water, the victim was placed in a small tin box or in a kind of chicken coop and then prodded with bamboo sticks. Fake executions were one of the most popular mental tortures.

The Torture of Miss U

Rosena Utinsky, a Lithuanian woman in Manila, was not interned because she was able to obtain fake identification as being "non–Allied." She was responsible for numerous underground actions to help POWs and civilian internees obtain and smuggle extra food and medical supplies until she was caught and then taken to the infamous Kempeitai headquarters.

The following is an abbreviated account of the tortures she had to endure, taken from her book, *Miss U*:

> I was in a cell about eight feet long and five feet wide. The only light came from an aperture above the door. At one end of the cell was a bucket of drinking water, but no water in which to wash. At the other end there was a hole in which a covered bucket was lowered, the only sanitary facility provided. Every morning the bucket was taken from behind the wall, emptied and returned to the hole.
>
> That night there were seven women in the cell. I crumpled down on the floor with weariness. There was no place to sit. We slept at night on the floor without even a newspaper to cover us. I began to see now why the other women in my cell were in such terrible condition. Some of them had not washed or changed their clothes in at least three months. No care of any sort was permitted them. They had menstruated at first with no protection. After a while that stopped; they were all so undernourished that it could not go on. It was the fifth day I remembered best because that was the day the torture started. The officer made a gesture and the interpreter got up and pushed a bench near the table. He pointed to it. The unusual feature of the bench was that it had split bamboo across it for a seat—and split bamboo is as sharp as knives. I pulled down my skirt and sat down easily, carefully. "No, no," the interpreter yelled, "Kneel on it."
>
> So I sat back on my heels, the bamboo cutting into my legs. It went on for hours, the sharp edges of the bamboo cutting deeper and deeper into my legs. The bone is close to the surface on the shins. The muscles in my hips and thighs ached. He slapped me over and over. But I was in so much pain every other way, with my legs bleeding, my muscles cramped, that a slap more or less hardly counted.
>
> The next day the Kempeitai decided to try something else. They tied my hands behind my back, attached a rope to my wrists and jerked me up several feet above the floor, and beat me with their fists. I lived through thirty-two days of such torture. Sometimes, just for variety, when his cigarette was burning brightly, the officer ground the burning coal into my arm.
>
> All that time, all those days and days, I never screamed. But toward the end when my shins were a mass of running sores, they took a stick, and scraped the sores.
>
> I yelled then.[10]

NOTES

1. C. Hosoya et al., *The Tokyo War Crimes Trial*, Tokyo, 1986, pp. 7–8.
2. Dr. B. V. A. Röling and Dr. C. F. Ruter, *The Tokyo Judgment*, Amsterdam, 1977, Vol. 1.
3. C. Hosoya et al., *The Tokyo War Crimes Trial*, p. 53.
4. Röling and Ruter, *The Tokyo Judgment*, p. xiii.
5. IMTFE, record pp. 13484; 14426; 27200; 27229; 49723; RvO IC 775; 778; 2158; 5278.

6. Arnold C. Brackman, *The Other Nuremberg: The Untold Story of the Tokyo War Crimes Trial*, New York, 1987, pp. 265–266.
7. Laurens van der Post, *The Night of the New Moon*, London, 1970, pp. 151–152.
8. Adolf Frank Reel, *The Case of General Yamashita*, Chicago, 1949, p. 144.
9. *Ibid.*
10. Margaret Utinsky, *Miss U*, San Antonio, 1948, pp. 99–106.

SOURCES

Appleman, John Alan. *Military Tribunal and International Crimes.* Indianapolis, 1954.
Blewett, George F. "Victor's Justice: The Tokyo War Crimes Trial," *American Perspective* 4(3) (1950).
Brackman, Arnold C. *The Other Nuremburg: The Untold Story of the Tokyo War Crimes Trial.* New York, 1987.
Cho, Sung Yoon. "The Tokyo War Crimes Trial," *Quarterly Journal of the Library of Congress* 24(4) (1967), 309–318.
Creel, George. *War Criminals and Punishment.* New York, 1944.
Dull, Paul S., and Michael Takaaki Umemura. *The Tokyo Trial: A Functional Index to the Proceedings of the IMTFE.* Ann Arbor, MI, 1957.
Falk, Richard A., et al. *Crimes of War: A Legal, Political Documentary and Psychological Inquiry into the Responsibility of Leaders, Citizens and Soldiers for Criminal Acts of War.* New York, 1971.
Glueck, Sheldon. *War Criminals.* New York, 1944.
Gozawa, Sadaichi. *Trial of Gozawa Sadaichi and 9 Others*, edited by Colin Sleeman and S. C. Silkin. London, 1948.
Hanson, John F. "The Trial of Lt. Gen. Masaharu Honuma." Unpublished doctoral dissertation, University of Mississippi, 1977.
Hewton, T. *Webb's Justice: The Role of Sir William Flood Webb in the Tokyo Trial.* Adelaide, Australia, 1976.
Horwitz, Solis. *The Tokyo Trial.* 1950.
Hosoya, C., et al. *The Tokyo War Crimes Trial: An International Symposium.* Tokyo, 1986.
Junji, Kinoshita. *Between God and Man: A Judgment on War Crimes.* Washington, DC, 1979.
Kenworthy, Aubrey. *The Tiger of Malaya: The Story of General Tomoyuki Yamashita and Death March General Masaharu Homma.* New York, 1953.
Kirchman, Charles, revised by Gary D. Ryan. *Preliminary Inventory of the Textual Records IMTFE.* National Archives, Washington, DC, 1965.
Lael, Richard L. *The Yamashita Precedent: War Crimes and Command Responsibility.* Wilmington, DE, 1982.
Lewis, John R. *Uncertain Judgment: A Bibliography of War Crime Trials.* Santa Barbara, CA, 1979.
Mallal, Bashir A., ed. *The Double Tenth Trial: War Crimes Court.* Singapore, 1946.
Minear, Richard H. *Victor's Justice: The Tokyo War Crimes Trial.* Princeton, NJ, 1971.
National Archives. *Reviews of Yokohama Class B and Class C War Crime Trials, 1946–1949.* Washington, DC, 1981.
Pal, Radhabinod. *IMTFE: Dissentient Judgment.* Calcutta, 1953.

Piccigallo, Philip. *The Japanese on Trial: Allied War Crimes Operations in the East, 1945–1951.* Austin, TX, 1979.

Powell, J. W. "A Hidden Chapter in History—Japan's Biological Weapons 1930–1945." *Bulletin of Atomic Scientists* 37(8) (October 1981), 44–52.

———. "Japan's Germ Warfare: The U.S. Coverup of a War Crime." *Bulletin of Concerned Asian Scholars* 12(4) (1980), 2–17.

Pritchard, R., John Zaide and Sonia Zaide, eds. "An Overview of the Historical Importance of the Tokyo War Trial" (Nissan Paper Series No. 5), Oxford, 1987.

———. "A Survey of Tokyo War Trial Records in Britain." *History and International Relations* 1(1) (1976), 131–150.

———. *The Tokyo War Crimes Trial—The Complete Transcripts of the Proceedings of the IMTFE* (21 vols.). New York, 1981.

Redford, Larry H. "The Trial of General Tomoyuki Yamashita: A Case Study in Command Responsibility." Unpublished master's thesis, Norfolk, 1975.

Reel, Adolf Frank. *The Case of General Yamashita.* Chicago, 1949.

Röling, Dr. B. V. A., and Dr. C. F. Ruter. *The Tokyo Judgment: The IMTFE: 29 April 1946–12 November 1948* (2 vols.). Amsterdam, 1977.

Sissons, D. C. S. "War Crimes Trials," *Australian Encyclopedia* (Vol. 10). Sydney, 1983, pp. 204–207.

Spurlock, Paul E. "The Yokohama War Crime Trials: The Truth About a Misunderstood Subject." *American Bar Association Journal* 36(5), May 1950.

Taylor, Lawrence. *A Trial of Generals: Homma, Yamashita, MacArthur.* South Bend, IN, 1981.

Tutorow, Norman E. *War Crimes, War Criminals and War Crime Trials: An Annotated Bibliography and Source Book.* New York, 1986.

Sources with Reference to IMTFE Documents and Records

National Archives: Washington, DC:

Preliminary Inventory No. 180, Record Group 238: Records of IMTFE, 1975, 13 pp., by Jarritus Wolfinger.

Record Group 107, 60 linear feet: Some documents on war crimes, Records of the Secretary of War.

Record Group III: Some films on war crime trials in Germany and Japan, Records of the Office of the Chief Signal Officer.

Record Group 153: Two files—(a) 151 linear feet in WNRC Records of the War Crimes Division and (b) 336 linear feet in Records of the International Affairs Division (Judge Advocate General).

Record Group 238: Audiovisual records: including 5,022 photographs, 149 linear feet, and 62 rolls of microfilm.

Library of Congress:

Documents, exhibits for the defense, nos. 1–3088, January 27, 1947–February 10, 1948.

Note: One of the more complete sets of IMTFE records is at the University of California at Berkeley.

Records of proceedings, 1946–1948, 36 reels of microfilm.
Proceedings, April 29, 1946–November 12, 1948, Nos. 1–49858.
Prosecution documents that were not offered or were rejected, Law 133.
Documents, exhibits for the prosecution, Nos. 1–2282: May 4, 1946–January 12, 1947.

Supreme Commander Allied Forces, Tokyo:

IPS documents for the prosecution, IMTFE 1946–1947.
Numerical list of IPS documents, IMTFE, 1947.
Addendum to revised index of documents, IMTFE, 1947.
Index to documents by phrase and subject, IMTFE, 1947.
General index of the records of the defense, IMTFE, 1947.

War Memorial, Canberra, Australia:

AWM 54: written records following broad categories.
1010/-/-: Statements by former POWs and internees.
779/1/-: Investigation reports of particular areas.
779/3/-: Examination and interrogations.
779/4/-: Statements by Japanese.
781/-/-: POW statements.
229/-/-: Courts of inquiry.
233/-/-: Crimes and offenses.
AWM 52: War diaries 1939–1945.
AWM 166: Files of the adjutant general dealing with trials of war criminals (1 box).
AWM 83: IMTFE—proceedings, exhibits, etc., Tokyo, March 1947–January 1948.
3DRL: Sir William Webb papers.
AWM 51: Report on the atrocities and breaches of the rules of warfare by Justice Webb, March 15, 1944.
AWM 54 1010/0/129: Report on war crimes by individual members of the armed forces.
AWM 226 (6): War crimes commission evidence; Vol. 1, pp. 1–227.
AWM 226 (8): Australian War Crimes Board of Inquiry Report, Vol. 1.

Specific IMTFE record page numbers concerning war crimes:

IMTFE, record pp. 12345–15496: prosecution records.
IMTFE, record pp. 27117–27963, 28058–28088: defense record pages.
IMTFE, record pp. 39992–40537: prosecution summation.
IMTFE, record pp. 42618–42691: defense summation.

Chapter 6
Conscript Asian Labor: Native Prisoners

The Story

From the diary entries of Ronald Hastain, POW on the Burma-Siam railroad:

> May–June, 1943: Gangs of native workers driven up country— Chinese, Malays, Tamils from Singapore and Malaya; Annamese from Indo China; Burmese from Burma.
> Commanded to make their own way—no medical facilities—put straight to work—living conditions were of indescribable squalor— disease and starvation stalked among this human flotsam—flies were breeding on the unmoved filth, excreta and corpses.
> September 1943: Native workers made their way to Three Pagoda Pass for the building of the last lap that would connect an extension from Moulmein, on the Burma side—like skeletons and in the final throes of disease and degradation.[1]

This excerpt describes a tiny part of the untold and often ignored story of Japanese prisoners who had no registered camps, of whom no records exist, and about whom no books have been written.

These were conscripted Asians—prisoners, to be exact—Javanese, Malays, Burmese, Tamils, and some Chinese, who were lured by the Japanese to work on a wide variety of projects all over Southeast Asia and the Pacific. As Allied prisoners of war were transported from the Dutch East Indies and Singapore to Burma and Siam to work on the railroad, native laborers followed them or had preceded them to provide extra manpower.

Similarly, all over the Dutch East Indies indigenous labor was used to work on numerous construction projects. In Malayan and Indonesian newspapers, the Japanese placed advertisements seeking laborers for work periods of up to three months.

Propaganda for the Recruitment of *Romushas* (Indonesian Workers)

In need of labor for a wide variety of war-related projects, the Japanese instituted a well-thought-out propaganda plan. In principle, they played on the theme of "warriors of labor," to be honored by their families and the community. The Japanese propaganda methods consisted of organized meetings from the village level to the large cities; speeches, movies and wayang [puppet] performances. Radio, magazines, and newspapers hammered on the theme "all the people must work." Awards and trophies were handed to those whose films, plays, posters, songs, and stories were chosen for use in the propaganda activities. Finally, the homes in which a "warrior of labor" had registered himself would be marked with a special "honor plaque," so all in the village or town could see who had to be honored and supported.[2]

Free rail travel, housing, food, and medical services were offered, together with pay at the rate of one dollar or one rupiah a day. The response was negligible, so the Japanese resorted to more stringent methods, such as "mobilizations."

Japanese Plan of Mobilizing Javanese Labor

In a meeting of the Japanese armed forces staff on October 6, 1943, in Singapore, plans were made to mobilize and utilize the excess indigenous labor forces of Java. Besides propaganda methods, more specific rules and methods for the mobilization of romushas were issued after September 15, 1944.

The Japanese urged the Javanese people to feel a "love and willingness to work." They instituted a number of specific methods, such as (1) registration of labor, (2) transportation of romushas and their care and feeding, (3) instituting *asramas* (boarding centers), (4) mobilization of the jobless, (5) increased productivity, so that workers could be freed to become romushas, (6) use of more women as workers, again to free the men to be used as romushas, (7) improvement of the concept of the volunteer labor force so everyone would become a "worker."[3]

The three-month contract the Japanese had envisioned proved worthless because no laborers returned to their homes in Malay and Java during the first 18 months. At the points of destination—Burma-Siam, Sumatra, and other islands—the laborers found themselves herded into unhygienic, half-built camps with no medical facilities and inadequate rations and were forced to a relentless grind of slave labor in which nothing mattered but completion of the project.

On the Burma–Siam railway, out of the mire of rain-sodden jungle and earth, the most fearful specter of all emerged: cholera. Unlike the Allied POWs, the native laborers had no doctors, male nurses, medicines, or supplies; all along the route of the railway they died by the thousands.

Wrote POW John Coast:

> The Tamils' work was just the same as ours though they seemed to do more of the breaking of stones for ballast than we did. Their rations were worse, likewise their accommodations. But the medical side!! Our poor Dr. Andrews was driven almost crazy within a week. The Nips regarded their fellow Asiatics as machines pure and simple, and utterly failed to regard them as men—as human beings. Consequently, when, as was inevitable, cholera hit the camp after only a few days, the Nips forbade our medical officer to waste time on them. Their (the Japanese) way of thinking was that the Tamil who got cholera would die, therefore don't bother with him, let him die; but just try to keep enough of them fit till the railway was through in that sector, as it should be in a few weeks.[4]

The IMTFE began to pay interest in mid–December 1946 to the cruelties the Japanese had meted out to the Asian slave laborers:

> Several of the western survivors testified that the Japanese treatment of the Asian slave workers was far worse than the treatment accorded European and American prisoners. Indonesian coolies who suffered from cholera, for example, were often forced into common pit graves and buried alive. Other coolies were regularly beaten and humiliated; women among them were insulted and violated; disinfectant was sprayed into the eyes of some laborers, ostensibly as a joke; one Japanese doctor viciously beat the coolies he examined for cholera, whether they had the disease or not (it made no sense that he struck them).
>
> The western prisoners looked on in shock at this inhuman behavior, but a Japanese physician explained lightly to the Europeans that "coolies are subhuman and not worthy of consideration."
>
> According to one affidavit, workers at one camp who could not walk were injected with a "red, unknown fluid." All died within a few minutes. On another occasion sick coolies were offered a large tin of brown sugar. Those who ate the sugar, which turned out to be poisoned, died in agony later the same day.
>
> When the clothes the Asian laborers had brought from home began to fall into rags, they were provided with gunny sacks for wearing apparel and as blankets. There was no change of clothing, so that in a short time "the clothes of almost all laborers was crawling with vermin, and most of them [were] suffering from a virulent type of skin disease," according to the evidence. When cholera broke out, the Japanese often sought to check the spread of the epidemic by cremating not only the dead but also persons whom they considered incurable. "There are many authentic cases of live cremations," one witness told the tribunal.
>
> One of the tragedies of the period is that the Japanese kept no complete records of their coolie laborers as they did of prisoners of war—although, of course, most of the latter records were burned at the Japanese surrender.

Thus, the names of tens of thousands of Asians who perished along the Siam-Burma track are not known, nor are their graves marked. Among them were, for example, many of the 200,000 Indonesians contracted as day laborers during the war who subsequently disappeared.[5]

The following personal observation by Dutch POW Bernard Schoonenberg in Sumatra may serve as a last disturbing image of this subject:

> Walking along a small path in the jungle the author comes upon a scene of rotting corpses, skeletons and recently expired Indonesian laborers. There must have been hundreds.
> When someone appears, it is the shadow of an Indonesian—bones held together by leathery skin. The man tells the story of young men rounded up in villages in Java and shipped to Sumatra to labor on the railroad. There were originally 600 of them—cutting trees, constructing a road. Food was not given or prepared and all had to scrounge for themselves. When more and more of the men became sick and unable to work, the Japanese took the more healthy ones away and left the rest back in the jungle to die—without food, medicine. No one to bury the dead.[6]

NOTES

1. Ronald Hastain, *White Coolie*, London, 1947.
2. RvO IC 6900.
3. RvO IC 5036.
4. John Coast, *Railroad of Death*, London, 1946, p. 130.
5. Arnold C. Brackman, *The Untold Story of the Tokyo War Crimes Trial*, New York, 1987, pp. 256–257.
6. Bernard Schoonenberg, *De Poorten der Hel* [The Gates of Hell], Bussum, the Netherlands, 1978, p. 207.

SOURCES

There are no books or personal accounts on the subject of conscripted Asian labor or native prisoners. The Netherlands Institute for War Documentation (Rijksinstituut voor Oorlogsdocumentatie)—RvO IC—has some documents on this topic: Nos. 6900, 5036, 4519, 5038, 5037.

One book, *Nederlandsch Indie onder Japanse Bezetting* [The Dutch East Indies Under Japanese Occupation], by Dr. I. J. Brugmans et al., Franeker, 1960, includes a number of accounts of native prisoners. Especially worthwhile are accounts 87, p. 196, and 346, p. 500. In addition most of the books and bibliographies listed in the sources to chapter 5 have some references to the subject.

Chapter 7
The POW Medal

The U.S. POW Medal

On November 8, 1985, the U.S. Congress passed Public Law 99-145, authorizing the Prisoner of War Medal, which was signed by the president without delay. The law authorizes the issuance of the POW Medal to all who were captured and who served honorably during captivity during all wars since World War I.

The design is that of a tricolor ribbon with a circular medal attached. The symbolic description is as follows:

> • Front side: the eagle, symbol of the United States and the American Spirit, though surrounded by barbed wire and bayonet points, stands with pride and dignity, continually on the alert for the opportunity to seize hold of beloved freedom, thus symbolizing the hope that upholds the spirit of the POW.
>
> • Reverse side: at top, below the words "Awarded to" is space for engraving the recipient's name; below it is the inscription: "For Honorable Service While a Prisoner of War." Appearing below the inscription is the shield from the coat of arms of the United States and the words "United States of America" bordering the bottom of the medal.

Why the Medal?

The military community has questioned why a person should get a medal for being a POW. Even some ex-POWs have questioned the validity of such a decoration.

The POW Medal: What It Means

In a short paper, Dr. Guy Kelnhofer, himself an ex-POW, wrote the following:

A short time ago, I received in the mail a new military decoration, the prisoner of war medal. My eligibility for the award was earned by serving almost four years as a prisoner of the Japanese during WW II. The medal was received with mixed emotions by me and by my comrades in arms.

In one sense I was offended by the medal. It was so belated, coming as it did more than forty years after my liberation from prison camp. Moreover, it was such an inadequate recognition, representing the only official acknowledgement we had ever been accorded for the suffering we had endured for our country. The manner of its presentation left a great deal to be desired. How such significance can be given to a decoration that is sent to the recipient in the mail without the minimal courtesy of an accompanying letter of explanation or gratitude? Where is the honor in that?

The medal lost some of its luster too, by the unfriendly reception it was given by the military community. Some, in their ignorance, complained that men were being honored, not for fighting but for giving up. This kind of condemnation by misinformed critics has cast a cloud on the award. Unfortunately, these protestations also reflect a widespread misconception about the prisoner of war experience.

The prisoner of war medal is given to those members of the armed forces who exhibited unusual courage and steadfastness during prolonged periods of extreme stress and maximum danger while in the hands of the enemy. Despite years of torture, starvation, beatings, humiliations and slave labor, these men and women conducted themselves so as to preserve and defend the honor and integrity of the United States. Their unswerving loyalty, discipline and patriotism remained intact under the most trying conditions in which the human mind and body can be subjected.

Unlike the benign conditions portrayed in movie versions of life in prison camps, the prisoner of war was usually treated brutally by his captors. Nearly all of the men who were captured had no decision in the surrender. Either they were shot down over enemy targets or they were ordered by their officers to lay down their weapons. For strategic reasons, men and women who were captured in such Pacific outposts as Guam, Wake Island, Bataan and Corregidor in WW II were deliberately sacrificed to the enemy by a nation that lacked the necessary resources to supply and reinforce them.

Military prisoners of war, for the most part, were given no parades, no ceremonies of homecoming, and no attention to the serious aftereffects of their imprisonment experiences. It is time for this nation to acknowledge with this small token its debt to those who gave so much in defense of their country. The prisoner of war medal deserves respect from the military family.[1]

The POW Medal: Who Needs It?

Some POWs asked whether the medal is an adequate recognition of their POW experience. There is, of course, nothing that can adequately "pay" for the experience of being a POW in World War II.

To acknowledge the POWs, however, is to recognize the source of their terrible pain and struggles during captivity. To acknowledge them is to honor and affirm each life that ended in those years of captivity—lives that could have contributed to our society through their talents and love.

To many who are associated with the POWs, the medal is more than a recognition of past sacrifice and suffering. It honors the sacrifices of those who helped others to learn what humans do to other humans.

Should a POW Be Awarded a Medal?

Dr. Thomas Nixon, an ex–POW himself, asked this question. He then answered it by saying:

> I can only answer the question based on my personal knowledge of being a prisoner of the Japanese for nearly four years. Though each prison camp and experience was different, the theme was similar: continue fighting the enemy from within. I most assuredly believe that any POW who came out of imprisonment with his or her honor unblemished certainly deserves the recognition bestowed upon them by the award of a medal.[2]

International POW Medal

The National Ex-Prisoners of War Association in England announced in 1990 the striking of a commemorative medal for all Allied ex–POWs. The medal is available only to bonafide ex–POWs or their next of kin whose countries were Allies with Britain at the time of their capture, irrespective of whether the United Kingdom was itself involved in the conflict or not.

The ribbon is woven 32 mm wide with a symbolized strand of white barbed wire 2 mm wide at its center. It is bounded on either side by 4 mm black bands representing the despair of the camp. These bands, in turn, are edged by two white 2 mm bands representing the second and third fences of the camp compound. Outside these bands are 7 mm bands of green, reminiscent of the grassy fields at home, and, finally, both edges consist of 2 mm red bands symbolizing the burning faith of those who interned.

The obverse shows a strand of barbed wire that has entrapped a young bird, symbolic of freedom itself.

These elements surmount a globe of the world, indicative of the international parameters of the medal. The words "International Prisoners of War" encircle the entire design. The reverse shows the haunting and vicious barb of the ever-present wire, symbolically dividing this side into four elements, each bearing one of the words in the phrase "Intrepid against all adversity."

NOTES

1. Guy J. Kelnhofer, Ph.D., "The POW Medal: What It Means," *Ex-POW Bulletin*.
2. Thomas Nixon, Ph.D., "Should a POW Be Awarded a Medal?" *Ex-POW Bulletin*, 1986.

Chapter 8
Andersonville National Historic Site and POW Museum

Short History of the Site

> I am dying comrades, dying
> Far away from friends and home
> In this rebel den I'm lying
> Suffering, starving all alone
> —*from a poem by an unknown Andersonville POW.*

Andersonville, or Camp Sutter (in Andersonville, Georgia) as it was known officially, was the largest of many Confederate military prisons established during the Civil War. It was built in early 1864 after Confederate officials decided to move the large number of federal prisoners in and around Richmond to a place of greater security and more abundant food. During the 14 months it existed, more than 45,000 Union soldiers were confined there. Of these, almost 13,000 died from disease, poor sanitation, malnutrition, overcrowding, or exposure to the elements.

The prison pen initially covered about 16½ acres of land enclosed by a 15-foot-high stockade of hewed pine logs. It was enlarged to 26½ acres in June 1864. Sentry boxes, or "pigeon roosts," as the prisoners called them, stood at 30-yard intervals along the top of the stockade. A branch of Sweetwater Creek flowed through the prison yard. It supplied water to most of the prison.

The first prisoners were brought to Andersonville in February 1864; by August, there were 45,000. Because of deteriorating economic conditions and inadequate logistics, the Confederate government was unable to provide adequate housing, food, clothing, and medical care to the federal captives.

When the war ended, Captain Henry Wirz, the camp's commandant, was arrested and charged with conspiring with high Confederate officials to "impair and injure the health and destroy the lives of federal prisoners and murder in violation of the laws of war." Such conspiracy never existed, but public anger demanded appeasement. Tried and found guilty by a military tribunal, Wirz was hanged in Washington, DC, on November 10, 1865.

The Daughters of the Confederacy erected a large monument to Wirz on Andersonville's main street "to rescue his name from the stigma attached to it by embittered prejudice." In 1981 Wirz was posthumously awarded the Confederate Medal of Honor.

Andersonville prison ceased to exist when the war ended in April and May 1865. During July and August 1865, Clara Barton, a detachment of laborers and soldiers and a former prisoner named Dorence Atwater, came to Andersonville cemetery to identify and mark the graves of the Union dead.

The prison reverted to private ownership in 1875. In December 1890 it was purchased by the Georgia Department of the Grand Army of the Republic (GAR), a Union veterans' organization. Unable to finance improvements needed to protect the property, this group sold it for $1 to the Woman's Relief Corps (WRC), the national auxiliary of the GAR.

In 1910 the WRC donated the prison site to the people of the United States. The site was administered by the War Department and its successor, the Department of the Army, through 1970, when it was made a national historic site. The National Park Service took over administration on July 1, 1971.

Cemetery

Andersonville's cemetery is a "working" cemetery. All military veterans discharged under conditions other than dishonorable and their wives or their dependent children can be buried at Andersonville. The cemetery can bury four deep per grave if necessary.

After the Civil War 13,699 bodies were buried in the cemetery, including the 779 who were brought in from battlefields throughout Georgia. Today, approximately 16,700 are buried there, with space for another 8,000.

Andersonville has two to three burials per week. Two Medal of Honor winners are buried there: Corporal Luther H. Story, from the Korean War, and James Wiley, who captured a Georgia flag at Gettysburg during the Civil War. There are 12 memorial stones for individuals whose bodies were never recovered.

POW Museum

The National Prisoner of War Museum at Andersonville is the only one of its kind in the nation. It has been operated since November 1987 by the National Park Service, in cooperation with the American Ex-Prisoners of War, Inc. The temporary museum is filled with memorabilia from POWs of World Wars I and II, Korea, and Vietnam. The museum's purpose is to tell the POW story—and that of the civilian internees—to the American people through interpretive exhibits. On display are letters from POWs and internees, prison camp diaries and artwork, photographs of prisoners, and maps showing camp locations.

William J. Thompson's haunting sculpture of a crippled POW leaning on a crutch stands in front of hundreds of marble headstones marking the burial place of Andersonville prisoners. Presented by Georgia in 1976, the statue honors all American prisoners involved in all the nation's wars and carries the words of Zechariah: "Turn you to the stronghold, ye prisoners of hope."

The design of a new museum was nearly halfway complete at this writing. Architects from the Denver Service Center had moved from conceptual design to more detailed plans for the 10,000-square-foot facility. The Ex-Prisoners of War liaison committee approved the design at the organization's national convention in Seattle in October 1990.

Congress appropriated sufficient funds to build the necessary utilities for the new museum. The total cost of the project is shared by the National Park Service and the American Ex-Prisoners of War, Inc.

A Short Tour

In the beauty and serenity of the present-day prison site, it is difficult for visitors to visualize the scene 126 years ago, when a wretched crowd of 33,000 sick, starving, dirty human beings existed in filth and squalor in thousands of huts, lean-tos, and dugouts, all massed together in a stockaded area of 26 acres.

Today, on the lush, immaculate green grounds, visitors can view the outline of the famous stockade. They can see deep wells dug by prisoners with their bare hands or with improvised tools in their frantic search for fresh drinking water when Stockade Creek became polluted. Tunnels, which the prisoners fashioned for escapes and where many perished in cave-ins, can also be viewed. Providence Spring, which legend says gushed forth in answer to the prayers of prisoners dying of thirst, is still bubbling pure water.

In the cemetery, headstones mark the final resting place of 12,912

Union soldiers who died there between February 1864 and April 1865. Most stones bear the name, home state, and monument number of the man buried under them. On more than 500 stones there is only one word: "Unknown."

Towering high above the individual tombstones are larger statuary dedicated by various states to their own dead. Most of these monuments have been erected since 1900. New Jersey took the lead in 1899 by erecting a $2,000 monument to her 235 sons who died at Andersonville. Other states that contributed monuments were Massachusetts, with 767 known dead; Maine, with 252; Pennsylvania, with 1,849; Iowa, with 214; Indiana, with 702; Rhode Island, with 79; New York, with 2,261; Wisconsin, with 378; Connecticut, with 290; Illinois, with 850; Tennessee, with 1,284; Ohio, with 1,055; Michigan, with 638; and Minnesota, with 79.

Specific Needs of the Park

- Computer and specific programs listing POWs to which visitors can gain access.
- The treatment, restoration, and preservation of existing artifacts and the purchase of additional items.
- Additional funds for the construction of the visitors' center and museum.
- Educational exhibits and equipment.
- Audiovisual equipment.
- Maintenance and improvement projects.
- Cleaning and restoration of monuments in the park.
- Research projects.
- Acquisition of research and library books.
- Gravesite flags and poles.

POW Questionnaire

As stated in the Act of October 18, 1970 (P.L. 91-465), Andersonville National Historic Site has been set aside "to provide an understanding of the overall prisoner of war story and to interpret the role of prisoner of war camps in history and to commemorate the sacrifice of Americans who lost their lives in such camps."

Therefore, the POW questionnaire is an ongoing park research effort to obtain the facts and information necessary to understand and successfully interpret the story of POWs and civilian internees.

All former POWs are encouraged to complete the form and return it to the Andersonville National Historic Site, Andersonville, GA 31711. A sample follows.

1. Basic biographical data:

    Name: Age:

    Current Address:

2. In what war were you held as a prisoner of war or civilian internee?
3. Where were you held captive?
4. Dates of capture and release.
5. Country of capture?   Country of release?
6. What was [were] the official name or names of your camp or camps? The unofficial name or names?
7. Do you feel that you were treated in accordance with the minimum standards for humane treatment set forth in the Geneva Convention?
8. Can you describe what type of housing or barracks were provided?
9. Describe a typical day's routine: work, meals, recreational and religious opportunities.
10. Can you provide the names and addresses of other POWs?
11. Do you have any memorabilia, artifacts, or documents related to your POW or civilian-internee experience that you would like to lend or donate to the National Park Service for display in the museum?
12. Are there other information, stories, or experiences that you would like to mention?

Chapter 9

Statistics

U.S. Department of Defense Statistical Data: POWs

General

The United States Department of Defense, National Research Council, National Archives, and other sources have presented American Ex-POWs, Inc., with data that reflect a consensus about the accuracy and acceptability of the information presented. Since this book is solely concerned with information related to prisoners of the Japanese in World War II, when possible and applicable, only figures on the Pacific are listed.

The following are figures current as of January 1, 1989, for Americans captured in all areas of the Pacific:

```
WW II:  Captured and interned ...................... 130,201
        Died while POW ............................. 14,072
        Returned to U.S. control ................... 116,129
        Alive on January 1, 1982 ................... 87,996
        Alive on January 1, 1989 ................... 71,620
```

These data do not include United States Merchant Marine casualties, which were 4,780 missing, 882 dead (including 57 POWs), 572 POWs released, and 1 POW unaccounted for.[1]

When totaling the figures, I arrive at the following:

```
WW II:  Captured and interned ...................... 130,830
        Died while POW ............................. 14,129
        Unaccounted ................................ 1
        Returned to U.S. control ................... 116,701
```

The research done by this author reveals that it is impossible to arrive at figures that are completely accurate. There are numerous discrepancies because the Japanese records were destroyed shortly after the date of surrender and the Allied records were not always accurate because of the Japanese practice of moving POWs around on a minute's notice. The information presented in this chapter is based on the most reliable and authoritative figures available.

The Philippines

Japanese forces captured approximately 17,000 American nationals, 12,000 Filipino scouts, and about 30,000 Filipino troops. In addition, some 7,300 American civilian men, women, and children were interned.

During the first year of captivity, a reported 30 percent of the Americans and about 80 percent of the scouts died. Although the proportion of each group who survived to repatriation is not clear, a rough estimate is that 11,000 Americans and about 4,000 scouts survived.

This information is based on military records kept during the war; no accurate breakdown was made after repatriation.

Guam and Wake Islands

Originally there were 1,146 construction workers on Wake Island and 25 Pan American Airways employees on Guam, for a total of 1,171. An estimated 600 were evacuated, and approximately 600 may have been captured.

Other Data

In the epilogue of his book *War Without Mercy*, John W. Dower listed figures for native and European prisoners in the Dutch East Indies. European internees numbered 130,000, of whom 30,000 died during captivity. From 300,000 to 1 million Indonesians and Chinese were mobilized as forced laborers. After the war, the United Nations accepted a figure of 300,000 deaths. Of the 73,000 Malays who were mobilized, 25,000 were reported to have died.[2]

In *Last Stop Nagasaki* and *A Life for Every Sleeper*, Hugh V. Clarke presented the following breakdown of the 138,708 Allied, non–American troops in Singapore and Malaya:

British troops	38,496
Australian troops	18,490
Indian troops	67,340
Local, volunteer troops	14,382

Of this number, about 130,000 became POWs. Concerning the Australians, Clarke calculated that of the 18,490 POWs, 7,777 died and the remainder were recovered. However, when he listed those who did *not* return from Japanese prison camps by area and included other reasons, he came up with a higher total, as follows:

Siam	2,336
Borneo	1,783
Ambon	718
Burma	479
Malaya	284
New Britain	200
Japan	190
Lost at sea	1,515
Executed for attempted escape	27
Other reasons	193
Unknown reasons	375
	8,100 men died

One may assume that the difference of 323 between the first and second totals is part of the 375 executed for unknown reasons.[3]

In *Surrender and Survival: The Experience of American POWs in the Pacific 1941–1945*, Bartlett E. Kerr assembled the following totals of U.S. POWs captured by the Japanese.

1. *Captured by Japanese*

The Philippines	22,000
Wake Island	1,555
Java	890
Japan and elsewhere	300
Celebes	255
Guam	400
China	200
	25,600

2. *Died After Capture*

The Philippines	5,135
On prison ships	3,840
Japan	1,200
Manchuria	175
Burma	130
Wake Island	100
Korea	70
	10,650

3. *Liberated*

Japan	11,400
The Philippines	1,500
Manchuria	1,200
Burma-Siam	480
Celebes	200
Korea	150
China	20
	14,950

Sources listed by Kerr include Philippine Department, U.S. Army, Machine Records Unit (station strength and miscellaneous), November 1941; Philippine Harbor Defense report of operations; "Operations in the Pacific in World War II"; "The Rising Sun in the Pacific" by S. E. Morrison; Records of the Lost Battalion Association; U.S. POWs, Provost Marshal General's general estimate, December 20, 1944; Japanese report on American POWs, June 1946; official records of death from the Cabanatuan and O'Donnell camp records; diaries and postwar statements by POWs pertaining to Manchuria and Korea; and Japanese testimony during the Allied War Crimes Trials.[4]

Data from the Netherlands Institute of War Documentation (RvO IC) include 37,000 POWs in the Dutch East Indies, of whom 8,500 died and 28,500 were liberated.

In *Indonesian Society in Transition*, W. F. Wertheim mentions that of the 300,000 Indonesian forced laborers (romushas) who worked with the Allied POWs, only about 70,000 survived the war.[5]

With regard to undocumented native prisoners, of the approximately 300,000 laborers who were used on the Burma-Siam railroad, about 60,000 died.

Conclusions on Allied POWs and Native Prisoners

From Clarke's list of *British, Australian, Indian and local* POWs:

POWs: ±130,000   died: ±8,100 (±6.2%)

From Kerr's list of *American POWs:*

POWs: ±25,600   died: ±10,650 (±41.6%)

From the RvO IC list of *Dutch* POWs:

POWs: ±37,000   died: ±8,500 (±23%)

Total POWs: ±192,600   died: ±27,250 (±14.1%)

From Wertheim's list of *Indonesian forced laborers:*

Laborers: ±300,000   died: ±230,000 (±76.6%)

From the list of *undocumented native prisoners:*

Laborers: ±300,000   died: ±60,000 (±20%)

Total Laborers: ±600,000   died: ±290,000 (±48.3%)

According to some figures, of the 235,473 United States and Allied prisoners captured by the Germans, 9,348 (about 4 percent) died. Other figures show a death rate for POWs captured by the Japanese as high as 27 percent. On the Burma-Siam death railway, 46,000 POWs were put to work, of whom 16,000 (or ±34.7 percent) died. From all these figures, the 31.4 percent overall death rate for POWs seems to be a reasonable figure.

Civilians

In *De Japanse Burgerkampen* [The Japanese Civilian Camps], an exhaustive study of civilian internment centers, Dr. D. van Velden has assembled the following figures on *all* civilians in the Pacific theater[6]:

Country	Men	Women	Children	Total	Died	%
Japan	480	190	20	690	32	4.6
China	4,500	3,350	1,500	9,350	250	2.6
Indochina	50	10	5	65	1	1.5
Siam	155	35	10	200	9	4.5
Hong Kong	1,300	920	315	2,535	127	5.0
Philippines	4,200	2,300	1,300	7,800	453	5.8
Burma	170	20	10	200	?	—
Malaya	3,175	1,020	330	4,525	218	4.8
Subtotals				25,365	1,090	4.3

The Dutch East Indies

Country	Men	Women	Children	Total	Died	%
Sumatra	4,000	4,500	4,700	13,200	1,300	9.8
Java	29,000	25,000	29,000	83,000	11,000	13.2
Borneo, North	250	250	30	530	30	5.6
Borneo, South	70	80	90	240	30	12.5
Celebes, South	600	820	835	2,255	84	3.7
Celebes, North	155	300	100	555	98	17.6
Other Islands	2,635	1,100	2,015	5,750	1,025	17.8
Subtotals				105,530	13,567	12.8
Total of *all* camps				130,895	14,657	11.2

These figures show a death rate among civilian internees that was one-third that of the POWs. This rate is not surprising, since civilians were not put to work on death railroads or transported on "hellships."

Final Data

If all the various figures listed in this chapter are added up, the following approximate conclusions can be reached:

Allied POWs: ±193,000   died: ±60,600 (±31.4%)
Native prisoners: ±600,000   died: ±290,000 (±48.3%)
Civilian internees: ±130,895   died: ±14,650 (±11.2%)

Total prisoners: ±923,895   died: ±365,250 (±39.5%)

Out of about 1 million captives, well over *one-third* died—a needlessly and tragically high figure.

NOTES

1. From *Summary of Merchant Marine Casualties: World War II*, U. S. Coast Guard, Washington, DC, July 1, 1950.
2. John W. Dower, *War Without Mercy*, New York, 1986, p. 296.
3. Hugh V. Clarke, *Last Stop Nagasaki*, Sydney, 1984, and *A Life for Every Sleeper*, Sydney, 1986, p. 124.
4. Bartlett E. Kerr, *Surrender and Survival*, New York, 1985, pp. 339–340.
5. W. F. Wertheim, *Indonesian Society in Transition: A Study of Social Change*, The Hague–Bandoeng, 1956, pp. 263–266.
6. Dr. D. van Velden, *De Japanse Burgerkampen* [The Japanese Civilian Camps], Franeker, the Netherlands, 1977, pp. 519–544.

II
REFERENCE TO INDIVIDUAL PRISON SHIPS AND CAMPS

Chapter 10

The Prison Ships: The Overseas Transports

Introduction

During the American Revolution, the British considered the American rebels traitors, so that capture could mean trial for treason or confinement on a British ship stationed in Wallebout Bay, New York. Why England chose to use ships for prisons is not known, since she had many buildings in New York that could have served as prisons. This was perhaps the first time in history that the term *prison ship* was used.

The conditions on these ships were far from pleasant. The following two accounts speak for themselves, and they set the stage for what is to follow in this chapter on prison ships, referred to by all POWs who were transported on them as "hellships."

> In June 1778 Robert Sheffield, a shipmaster of Stonington, Connecticut, made his escape from a New York prison ship after six days. He said there were three hundred and fifty men on board confined below and that the heat was so intense they were all naked. Some were delirious, raving and storming; some groaning and dying, all panting for breath. The air was so foul at times a lamp could not be kept burning by reason of which the boys were not missed until they had been dead for 10 days. There were five or six deaths per day.

> The "Jersey" was, indeed, a derelict among derelicts. There was never enough food and seldom enough water. As many as 1200 prisoners were confined aboard her at one time. During the day they were permitted on deck, but at night everyone had to go below without regard for their condition. The air was so foul and nauseous that it was considered a privilege to sleep near one of the holes in the sides of the ship. The sick were doubtless made sicker and the dying were speeded on their way by the heat, the vermin and the stench. Dysentery, smallpox and yellow fever were prevalent and helped to produce an appalling death rate.[1]

Because the conditions on a prison ship in the late 1700s were essentially the same as those on Japanese prison ships from 1942 to 1945, except for a few unique situations and circumstances, the basic conditions on each prison ship listed in this chapter will not be repeated.

One hundred sixty-five years after the events just described, the Japanese used ships for the same purpose as the British, except that they sailed the ships from place to place and the prisoners called them "hellships," not "prison ships."

From the autumn of 1942 through the beginning of 1945, the Japanese moved nearly 40,000 American and Allied POWs from Java, the Dutch East Indies, to other islands and destinations; from Singapore to Burma, Formosa, Manchuria, and Japan; from the Philippines to Japan; and from and to other places. Their reasons for doing so are unclear.

Some answers were given in earlier chapters. Sir John Fletcher-Cooke offered a typical British viewpoint:

> Why had a hundred or so POWs, already weakened by malnutrition and singularly lacking in the skills required for shipbuilding, been brought thousands of miles from Java to this little island on the Seto Inland Sea?
> Not to step up output! But to boost up the morale of the dockyard mateys!![2]

Whatever the Japanese reasons were, the prisoners fared even worse on the ships than they did in the camps.

One aspect of these transports that also came up in the War Crimes Trials was that the ships were unmarked. As POW William R. Evans commented:

> Of all the atrocities [the worst] was the decision to transport POWs in unmarked ships, in convoys of war ships, tankers, freighters and other craft, making prison ships legitimate targets for U.S. war planes and submarines.[3]

The answers lie somewhere buried deep in the affidavits and testimonies of the Tokyo War Crimes Trial and the various local trials. Another unanswered question is why all POWs received uniformly inhumane treatment aboard the hellships, yet in the camps some commandants treated their captives better or worse than others.

As early as December 1942, the War Ministry in Tokyo issued instructions that "prisoners should arrive at their intended destinations in suitable condition to immediately perform their assigned duties." The orders had no real effect.

Since Japan's offensive stance, which began with the attack on Pearl

Harbor, changed into a defensive one by the end of 1942, the prisoners' continuous bad treatment on the transport ships can perhaps be interpreted as a face-saving action by individual Japanese commanders. Whatever the reasons for the Japanese attitudes, the facts are that the Japanese showed no concern for their "passengers."

Conditions Aboard the Ships and the Treatment of POWs

Hell on the Prison Ships

Although the conditions on the British prison ships during the American Revolution and on the Japanese prison ships were similarly harsh, the Japanese prison ships differed in two important aspects: They traveled from place to place, and they were often sunk by Allied planes or submarines, with the added challenge for the prisoner of surviving in the ocean. As one American POW wrote:

> The damned, dark world of the hellship lies buried beyond the reach of memory or imagination. It was a world providing only scenes and experiences unrelieved by humor or light, unvaried in routine and setting, unfathomable for reader or viewer. To make a movie of this, or painting, or write a novel, would, like the astronomer's black hole, only collapse onto itself, shedding no light, yielding no understanding. Hellships represent a kind of depravity, a supreme pure form of evil, beyond the scope of history, beyond the creative imagination even of those who survived them.[4]

There is no other way to support the general portrait of conditions on these ships than by citing a number of dramatic and sensitive accounts written by survivors. More than 62,000 POWs were transported in 56 ships, of which 19 were torpedoed or bombed (and sunk) and one was lost in a typhoon. More than 22,000 (35.2 percent)—or more than one in three—lost their lives.

"You are bred like rats, and you will die like rats."

> It was unbearable down in the hold—almost every man had finished the small ration of water in his water bottle. Eventually, a few containers were lowered in the holds. In them was foul and polluted water, covered with thick, greenish scum. Nimorri, the interpreter, played his sadistic card. He lowered two more containers: one was full of seawater and the other contained urine. His parting words were: "You are bred like rats and you will die like rats."[5]

"Here! Here! Help!"

> After the ship sank I floated for twenty-four hours in an empty tea box, with my knees touching my chin. I took my shirt off and placed it on my head to prevent sunstroke. I was stark naked. My body was one lump of pain and cramps. The night seemed an eternity. I prayed to the moon. When daylight came I noticed a ship with Japs picking up survivors. I screamed, "Here! Here! Help!" a hundred times. Finally they pulled me out of the crate and on the deck. The ship was loaded with wounded and survivors. I was on the point of losing consciousness when we stopped some place. We trucked to Padang. Someone, I think a Sumatran, gave me a red blanket.[6]

Attitudes of decency. Among all the horror and terror, among the filth and human decay often so prevalent on the hellships, there were men who refused to let the horrible atmosphere get hold of them. They showed that the proper values could prevail.

> For the most part the atmosphere of desolation and hopelessness ruled out civility and charity. Each man, in his personal agony and struggle to survive, seemed to grow numb to the misery of others. Yet, occasional acts of decency and tenderness surfaced. Over the dead body of a dear friend, a man would stand in an attitude of prayer with tears dripping down his cheeks. Another would share with a fever-ridden buddy a cup of precious water, purchased from a guard at the price of a treasured wedding band. More than once I saw a weak, starving prisoner, with nothing but hope left in his own heart, cradle the head of a comrade in his arms and plead with the dying man to hang on.[7]

Individual Prison Ships

With the destruction of all POW-related documents by the Japanese just before the official signing of surrender and the impossibility—at times—for the Allied officers in charge of prison-camp administration to keep up the necessary data and information, what is known about the prison ships is by no means complete.

The data that follow have been compiled from thousands of pages of books, documents, and other papers. Although not all-encompassing, they provide sufficient basic information for future researchers. The ships are listed by number (PS 1 and so forth), as well as by name. Sixteen of the 56 transport ships listed were sunk, or 30 percent of all the transports, killing 20,920 of the 68,063 men being hauled from one place to another, or 30 percent of the total.

- *PS 1: Name unknown*
  From: Batavia, Dutch East Indies, December 30, 1942
  Destination: Formosa, February 1, 1943
  Aboard: 74 of the highest-ranking military officers and civilian authorities: Lieutenant General H. ter Poorten, Dutch Army Chief of Staff; 7 Dutch major generals; 22 colonels; Tjarda van Starkenborg Stachouwer, governor general of the Dutch East Indies; Paul Mattbey, British air vice marshall; 2 air commodores; 1 British major general; 1 British brigadier general; other officers.

From the diary of a field officer:

> Wednesday, December 30, 1942: On Monday, 28 December by truck to Batavia harbor. Speech by transport commander, a warrant officer. The Governor General of the Dutch East Indies [the highest authority in the land] and generals placed in automobiles—other officers in three trucks. We were allowed to take all our bedding and luggage with us.
> In the harbor, Lt. Gen. Yaheita Saito, Commander of the Japanese 25th Army himself, was present, together with a number of other officers.
> The ship was an old, rusty steamer, about 4000 BRT [bruto registered tons]. Saito had a few presents for the Governor General: mosquito coils, 25 cigars, eau de cologne. He conversed with many of us. All very friendly. We talked about corresponding with our families. —"War is not pleasant," they said.
> We went aboard. On the 1st level of the hold, in two layers were the Japanese. On the 2nd level also in two layers were we located—also the Governor General. Forward hold: two layers thick. Everything too low to stand straight up. Cramped sleeping places. Japanese soldiers were in the same situation. No angry mood. Food the same for everybody: rice, three times a day. Latrines were a joke—transparent wooden huts—urinating done in public view—difficult for some. Stinking mess. We wash ourselves with our own sweat.
> The Governor General holds himself up quite well, considering the circumstances.

This was symbolically a fascinating historic occurrence. After more than 300 years of colonial rule, the highest Dutch ruler, the governor general and other high-ranking officers in the ex-colony were herded away in a small, rusty old steamer. When the Dutch arrived 300 years earlier, they came with numerous beautiful schooners, built in the "golden age" of Holland. Neither Governor General Tjarda van Starkenborg Stachouwer nor many of the other high officials saw the "Dutch East Indies" again.

Special sources: 1. Colonel William C. Braly, *The Hard Way Home*, Washington, DC, 1947.
2. RvO IC 6884.
3. Dr. I. J. Brugmans, *Nederlands Indie Onder Japanse Bezetting*, Franeker, 1960.

- *PS 2: Name unknown*
    From: Singapore; June 1, 1944
    Destination: Japan (POWs were transferred in Formosa to the PS47, *Tomohuko Maru*)
    Aboard: 766 POWs: 267 Australians, 190 British, 43 Americans, and 266 Dutch

- *PS 3: Name unknown*
    From: unknown—most likely Singapore
    Destination: most likely Japan
    Aboard: about 1,100 British and Dutch POWs
    Sunk: bombed in Manila Harbor on September 22, 1944
    Casualties: more than 900 men
    Specific source: E. Bartlett Kerr, *Surrender and Survival*, New York, 1985.

- *PS 4: Name unknown* (known by POWs as "October Ship")
    From: Manila, the Philippines, October 11, 1944
    Destination: Japan
    Aboard: 1,800 POWs
    Sunk: torpedoed on October 25, 1944, between Hong Kong and Formosa
    Casualties: 1,796
    Note: Four survivors were picked up and transported to Formosa where they were put together with another contingent of POWs who had just arrived.
    Special sources: 1. Colonel William C. Braly, *The Hard Way Home*, Washington, DC, 1947.
    2. Liaison and Research Branch, American Prisoner of War Information Bureau, statement by Boatswain M. Binder, July 31, 1946.

- *PS 5: Amagi Maru*
    From: Soerabaja, Dutch East Indies, April 1943
    Destination: Haroekoe, Ceram Island, Dutch East Indies, 17 days later
    Aboard: 2,000 POWs
    Special source: Captain Korteweg, *DE 1000 van Amahei*, 1946.

- *PS 6: Argentina Maru*
    From: Guam Island, January 10, 1942
    Destination: Japan, January 16, 1942
    Aboard: over 400 POWs from Guam

Specific source: E. Bartlett Kerr, *Surrender and Survival*, New York, 1985.

- **PS 7: *Arisan Maru* (6,886 BRT)**
  From: Manila, October 10, 1944
  Destination: Japan
  Aboard: ±1,800 American POWs
  Sunk: torpedoed (3 torpedoes) east of Hong Kong on October 24, 1944, by *USS Snook* (Shark?)
  Casualties: about 1,792
  Note: Only eight men survived the sinking. Five of them, while floating in the waters, came across a life boat, then a mast and sails, then a five-gallon keg with drinking water and then a tin box filled with biscuits. The story becomes more unbelievable: In typhoon weather the men raised the sail (the rigging of a sail in typhoon weather is against all navy instructions) and covered 300 miles. With some knowledge of astronomy, they reached the coast of China, amazingly in an area where there were no Japanese.
  "Disembarking their boat, these five physical wrecks walked down the main street of a city of 150,000 people just like they came into this world—naked, hungry and weak." These men eventually reached the United States. Three other survivors of the *Arisan Maru* were picked up by the Japanese and interned in Formosa. One of them died a short time later.
  Specific sources: 1. Calvin Graef (one of the five survivors), testimony to the Office of the Provost Marshall General.
  2. Manny Lawton, *Some Survived*, Chapel Hill, 1984.
  3. E. Bartlett Kerr, *Surrender and Survival*, New York, 1985.

- **PS 8: *Asaka Maru***
  From: Singapore, July 4, 1942
  Destination: Japan
  Aboard: 700 POWs
  Sunk: shipwrecked in a typhoon, August 13, 1942, on an island of the Bashee Group, south of Formosa
  Casualties: unknown, but can be assumed to be few
  Note: After floating around for three days, the Japanese crew and guards and the POWs were picked up by Japanese destroyers and taken to Kilung, Formosa. The POWs were subsequently transported by the *Hakusan Maru* (PS 18) to Japan.
  Special source: Ronald Hastain, *White Coolie*, London, 1947.

- *PS 9: Benjo Maru* (so called by the POWs because of the difficulties of going *benjo* [going to the toilet])
    From: Manila, January 1945
    Destination: Japan
    Aboard: about 230 American POWs
    Specific source: E. Bartlett Kerr, *Surrender and Survival*, New York, 1985.

- *PS 10: Brazil Maru*
    From: Lingayen Gulf, the Philippines, December 27, 1944
    Destination: Japan
    Aboard: 1,105 of the 1,341 survivors of the PS 38 *Oryoku Maru* disaster (236 survivors embarked on the *Enoura Maru*, PS 14).
    Note: En route to Japan, the *Brazil Maru* and the *Enoura Maru* traveled via Takao, Formosa, where they arrived on December 31, 1944. On January 8, 1945, American navy planes attacked Takao Harbor. The *Enoura Maru* was hit. It is not known how many were actually on board the *Enoura Maru* and how many survivors of this ship were transferred to the *Brazil Maru*. The final numbers of survivors and those who perished are also not known for certain. Whatever data there are are listed under PS 38, *Oryoku Maru*.

- *PS 11: Coral Maru*
    From: Manila, October 1943
    Destination: most likely Japan
    Aboard: about 800 POWs
    Note: No other information

- *PS 12: Dai Nichi Maru*
    From: Singapore, October 30, 1942
    Destination: Moji, Japan, November 24, 1942
    Aboard: About 500 Dutch and British POWs from PS 55, the *Yoshida Maru*, plus an unknown number from the Singapore camp
    Note: The ship sailed via Saigon, where it arrived on Tuesday, November 3, 1942. In mid–November it left for Takao, Formosa, where it stayed for three days and three nights. The total journey to Japan was almost one month.
    Specific source: Sir John Fletcher-Cooke, *The Emperor's Guests*, London, 1971/1982.

- *PS 13: England Maru*
    Aboard: about 1,000 POWs
    Note: No other information

The Prison Ships: The Overseas Transports 157

- *PS 14: Enoura Maru*
  From: San Fernando, the Philippines, December 27, 1944
  Destination: Japan
  Aboard: 236 survivors from the *Oryoku Maru* (PS 38) disaster
  Note: En route to Japan, the ship arrived in Takao, Formosa, on December 31, 1944. On January 8, 1945, it was attacked by U.S. Navy planes. The ship was hit several times, and the casualties were heavy. Survivors were transferred to the *Brazil Maru* for further transportation to Japan. The numbers listed in the various accounts and those in the report of the Liaison and Research Branch, American Prisoners of War Information Bureau, do not coincide.

- *PS 15: Fukai Maru*
  From: Singapore, August 16, 1942
  Destination: Takao, Formosa, August 29, 1942
  Aboard: High-ranking military personnel and civilian officials from Malaya and Singapore
  Note: No other information

- *PS 16: Fuku Maru* (also listed as *Hofuku Maru*, *Toyofuku Maru*, and *Fuji Maru*—5,000 BRT)
  From: Manila, September 20, 1944
  Destination: most likely Japan
  Aboard: 1,289: 213 Dutch and 1,076 British POWs
  Sunk: by Navy dive bombers on September 21, 1944, near San Narciso in Subic Bay
  Casualties: 1,226: 193 Dutch and 1,033 British
  Note: The 63 survivors were later taken aboard the *Oryoku Maru* (PS 38) on December 13, 1944; that ship was also sunk.
  Specific source: RvO IC 6779.

- *PS 17: Fukuji Maru*
  From: Moji, Japan, November 9, 1944
  Destination: Fusan, Manchuria
  Aboard: 354 high-ranking military officers and civilians
  Note: No other information
  Specific source: Colonel William C. Braly, *The Hard Way Home*, Washington, DC, 1947.

- *PS 18: Hakusan Maru*
  From: Kilung, Formosa
  Destination: Japan
  Aboard: about 700 POWs taken from the damaged PS 8 *Asaka Maru*.

- *PS 19: Haru Maru*
    From: Manila, October 3, 1944
    Destination: Takao, Formosa, October 25, 1944
    Aboard: about 1,100 American POWs
    Note: POWs boarded the ship on October 1, 1944, and were put in two holds—one partially filled with coal and the other with horse manure. Only four buckets were available for human waste. The ship stopped in Hong Kong on October 13, 1944. When it arrived in Takao, Formosa, 60 men had died. The survivors of the PS 7 *Arisan Maru* were added to this transport.

From Dr. Julien M. Goodman's diary:

> October 8, 1944: Hatred among the men is becoming more and more evident and bitter in the hold. A week with no rest, insufficient water and squatting in a hollow scooped out of coal changes anyone into an animal. There have been five deaths from exhaustion coupled with other things, since last night. Good Lord, how long? How long?

Specific sources: 1. Dr. Julien M. Goodman, *M.D.P.O.W.*, New York, 1972.
2. E. Bartlett Kerr, *Surrender and Survival*, New York, 1985.

- *PS 20: Harukiku Maru* (3,040 BRT)
    From: Medan, East Sumatra (Dutch East Indies)
    Destination: Singapore
    Aboard: Unknown number of POWs
    Sunk: torpedoed in Malacca Strait on June 26, 1944, by HMS *Truculent*
    Casualties: about 178
    Specific source: RvO IC 3155.

- *PS 21: Junyo Maru* (5,015 BRT)
    From: Batavia, West Java, September 15–16, 1944
    Destination: Padang, West Sumatra
    Aboard: 2,200—about 1,700 Dutch, British, Australian POWs; 14 American POWs; and 506 Ambonese and Menadonese (Indonesian) POWs—and about 4,320 Javanese conscript laborers (native prisoners).
    Sunk: torpedoed on September 18, 1944, west of Benkulen, West Sumatra, by HMS *Tradewind*, under the command of Captain Maydon.

Note: Here the author wishes to insert his personal observations. The *Junyo Maru* disaster has been the least reported in the annals of POW history. It was the largest maritime disaster in world history: 5,640 men lost their lives in a single shipwreck. Why then has history paid little attention to this occurrence? Could it be because more than two-thirds of the victims were Indonesian natives, and not westerners? There is no way to answer these questions. The author himself is one of the few remaining survivors of the *Junyo Maru* sinking.

The following figures speak for themselves:

POWs aboard:	2,200	died 1,520	survived 680
Laborers:	4,320	died 4,120	survived 200
Total	6,520	died 5,640	survived 880

There are a couple of interesting facts connected with the *Junyo Maru*. First, on only one occasion did the Japanese ever issue a "death certificate" on a drowned POW—to the family of merchant marine Philip McKeever. Second, Captain Maydon, commander of the submarine *Tradewind*, discovered only in 1962 that he had torpedoed a ship loaded not only with cargo, but with prisoners.

From a letter by Captain Maydon to George Duffy, ex–POW and merchant marine officer in Pakanbaroe camp:

> Do you know what was the cargo of this vessel? Did she have on board any Allied prisoners of war? We were often anxious that we might scupper our own people but you could not stop to ask.

To which letter Duffy replied:

> Actually, it seems incredible that, throughout all of the years since the war's end, you have learned nothing of *Junyo Maru*. For you see, your fears "that we might scupper our own people" were realized that afternoon off the Sumatra coast. *Junyo Maru* was carrying prisoners of war.

- *PS 22: Kachidoki Maru* (10,509 BRT)
  From: Singapore
  Destination: Most likely Japan
  Aboard: about 900 British POWs
  Sunk: torpedoed near Hainan Island on September 5, 1944, by USS *Pampanito*
  Casualties: about 400

Specific source: Joan and Clay Blair, *Return from the River Kwai*, New York, 1979.

- *PS 23: Kamakura Maru* (15,000 BRT)
  From: Singapore, November 29, 1942
  Destination: Japan, December 8, 1942
  Aboard: about 2,200: about 563 Australian, 500 American, 950 Dutch, and 200 British POWs

- *PS 24: King Kong Maru* (5,000 BRT)
  From: Batavia, West Java, October 8, 1942
  Destination: Singapore, October 11, 1942
  Aboard: about 1,500 POWs
  Note: In Singapore, the party was augmented by about 300 men and transported to Moulmein, Burma (see PS 30, *Mayebassi Maru*, and PS 54, *Yinagata Maru*).
  Specific source: Rohan D. Rivett, *Behind Bamboo*, Sydney, 1947.

- *PS 25: Kurimata Maru*
  From: Soerabaja, East Java, April 22, 1943
  Destination: Ambon, the Moluccas, April 29, 1943
  Aboard: about 1,500 POWs
  Specific source: Captain Korteweg, *DE 1000 van Amahei*, Amsterdam, 1946

- *PS 26: Kyokko Maru*
  From: Singapore, April 26, 1943
  Destination: Japan, May 21, 1943
  Aboard: 1,500 Dutch, 300 British, and 200 Australian POWs

- *PS 27: Lisbon Maru* (7,053 BRT)
  From: Hong Kong, September 25, 1942
  Destination: Japan
  Aboard: 1,816 British POWs
  Sunk: torpedoed on October 2, 1942, near Hong Kong by USS *Grouper* under the command of Lieutenant Commander Rob McGregor
  Casualties: 846
  Note: The 970 survivors were assembled in Shanghai and were then transported by PS 43, the *Shinsei Maru*, to Japan. Six other survivors managed to get picked up by Chinese junks; they subsequently reached the United States.
  Specific sources: 1. Lord Russell of Liverpool, *The Knights of Bushido*, London, 1958.

2. Tim Carew, *Hostages to Fortune*, London, 1971.

- *PS 28: Maros Maru* (600 BRT)
  From: Ambon, the Moluccas, September 17, 1944
  Destination: Soerabaja, East Java
  Aboard: about 500 British and Dutch POWs—about 150 more were picked up en route
  Note: The ship had to lay over for 40 days in Makassar, South Celebes, for repairs. For 40 days the men were not allowed to leave the ship.
  Specific sources: 1. Lord Russell of Liverpool, *The Knights of Bushido*, London, 1958.
  2. Captain Korteweg, *De 1000 van Amahei*, Amsterdam, 1946.

- *PS 29: Canadian Inventor*, or *Matti Matti Maru*
  From: Manila, July 1944
  Destination: Japan, September 1, 1944—the longest journey of any prison ship: more than 60 days
  Aboard: 500 American POWs from Davao and 500 from Cabanatuan-Bilibid camps
  Specific source: E. Bartlett Kerr, *Surrender and Survival*, New York, 1985.

- *PS 30: Mayebassi Maru*
  From: Singapore, end of 1942
  Destination: Moulmein, Burma
  Aboard: the 1,500 POWs from the PS 24, the *King Kong Maru*, and another 300 from the Singapore camp. In Moulmein, POWs were transferred to PS 54, *Yinagata Maru*.

- *PS 31: Montevideo Maru* (7,267 BRT)
  From: Rabaul, New Britain
  Destination: unknown
  Aboard: about 1,050 POWs and civilians
  Sunk: torpedoed on July 1, 1942, near Luzon
  Casualties: about 1,035

- *PS 32: Nagato Maru*
  From: Manila, November 7, 1942
  Destination: Japan, November 25, 1942
  Aboard: about 1,700 American POWs

Casualties: 157 men: 7 men died en route and 150 dying men were left on the docks in Moji, Japan, and were never seen again

Specific sources: 1. Lieutenants Edward Erickson and Robert Powell, U.S. Army Air Corps, and Lieutenant Frank Burwell, U.S. Army, Packet No. 10, p. 34, American Ex-POWs, Inc.
2. E. Bartlett Kerr, *Surrender and Survival*, New York, 1985.
3. Colonel E. B. Miller, Bataan, *Uncensored*, 1949.
4. John S. Coleman, *Bataan and Beyond*, 1978.

- PS 33: *Natoru Maru*
  From: New Britain, July 15, 1942
  Destination: Yokohama, Japan
  Aboard: 60 POWs and 19 women, including 6 Australian Army nurses

- PS 34: *Nissyo Maru*
  From: Manila, July 17, 1944
  Destination: Japan
  Aboard: about 1,500 American POWs
  Note: about 1,000 men were put in the aft hold and about 500 were put into one small midship hold.

- PS 35: *Nitta Maru*
  From: Wake Island, January 12, 1942
  Destination: Yokohama, Japan, January 18, 1942
  Aboard: 489 POWs and 746 civilians
  Note: The ship laid over for two days in Japan and continued its voyage to Shanghai, China—a two-day journey. Special "instructions" were issued to each prisoner, that "talking without permission or raising the voice" would be punished with immediate death. On the second day out from Yokohama, Captain Saito—the Japanese officer in charge—ordered five Americans to be executed by beheading with the sword. Before the execution, he read the following statement: "Since you have committed a crime, it will do no good to the world to let you live. I hope you will find happiness in the next world. When you are born again, I hope you will become peace-loving citizens."
  Special sources: 1. Lord Russell of Liverpool, *The Knights of Bushido*, London, 1958.
  2. E. Bartlett Kerr, *Surrender and Survival*, New York, 1985.

- *PS 36: Nitimei Maru* (4,074 BRT)
  From: Singapore, January 10, 1943
  Destination: Moulmein-Rangoon, Burma
  Aboard: about 1,000 POWs
  Sunk: attacked by Allied planes on January 15, 1943, about 80 miles from the Burma coast in Martaban Bay.
  Casualties: about 35

- *PS 37: Noto Maru*
  From: Manila, September 1944
  Destination: Japan
  Aboard: 985–1,035 POWs
  Specific source: E. Bartlett Kerr, *Surrender and Survival*, New York, 1985.

- *PS 38: Oryoku Maru* (7,000 BRT)
  From: Manila, December 14, 1944
  Destination: Japan
  Aboard: 1,619 American POWs
  Sunk: bombed by U.S. planes off Bataan Peninsula on December 15, 1944
  Casualties: 1,122, including those who died when they were attacked a second time while on PS 14, the *Enoura Maru*, Takao harbor, Formosa
  Note: This ship has been written about more than any other prison ship. The 1,341 men who survived the sinking of the *Oryoku Maru* were divided into two groups. One group, of about 235 men, were placed on PS 10, the *Brazil Maru*. The second group, of about 1,000 men, went aboard PS 14, the *Enoura Maru*. The *Oryoku Maru* had been used in October 1944 before her demise for the transportation of high-ranking military officers and civilian authorities from Formosa to Manchuria. "As we marched off," wrote Col. William C. Braly, "I took one last look at our most recent hate, the *Oryoku Maru*, little dreaming of the horror that was awaiting her POW passengers on her next trip."
  Specific sources: 1. Reports of the American Prisoners Liaison and Research Branch, American POW Information Bureau, July 31, 1946.
  2. Major G. J. Anloff, "I Was on the Oryoku Maru," *Ex-POW Bulletin*, September 1949.
  3. "Forty Nine Days in Hell: The Story of the Oryoku Maru," *Ex-POW Bulletin*, September 1952 through May 1953.

4. E. Bartlett Kerr, *Surrender and Survival*, New York, 1985.
5. Colonel William C. Braly, *The Hard Way Home*, Washington, DC, 1947.
6. Manny Lawton, *Some Survived*, Chapel Hill, 1984.

- PS 39: *Rio de Janeiro Maru*
  From: Makassar, South Celebes, October 2, 1943
  Destination: Batavia, West Java, October 5, 1943
  Aboard: 200 POWs
  Note: The following observation was made by one of the POWs on arriving at Batavia's harbor: "The harbor was empty, completely devoid of shipping, except for our own transport and a salvaged wreck rotting with rust. They've lost the war. The end is only a matter of time."
  Specific source: C. T. Cooper and D. Holman, *Ordeal in the Sun*, London, 1963.

- PS 40: *Ryukyu Maru*
  From: unknown
  Destination: unknown
  Aboard: unknown
  Sunk: torpedoed on November 17, 1943, west of Timor Island
  Casualties: about 41 (?)

- PS 41: *Rokyo Maru* (9,419 BRT)
  From: Singapore
  Destination: Most likely Japan
  Aboard: about 1,318 British and American POWs
  Sunk: torpedoed on September 5, 1944, near Hainan Island by USS *Sealion* — the same day as PS 22, the *Kachidoki Maru*
  Casualties: about 1,159
  Specific source: Joan and Clay Blair, *Return from the River Kwai*, New York, 1979.

- PS 42: *Shinsei Maru*
  From: Shanghai, October 5, 1942
  Destination: Japan
  Aboard: 840 British POWs, survivors from PS 27, the *Lisbon Maru*

- PS 43: *Shinyo Maru*
  From: Zamboanga, Mindanao Island, the Philippines, September 3, 1944.

Destination: most likely Japan
Aboard: 750 American POWs
Sunk: torpedoed on September 7, 1944, at Sindangan Point by USS *Paddle*.
Casualties: 667 men
Specific sources: 1. Major Manny Lawton and Master Sergeant George Robinett, *The Japanese Story*, Packet No. 10, American Ex-POWs, Inc.
2. E. Bartlett Kerr, *Surrender and Survival*, New York, 1985.

* *PS 44: Singapore Maru* (5,800 BRT)
  From: Singapore, October–November, 1942
  Destination: Japan, November 20, 1942
  Aboard: 1,100 POWs
  Casualties: 240 men: 60 men died en route and about another 180 men died within a few weeks of their arrival.
  Specific source: Lord Russell of Liverpool, *The Knights of Bushido*, London, 1958.

* *PS 45: Suez Maru* (4,646 BRT)
  From: Ambon Island, the Moluccas, November 1943
  Destination: Soerabaja, East Java
  Aboard: about 1,150 POWs
  Sunk: torpedoed on November 29, 1943, near Kamean Islands by USS *Bonefish*.
  Casualties: about 540 men
  Specific source: Captain Korteweg, *De 1000 van Amahei*, Amsterdam, 1946.

* *PS 46: Taga Maru*
  From: Manila, September 1943
  Destination: Japan
  Aboard: about 850 American POWs
  Casualties: about 70 men died en route

* *PS 47: Tango Maru*
  From: unknown
  Destination: unknown
  Aboard: about 3,500 POWs
  Sunk: torpedoed on February 25, 1944, east of Java
  Casualties: about 3,000 men

- *PS 48: Thames Maru* (5,000 BRT)
    From: Singapore, May 5, 1943
    Destination: Babelthuap Island, one of the Palau Islands, north of New Guinea, June 8, 1943
    Aboard: 2,000 Indian POWs and 150 Indonesian prisoners
    Casualties: about 200 men died en route
    Specific sources: 1. Lord Russell of Liverpool, *The Knights of Bushido*, London, 1958.
    2. Lieutenant Colonel Colin Sleeman, *The Trial of Gozawa Sadaichi and Nine Others*, London, 1948.

- *PS 49: Tomohoku Maru* (6,780 BRT)
    From: Takao, Formosa
    Destination: Japan
    Aboard: 772 POWs: 267 Australian, 196 British, 43 Americans, and 266 Dutch
    Sunk: torpedoed on June 24, 1944, near Nagasaki by USS *Tang*
    Casualties: 559 men: 195 Australian, 154 British, 29 American, and 181 Dutch

- *PS 50: Tottori Maru*
    From: Manila, October 8, 1942
    Destination: Pusan, Korea, November 8, 1942
    Aboard: 1,930 POWs
    Casualties: 10
    Specific sources: 1. Provost Marshall General, Packet No. 10, p. 34, American Ex-POWs, Inc.
    2. E. Bartlett Kerr, *Surrender and Survival*, New York, 1985.

- *PS 51: Toyama Maru*
    From: Hong Kong, December 1942
    Destination: Japan
    Aboard: Canadian POWs

- *PS 52: Umeda Maru*
    From: Manila, November 7, 1942
    Destination: Japan, November 25, 1942
    Aboard: about 1,500 American POWs
    Casualties: about 15
    Specific source: Lieutenant Samuel Goldblith, Packet No. 10, American Ex-POWs, Inc.

- *PS 53: Weills Maru*
  From: Singapore, May 16, 1943
  Destination: Japan, July 7, 1943
  Aboard: about 950 POWs: 300 Australian, 600 British, and 50 American

- *PS 54: Yashu Maru*
  From: Davao Island, the Philippines, June 6, 1944
  Destination: Zamboanga, Cebu Island, and then to Manila, June 26, 1944
  Aboard: about 1,240 POWs
  Specific source: E. Bartlett Kerr, *Surrender and Survival*, New York, 1985.

- *PS 55: Yinagata Maru*
  From: Rangoon
  Destination: Moulmein, Burma
  Aboard: 1,799 POWs from PS 30, the *Mayebassi Maru*

- *PS 56: Yoshida Maru* (3,000 BRT)
  From: Batavia, West Java, October 22, 1942
  Destination: Singapore, October 25, 1942; on October 28, 1942, the men were transferred to PS 12, the *Dai Nichi Maru*.
  Aboard: 3,000 POWs and Javanese prisoners

Final Tally of the Prison Ships

	Ship	On Board	Sunk	Died	Departure
PS	1: Name unknown	772			6/1944
PS	2: Name unknown	74			12/1942
PS	3: Name unknown	1,000	9/22/1944	910	9/1944
PS	4: Name unknown	1,800	10/25/1944	1,796	10/1944
PS	5: *Amagi Maru*	2,000			4/1943
PS	6: *Argentina Maru*	400			1/1942
PS	7: *Arisan Maru*	1,800	10/24/1944	1,792	10/1944
PS	8: *Asaka Maru*	700	8/13/1942	50	7/1942
PS	9: *Benjo Maru*	230			1/1945
PS	10: *Brazil Maru*	236			12/1944
PS	11: *Coral Maru*	800			10/1943
PS	12: *Dai Nichi Maru*	1,000			10/1942
PS	13: *England Maru*	1,105			?
PS	14: *Enoura Maru*	1,105			1/1945
PS	15: *Fukai Maru*	?			8/1942
PS	16: *Fuku Maru*	1,289	9/21/1944	1,224	9/1944

Ship	On Board	Sunk	Died	Departure
PS 17: Fukuji Maru	354			11/1944
PS 18: Hakusan Maru	700			7/1942
PS 19: Haru Maru	1,100		60	10/1944
PS 20: Harukiku Maru	?	6/26/1944	178	6/1944
PS 21: Junyo Maru	6,520	9/18/1944	5,640	9/1944
PS 22: Kachidoki Maru	900	9/05/1944	400	9/1944
PS 23: Kamakura Maru	2,200			11/1942
PS 24: King Kong Maru	1,500			10/1942
PS 25: Kurimata Maru	1,500			4/1943
PS 26: Kyokko Maru	1,500			4/1943
PS 27: Lisbon Maru	1,815	10/02/1942	845	10/1942
PS 28: Maros Maru	650		250	9/1944
PS 29: Matti Matti Maru	1,000			7/1944
PS 30: Mayebassi Maru	1,800			1942
PS 31: Montevideo Maru	1,050	7/01/1942	1,035	7/1942
PS 32: Nagato Maru	1,700		160	11/1942
PS 33: Natoru Maru	79			7/1942
PS 34: Nissyo Maru	1,500			7/1944
PS 35: Nitta Maru	1,235			1/1942
PS 36: Nitimei Maru	1,000		35	1/1943
PS 37: Noto Maru	985			9/1944
PS 38: Oryoko Maru	1,619	12/15/1944	1,122	12/1944
PS 39: Rio de Janeiro Maru	200			10/1943
PS 40: Ryukyu Maru	?		41	11/1943
PS 41: Rokyo Maru	1,318	9/05/1944	1,159	9/1944
PS 42: Shinsei Maru	840			10/1942
PS 43: Shinyo Maru	750	9/07/1944	670	9/1944
PS 44: Singapore Maru	1,100		240	10/1942
PS 45: Suez Maru	1,150	11/29/1943	540	11/1943
PS 46: Taga Maru	850		70	9/1943
PS 47: Tango Maru	3,500	2/25/1944	3,000	2/1944
PS 48: Thames Maru	2,150		200	5/1943
PS 49: Tomohoku Maru	772	6/24/1944	559	6/1944
PS 50: Tottori Maru	1,930		10	10/1942
PS 51: Toyama Maru	?			12/1942
PS 52: Umeda Maru	1,500		15	11/1942
PS 53: Weills Maru	950			5/1943
PS 54: Yashu Maru	1,240			6/1944
PS 55: Yinagata Maru	1,800			1942
PS 56: Yoshida Maru	3,000			10/1942
	68,068		22,001	

NOTES

1. Maude Gallman Brown, "Prison Ships During the American Revolution," *Ex-POW Bulletin.* M.p., M.d.
2. Sir John Fletcher-Cooke, *The Emperor's Guests*, London, 1971/1972.

3. William R. Evans, *Soochow and the 4th Marines*, Rogue River, OR, 1987, p. 129.
4. Preston John Hubbard, *Apocalypse Undone*, New York, 1990, p. 164.
5. Tim Carew, *Hostages to Fortune*, London, 1971, p. 123.
6. Bernard Schoonenberg, *De Poorten der Hel* [The Gates of Hell], Bussum, the Netherlands, 1978, p. 171.
7. Manny Lawton, *Some Survived*, Chapel Hill, NC, 1984, p. 203.

SOURCES

Beets, N. *De Verre Oorlog*. Amsterdam, 1981.
Blair, Joan, and Clay Blair. *Return from the River Kwai*. New York, 1979.
Braly, Col. William C. *The Hard Way Home*. Washington, DC, 1947.
Brown, Lt. Col. Charles M. *The Oryoku Maru Story*. Magalia, CA, 1983.
Brugmans, Dr. I. J. *Nederlands Indie Onder Japanse Bezetting* [Dutch East Indies Under Japanese Occupation]. Franeker, the Netherlands, 1960.
Campbell, Jim. *I Survived a Hell Ship*. Sydney, 1951.
Carew, Tim. *Hostages to Fortune*. London, 1971.
Clarke, Hugh V. *A Life for Every Sleeper*. Sydney, 1986.
———. *Twilight Liberation*. Sydney, 1985.
Coleman, John S. *Bataan and Beyond*. 1978, M.p.
Cooper, C. T., and D. Holman. *Ordeal in the Sun*. London, 1963.
Erickson, Lt. Edward, and Robert Powell. *Hell Ship*. Packet No. 10, p. 34. American Ex-POWs, Inc.
Evans, William R. *Soochow and the 4th Marines*. Rogue River, OR, 1987.
Fletcher-Cooke, Sir John. *The Emperor's Guest*. London, 1982.
Fluckey, Captain Eugene B. *The Terrible Trek of the Submarine Barb*. New York, 1955.
Goodman, Julien M., MD. *M.D.P.O.W.* New York, 1972.
Hamilton, Geoffrey C. *The Sinking of the Lisbon Maru*. Hong Kong, 1966.
Harrison, K. *The Brave Japanese*. London, 1967.
Hartley, Peter. *Escape to Captivity*. London, 1952.
Hastain, Ronald. *White Coolie*. London, 1947.
Hubbard, Preston John. *Apocalypse Undone*. Nashville, TN, 1990.
Kerr, E. Bartlett. *Surrender and Survival*. New York, 1985.
Korteweg, Capt. *De 1000 van Amahei* [The 1,000 of Amahei]. Amsterdam, 1946.
Lawton, Manny. *Some Survived*. Chapel Hill, NC, 1984.
Melis, Ed, et al. *Eresaluut Boven Massagraf* [Honor Salute over a Mass Grave]. Nijmegen, the Netherlands, 1984.
Miller, Col. E. B. *Bataan Uncensored*. 1949, M.p.
Neumann, H., and E. van Witsen. *De Pakanbaroe Spoorweg* [The Pakanbaru Railroad]. Leerdam, the Netherlands, 1982.
Nordquist, Ernest. *Our Paradise: A GI's War Diary*. Hancock, 1989.
Rivett, Rohan D. *Behind Bamboo*. Sydney, 1947.
Russell, Lord of Liverpool. *The Knights of Bushido*. London, 1958.
Scoonenberg, B. H. *De Poorten der Hel* [The Gates of Hell]. Bussum, the Netherlands, 1978.
Sleeman, Lt. Col. (retired) Colin. *Trial of Gozawa Sadaichi and Nine Others*. London, 1948.
Stulemeyer, J. E. *Kamptoestanden in Nederlands Oost Indie*. Amsterdam, 1978.

Sweeting, A. J. "Montevideo Maru: Myth or Merchantman?" *Australian Territories* (February 1961), pp. 36–38.
van Witsen, E. *Krijgsgevangenen in de Pacific Oorlog*. Franeker, the Netherlands, 1971.
Waldron, Ben D., and Emily Burneson. *Corregidor: From Paradise to Hell*. Freeman, 1980.
Wright, Lt. Gen. John M., Jr. *Captured on Corregidor*. Jefferson, NC , 1988.

OTHER SOURCES

Australian Archives, Melbourne, MP 1587/1, File 20S; MP 742/1, File 255/15/579; MP 1049/5, File 1951/2/99; MP 729/6, File 63/401/728.
Australian War Memorial, Canberra, CRS A2663, records file 1010/9/109.
Liaison and Research Branch, American Prisoner of War Information Bureau, Washington, DC, Office of the Provost Marshall General, Washington, DC.
Public Records Office, Kew Gardens, London, Secret Files C-10-F-24045 and Files FO-371/41791.
Rijksinstituut voor Oorlogsdocumentatie [Netherlands Institute for War Documentation], Amsterdam, the Netherlands—RvO IC 6884; unknown Maru, RvO IC 6779: Fuku Maru, RvO IC 3155: Harukiku Maru, RvO IC 015871; 015961; 029292; 010890–96; 010879–89; 000126–136/4272; 000387–8; 029410; 029411: Junyo Maru.
U.S. Naval Historical Center, Navy Yard, Washington DC. Reports on submarine activities: USS *Barb, Fulton, Growler, Pampanito, Queenfish, Stallion,* and *Tunny.*

Chapter 11
Prison Camps

Introduction

After Japan had occupied large parts of Asia and all of Southeast Asia, it had no political, logical, or philosophical problems about how to handle the captured Allied forces: They were to become prisoners of war, locked up in camps behind barbed wire.

The location of the prison camps is known, but the exact number of POWs and internees held in these camps and of those who perished during captivity can only be estimated because records either were not kept or were lost or destroyed after the war. The Japanese tactics of frequently moving prisoners from one camp to another made record keeping by Allied camp leaders almost impossible (see the story of POW Bulcock's 15 moves later in this chapter). For example, of the 358 civilian internment centers in use throughout the Pacific area some were closed and some were opened, and some internees were moved from one camp to another, while others stayed behind. The chaos was oftentimes indescribable.

> Why a uniform policy was not adopted for the operation of all internment camps was beyond our comprehension. It seemed that each military district was a law unto itself and the commanding officer did as he pleased.[1]

The Japanese regulations on prisoners provided that barracks, schools, prisons, and other buildings were to be used as camps. In many larger cities in the Dutch East Indies, whole city blocks—whole neighborhoods—were surrounded by barbed wire and bamboo fences and civilian internees were herded into them for, as the Japanese called it, "protection of the civilians"; the camps were even called "protection centers."

In many instances, it was common practice for the prisoners to build their own camps from wood and bamboo, with coconut-leaf (or atap) roofs. Until the huts, barracks, or shelters were completed, the prisoners had to live in the open and were exposed to the weather at all times.

Sometimes the prisoners were spared the labor of building their own camp by taking over a site previously used by other prisoners. But this practice also had its disadvantages: The previous occupants, not knowing that fellow prisoners would occupy the huts or barracks, would strip the site clear of all useful items.

The 15 Moves of an Australian POW

Roy Bulcock, an Australian POW, together with a group of fellow prisoners (not always the same individuals), was moved 15 times from one camp to another and from one building to another in a camp. His group was never sent overseas, but they had to face the trauma of frequent packing and unpacking.

Bulcock described his experiences as a POW in his book, *Of Death But Once*:

- Between March 1942 and December 1942:
1. Racecourse camp, Tasikmalaja, West Java.
2. School buildings in Djokjakarta, Central Java.
3. Airfield in Djokjakarta.
4. Convention building in Soerabaja, East Java.
5. School compound in Soerabaja.

- Between January 1943 and December 1943:
6. Back to convention building in Soerabaja.
7. Military barracks in Tjimahi, West Java.
8. Prison in Bandoeng, West Java.
9. Military barracks in Batavia, West Java (cycle camp).
10. Makassar camp, farm plot, in Batavia.

- Between January 1944 and December 1944:
11. Back to military barracks (cycle camp), Batavia.
12. Prison camp in Bandoeng, West Java.

- Between January 1945 and December 1945:
13. Reform-school building in Bandoeng, West Java.
14. Military barracks (cycle camp), Batavia, West Java.
15. Jail in Bandoeng, West Java.

Bulcock said the following about his experience:

And so we say farewell to Java—the land of plenty where we starved—the land of riches where we lived in poverty—the country of happy people, where we were humiliated and enslaved—the last paradise, which we found a hell—in short: the green land, where we were browned off.[2]

Locations of Prison Camps and the Japanese Command Structure

Camp Locations: General

From the autumn of 1942 to the end of 1944, the Japanese moved nearly 70,000 American and other Allied POWs from the Philippines, Malaya, and other southern areas to the north, principally to camps in Japan. Nearly half of the POWs were being held in Japan proper by the end of the war.

Outside Japan, the Hoten camp near Mukden, Manchuria, and a camp near Shanghai held POWs. Similar groups, mostly of British prisoners along with a few Americans, were held in camps in Korea, Hong Kong, and Formosa. The remainder of the prisoners—British, Dutch, Australian, and Americans—were held in numerous locations in French Indochina, Siam, Burma, Malaya, Singapore, and the Dutch East Indies.

In December 1941, for the first time in U.S. history, a large group of civilians was interned in the Philippines. Many of these civilians had a vested interest in the future of the islands, and some were owners of factories and businesses or were professionally employed. The American internees all faced three years of mental deprivation, abuse, and slow torture.

In China, the majority of civilian internees were held in four camps: Lunghwa, Weihsien, Chapei, and Pootung.

Those interned in the Dutch East Indies were the largest group of civilian internees.

Japanese Command Structure and Control of Prison Camps

In Japan proper the Ministry of Internal Affairs was charged with the supervision of all foreign nationals and the internment and prison camps. The POW camps were controlled by the Ministry of Defense, Bureau of Military Affairs.

In Korea and Formosa, this duty was assigned to the Ministry of Overseas Territories. The situation in China was more confusing; the supervision of the camps was left entirely to Japanese civilians and military forces reporting to the Japanese consul-general.

In the Southern Territories—everything south of Formosa and China—the Ministry of Defense, the War Department, was assigned all the administrative and supervisory duties regarding all prison camps.

The military government that was organized in the occupied territories instituted a special section that was responsible for the administration and supervision of all civilian internment centers. In 1944, this supervision was absorbed by the army command structure; the actual guard duties of some camps were performed by local policemen.

Imperial decree No. 1246 of December 27, 1941, established the Bureau of Information on POWs. Facts and data on POWs were transmitted by this department to the International Red Cross.

On March 31, 1942, the Bureau for Control and Administration of Prisoners of War was established as a subdepartment of the Bureau of Military Affairs.

The dissemination of information, data, and orders up and down the military hierarchical line was confusing, slow, and disorganized. It took months for the extensive and detailed information on the camps and conditions of the prisoners to reach Tokyo, where they were most likely not intensively studied because of their outdatedness.

The civilian camps, which were under the management of the military government from 1942, came under the jurisdiction of the army by an imperial order dated November 7, 1943. Here again there were inconsistencies: Hong Kong was under army control from January 1944, whereas the Philippines were under army control from February 1944, and Java, Sumatra, and Malay from April 1944.

The rules and instructions coming from Tokyo had to travel an extensive chain of command that was not adequately controlled by Tokyo. Camp commanders, for example, had the power to choose who was going "on transport" and who was not. All they needed was a request from headquarters in Singapore.

Interrogation of Major General Masatoshi Saito

The following is from the interrogation of Major General Masatoshi Saito, on May 1, 1946, in answer to the question, "Who ordered the deportation of POWs from Java?"

> The Minister of War himself. The order was transferred to the Army commanders, who then relayed them to the commanders assigned to the POWs. The procedure was as follows: Field Marshall Terauchi received his orders from the Minister in Tokyo. He then relayed this order to the Akatsuki Butai [Maritime Department of the Army] for shipping accommodation and the orders to have available a specific number of POWs. These orders were distributed to the various camp commanders.[3]

Organization of a POW Camp

The following report, made after the war, illustrates the organization of camps in Java and the responsibilities of the guards.

Report from a Korean official—November 1946: The head of the POW camps was responsible for the overall command. In March 1944, he also became responsible for the civilian internment centers. He was assisted by a field officer, and other officers and NCOs in the following departments:

a) Two officers handled the administration and other personal affairs of the Japanese military and civilian camp personnel.

b) The POW department—and also later the civilian internees—handled: movement of prisoners; distribution of special identifications to certain prisoners; handling of affairs concerning deceased prisoners; execution of labor plans and work details for prisoners.

c) The Army Service Corps took care of the Japanese camp personnel. It was also responsible for paying wages to the prisoners for work and jobs done; for the purchase and distribution of food rations, vegetables and cooking fuel; for the distribution and mending of clothes and the administration and management of confiscated items.

d) The Medical Department was not only responsible for the care of the Japanese personnel, but also of the hospital for the prisoners, replenishment of medicines, for determining and registering the cause of death of a prisoner and issuing death certificates and for the funeral or cremation.

In each department there were two to three NCOs doing the work, mostly Koreans.

The whole organization was under the command of the 16th Army. Headquarters was located in Batavia, with branches in Bandoeng and Tjilatjap—West Java—and Soerabaja and Malang—East Java.[4]

The Korean Guards

From the testimony of a translator, July 1947:

In August 1942 the guarding of POWs and internees in Java and elsewhere was taken over by Koreans. They were basically civilian officials in the Japanese army, but they acted as if they were regular Japanese soldiers and were introduced to the captives as such by the Japanese officers and NCOs.

Korea became part of Japan in 1910. When Southwest Asia was occupied by the Japanese, the Koreans were promised that they could participate actively in governing the territories. Instead, all they were assigned to do was guard duties of prison and internment camps on a two-year contract. When this contract expired, they expected to return home. This did not happen, and the Koreans lost faith in and respect for the Japanese. They turned their hostility towards the prisoners and internees and forced many of them to sell their valuables, such as watches, fountain pens, rings, etc., for laughably low prices. When the captives resisted they were beaten and tortured under the pretext of "not following Japanese rules."[5]

Note: Research is limited regarding the role of the Koreans as guards of prison camps and civilian internment centers.

Often in the literature the Japanese have been accused of cruelties and atrocities against their captives. In many books by former POWs and internees, however, the authors complain about the attitude and behavior of the Korean guards. In local war crime trials Korean guards were indicted and sentenced for their atrocities against the prisoners.

In many instances the source of the Koreans' behavior can be traced back to their "masters": the Japanese. This was, in the eyes of many captives, not a valid excuse for cruel behavior against them.

The Japanese High Command

Japanese Prime Minister
October 18, 1941–July 22, 1944   General Hideki Tojo
July 22, 1944–April 7, 1945   Kuniaki Koiso
April 7, 1945–August 17, 1945   Admiral Kantaro Suzuki
After August 17, 1945   General Higasikumi

Minister of War (Defense)
October 18, 1941–July 22, 1944   General Hideki Tojo
July 22, 1944–April 7, 1945   Field Marshal Hajemei Sugiyama
April 7, 1945–August 13, 1945   General Korechika Anami
August 13, 1945–August 17, 1945   Lieutenant General Sadamu Shimomura
After August 17, 1945   General Higasikumi

Chief of Staff, Japanese Imperial Army
October 3, 1940–February 18, 1944   Field Marshal Sugiyama
February 18, 1944–July 18, 1944   General Hideki Tojo
July 18, 1944–September 1945   Yoshijiro Umezu

Minister of the Navy
October 18, 1941–July 17, 1944   Admiral Shigetaro Shimada
July 17, 1944–July 22, 1944   Admiral Naokuni Nomura
July 22, 1944–August 17, 1945   Admiral Mitsumasa Yomai

Minister of Greater East Asia
November 1, 1942–July 22, 1944   Kazuo Aoki
July 22, 1944–April 7, 1945   Mamoru Shigemitzu
April 7, 1945–April 9, 1945   Admiral Kantoro Suzuki
April 9, 1945–August 17, 1945   Shigenori Togo

Minister of Foreign Affairs
August 17, 1945 and beyond   Mamoru Shigemitzu

Supreme Commander, Southern Territories
(all territories except China and Manchuria)
October 1941–September 1945   Field Marshal Hisaichi Terauchi
   Headquarters:
      October 1941–1942:   Saigon

March 1942–June 1944:   Singapore
June 1944–November 1944:   Manila
November 1944–September 1945:   Saigon

Chief of Staff of the Southern Armies
November 1941–July 1942   Lieutenant General Osamu Tsukada
July 1942–May 1943   Lieutenant General Shigenori Kuroda
May 1943–March 1944   Lieutenant General Shigenori Kuroda
March 17, 1944–December 1944   Lieutenant General Minoru Imura
December 1944–September 1945   Lieutenant General Takazo Numata

Supreme Commander, Seventh Army—Singapore
March 21, 1944–April 7, 1945   General Kenji Doihara
April 7, 1945–September 12, 1945   General Seishiro Itagaki

Commander in Chief, 16th Army—Java
March 1942–November 1942   Lieutenant General Hitoshi Imamura
November 1942–April 1945   Lieutenant General Kumakishi Harada
April 1945–September 1945   Lieutenant General Yosiuchi Nagano

Chief of Staff and Head of Military Rule
March 1942–May 1943   Lieutenant General Seisaburo Okazaki
May 1943–November 1944   Lieutenant General Shinsichiro Kokubu
November 1944–September 1945   Major General Moichiro Yamamoto

Commander in Chief, 25th Army—Sumatra
March 1942–March 1943   Lieutenant General Yaheita Saito
March 1943–September 1945   Lieutenant General Moritake Tanabe

Chief of Staff and Head of Military Rule
March 1942–October 1944   Lieutenant General Funio Shimura
October 1944–September 1945   Major General Yahagi

Navy Territories—Borneo, Celebes, and everything east of these islands—under command of the Southwest Fleet, with elements of the First, Second, and Third South fleets.

Commander Southwest Fleet, Headquarters: Makassar, South Celebes
April 1942–September 1942   Vice Admiral Ibo Takhahashi
September 1942–June 1944   Vice Admiral Shiru Takasu
June 1944–November 1944   Vice Admiral Gunichi Mimura
November 1944–August 1945   Vice Admiral Denshichi Ohkochi

Chief of Staff
April 1942–November 1942   Rear Admiral Toshihisa Nakamura
November 1942–February 1944   Rear Admiral Takeo Tada
February 1944–October 1944   Rear Admiral Hidemi Nisho
October 1944–August 1945   Rear Admiral Kaoru Arima

Commander, Second South Fleet, East Borneo, Java
April 1942–September 1942   Vice Admiral Ibo Takahashi

September 1942–April 1943   Vice Admiral Shiru Takasu
April 1943–September 1943   Vice Admiral Seiichi Iwamura
September 1943–June 1944   Vice Admiral Gunichi Mimura
June 1944–January 1945   Vice Admiral Shiro Kanase
January 1945–August 1945   Rear Admiral Yaichiro Shibata

Chief of Staff
April 1942–October 1942   Rear Admiral Toshihisa Nakamura
October 1942–May 1943   Rear Admiral Takeo Tada
May 1943–January 1945   Rear Admiral Akira Matsuzaki
January 1945–August 1945   Rear Admiral Shinsaburo Hase

Supreme Commander, Second Army, which moved in command position
October 1943–December 1943   Lieutenant General Ichiro Nanada
December 1943–August 1945   Lieutenant General Fusutaro Toshina

Chief of Staff
October 1943–December 1944   Lieutenant General Takazo Numata
December 1944–August 1945   Major General Tasao Fujizuka

POW Camps: General

For the most part, POWs in the Pacific theater of World War II faced much harsher conditions in the camps than did their counterparts in Europe. They also endured longer terms of imprisonment. The average length of captivity for a POW in the Pacific was 1,148 days, compared to 347 days in Europe.

The Japanese originally captured and interned about 192,600 Allied POWs: American, British, Dutch, Australian, and New Zealanders, plus native, indigenous prisoners.

Not all POWs were interrogated before entering the prison camps. When they were, the Japanese often used violence before, during and after the interviews to enforce their demands for accurate information.

Captivity usually began with a long march on foot carrying all baggage. Prisoners captured in small groups often had their valuables taken from them, whereas those surrendering in large units were better able to retain them. Although they did not realize it at the time, the clothes they were wearing and brought with them into camp were likely to have to last them the three or more years of their imprisonment. Prudence in selecting "kit" to take into the camps paid heavy dividends. Few, however, realized that relief was a number of years away.

The first living quarters allotted to newly captured POWs were usually the worst of their captivity. To some extent, this situation was due to the exigencies of war and in part, to the unpreparedness of the Japanese to accept the surrender of larger numbers of military men than they had anticipated. Frequently, the men were given no food at all during the first two to three days of captivity.

The brutality of the Japanese treatment of prisoners in general has been described in Chapter 2, but a detailed account by a physician—POW Major Livingstone P. Noell, Jr., Medical Corps, U.S. Army Air Force—provides some valuable reference information:

> During 34 ghastly months I saw every manifestation of dietary deficiency merely by looking at people around me—the terrible pain and toe-dragging gait of beriberi, the hemorrhages from scurvy, the mental stupor and hardened skin of pellagra, the barrel-like bloat and withered muscles of hypothermia.
>
> At first, malaria and dysentery plagues slaughtered our people. Quinine would have prevented the malaria deaths; sanitation alone, if we had been permitted to enforce it, would have wiped out the dysentery.
>
> The starvation program began its awful execution with the diseases of prolonged food deficiency. There was dry beriberi, bringing its burning, stinging and crawling sensation of the skin on legs and feet, its terrible painful neuritis, its paralysis of the muscles which lifts the foot [making] it necessary for those walking skeletons in our camp to take high steps to keep their toes from dragging. Also prevalent was the wet type of beriberi, bringing its dropsy, which waterlogs bulging legs, balloons abdomens and faces, and before death, effects a bloating of the entire body—excruciating penalties for lack of vitamin B_1, or thiamine chloride.
>
> Other diseases included pellagra and ariboflavinosis, which were seen with dermatitis, a colored or thickened skin, swelling of the tongue, diarrhea, mental confusion and, ultimately, dementia. Vitamin B_2 deficiency resulted in cracked lips, sores on the nose, and ulcers on the legs.
>
> Scurvy was caused by vitamin C deficiency and resulted in broken blood vessels, bleeding gums and the loss of teeth. Vitamin A deficiency resulted in ulcering and scarring of the eyes and ultimately, total blindness.[6]

Escapes

Some POWs asked themselves, "Where to escape to?" The whole of the Dutch East Indies was in Japanese hands, and the Indonesian people were not inclined to assist any subversive Allied actions, including escapees.

Siam, Burma, the Malay Peninsula, and Singapore were totally occupied by Japanese forces. In contrast to the Dutch East Indies [Indonesia], however, on the Malay Peninsula and in Singapore, a large segment of the indigenous population consisted of Chinese, of whom many were fervently anti–Japanese. Many of them are known to have performed underground activities against the Japanese. They helped the few Allied POWs who escaped by giving them weapons, food, and radio equipment.

Escape depended on a combination of magnificent courage, stupidity, and luck. Bates, Bradley, Chapman, Crawford, and Skidmore were some of the few who made it, and their exploits are described in the books they wrote.

Escape from territories in China was as difficult and perilous as anywhere else. The problem was basically fear. Although many native people in Malaya, Hong Kong, China, Borneo, and the Philippines were anti-Japanese, most of them were petrified of Japanese reprisals if it was discovered that they had assisted escaped POWs. The Japanese didn't blink an eye before wiping out whole villages as a mere punishment for aiding and abetting escaped prisoners.

But, just as some POWs in Malaya managed to escape successfully from their camps, so did a number of them in China and the Philippines.

One of the most spectacular escapes from a POW camp was on April 4, 1943, at the Davao Penal Colony on the island of Mindanao. Among those making the successful bid for freedom were Lieutenant Commander Melvyn H. McCoy, Captain Ed Dyess, Captain Austin Schofner, Lieutenant Michael Dobervitch, and Lieutenant Jack Hawkins. When these men arrived safely in Australia, they gave General MacArthur his first in-depth report on the atrocities committed by the Japanese against American and Filipino POWs. However, their information was not made public until the early months of 1945, for fear of spurring reprisals by the Japanese.

Another equally spectacular and dramatic escape was that of two groups of POWs from Sandakan camp in North Borneo. These men made their way successfully over water to friendly Filipino guerrillas on the southernmost Philippine islands. One group consisted of Jock McLaren, Jim Kennedy, and Rex Butler. In the other group were Walter Wallace, Ray Steel, Miles Gillon, Charlie Wagner, and Rex Blow. Their exploits have also been immortalized in a number of books.

The "No Escape" Document

The biggest initial problem the Japanese had with the POWs was the signing of the "no escape" document, which was met with massive refusals by the POWs resulting in subsequent harsh reprisals by the Japanese. To prevent further brutalities against the men, the officers finally relented and signed the document "under duress."

The Japanese thought it necessary to include Allied POWs in the administration and responsibility of their army. According to these rules, POWs were war booty and had basically no right to live. By signing the documents, the POWs became "real" POWs.

The following is an example of an order given by a Dutch senior officer to his men concerning the signing of the "no escape" document—an order he passed on from the Japanese command:

July 31, 1942:
1. Oath of loyalty forms are available in my office—they are in Japanese and Malay.
2. It states, "I, the undersigned, swear solemn loyalty and obedience to all orders given by the Japanese Army. Date. Name. Signature."
3. To be signed by August 1.
4. The consequences are very severe should you refuse to sign this form.[7]

A Little Propaganda

That the Japanese were not averse to presenting a "pretty picture" about the POWs for whom they were responsible can be learned from a radio program received by Allied listening posts. Most likely, the story refers to "Tjilatjap" camp on Java's south coast.

Domei Agency message intercepted by Allied listening posts—18 December 1942:

> At the edge of a beautiful coastal town is a prison camp, occupied by 2,000 prisoners of war. Just outside the camp is a "Waikiki beach," where trade winds and cool rains offer a paradise-like climate.
> Reveille is at 6:00 A.M. and the prisoners do light exercises at 6:30 A.M. Then, coffee and scrambled eggs are served. The officers study Japanese in the morning. The soldiers occupy their time with light labor, washing clothes and swimming.
> Lunch is followed by a two-hour siesta, after which the men do some more light work.
> Once in a while the prisoners are kept up to date with the latest news from the war fronts.
> On Sundays, the church services are followed by sports—soccer, basketball and the like. After dinner the prisoners are free to do as they wish. Bedtime is at ten o'clock.[8]

All POWs have wished that the treatment by their captors and the conditions were as described in this propaganda story. Their actual experiences belie this story.

Civilian Internment Centers: General

Introduction

Just as the internment of Allied soldiers could be considered complex because of the lack of immediately available facilities to lock up an unexpected number of 192,600 men, the internment of civilians was a massive undertaking for which the Japanese were also not prepared. Men, women, and children had to be interned because the Japanese were determined to get the civilians "off the streets" to wipe out any further bond or influence that still might exist between them and the local people.

The initial Japanese policy was to let the Allied citizens keep their money and personal belongings so that, as a group, they could stay alive in an assigned city block (or blocks) without any possibility of contact with the indigenous peoples.

This policy was based on the assumption that Japan would win a short war. When it became apparent that the war could go on for a long time, the Japanese simply dumped civilians behind guarded gates of certain city blocks, fenced in by barbed wire and bamboo matting, and left them to fend for themselves. This practice was followed primarily in the Dutch East Indies.

Others were locked up in a wide variety of camps—including old army barracks, schools, jails, and convents—in Japan, China, Manchuria, Malaya, Singapore, Burma, the Philippines, the Dutch East Indies, and wherever "white-skinned" people were still present.

There is not one consistent description of the internment of almost 131,000 men, women and children. The character of the internments depended upon the Japanese commander in each area.

The often arbitrary rules created chaos among the Westerners in the various Japanese occupied territories. The *general instructions* concerning correspondence with those outside the camps, for example, consisted of 19 different rules—all confusing and "strange":

> Instructions concerning correspondence:
>
> a) Standard sentences for postcards from internees:
>   1. I hope you are all well? How are the children? Do you have enough money to subsist?
>   2. We have a well-equipped hospital and a rest house.
>   3. The children are healthy and are very helpful.
>   4. Such and so have grown up; they remember you well.
>   5. Our camp is set up well and comfortably equipped.
>   6. We have a sewing club and we can all use the machines.
>   7. We receive an English newspaper and several local magazines which keep us up to date with what's happening.
>   8. We are allowed to grow our own vegetables and flowers if we want to. We enjoy the work in the open air.
>   9. I've received letters from home and all are doing well.
>   10. I long for the end of this miserable war and for my homecoming.
>   11. I think continually about you. How beautiful it would be to see each other again.
>   12. Take care of yourself and keep the faith.
>
> b) General instructions for the writing of postcards:
>   1. It is not allowed to write about military, political or economical affairs.

2. A prisoner may not correspond with another prisoner; a male internee not with another male internee, and similarly female internees with other female internees.
3. It is not allowed to use numbers, invisible ink or braille.
4. The name of the camp has to appear in code on the front of the card, such as "Java CP."
5. Write in Japanese or Malay. English is only allowed for destinations outside the territory.
6. Make a choice from the texts described above—which have to be used verbatim. Twenty "free" words may be added to that.
7. The cards have to be written on the back side parallel with the long side—in capital block letters only.[9]

Conditions in Civilian Internment Camps

Finding many camps scantily equipped for even the most elementary purposes, the internees used their skill and ingenuity to set up suitable kitchens, hospitals, and dispensaries; to improve toilet and plumbing facilities; and to build beds, furniture, stages, playgrounds, and many other things necessary to make their new homes reasonably livable.

In several camps gardens were planted, often under the direction of an agricultural expert, to provide fresh vegetables to supplement the internees' diets. For example, in one record month at Santo Tomas (Manila, the Philippines), 15,000 pounds of tolinum (a green similar to spinach) were harvested. All work in the camps was done by the internees themselves.

All the internment centers were crowded, resulting in a complete lack of privacy. The buildings in most camps were not designed for such a large number of people, and it was only through the constant efforts of the internees themselves that the camps were made passably comfortable.

Sleeping quarters were usually "dormitory" style, with only a minimum of space per person. In the camps where houses were available, several persons occupied the limited space. Beds or cots were brought to the camps by a few people when they entered; others managed to obtain beds after their entrance to the camps or built them from pieces of lumber scrounged from somewhere.

Depending upon the internment facility, toilet and bathing facilities, at first very inadequate, were gradually improved by the internees' plumbing and construction squads. Lines waiting for a bath were the rule in the early days and were common throughout the war in many camps.

By good fortune, most of the internment centers were favored by the presence of competent physicians among the internees. These physicians, working with a minimum of equipment and medical supplies, performed wonders in treating the sick.

Internees generally expressed concern over the lack of mail and cables from home, and the same lack of communication from the Far East was a matter of great anxiety to the internees' relatives and friends.

Internees, although occupied for several hours daily with the many tasks about the camps, had much free time. To relieve the monotony and boredom of existence, sports and recreation committees were organized for indoor and outdoor games, plays, musical entertainments, and various other forms of recreation. Educational committees organized schools not only for the children, but for adults as well.

Religious groups developed a well-rounded program of activities, including church services, prayer meetings, and discussion groups.

The extent of all these programs depended greatly, however, on the area in which the camp was located and the leniency or strictness of the specific Japanese commandant.

Explanation of Individual Listings

Sixteen locations on the individual listings of the camps are in the following sequence: Japan, Formosa, Korea, Manchuria, China and Hong Kong, French Indochina, Burma and Siam (the Burma-Siam railroad, Burma, and Siam), and the Philippines, Malaya and Singapore, Sumatra, Java, North Borneo and West Borneo, East and South Borneo, and other islands and territories.

In a map prepared by Frances Worthington Lipe based on documents from the National Archives and other sources, the locations of numerous camps and internment centers are identified. A listing of these camps and centers accompanies the map. Certain discrepancies between Lipe's listings and those compiled by this author could not be resolved.

This author followed Lipe's listings for camps and centers located in certain areas, including Japan, Korea, Formosa, and Manchuria. In these countries no foreigners were living outside the camps and centers, so there was no information to be added to what was provided by the prisoners and the Japanese.

In the other countries, however, such as the Philippines, the Dutch East Indies, Malaya, and Singapore, indigenous people who were loyal to their old colonial masters and who lived outside the camps and centers provided valuable information on camps and centers in addition to what was provided by the captives themselves. Therefore, for these countries, this author relied on a combination of data from various sources. The resulting compilation of information represents an attempt to provide the most accurate records possible of a chaotic situation.

The chapter is arranged by country or geographical area. Each section contains listings of individual POW camps located in that area, followed by a listing of the civilian internment centers. Each camp is numbered sequentially (POW1, POW2, etc.) as is each civilian internment center (CIC1, CIC2, etc.).

NOTES

1. R. Renton Hind, *Spirits Unbroken*, San Francisco, 1946, p. 62.
2. Roy Bulcock, *Of Death But Once*, Melbourne, 1947.
3. RvO IC 5278.
4. RvO IC 5252.
5. RvO IC 5251.
6. Gardner Hatch, ed., *American Ex-POW History Book*, Paducah, 1988, p. 34.
7. RvO IC 5256.
8. RvO IC 5260.
9. RvO IC 5264.

SOURCES, CAMPS: GENERAL

IMTFE 979: The fundamental principles of Japan's National Policy, August 11, 1936.
IMTFE 628: Outline of Japanese policy, September 28, 1940, and tentative plan for policy towards the Southern Regions, October 4, 1940.
IMTFE 878, 1169: Fundamental foreign tenets concerning education of the national policy, Imperial conference, November 5, 1941.
IMTFE 1167, 1169: General outline for hastening conclusion of the war against the United States, Great Britain, the Netherlands and the Chunking Regime, November 12, 1941.
IMTFE 877: Details of execution of administration of the Southern occupied territories, November 20, 1941.
IMTFE 1333A: Summarizes plan for the management of the South area, December 1941.
IMTFE 1332: Outline for the economic counterplans for the Southern area, December 12, 1941.
IMTFE 1334: The fundamental principles of the remedial measures for Southern regions to be occupied as a result of the Great Asia war and for land disposal within the Greater Asiatic Co-Prosperity Sphere, December 1941.
IMTFE record 27133 and on: Duties of the Ministry of Overseas Territories.
IMTFE record 49598: Supervision and administration of POW camps in Japan.
IMTFE 1983A and B, 1984A and B: Places and numbers of POW camps assigned.
IMTFE 14285: Twice-a-week discussions at the Ministry of Foreign Affairs concerning treatment and malnutrition of POWs.
IMTFE 13484, 14426, 27200, 27220, 49723, and RvO IC 775, 778, 2158, 5278: Conference meetings of the Bureau of Control and administration of POWs and the destruction of documents related to reports of these meetings.
IMTFE 28725, 30228 and RvO IC 2365: Inconsistencies of transfer of orders concerning POWs under Field Marshal Terauchi.

IMTFE 5387, September 1942: POW camps in Malaya fall under control of the Bureau of Control and Administration of POWs.
IMTFE 14839–90; 27198–99: Prisoner of war control.
IMTFE 14197–261; 14270–80; 14901–09; 27803–78: Affidavits and testimonies concerning camps.
IMTFE 14539–42: Censorship of news received.
IMTFE 17530–31: Imperial ordinance concerning establishment of camps.
IMTFE 27837–41: Improvement of camps—investigations concerning undernourishment of prisoners.
IMTFE 27806–07: Regulations concerning camps.
IMTFE 27809; 27811–12: Study of prison camps.
IMTFE 12873–74: Testimonies on the inspections of prison camps.
IMTFE 27918: Affidavit concerning religious services in camps.
IMTFE 27797, 27788–96: Affidavits concerning food supplies to camps.
RvO IC 2365: Complaints from internees and existence of abuses were never received in Tokyo.
RvO IC 2171: Dissemination of camp reports from Java to Tokyo.
RvO IC 4225, IMTFE 1983A: Establishment of Department of Information on POWs.
RvO IC 6227: Organization of office of civilian internee affairs.
RvO IC 3303, 5280: Administration and supervision of internment camps.

National Archives, Washington, DC:

- POW Camps in Japan and Japanese Controlled Areas, Box 1584, 12W3/6/31/d, 233 pp.
- POW Camps in Areas Other Than the Four Principal Islands of Japan, Box 1584, 12W3/6/31/d, 83 pp.
- Locations and Strengths of POW Camps and Civilian Assembly Centers in Japan and Japanese Occupied Territories, Box 1584, 12W3/6/31/d, 50 pp.

SOURCES, ESCAPES

Bates, H. F. *Vlucht uit Burma* [Escape from Burma]. Utrecht, 1961.
Bradley, James. *Towards the Setting Sun: An Escape from the Thailand-Burma Railway 1943.* London, 1982.
Chapman, F. Spencer. *The Jungle Is Neutral* [Escape on the Malay Peninsula]. London, 1949.
Crawford, H. *The Long Green Tunnel* [Escape on the Malay Peninsula]. London, 1967.
Dyess, Lieutenant Colonel William E. *The Dyess Story* [Escape in the Philippines]. New York, 1944.
McCoy, M. H., et al. *Ten Escape from Tojo* [Escape in the Philippines]. New York, 1944.
Marsman, Jan Hendrik. *I Escaped from Hong Kong.* New York, 1942.
Mellnik, Brigadier General Steve. *Philippine Diary, 1939–1945* [Escape in the Philippines]. New York, 1969.
Reynolds, Quentin. *Officially Dead* [Escape in China]. London, 1946.
Richardson, Hal. *One-Man War: The Jock McLaren Story* [Escape in North Borneo]. Sydney, 1957.

Skidmore, Ian. *Escape from Singapore.* New York, 1973.
United States War Department. *Military Personnel Escaped from Enemy Territory.* Washington, DC, July 11, 1944.
_____. *Publicity in connection with escaped, liberated or repatriated POWs, to include evaders of capture.* Washington, DC, March 29, 1945.
Wallace, Walter. *Escape from Hell: The Sandakan Story* [Escape in North Borneo]. London, 1957.

JAPAN

POW Camps

Introduction. The POW camps in Japan were usually attached to some industry: a shipbuilding yard, a steel works, a coal mine, or the wharves of a large port. Some were on Hokkaido, the northern island of Japan, where the winter is rigorous and the summer is prolific with mosquitoes. Most of the prisoners going to Japan were given uniforms of a rough, sacklike material that was inadequate to keep out the cold in a region whose inhabitants wore fur in the winter.

Much of the work done by the POWs consisted of heavy menial labor. The treatment and conditions in the camps varied enormously, depending on the character of the particular Japanese officer in charge. Generally, POWs taken to the Japanese home islands were not better treated—except in some minor ways—than were those who remained in the newly conquered Co-Prosperity Sphere in other areas of Asia and Southeast Asia.

In some places the Japanese civilians were friendly to the POWs, but in other areas—especially those that were continually bombed by American planes—they were quite hostile. In some cases, the gentleness and good manners of the civilians stood in sharp contrast to the behavior of the military guards. Many were glad to barter in exchange for their own increasingly meager supplies of food. At considerable risk, some men were able to get out of their camps at night to forage, but it was hopeless to attempt to escape. The food shortage in Japan weighed on the civil population just as heavily as on the POWs and gave everyone a fair idea of the trend of the war.

Although representatives of the Red Cross and of some of the neutral powers were allowed to visit some camps, they were never allowed to speak to the prisoners. More Red Cross parcels were distributed in Japan than elsewhere in the occupied territories, but many guards pilfered the parcels mercilessly, saying that everything belonging to the POWs was legally the property of the Japanese government.

The following anecdote, taken from the American Red Cross *Prisoner of War Bulletin*, presents a vivid picture of some of the actions the POWs took while imprisoned by the Japanese:

> We were working on the shipyard. Lots of times the man heating the rivets would just about burn them up. As long as they were hot you could batter a head on them. When they got cold, they were coved with red lead, then painted. They looked good but we knew they would not hold very long. We did this to a lot of outside plates of a ship and also on the inside water tight compartments.

Individual Listings of the POW Camps

Hokkaido Group: POW1–POW13

POW1: Hakodate No. 2

Location: Island of Hokkaido, approximately 18 miles south and west of Takikawa, and about 10 miles northeast of Hakodate—43°24'N and 142°06'E.

Prisoners: The camp was occupied for the first time in early 1945 by 130 Americans from China and 150 British from Singapore. Senior officer: Major Murray of the British.

Guards: Lieutenant Tindo, commandant, plus one interpreter and three army sergeants.

Housing: The compound was 180 feet by 120 feet, surrounded by a high wood fence on three sides. The fourth side was a steep cliff paralleling the river. There were three wooden, single-story barracks—one for the Americans and two for the British. Each was 60 feet by 40 feet, with lap siding walls, a leaky wood-shingled roof, and dirt floors into which had been built four wooden sleeping platforms running the length of each building. Mosquitoes, fleas, lice, and rats infested the barracks.

Sanitary conditions: Three latrines were joined to all the barracks at one end by intervening wash racks. They were of wood with cement floors, with concrete-lined pits under an open hole in the floor. At intervals POWs dipped out the excrement and deposited it in the garden.

Bathing: At the river side of the compound, there was one bathhouse with two wooden tubs 3½ feet by 3½ feet. Hot water and soap were provided.

Food: The British POWs did the central cooking—rice, soup, seaweed, and some dried fish flakes. The crops in the camp garden were raided by the guards.

Medical conditions: There were two army physicians in camp—Major Murray, British, and Major Lynch, Canadian. Many of the sick should have been bed patients, but went to work anyway because collapse was an invitation to beating and withholding of the evening meal. Medical supplies and medicines were withheld. There was no hospital. Two small rooms—15 feet by 20 feet—were used as dispensaries and bedding for those who were not ambulatory.

Work: coal mining in an old, worn-out mine. There were no fatal accidents, but many were badly hurt by falling rocks. The mine was always wet; the prisoners worked in the water in two shifts beginning at 6:30 A.M. Each 11th day was a rest day.

General treatment: The camp officials were not particularly brutal, but the guards in the mine were. No Red Cross parcels were distributed. No ingoing or outgoing mail was permitted.

Recreation and religious activities: None.

Attitude: Morale was always high.

Liberation-release date: September 15, 1945.

POW2: Hakodate No. 3

Location: Outside the town of Utashinai, 12 miles east of Takikawa, and approximately 15 miles west of Ashibetsu. Coordinates: 43°31'N and 142°03'E.

Prisoners: The camp was occupied on July 7, 1945, by 285 Americans and about 45 British, originally from Hong Kong. Senior officer: Lieutenant E. G. F. Pollard, USN Dental Corps.

Guards: Captain Kinsaburo Niizuma, weak and indifferent; Sergeant Major Kozo Ishigooka; Sergeant Seizaburo Isa; Corpsman Unesaku Nakao; and Private Hisao Kawasaki.

Housing: A single, two-story building made of wood with a wooden roof and floors, divided into eight sleeping sections. There were two ladder-high sleeping galleries, 8 feet by 15 feet, in each section—a total of 16 galleries for 10 men each, or 160 men on each level.

Sanitary conditions: There was a latrine adjacent to the sleeping quarters with 10 openings in the floor and a cement vat underneath. The vat was emptied with buckets, and the excrement was used as fertilizer.

Bathing: A shed in the rear of the barracks had one wooden tank, 12 feet by 15 feet.

Food: central cooking—500 grams of rice a day, weedlike stalks, and a small amount of dry fish. The food was carried in buckets to the sleeping quarters, where it was eaten.

Medical conditions: There was no hospital and virtually no medicines or supplies.

Work: coal mining in a 42-year-old mine. There were regular cave-ins and accidents and constantly wet conditions.

General treatment: No Red Cross parcels and no incoming mail were

permitted; one outgoing postcard was allowed. There were frequent beatings and considerable nagging.
Recreation and religious activities: None.
Attitude: Morale was high at first, but dropped under the oppressive working conditions.
Liberation of camp: September 15, 1945.

POW3: Asahigawa
POW4: Bibai-Machi
POW5: Hakodate Main Camp
POW6: Hakodate Divisional Camp
POW7: Kamiso Subcamp
POW8: Mitsuishi
POW9: Muroran
POW10: Otaru
POW11: Sappo Penitentiary
POW12: Teniya Park Stadium
POW13: Tomakomai

Tokyo Group: POW14–POW76

POW14: Sendai Camp No. 11
Location: 12½ miles south of Aomori and 20 miles west of Lake Ogawahara. Coordinates: 40°30'N and 141°20'E.
Prisoners: The camp was occupied on July 7, 1945, by 198 Americans from Fengtai Camp, China (POW207), 186 civilians originally from Wake Island, and 12 military prisoners from that island.
Senior Officer: Commander William Foley, U.S. Navy Medical Corps.
Guards: Second Lieutenant Uozumi, the camp commandant, committed suicide on August 8, 1945. Sergeant Major Subano, a sadist, took over; he was held captive after the war to stand trial for brutalities.
Housing: One two-story building, 40 feet by 80 feet, with a wood-shingled roof and a wooden floor, in a compound 300 feet by 300 feet, enclosed by a wooden fence.
Sanitary conditions: There was a shed 20 feet by 10 feet with holes in the floor and buckets underneath.
Bathing: There was a detached frame building, 40 feet by 20 feet, with a wooden tub, 10 feet by 10 feet. The water was electrically heated. Bathing was done by dipping water from the tub and splashing it over the body.
Food: Rice, a soybean mixture, and weeds were cooked by the prisoners in iron cauldrons. The food was served in the barracks.

Medical conditions: There were no hospital and no supplies, equipment, or medicines. Eight beds on the ground floor of barracks were provided for the sick.

Work: Hard labor in an open-pit iron mine. Reveille was at 4:30 A.M. The men went to work at 5:30 A.M., descended a 750-foot cliff, trekked 2 miles down the valley, and climbed 1,000 feet up the mountain to the mine.

General treatment: On reaching the camp all POWs were stripped of their personal belongings and food and medicine from Red Cross parcels received in China. They had little clothing. The guards frequently counted the POWs during the night. The flea infestation was severe. The camp was called "hell hole" by the prisoners.

Note: After the war, Red Cross parcels were found stacked in a nearby storeroom.

Recreation and religious activities: None.

Attitude: Very low morale.

Camp liberated: September 12, 1945.

POW15: Hanawa Sendai No. 6

Location: 50 miles from northern tip of Honshu Island. Coordinates: 40°11'N and 140°48'E.

Prisoners: The camp opened on September 9, 1944, with 500 American and 50 British POWs.

Senior officer: Colonel Walker, U. S. Army Air Force.

Guards: Lieutenant Osaka, commandant.

Housing: Three barracks, each 20 feet by 150 feet, in a 130 foot by 325 foot compound surrounded by a 12-foot wooden fence.

Sanitary conditions: Latrine holes with buckets underneath.

Bathing: Two wooden tubs, each 12 feet square and 4 feet deep. Hot water was available.

Food: Rice, barley, and putrid fish were prepared in a galley in iron cauldrons.

Medical conditions: There were a hospital and a first-aid room, a physician's office, and corpsmen's quarters in two buildings. The medical supplies and medicines were insufficient.

Work: A copper mine and a smelting plant.

General treatment: The men were worked hard and were hungry most of the time, but there was no evidence of sustained cruelty.

Recreation: None.

Religious Services: At Christmas and Easter.

Attitude: High morale.

Camp liberated: September 13, 1945.

POW16: Matsusima, Camp 2-D

Location: Central island, eastern banks Tenryu river. Coordinates: 35°55'N and 137°39'E.

Prisoners: This camp was first opened in November 1942 and was occupied by American, Dutch, and British POWs, who were moved about. On August 12, 1944, about 313 men—96 Americans and 217 British—were in the camp.

Guards: A commandant assisted by 8 to 12 guards.

Housing: Thirteen wooden structures surrounded by a 20-foot-high wooden fence. There were living barracks, 18 feet by 75 feet, for 120 prisoners; each prisoner was allowed 30 inches by 73 inches of sleeping and living space.

Sanitary conditions: Two latrines in separate wooden buildings for 30 men at a time with a "straddle trench."

Bathing: One tub, 6 feet by 6 feet by 3 feet deep, was filled once every 10 days. The water was heated.

Food: Barley, rice (ratio of 8:2), and occasionally some beans and vegetables were cooked by American personnel.

Medical conditions: One British physician and later one American physician. Little medicine was provided.

Work: As requested by each contractor in the area.

General treatment: The guards were rough and made their own rules each time there was a change of guard. "Very severe" was the general description of the treatment in this camp.

Recreation: None. *Religious activities*: Occasional church services.

Attitude: The high morale was attributed to the POWs' ability to steal and purchase newspapers and keep up to date on the advances of the American forces.

Camp liberated: September 4, 1945.

POW17: Hitachi, Ibargi-ken Camp D-12

Location: The western side of Mount Juragaki, 70 miles northeast of Tokyo. Coordinates: 36°38'N and 140°36'E.

Prisoners: The camp was occupied from April 11, 1944, to August 11, 1944, with a total of 300 American POWs.

Senior officer: Major Arthur G. Christensen.

Guards: Captain Nimoto plus 8 to 12 guards.

Housing: There were 13 flimsily constructed buildings. Six buildings were used for POWs; three were 60 feet by 16 feet, for 32 men, and three were 140 feet by 16 feet, each for 68 men.

Sanitary conditions: A regular straddle trench.

Bathing: One tub, 6 feet by 12 feet by 3 feet, with hot water and small buckets to splash over the body.

Food: Barley, millet, maize, rice, and occasionally small bits of fish or meat and vegetables were cooked by the Americans under Japanese supervision.

Medical conditions: Medical supplies that were brought from the Philippines were confiscated upon arrival in Japan; they were occasionally supplemented with Japanese medicine. A small barracks for 16 patients functioned as a hospital. There was one American physician and one corpsman.

Work: in the coal mines.

General treatment: fair.

Recreation and religious activities: None.

Attitude: The morale was initially low, but it increased considerably when the men smuggled newspapers into camp and learned about the American advances.

POW18: Niigata, Sub-camp 5

Location: On the Japan seaboard.

Prisoners: Ex-POW George Francis made a return trip to Niigata camp, accompanied by his wife, more than 40 years after his imprisonment there. The following is a short excerpt of his impressions:

> I dreamt fitfully that night in the hotel of Niigata, pushing and straining against an old two-wheeled cart I had pushed many times before in the coal yards of Rinko. In my dreams it would hardly move, or would the sheets in my bed. I woke tired, fretful to see my wife Bertie already dressed and my travel clock reading 4 A.M. It seemed only minutes before we had sunk exhausted on the bed, but she was up and as excited as I was.
>
> We had talked at dinner the night before of what we might expect in Niigata. Would the old camp be there? Was I emotionally ready to look back at all those days of misery to remember the tragedy, the constant hunger, the death, the brutality in a camp identified as the worst of all POW camps? Would I see "Cyclone Pete," the honcho domo of Camp 5B, swaggering down the dirt paths, his samurai sword in hand, yelling, "Bacca, konyero," at the coal blackened faces of the POWs in 5B. There too, were the stark white faces from the Marutsu gang. They worked the docks unloading ships of soy beans, metholine and other commercials. We envied them and their opportunity to enhance their food supply.
>
> In late 1945, back in the land of milk and honey, I was able to put my hostilities to rest. There were many reasons I could not live with hate. "A man came to me with hostility and I let him keep his gift," I would teach my sons that simple Confucian parable, but now at the gate to Niigata I was not so sure. The camp was gone, a few empty buildings in their place. My wife and I embraced, the tears flowing from our eyes. She knew this place as well as I. She had heard all the stories, knew all the people who had died here. Somehow we became quiet and yet elated that we had come this long way. We knew, too, that we could go home again.[1]

POW19: Omori Main Camp
Location: Just outside Tokyo.
Prisoners: Ex-POW Minos D. Miller wrote about his experiences in this camp. The following is a brief excerpt.

> Pappy Boyington was in our group and it was at Omori where I got to know Pappy well. Omori was a registered POW camp, but we were not registered as POWs when we got there (shot-down pilots). We "Ofuna" prisoners were separated from the registered POWs and placed in one large hayloft arranged as a dormitory. Rats ran across us while we were sleeping—every night. We learned to tolerate the continuous problem with lice and would pick lice off one another. The Omori camp was an island in Tokyo Bay—connected to the mainland by a wooden causeway. More than 1,500 POWs were confined there, all "registered" POWs, except those of us shot down over the "homeland" were never registered POWs.[2]

Ray "Hap" Halloran, navigator on a B-29 Superfortress, was shot down over Tokyo during the war. In September 1985, he shook the hand of Isamu Kashiide, the pilot who had shot down his plane on January 27, 1945. After he parachuted safely out of the plane, Ray Halloran was kept as an "unregistered" POW in Omori camp. His decision to meet with Kashiide was to "complete the cycle of life." As he put it, "It would be the ultimate epilogue." It worked: he stopped getting nightmares and his bitterness about Japan was giving way to new feelings.

POW20: Achi Yamakita
POW21: Akasaka
POW22: Akita
POW23: Aomori
POW24: Ashikago
POW25: Atami
POW26: Chiba
POW27: Chugenji
POW28: Furumaki
POW29: Futatsui City
POW30: Fuji
POW31: Franciscan Monastery
POW32: Hakone
POW33: Hiraoka, Subcamp No. 3
POW34: Hayashi Village
POW35: Hitachi Motoyama
POW36: Kagawa Christian Fellowship Home
POW37: Kanagawa Tokyo 2

POW38: Kanagawa Kneko
POW39: Kamitan Kozan, Sendai No. 11
POW40: Kanazawa
POW41: Kawasaki No. 1
POW42: Kawasaki Dispatch Camp No. 5
POW43: Kawasaki Subcamp No. 2
POW44: Kita Cotygara
POW45: Kosaka
POW46: Mizonkuchi
POW47: Mito
POW48: Morioka
POW49: Murakami
POW50: Narashino Airport
POW51: Nogeyama Park
POW52: Nooetzu Camp (Niigata Ken)
POW53: Odate
POW54: Ofuna
POW55: Ohashi
POW56: Old City Hall
POW57: Park Central Camp
POW58: Park Central Stadium
POW59: Sekiguchi
POW60: Shibaura
POW61: Shimodate
POW62: Shimomago Hitachi
POW63: Shinagawa Main Camp
POW64: Shinjuku Camp No. 1
POW65: Shizuoka
POW66: Sumidagawa
POW67: Suzuki Aio No Moto Factory
POW68: Takadanobaba
POW69: Toyama
POW70: Tsurumi Subcamp No. 5
POW71: Uraga
POW72: Utsonomiya
POW73: Wakasen
POW74: Yamashita Camp No. 1
POW75: Yokohama No. 5
POW76: Uywake (Iwake)

Osaka-Kobe Group: POW77–POW119

POW77: Kobe POW Hospital
   Location: City of Kobe, on a quiet hillside in a former mission school.

In August 1944, a delegate of the International Committee of the Red Cross visited this POW hospital. The report of the delegate was published in the November 1944 issue of the American Red Cross's *Prisoner of War Bulletin*. The delegate was very complimentary about the treatment the prisoner-patients received. "The prisoners' diet was reported to correspond to that of the camp guards in quantity and quality," he stated. "Caloric value was 3000. Drug supply, mainly from American Red Cross supplies, was sufficient."[3]

POW78: Sakurajima
   Location: Across the bay from Kobe. Coordinates: 34°40'N and 135°26'E.
   Food: Central cooking—rice, soup, weeds, sometimes spoiled fish, and 15–20 pounds of meat monthly for 300 prisoners.
   Medical conditions: In one small sickbay, two American and two British physicians successfully held death to a minimum. There were inadequate supplies of medicine and equipment. In extreme cases, the patients were sent to the hospital at Kobe, although the facilities were crude.
   Note: The statements concerning the conditions in the camp and the hospital in Kobe were made by POWs after their return to the United States. The POWs' experiences and observations completely contradict those of the Red Cross delegate. As the evidence presented in this book demonstrates, the value of sending Red Cross representatives to prison camps was highly questionable. It has been proven that it takes just a little time and imagination for the captors to pull the wool over the eyes of inspectors.

POW79: Sakurajima Ichioka School
   Prisoners: 150 POWs from Guam who were interned here from June 1942 to the end of 1942, when they were dispersed to other camps.

POW80: Umeda Bonshu
   Location: Suburb of Osaka. Bounded by a freight yard on one side and by the main railroad station of Osaka on the other side. Coordinates: 34°40'N and 135°29'E.
   Prisoners: The camp was first occupied on November 26, 1942, by 458 American POWs. Another detail of 330 men arrived on May 13, 1943. Total: 788, of whom 118 died. Senior Officer: Lieutenant Colonel G. L. Fields.
   Guards: Lieutenant Yamada, succeeded by Sergeant Major Kanori.
   Housing: In a camp compound, 150 feet by 200 feet, enclosed by a wooden fence, there was a three-story stucco building with a tile roof. The double-deck sleeping platforms with straw mats were infested with vermin.

Sanitary conditions: There were 16 straddle-type latrines. Holes were cut in the cement floor, and the cement tanks were emptied by Japanese laborers.

Bathing: There were two four-man tubs, one eight-man tub, and eight cold-water showers.

Food: Low in quantity and quality—570 grams of cereal daily per man. In 1943 the ration was reduced to 470 grams.

Medical conditions: Two American physicians worked under the supervision of a Japanese medical attendant who constantly overruled their decisions. Practically no medicines or instruments were furnished. Dysentery, malaria, beriberi, and pneumonia were rampant and caused many deaths.

Work: In the freight yard of Nippon Tsuun Kaisha, loading and unloading freight cars and barges. Heavy and dangerous work.

General treatment: Five Red Cross parcels a man were distributed to each man between Christmas 1943 and Christmas 1944. Some clothing was issued. Blankets were thin. Prisoners endured rough and cruel treatment, including forced calisthenics. They were allowed no paper or writing materials.

Recreation and religious activities: None.

Attitude: Morale was good to very high.

Movements: In May 1945, the POWs were moved to four other camps.

Note: Since the differences among the various camps that follow are negligible, the information on these camps will be presented in a one- or two-paragraph narrative.

POW81: Akenobe, No. 6-B

About 75 miles northwest of Osaka and about 20 miles from the coast of the Japan Sea. Coordinates: 34°20'N and 134°35'E. Number of POWs: 307 (96 Americans, 166 British, 45 Australians). The crowded, poorly ventilated, poorly heated barracks were so heavily infested with fleas that sleeping through the night was impossible. The work project was mining copper for the Mitsubishi Mining Company. Conditions were dangerous— falling rocks and crude implements. The suffering of the POWs was made increasingly unendurable by starvation, long working hours, inadequate clothing, and the lack of medicines.

POW82: Funatsu

Located 70 miles in the hills near Osaka, the camp housed a total of 360 POWs—155 Americans and 205 Australians. Housing was in two two-story barracks. The POWs worked in two smelting factories; in one they extracted lead and zinc, and in the other, tin.

Staff sergeant Larry W. Wozniak said the following:

> Punishments were constant. We would be punished for lying on beds in daytime, or failing to salute some Jap soldier, and many other things. Slapping, beating, standing in front of the guardhouse naked in wintertime, while sentries threw buckets of cold water on you, or withholding your food, were some of the punishments meted out.[4]

POW83: Notogawa, No. 9B

The camp was located on the east bank of Lake Buva, in the town of Iba, at the western edge of Notogawa city (no exact location could be determined). There were 301 POWs—110 Americans, 66 British, 69 Dutch, and 56 Australians, all transferred from another camp in the Osaka district. The living conditions were extremely crowded and poor. There was no heating, poor lighting, and a horrible infestation of bed bugs. The work consisted of building dikes and digging irrigation canals in the rice paddies. The general treatment was harsh—slappings and kickings.

POW84: Oeyama, Osaka No. 3

The camp was located on Wakasa Bay, north of Miyazu (coordinates: 35°53'N and 136°10'E). At liberation there were 645 POWs—384 Americans, 177 British, 73 Canadians, 3 Australians, 3 Dutch, and 5 Norwegian merchant marines. The housing conditions were poor, with insufficient heat and a heavy infestation of fleas. The men worked in the nickel mine with picks and shovels and in the adjoining refinery. The treatment was not particularly harsh, but there were numerous complaints about the meager food and lack of medication.

POW85: Roku Roshi

The camp was located in a picturesque valley at an elevation of 6,500 feet, 25 miles from the Japan Sea (coordinates: 35°54'N and 136°01'E). At liberation, there were 380 Americans and 15 British and Dutch POWs, mostly officers. The outward appearance of the barracks was pleasant and restful, surrounded by green timber. Inside, there was a dirt floor, no running water, and one fire pit—with no flues for smoke evacuation—which was the only source of heat. Bunk space allowed: 22 inches. Agricultural projects, road building, and wood cutting were the assigned tasks.

POW86: Tsuruga, Divisional Camp 5B

The camp was located at the extreme southern end of Wakasa Bay, 30 miles northeast of Osaka. From May 16, 1945, to liberation in September 1945, POWs occupied four different camp sites, three of which were bombed and burned during American air raids. Coordinates: 35°38'N and 136°03'E. There were a total of 400 POWs—382 Americans and 18 Dutch. The last housing of the four sites was a dilapidated structure. Work consisted of manually loading and unloading cargo-carrying ships and railroad freight cars of coal, bombs, and the like. For example, a crew of 10 men was required to load 1,880 sacks of beans, each sack weighing 220 pounds, in one day. All the men agreed that the treatment was brutal. But the morale was high, as long as the air raids increased.

Note: This information was obtained from reports of interned POWs to the Liaison and Research Branch, American Prisoner of War Information Bureau, John M. Gibbs, July 31, 1946.

The following is an extract from a report titled "Prisoner of War Camps in Japan-Osaka," published in the American Red Cross's *Prisoner of War Bulletin*:

> The camps are reported to be clean, tidy and free of vermin. They are electrically lighted and some stoves provide heat during January and February. The food, prepared by army cooks, consists of bread, rice, barley, fish, vegetables, potatoes, some fruit, salt, sugar, a small amount of meat and some margarine from time to time.
> The report on health conditions reveals a considerable amount of sickness, but the indications are that the situation is improving. Four Japanese army surgeons, two civilian doctors, and medical orderlies visit the camps two or three times a week and there is a prisoner surgeon in each camp. Since dental facilities are not provided in the camps, when permitted, prisoners are obliged to visit civilian dentists in the nearby towns.
> The men are working in shipyards, ironworks, oil factories, and as stevedores and dock workers. Including the journey to and from work, the men work eight hours a day, six days a week, with Sundays free. Working conditions are said to be fair.
> Recreational activities consist of some outdoor sports such as football and deck tennis. Some camps have ping pong sets.[5]

The contrasts between the reports given by ex–POWs and those by the Red Cross are obvious.

POW87: Hirohata Divisional Camp
Housing: Two wooden buildings 50 feet by 100 feet with tile roofs and wooden floors, not insulated or heated. For sleeping, there were two layers of platforms with straw mats, so infested with lice and fleas that sleeping was almost impossible. A starvation diet was maintained (ration of 575 to 750 grams a day); only the theft of food from Japanese ships prevented the death rate among POWs from climbing very high. Sick men were detailed

to catch frogs, snakes, and grasshoppers which were cooked in the galley for all men. General treatment: The men were cruelly beaten, forced to maintain a back-breaking pace at heavy work while too sick to work, given a starvation diet, and denied medicines and medical supplies.

The following is the report on Hirohata Division Camp as published in the Red Cross's *Prisoner of War Bulletin*:

> Hirohata Divisional Camp: The Delegate reported the buildings were well ventilated with heating available in the evening. Conditions appear to be better in this camp than at the others. The food supply is larger and the canteen is better supplied. Also walks in the country are permitted on Sundays. By and large it seems this camp, like others situated in country districts, is better than camps located in or near large industrial cities.[6]

This bulletin, which was read by many friends and relatives of those held captive by the Japanese, demonstrates the gross inaccuracy that was characteristic of the reports written by announced observers. These positive portraits, contradicted by the unanimous testimony of the prisoners, reveal the uselessness of the inspection system that was used.

POW88: Aioshi
POW89: Amagasaki Subcamp
POW90: Furashi
POW91: Fuse
POW92: Gifu—Nagara hotel
POW93: Harina, Camp No. 29
POW94: Himeji
POW95: Kamioka
POW96: Kawasaki Camp—Kobe
POW97: Kobe, Divisional Camp
POW98: Kobe, Camp No. 31
POW99: Koshian Hotel
POW100: Kyota—branches Hakata, Kaira
POW101: Maibara
POW102: Maisure
POW103: Nagoya Main Camp
POW104: Narumi, Nagoya Subcamp No. 2
POW105: Nagoya, Subcamp No. 10
POW106: Minato-ku
POW107: Osaka Central Market
POW108: Osaka No. 1 Headquarters Camp
POW109: Shingu

POW110: Suzurandai
POW111: Sumiyoshi-ku
POW112: Sakai Prison
POW113: Tanagawa
POW114: Toyoka
POW115: Wakayama
POW116: Yodagawa Bunsho
POW117: Yokkaichi
POW118: Yonago
POW119: Yura

Zentsuji Group: POW120–POW137

POW120: Zentsuji Headquarters Camp
This camp was located on the southern outskirts of Zentsuji (coordinates: 34°13'N and 133°47'E). In June 1945, when POWs were moved to another camp, there were 957 men, the majority of them officers. Housing consisted of two two-story warehouse buildings of wood and stucco. Latrines were of the regular squatting type. The meager food was the monumental complaint at this camp. It ranged from fair during the early months of occupancy to a starvation level in 1944. A steady starvation diet and humiliation were common. The interesting feature of this camp was a library of about 2,000 volumes, started with a set of books donated by Ambassador Grew before his return to the United States. The morale was excellent.

POW121: Camp No. 23
POW122: Higashi-Misone, Subcamp No. 10
POW123: Imoshima Island, Subcamp No. 2
POW124: Kochi
POW125: Kure
POW126: Mitsu, Branch Camp No. 5
POW127: Motoyama, Subcamp No. 8
POW128: Myoshi
POW129: Niihama, Branch Camp No. 2
POW130: Ohama, Subcamp No. 9
POW131: Omine, Subcamp No. 6
POW132: Onada, Branch Camp No. 8
POW133: Onada, Branch Camp No. 9
POW134: Shimonseki
POW135: Tamano, Branch Camp No. 3
POW136: Ube, Subcamp No. 7
POW137: Zentsuji, Subcamp No. 3

Fukuoka Group: POW138–POW160

The accounts of the camps under this group are confusing. In the reports of the Liaison and Research Branch of the American Prisoner of War Information Bureau, a number of these camps are listed as "Fukuoka No. 1" and so on, while the National Archives used a different name for these camps. In the listings below, both nomenclatures are identified. Most of the Fukuoka camps were located on the island of Kyushu.

POW138: Kashii Camp No. 1 (Fukuoka 1)

This camp had three locations within a period of 10 months from March 1944 to January 1945. There were 913 men in the camp—493 Americans, including 100 civilians from Wake Island and 193 survivors from the prison ship *Oryoku Maru*; 150 British; 250 Dutch; and 20 Australians. The enlisted men worked 10 hours a day at hard labor in the construction of airfield bomb shelters and in coal mining. They were exposed to bombing raids and subjected to frequent beatings by the guards and stoning by the civilian population.

POW*139*: Koyagi Shima (Fukuoka 2)

It was necessary in this hilly place in the country to cut a place out of the side of the hill to build the camp. In April 1946, there were 1,422 POWs—all Americans. The work carried out was shipbuilding and ship repairs. Many POWs were killed and a large number were seriously wounded because of the lack of safety measures. Morale in this camp was poor because of the harsh treatment.

POW140: Tobata (Fukuoka 3)

The camp was located about 500 yards from a massive powerplant built on a hill, with smoke stacks about 100 feet high. It was never bombed by American planes because it served as an excellent landmark. The camp population was about 1,200, of which 500 were Americans, including civilians from Wake Island; 130 were British; 3 were Australians; 150 were Indians; 345 were Dutch; and 72 were Malayan and Portuguese. The Japanese employed coercive measures to cause the men to work as stevedores, mechanics, and machinists, especially a decrease in the already inadequate rations when the POWs refused to do the labor. The treatment was consistently inhumane; the camp was rated "poor."

POW141: Futase (Fukuoka 10)

Located between the villages of Futase and Iizuka, the camp held 552 POWs—200 Americans, 350 Dutch, and 2 British prisoners. The men worked in the coal mines. The conditions and treatment were as bad as in the other camps.

POW142: Camp No. 11 (Fukuoka 11)

The camp was located in a small unidentified mining town, 50 miles south of Moji and 40 miles east of Fukuoka. Of the 590 POWs, 69 were Americans, 251 were British, and 270 were Dutch. The men were assigned to work in the coal mines in three shifts of eight hours each. Cave-ins were common; because the POWs were constantly aware of this possibility, their anxiety added to the menace to their health posed by the actual work. The general treatment was sadistic.

POW143: Omuta, Camp 17 (Fukuoka 17)

The camp was located 17 miles northwest of Kumamoto and 40 miles south of Fukuoka. There was much movement to and from this camp. At one time 814 American POWs were in the camp. Later, British, Australian, and Dutch prisoners arrived, all in desperate condition from the treatment on the prison ships. At the time of liberation, there were 1,859 men: 821 Americans, 562 Australians, 218 British, and 258 Dutch. Work was done in the coal mines and zinc smelters in three shifts a day.

Morale was low not only because of the inadequate food, long hours, and hard work, but especially because the men were harassed even during sleeping hours, which made rest virtually impossible. The situation was so detrimental to the men that the medical staff prepared a report, completed on August 25, 1945, while they were still together and able to recall the period. This report was accepted into the Australian Army Museum.

In August 1945, a number of men scavenged the city of Omuta as Colonel Thomas H. Hewlett, MD, U.S. Army retired, reported:

> Early in the exploration we found several warehouses packed with Red Cross food and medical supplies. The dates of receipt and storage indicated that these items had reached Japan prior to August 1943. Thus while we suffered from lack of food, essential medicines, surgical supplies and x-ray equipment, these items—gifts of the American people—were hoarded in warehouses during our two years in Japan. The reason we were denied these essentials remains a top secret of the Imperial Japanese Army.
>
> There is no summary to a nightmare that was permanently tattooed in our brains.[7]

POW144: Aokuma (Fukuoka 22)

The camp was located 30 miles southwest of Moji. It was a small camp with only 160 men. There were many movements of prisoners into and out of this camp.

POW145: Beppu

Located on the southwest coast of the Bay of Beppu, in the northeastern part of Kyushu Island, this camp was used to house POWs for only

13 days, from October 28, 1944, to November 10, 1944. These 169 POWs were the high-ranking military and civilian authorities en route from Formosa to Manchuria, and among them was General Wainwright. The camp itself consisted of five clean hotels, with natural hot springs and clean water. For the brief period of its operation, Beppu was considered by the POWs one of the best internment areas they had encountered.

POW146: Arao
POW147: Iizuka
POW148: Kumamoto
POW149: Kurume
POW150: Moji No. 2
POW151: Moji No. 4
POW152: Moji Hospital
POW153: Nacama No. 21 (Fukuoka 21)
POW154: Nagasaki No. 4
POW155: Nagasaki No. 2
POW156: Nagasaki No. 14

POW157: Nagasaki, Senryu No. 24

At liberation, there were 289 men in the camp—135 British, 36 Americans, 114 Australians, and 4 Dutch. Dr. Julien Goodman, MD, related a few interesting items about this camp.

> The only discomfort was the prevalence of lice, and everyone had them after about the third day out. They were a great annoyance because when one was just about asleep, they would begin to crawl slowly along some hairy area to arouse and awaken. Quickly exposing the infested part and catching the offending louse, crushing it between the thumbnails with a crack, which caused the nails to be bloodstained by rupturing their blood sacs, gave one a feeling of vengeful satisfaction, but this delight was only momentary. A few minutes later, as you again attempted to sleep, the same episode would be repeated, until in frustration, you tried to tolerate it rather than to delouse yourself one at a time.[8]

Dr. Goodman also made an interesting discovery:

> I learned a valuable lesson in ecology, not previously known. You can't have body lice and be in a flea-beset area at the same time. The fleas suck the blood from the lice and kill them before biting the human host.[9]

On the atomic bomb, Dr. Goodman observed:

> Suddenly, then it happened—a horrendous, loud, indescribable, earth-shaking sound assailed our ears. We both dived for the floor of the store-

room as the thunderous roar, which resembled that which would result from a myriad of 16-inch naval batteries fired in unison, filled the air and now was accompanied by the floor bumping up and down as during an earthquake. The earth and storeroom floor vibrated violently for a few moments, and the earth tremor stopped as suddenly as it started. A deathlike, all-encompassing silence now pervaded the area, followed by a sudden disruption by a violent hurricane wind which rocked the building, as its ever-increasing-in-strength gusts struck the walls and vigorously shook the window frames and rattled the doors.

Then this wind died away, and the stillness and quiet that was ominous of a catastrophe returned. Only then did John and I realize the siren had not yet sounded an all-clear after the cataclysm. The canyon and mountains running across the island north of Nagasaki had blocked from Senryu and our camp the maximum impact of the bomb. Thus natural barriers had protected us from explosive as well as radioactive effects.[10]

POW158: Sasebo
POW159: Subcamp No. 12 (Fukuoka 12)
POW160: Yawata, Camp No. 3

Civilian Internment Centers

Introduction. The morning after the attack on Pearl Harbor on December 7, 1941, many foreign journalists who were in Japan at that moment were arrested on alleged spy charges and interned in the Sugamo Jail in Tokyo. All were subsequently exchanged.

Other foreigners were interned in Western-style buildings and compounds. There were sufficient beds and other furniture. Sanitary conditions were generally excellent, with Western-style toilets and hot and cold water.

The internees had regular contact with the International Red Cross. Visits to the hospital and dentist were allowed, and they could shop regularly for extra food or other necessities. They could also correspond once a month with relatives overseas and once a week with friends, acquaintances, and family in Japan.

The upkeep of the internment buildings or compounds was quite good. The supply of foodstuffs, clothing, soap, medicine, and other necessities was adequate. Japanese cooks prepared the meals, and the Japanese in charge of the camps and the guards acted properly toward the internees.

Religious services and lectures, courses, concerts, and other forms of entertainment were allowed, as well as sporting events. Forced labor did not exist.

The number of internees fluctuated greatly; some people were interned later than 1942, and others were exchanged. There was no "general" internment policy for the civilians living in Japan. About 350 of them were never interned.

The situation was remarkably different in the internment camps set up for internees brought over from Guam, Wake, Rabaul, and other areas outside Japan.

As the Japanese suffered from the effects of war on food supplies, so did the internees as time progressed. Bread, rice, macaroni or potatoes, meat or fish, and fruit and vegetables were the daily fare in the early stages of the war, but in 1944 the rations decreased and certain foods, such as rice, were no longer available.

The Japanese people ate a mixture of rice and barley, soybeans, and fish and vegetables. Toward the end of the war, potatoes and sweet potatoes became the main fare; fruit and vegetables disappeared from the menu.

Individual Listings of Civilian Internment Centers: CIC1–CIC33

Tokyo

CIC1: Sumirejogakuen I

About 160 men from Tokyo and the surrounding area lived in a school building in the outskirts of the city from December 8, 1941, to October 1942. Some were exchanged; others were moved to CIC14 (Urawa-Saitama).

CIC2: Sumirejogakuen II

About 160 women and children from Tokyo, who were moved from CIC28 (Miyoshi I), from CIC16 (Mototerako), and from CIC30 (Shiroyama), lived in a school building in the suburbs from October 1942 to September 18, 1943. They were then moved to CIC3 (Denenchofu I).

CIC3: Denenchofu I

About 160 women and children moved from CIC2 (Sumirejogakuen II) to this convent in the suburbs, where they lived from September 18, 1943, to October 18, 1943. They then moved to CIC5 (Sekiguchi).

CIC4: Denenchofu II*

About 42 Italian diplomats were housed in this convent in the suburbs from October 18, 1943, to August 1945, when the camp was liberated.

**An asterisk denotes that the camp was liberated in August or September 1945.*

CIC5: Sekiguchi

About 60 women and children moved from CIC3 (Denenchofu II) to this seminary in the suburbs. They lived in the camp from October 18, 1943, to May 26, 1945. Some were exchanged; others moved to CIC6 (Seibo).

CIC6: Seibo*

About 37 women and children moved from CIC5 (Sekiguchi) to this hospital in the city, where they lived from May 26, 1945, to August 1945 when the camp was liberated.

CIC7: Keischico*

About 20 women and one man were housed in a police office in the town and were liberated in this camp.

Yokohama

CIC8: Negishi

About 50 men from the city and surrounding area lived in the jockey club outside town from December 8, 1941, to June 25, 1943. Some were exchanged; others moved to CIC11 (Yamakita).

CIC9: Yacht Club I

About 150 men from the city and surrounding area were housed in the club premises outside town from December 18, 1941, to June 1942. All were exchanged.

CIC10: Yacht Club II

Nineteen women from Rabaul and other Pacific Islands lived in the club premises outside town from August 1942 to July 1943. They were then moved to CIC12 (Totsuka).

This group of 18 Australian nurses from Rabaul (New Britain) and one American woman from Attu was one of the small groups that arrived in Japan unscathed from Allied attacks on Japanese transports from the Pacific area to the Japanese islands. The women were treated harshly and were forced to sew clothes for the Japanese army. This group was also one of the few civilian groups transported overseas.

Kanagawa

CIC11: Yamakita*

About 49 men from CIC8 (Negishi) lived in this summer country house near Odawara from June 25, 1943, to August 1945, when the camp was liberated.

CIC12: Totsuka*

The Australian nurses and the American woman first kept at CIC10 (Yacht Club II) were removed to this hospital outside Enoshina, where they lived from July 1943 to August 1945.

The food rations for these women were less than in other camps, and the women were never allowed contact with the Swiss Legation. Medical care was totally inadequate. The women did, however, receive Red Cross parcels on a regular basis. After the war no real reason was given by the Japanese authorities for their cruel treatment of the women. It may be assumed that these women were considered POWs when they were captured and that while they were in Japan, their status was not changed to civilian internees.

CIC13: Nanazawa*

About 26 men, women, and children from Yokohama lived in this hotel in the countryside from September 1943 to August 1945, when they were liberated.

Urawa

CIC14: Saitawa*

This camp housed about 56 men from CIC1 (Sumirejogakuen I) who were moved from CIC16 (Mototerako) and from CIC28 (Miyoshi I). The men lived in this camp from October 1, 1942, to August 1945, when they were liberated.

Fukushima

CIC15: Fukushima*

About 140 men, women, and children from a sunken transport ship — most likely the PS8 (*Asaka Maru*) — lived in this convent in the countryside from July 11, 1942, to August 1945, when the camp was liberated.

Sendai

CIC16: Mototerako

About 35 men and women from Sendai lived in a large house in the suburbs from December 8, 1941, to December 19, 1942. The men were moved to CIC14 (Saitawa), and the women were moved to CIC2 (Sumirejogakuen II).

CIC17: Kitaniban

About 20 women from Sendai lived in this house in the suburbs from

December 8, 1941, to December 19, 1942. The men were moved to CIC14 (Saitawa) and the women were moved to CIC1 (Sumirejogakuen I).

CIC18: Tatamiyasho*
This large house in the suburbs held 26 nuns from June 1944 to August 1945, when they were liberated.

The nuns were never considered "real" internees; contact with the Swiss Legation was allowed. Their position as nuns was an uncomfortable one for the Japanese authorities, who were not used to guarding such a group of women.

Nagoya

CIC19: Ishigase*
Twenty-two Dutch men, women, and children lived in a temple outside Okazaki. The men worked for Sumitomo Industries. The internees lived here from May 1945 to August 1945, when they were liberated.

The men were engineers from the radio laboratory in Bandoeng, West Java, which had become a part of the Sumitomo Concern. Despite their protests, the men and their families were transferred to Tokyo in January 1945. Sumitomo treated them very well; they were paid according to Japanese standards and were well provided for. Allied bombings of Tokyo were responsible for the group's move to Ishigase.

CIC20: Aichi*
This camp housed 16 Anti-Mussolino Italians in a temple outside Okazaki, where they lived from October 1943 to August 1945, when the camp was liberated.

Kobe

CIC21: Hyogo No. 1
About 60 men from Kobe and those transported from Guam (CIC357) lived in the Canadian University premises outside the city from December 9, 1941, to May 23, 1944, when they moved to CIC26 (Futababi).

Note: The Hyogo camps CIC21, CIC22, CIC23, and CIC24 held about 180 civilians who were captured during the surrender of Guam.

CIC22: Hyogo No. 2
About 42 men and women from Kobe, from CIC357 (Guam), and from Manchuria lived in this hotel outside Kobe from December 11, 1941, to July 1, 1944. The men were moved to CIC26 (Futababi), and the women were moved to CIC30 (Shiroyama).

CIC23: Hyogo No. 3

This camp was a large house in the suburbs in which 56 American men from CIC3357 (Guam) lived from January 23, 1942, to May 23, 1944, when they were moved to CIC26 (Futababi).

CIC24: Hyogo

This seamen's mission home in the city housed 77 American men from CIC357 (Guam) from January 23, 1942, to October 10, 1942. The men were then moved to CIC25 (Hyogo No. 4).

CIC25: Hyogo No. 4

The 77 men from CIC24 (Hyogo) lived in a large house in the suburbs from October 10, 1942, to May 23, 1944, when they were moved to CIC26 (Futababi).

CIC26: Futababi*

About 175 men, assembled from CIC21 (Hyogo No. 1), CIC22 (Hyogo No. 2), CIC23 (Hyogo No. 3), CIC24 (Hyogo), and CIC31 (St. Franciscus I) lived in a large boarding school outside Kobe from May 23, 1944, to August 1945, when they were liberated.

Okayama

CIC27: Okayama

Twelve nuns lived in this convent in the suburbs from December 1941 to April 1942, when they were moved to CIC28 (Miyoshi I).

Miyoshi

CIC28: Miyoshi I

About 20 men and women from the area, plus the nuns from CIC27 (Okayama), were housed in this school in the suburbs from December 13, 1941, to December 19, 1942. Then the men moved to CIC14 (Saitama), and the women moved to CIC2 (Sumirejogakuen II).

CIC29: Miyoshi II*

Forty-four men and women from the hospital ship *Op ten Noort* were illegally captured and held by the Japanese in a school in the suburbs from December 20, 1942, to August 1945, when they were liberated.

The hospital ship *Op ten Noort* was to be used in the Battle of the Java Sea, but was stopped by Japanese destroyers on February 28, 1942. Two days later, with survivors from the battle on board, it directed to Makassar, South Celebes. For nine months the ship was used as a hospital ship for the POWs in Makassar. On November 23, 1942, the ship steamed to Yokohama with a Japanese crew; the Dutch crew and hospital staff remained on board. The Dutch were interned in Miyoshi II camp. In September 1944 the ship sailed from Japan, under the Japanese flag, and disappeared under mysterious, never-clarified circumstances.

Nagasaki

CIC30: Shiroyama

About 30 men and women from Nagasaki and the surrounding area lived in this convent in the suburbs from December 9, 1941, to March 4, 1943. Some internees were exchanged; some men moved to CIC31 (St. Franciscus I), and some women moved to CIC2 (Shimorejogakuen II).

CIC31: St. Franciscus I

Fifteen men from CIC30 (Shiroyama) moved to this convent in the suburbs. They lived here from March 4, 1943, to May 1944, when they moved to CIC26 (Futababi).

CIC32: St. Franciscus II*

This convent in the suburbs housed 42 men and women from CIC22 (Hyogo No. 2) from May 1944 to August 1945, when the camp was liberated.

Hokkaido

CIC33: Hokkaido

Twenty-four men and women lived in some premises outside Port Otaru. Very little information is available on this site.

Concluding information on civilian internment centers. At one time or another the Japanese used approximately 160 facilities to incarcerate POWs and about 33 facilities for civilian internees—a total of 193 camps.

Whether or not this number is accurate, it reflects massive efforts by the Japanese to hold Allied captives in their homeland. More detailed and extensive research may reveal more information than is presented here.

The following approximate figures have been culled from Dr. D. van Velden's data on civilian internees:

Interned		Deaths
480 men	190 Americans	18 Americans
190 women	350 British	12 British
21 children	70 Dutch	2 others
691 persons	80 others	32 persons (4.6 percent)
	690 persons	

NOTES

1. George Francis, "Sayonara Niigata," *Ex-POW Bulletin* (March 1991), pp. 38–39.
2. Minos D. Miller, Jr., "Prison Experience," *Ex-POW Bulletin* (August 1990), p. 39.
3. International Committee of the Red Cross, "Reports from Japanese Camps," *Prisoner of War Bulletin* 2 (11) (November 1944).
4. Colonel William C. Braly, *The Hard Way Home*, Washington, DC, 1947, p. 232.
5. International Committee of the Red Cross, "Prisoner of War Camps in Japan," *Prisoner of War Bulletin* 1 (6) (November 1943), pp. 1, 10.
6. *Ibid.*, p. 10.
7. Thomas H. Hewlett, MD, F.A.C.S., Colonel U.S. Army retired, *Di Ju Nana Bunshyo Nightmare Revisited—The Japanese Story*, Packet No. 10, American Ex-POWs, Inc.
8. Dr. Julien M. Goodman, MD, *M.D.P.O.W.*, New York, 1972, p. 144.
9. *Ibid.*, p. 163.
10. *Ibid.*, pp. 200, 216.

SOURCES: CAMPS IN JAPAN

Adams, Geoffrey. *Destination Japan*. (POW). Dorset, 1980.
Beets, Dr. Nic. *De Krijgsgevangenen: Japan*. (POW). Meppel, the Netherlands, 1981.
Berger, Lee K. *Guest of the Emperor*. (POW). High Ridge, MO, 1987.
Blackwater, C. F. *Gods Without Reason*. (POW). London, 1948.
Booth, Martin. *Hiroshima Joe*. (POW). London, 1985.
Braly, Colonel William C. *The Hard Way Home*. (POW). Washington, DC, 1947.
Carew, Tim. *Hostages to Fortune*. (POW). London, 1971.
Clarke, Hugh V. *Last Stop Nagasaki*. (POW). Sydney, 1985.
———. *Twilight Liberation*. (POW). Sydney, 1985.
Devereux, James, P. S. *The Story of Wake*. (POW). New York, 1947.
Dunlop, E. E. *The War Diaries of Weary Dunlop*. (POW). Melbourne, 1986.
Eichelberger, Robert L., and Milton MacKay. *Our Jungle Road to Tokyo*. (POW). New York, 1950.
Evans, Frank. *Roll Call at Oeyama*. (POW). Wales, 1985.
Evans, William R. *Soochow and the 4th Marines*. (POW). Rogue River, OR, 1987.
Fletcher-Cooke, Sir John. *The Emperor's Guest*. (POW). London, 1982.
Gayn, Mark. *Japan Diary*. New York, 1948.
Harrison, K. *The Brave Japanese*. (POW). London, 1967.
Hastain, Ronald. *White Coolie*. (POW). London, 1947.
Hilfman, M. M. *Fukuoka 9: Arts in Krijgsgevangenschap*. (POW Physician). Utrecht, 1985.
Hofstede, N. W. *De Slaven van Roku Ban* [The Slaves of Roku Ban]. (POW). Franeker, the Netherlands, 1979.
Howard, Chris Pereze. *Mariguita: A Tragedy of Guam*. (POW). Suva, Fiji, 1986.

Hubbard, Preston John. *Apocalypse Undone.* (POW). Nashville, TN, 1990.
Kenny, Catherine. *Captives: Australian Army Nurses in Japanese Prison Camps.* (CIC). St. Lucia, 1986.
Kerr, E. Bartlett. *Surrender and Survival.* (POW). New York, 1985.
Lawton, Manny. *Some Survived.* (POW). Chapel Hill, NC, 1984.
Marek, Stephen (Victor Panek). *Laughter in Hell: The True Experiences of Lt. E. L. Guirey USN, and Technical Sgt. H. C. Nixon USMC and Their Comrades in Osaka and Tsuruga.* (POW). Caxton, 1953.
Norquist, Ernest. *Our Paradise: A GI's War Diary.* (POW). Hancock, 1989.
Parkin, Ray. *The Sword and the Blossoms.* (POW). London, 1968.
Prisoner of War Bulletin: 2 (2) (February 1944), 2 (10) (October 1944), and 2 (11) (November 1944).
Schafer, Rene. *Terug Naar Fukuoka 14* [Return to Fukuoka 14]. (POW). Amsterdam, 1985.
Stellingwerf, Dr. J. *Fatman van Nagasaki* [Fatman of Nagasaki]. (POW). Franeker, the Netherlands, 1980.
Trumbell, Robert. *Nine Who Survived Hiroshima and Nagasaki: Personal Experiences of Nine Men Who Lived Through the Atomic Bombings.* (POW). New York, 1957.
Tyson, G. G. *The Last Phase at Omine.* (POW). Launceston, 1946.
Velden, Dr. D. van. *De Japanse Burgerkampen* [The Japanese Civilian Camps]. (CIC). Franeker, the Netherlands, 1977.
Vander Londen, D. A. *Totdat de Atoombom Viel* [Until the Atom Bomb Fell]. (POW). Utrecht, 1946.
Waldron, Ben D., and Emily Burneson. *Corregidor: From Paradise to Hell.* (POW). Freeman, 1988.
Wormser, J. A. *Nacht van de Rijzende Zon* [Night of the Rising Sun]. (POW). Kampen, the Netherlands, 1989.
Wright, Lieutenant General John M., Jr. *Captured on Corregidor.* (POW). Jefferson, NC, 1988.

International Military Tribunal, Far East:

IMTFE 27880-83: Concerning Fukuoka camps.
IMTFE 27878-80, 27938-40: Concerning Tokyo camps.
IMTFE 27883-84: Concerning Zentsuji camps.
IMTFE 14197-261, 14270-80, 16258, 40217-20, 40251-55, 40279-83, 40305-07, 40236-29, 40362-72, 42669-72: Concerning camps in Japan, general.
IMTFE 27201-28, 27391-95, 27803-78, 27927-37, 28750-55, 28867-915, 29038-58: Concerning POWs in Japan—affidavits and testimonies.
IMTFE 27169-74, 36413-15, 36419-20, 36837-39: Concerning civilian internees in Japan—affidavits and testimonies.
RvO IC 6781: Slave labor as a miner in Japan.
RvO IC 238: Feeding of POWs in Japan.
RvO IC 1201: Bombing of Kobe, June 5, 1945.
RvO IC 1254: Atom bomb over Nagasaki and a Fukuoka camp.
RvO IC 6865: Liberation in Kamioka (POW9).

FORMOSA

POW Camps

Introduction. The name *Formosa* is used throughout to refer to the area that now makes up the nation of Taiwan, since all documents and literature use this name as it existed before and during the war.

According to the International Red Cross:

> Of the 1,500 prisoners reported in 1943, at least 500 were known to be Americans. When the camps were opened there was a considerably high incidence of colitis and diphtheria, aggravated by exhaustion from the journey from the south. Malaria was also a problem. The prison quarters consisted mostly of wooden military barracks.
>
> Food included rice and barley, with irregular quantities of meat and fish. The prisoners were allowed to raise some livestock and poultry. However, the food supplies were inadequate to provide a balanced diet. Red Cross shipments were not getting through. Prisoners' recreation consisted mostly of walking, gardening and sports, such as football and basketball, plus numerous indoor activities.[1]

The data were inconsistent. In June 1944, the International Red Cross reported 2,388 Allied POWs, with one unconfirmed, and an unidentified report stated that there were another 3,300 POWs from Java and Sumatra, bringing the total to 5,688 POWs.

A report prepared by MID, Washington, DC, and released on October 20, 1944, stated that "the food was good enough to exist on." One officer considered the three meals a day the "pleasure of the day and the food is filling. Rice is the staple and we are able to derive sufficient nourishment" (written February 15, 1944).

Also from the same letters, "We have now plenty of vegetable stews, and other things, such as pork, flour and soya beans."

The International Red Cross reported: "The food available consists of substantial quantities of meat and fish; vegetables, potatoes, fruit, small quantities of eggs, butter and cheese; and black tea, but practically no coffee."[2]

The personal accounts of those imprisoned on Formosa differ substantially from those given by the Red Cross and other neutral parties.

There were no civilian internment centers in Formosa.[3]

Individual Listings of POW Camps: POW161–POW169

POW161: Heito, Camp No. 3

Located in southern Formosa, about 6 miles east of Heito, this camp housed 301 men—243 British, 24 Australian, 26 American, 6 Dutch, and 2 Chinese.

POW162: Karenko

Red Cross Information: In this camp, near the town of Karenko, there were 248 prisoners. The food was estimated to contain 2,800 calories per day per man; in this camp the prisoners' weight is stated to have increased from an average of 114 pounds on arrival to 146 pounds at the end of May 1943.[4]

From *The Knights of Bushido*:

> In April 1943 all officers and all high civilian authorities were moved to Tamasata camp—they were told that this move was made as to give the prisoners better accommodations. He (the Red Cross Representative) walked through the camp, inspected the accommodation, and was allowed to talk to a few officers, but only in the presence of the Japanese.
>
> The prisoners were moved back to Karenko after the departure of the Red Cross Representative. A month later the Karenko prisoners were moved to Shirakawa.[5]

From *The Hard Way Home*: "The cookhouse was tucked behind a hedge at the backside of the compound. The food consisted of 2/3 bowl of watery vegetable soup, 1 teacup of rice, and occasionally tofu or soybean curd."[6]

Karenko camp was used to house all the high-ranking civilian governmental officials from the occupied "colonies" and military personnel from the rank of colonel up. These men were transported from the different places in Southeast Asia to Karenko between August 17, 1942, and February 1, 1943. In *The Hard Way Home*, Colonel William C. Braly listed all the prisoners by name, rank, and position.

POW163: Shirakawa

In June 1943, the prisoners in Karenko were moved to this old Japanese training billet. Barracks for the imprisoned generals had been built, but the wooden structures had gaping holes in the floor and leaky roofs. The officers had to sleep on bamboo beds. A central cookhouse with six cauldrons provided the food. Between June 1943 and June 1944, groups of officers continued to be transported to this camp from elsewhere. In

October 1944, this group of POWs was transported to Manchuria via POW145 (Beppu Camp) in Japan.

As Lord Russell of Liverpool stated:

> The Japanese discipline in Shirakawa was extremely harsh—notwithstanding that the captives were generals and high-ranking officials—and was enforced by brutal methods. Prisoners were severely beaten for the most trivial offenses, and often for no reasons at all. Offenses were "invented" in order to provide an excuse for chastising the prisoners.[7]

POW164: Taihoku Camp No. 2

Located in northern Formosa, this camp housed 779 British POWs who worked in the mines.

POW165: Taihoku Camp No. 5

Also located in northern Formosa, 6 miles from Taihoku town, this small camp of 32 prisoners housed the highest-ranking Allied military officers, who were moved from POW163 (Shirakawa).

POW166: Taihoku Camp No. 6

Located 5 miles from Taihoku, this camp housed 439 POWs—425 British, 13 Americans, and 1 Australian.

POW167: Taichu

A camp 10 miles south of Taichu, with 325 British POWs.

POW168: Keelung
POW169: Kingaseki

NOTES

1. American Red Cross, "Japanese Prisoner of War Camps in Formosa," *Prisoner of War Bulletin* 1 (4) (July–August 1943), p. 2.
2. *Ibid.*, p. 4.
3. IMTFE 27133.
4. American Red Cross, p. 3.
5. Lord Russell of Liverpool, *The Knights of Bushido*, London, 1958.
6. Colonel William C. Braly, *The Hard Way Home*, Washington, DC, 1947.
7. *Ibid.*, p. 167.

SOURCES: FORMOSA

Braly, Colonel William C. *The Hard Way Home*. Washington, DC, 1947.
Kerr, E. Bartlett. *Surrender and Survival*. New York, 1985.

Russell, Lord of Liverpool. *The Knights of Bushido.* London, 1958.
Velden, Dr. D. van. *De Japanse Burgerkampen* [The Japanese Civilian Camps]. Franeker, the Netherlands, 1977.
Wainwright, General Jonathan M. *General Wainwright's Story.* New York, 1946.

International Military Tribunal, Far East:

IMTFE 11547-9: Karenko camp.
IMTFE 14489-90, 14518-20, 14708-27: Internment of POWs.
IMTFE, exhibit 2015: Plans for the liquidation of POWs at Taihoku.
IMTFE 27133: No civilian internment camps in Formosa.

KOREA

POW Camps

Individual Listings of POW Camps: POW170-POW180

POW170: Jinsen

Jinsen camp, an officers' camp with a number of enlisted men to perform menial duties, was located on the outskirts of Jinsen city, about 30 miles from Keijo. It was first occupied by British and Australian POWs in 1942. In April 1945, 140 Americans arrived from Fukuoka, Japan. The camp was considered by far the best the Americans had been confined in. Voluntary work consisted of cultivating a vegetable garden and sewing button holes onto Japanese civilian uniforms.

POW171: Fusan

In August 1942 about 1,000 POWs from Malaya and Singapore marched through the streets of the city before a crowd of 120,000 Koreans and 57,000 Japanese. All were in poor physical condition and were jeered at.

POW172: Keijo 3
POW173: Keijo Main Camp
POW174: Keijo Branch Camp No. 1
POW175: Keijo Dispatch Camp No. 1
POW176: Konan
POW177: Rempo
POW178: Repho
POW179: Ryuzan
POW180: Seishin

Civilian Internment Centers

Introduction. Allied civilians in Korea were mostly missionaries and priests, and were eventually moved to Japan.

Individual Listings of Civilian Internment Centers: CIC34

CIC34: Koshuyu
   The American Methodist mission, in the outskirts of Taiden on the railroad between Fusan and Keijo, was used as an internment center. Six men, of whom five were priests, were interned from July 1, 1942, to August 1945. The internees were reasonably well supplied with food from the local police officials. Red Cross delegates from Tokyo paid these men several visits.

SOURCES: KOREA

Broughton, Douglas C. *Mongolian Plains and Japanese Prisons*. (CIC). London, 1947.

Velden, Dr. D. van. *De Japanse Burgerkampen* [The Japanese Civilian Camps]. Franeker, the Netherlands, 1977.

MANCHURIA

POW Camps

Introduction. Manchuria was visited on November 13, 1943, by a delegate of the International Red Cross. In some parts, the delegate's report painted a positive picture, but in other parts, it reflected the reality of the camps.

Individual Listings of POW Camps: POW181–POW185

POW181: Hoten Temporary

POW182: Hoten Main Camp
   The prisoners were moved in July 1943 from a temporary camp to this

new main camp on the outskirts of Mukden, on the railroad to Harbin. The first occupants were 1,170 Americans and 100 Australians and British. The number of POWs varied constantly because of deaths (over 200 died during captivity) and transfers. Senior officers and high-ranking civilians from Formosa arrived in this camp via Japan. They were then spread out over a number of camps.

There were many casualties during American air raids; two factories located near the prison camp were bombed. In contrast to the camps in Japan, there were numerous recreational activities—music, cabaret, reading (1,000 books were in the library), baseball, volleyball, and basketball. The POWs were transferred back and forth to three "work" camps.

POW183: Hoten "Work" Camp. No. 1
A tannery to which about 150 men were assigned.

POW184: Hoten "Work" Camp No. 2
A textile factory to which about 150 men were assigned.

POW185: Hoten "Work" Camp No. 3
A combination steel and lumber mill to which 125 men were assigned.

Civilian Internment Centers

Introduction. Politically and geographically, Manchuria became a Japanese "province" called Manchuko immediately after it was occupied. At the outbreak of the war, most foreign civilians were interned in Mukden. In May 1942 these civilians were transported to Japan; others remained in Mukden because of the lack of space on the ships.

Priests, nuns, and missionaries were interned within their own mission compounds. They were guarded and mostly well cared for by the Manchurian authorities. Whatever they lacked—and there was basically little they did not get—was supplied by Christians in the community, who regularly visited the missions.

Individual Listings of Civilian Internment Centers: CIC35–CIC38

Mukden

CIC35: Hoten*
About 50 men and women from all over Manchuria were interned in

---

*An asterisk denotes that the camp was liberated in August 1945.

the facilities of the British and American Business Men's Club. The work consisted mostly of maintaining the buildings and grounds. Some internees were transferred to Japan; others were exchanged for Japanese internees in other nations. The rest stayed until liberation in August 1945.

Szepingkai

POW36: Shinei*

About 60 missionaries, priests, and brothers were interned in one section of the convent. About 40 nuns were held in a separate section. The so-called lockup lasted from December 1941 to August 1945, when the camp was liberated.

Dairen

CIC37: Kabahashi

An unknown number of internees were held in a large house in the suburbs. Some were exchanged, and others were moved to CIC35 (Hoten).

Harbin

CIC38: Harbin

The camp was located near the germ warfare factory of Harbin. Before and during the war, the Japanese Army ran a biological warfare experimentation unit in Harbin, using prisoners as human guinea pigs. This program began in 1931 under the direction of Lieutenant General Shiro Ishii, a surgeon. In the war's final days, the Japanese destroyed the germ warfare test laboratories at Mukden, Pingfan, and Harbin before Soviet and American forces moved in.

Somehow, at some time, the U.S. government obtained from Japanese authorities the test results of these germ warfare experiments. The army's chief record keeper maintains that U.S. archives on the subject are skimpy and inconclusive.

Concluding Information on Civilian Internees

The following approximate data are available on the number of internees. No figures about deaths are available.

 50 men
 60 clergy
 40 nuns
 ±150 persons

SOURCES: MANCHURIA

Braly, Colonel William C. *The Hard Way Home.* (POW). Washington, DC, 1947.
Brougher, William E. *South to Bataan, North to Mukden.* (POW). Athens, 1971.
Broughton, Douglas G. B. *Mongolian Plains and Japanese Prisons.* (CIC). London, 1947.
Kerr, E. Bartlett. *Surrender and Survival.* (POW). New York, 1985.
Scholten, Major General P. *Op Reis met de Speciale Part* [Traveling with the Special Party]. (POW). Leiden, the Netherlands, 1971.
Velden, Dr. D. van. *De Japanse Burgerkampen* [The Japanese Civilian Camps]. (CIC). Franeker, the Netherlands, 1977.
Wainwright, General Jonathan M. *General Wainwright's Story.* (POW). New York, 1946.

International Military Tribunal, Far East:

IMTFE 31669-711, 27533-35: Employment of POWs.
IMTFE 27680-88, 27918-21: Camp reports.
IMTFE 28085-88: Affidavits and testimonies of civilian internees.

Sources on Harbin Germ Warfare Experimentations:

Army Center of Military History, Washington, DC.
Biological Warfare Research, Fort Detrick, Maryland.
Chen, Joseph C. Y. University of California at San Diego.
Dower, John. University of California at San Diego.
Harris, Sheldon. California State University at Northridge.
Powell, John W. Article for the *Bulletin of Atomic Scientists*, October 1981.
Professor Kei-ichi Tsuneishi, University of Nagasaki, Japan.
Professor Yoshiaki Yoshimi, Chou University in Tokyo, Japan.

CHINA and HONG KONG

POW Camps

Introduction. Both medicines and medical supplies were inadequate. Once American Red Cross parcels were allowed through, the situation changed markedly; more medicines and other needed supplies were available.

By the standards of Japanese prison camps, those in Hong Kong were relatively humane and well run. In Samshuipo camp there was a well-stocked library, as well as sports gear and instruments for a band. Malnutrition was common, however, and only the distribution of Red Cross parcels kept up minimum standards of health.

But even in these camps, the guards performed frequent acts of brutality, arrogance, and bad temper. Each guard could make up his own camp rules, so there was no end to the annoyances and interferences the prisoners had to endure.

Concerning the Chinese POWs, the Japanese considered the hostilities in China not a war but a "conflict," so they labeled the Chinese troops not as soldiers, but as bandits. According to the Japanese, the customs of war did not apply to the Chinese soldiers, who were often massacred or tortured and eventually drafted into labor camps.

This author's research could uncover information on only about 50 percent of the listed prison camps.

Individual Listings of POW Camps

Canton Group: POW186–POW190

POW186: Anton
POW187: Cheung Ping
POW188: Cheung Pang
POW189: Pakkai
POW190: Pokong

Hainan Island Group: POW191–POW197

POW191: Cheung Kong
POW192: Hachow
POW193: Hoihow
POW194: Paksha Kong [Patsho?]
POW195: Samal Naval Base
POW196: Shinhlushan
POW197: Tinduk Mine

Hong Kong Group: POW198–POW206

POW198: Argyle Street
This camp with 12 huts was used to intern high-ranking officers, including Major General Maltby and Commodore A. C. Collinson, Royal Navy, and about 430 officers and 116 men of other ranks. In August 1943 the officers were moved to Formosa. The camp was vacated in May 1944, when the rest of the POWs were moved to POW204 (Samshuipo).

POW199: Bowen Road Military Hospital
POW200: Kowloon Camp
POW201: Lai Chi Kok
POW202: Ma Tan Chaung [Matachung?]

POW203: North Point Camp
 Rows of wooden huts, 125 feet by 18 feet, were built over concrete floors. The bunks, with two tiers down each side, were well constructed. There were about 200 men in the camp.

POW204: Samshuipo
 On January 4, 1942, immediately after the fall of Hong Kong on December 25, 1941, 2,000 Allied POWs were interned in Samshuipo barracks. The camp had one large, three-story building and rows of long huts, with no window frames, no flooring, no plumbing, and no electricity. Work details consisted of various jobs at Kaitak airfield.
 On September 25, 1942, the men embarked on the *Lisbon Maru* for transport to Japan. On October 2 the ship was torpedoed, and about 850 men out of the ±1,800 lost their lives.

POW205: Stanley Camp
POW206: Yaumati Jail

Peking Group: POW207–POW208

POW207: Fengtai
 This camp was part of the "temporary camp system" of the Japanese authorities. The prisoners in this camp came from POW220 (Kiangwan), which in turn housed prisoners moved from POW222 (Woosung). The camp opened in May 1945, and of the ±1,000 prisoners, half were military and half civilians. Conditions in general were deplorable. The camp was overcrowded, and there was a huge open latrine pit with logs placed across it, one single fire hydrant for water, bad food, no medical supplies, and no recreation.
 In June 1945, the prisoners were divided into three groups. The first consisted of 500 men (436 American POWs and 64 British POWs); the second, 300 men (223 American civilians, 5 Norwegians, and 72 Italians); and the third, 196 men (108 American POWs and civilians and 88 Chinese). They traveled via Fusan, Korea, to Tokyo, Honshu Island, and Hokkaido Island.

POW208: Camp 407

Shanghai Group: POW209–POW222

POW209: Jessfield Road Police Station
POW210: Lin Cha Lu

POW211: Naval POW Camp
This camp was situated in the compound of the Shanghai meteorological station, formerly a Chinese hospital. The prisoners were officers and the crew of the USS *Wake*, survivors of the HMS *Petrel*, and officers and part of the crew of the SS *President Harrison*. From time to time, officers and crewmen from other captured merchant marine ships arrived in the camp. The total number of POWs varied from 70 to 210.

Conditions and treatment were quite good—friendly, polite guards; good housing facilities; generally good food, and medical treatment in a Japanese hospital.

The officers and crew of the *Wake* and *Petrel* were transferred to POW222 (Woosung) in January 1942. The merchant marine men were released and allowed to live in the International Settlement.

POW212: Power Station
POW213: Water Works
POW214: Ta Hsi Lu No. 65
POW215: Zikawei
POW216: Chin Hua
POW217: Civic Center
POW218: Hong Chi Salt Godown, Kinhua
POW219: Kiangsu Middle School

POW220: Kiangwan
The camp was located in the suburbs of Kiangwan, north of Shanghai on Tazang Motor Road. Prisoners in this camp—about 1,600 men, of whom 700 were American POWs—all came from POW222 (Woosung) on December 6, 1942. Conditions were fair, especially after the men made their own improvements in the latrines and campgrounds, planting vegetables and laying out a sports field. Medical supplies were adequate. Food supplies, delivered from the outside through the intermediary of the Red Cross and the American Association POW Committee, improved the conditions considerably. Work details—road building, drainage, ground leveling, and the like—were in the vicinity of the camp.

At the end of 1943, groups of men were transported to Japan. On May 9, 1945, Kiangwan was closed; the rest of the men moved to POW207 (Fengtai).

POW221: Lunghwa

POW222: Woosung
This camp was located 15 miles north of Shanghai and 5 miles northeast of Woosung Forts, next to a radio station. The first group of men to arrive came from the Naval POW Camp POW211. On February 1, 1942, about 750 POWs and 750 civilians arrived from Peking and Tientsin. In September 1942, 70 men were transported to Japan, and on December 6, 1942, the entire camp was moved to POW220 (Kiangwan).

Shantung Group: POW223–POW224

POW223: Swatow

POW224: Tientsin
This camp, used only a short time, was the Fourth Marine compound. The Tientsin marines—36 in all—were captured on December 8, 1941. Then, 21 marines, stationed in Chingwantao, were transported to this compound, followed by 205 marines of the Peking guards. The total number of POWs was 262.
The treatment was very good because the marines were on fairly good terms with the Japanese unit in that city before the outbreak of the war. The entire camp was moved on January 28, 1942, to POW222 (Woosung).

Yunan Group: POW225–POW230

POW225: Chaiotoukai
POW226: Huangsikan
POW227: Lunghing
POW228: Shangkiakai
POW229: Mangshih
POW230: Tengchung

Civilian Internment Centers

Introduction. It was not until October 1942 that small groups of Allied civilians were gradually interned on orders of the military, who became concerned about possible subversive actions of these civilians with the Chungking regime.
As a countermeasure against the American internment of Japanese Americans in assembly and relocation centers in the western states of the United States, the Japanese started full-scale internment of Allied civilians in China in February 1943. All camps were under the supervision of the

various Japanese consular offices, except for CIC57 (Amoy) and CIC43 (Haiphong Road).

The internees maintained the camp themselves and did the central cooking. Extra food supplies were purchased with money supplied by the Swiss Consulate, by borrowing money from the more well-to-do internees, by pooling all available funds into a camp fund, or by placing the money in a Japanese-controlled bank so that all internees could share in the purchase of the extra food supplies.

The Japanese supplied no clothing and very little medicines and soap. Medical treatment was generally good because of the many physicians and nurses from the mission hospitals who were interned with the civilians. The Red Cross and Swiss Consul regularly supplied the camps with medicines. They also paid for the treatment of the sick in hospitals outside the centers.

The morale in the internment centers was, on the whole, good. There was no forced labor, and religious services, study, and recreational activities, including concerts, dance evenings, and theater, were allowed.

Individual Listings of Civilian Internment Centers: CIC39–CIC60

Tsingtao

CIC39: Tsingtao CIC
Men, women, and children from the town and surrounding area were housed in this school in the city from December 1941 to March 1943. All were moved to CIC41 (Weihsien).

Che Foo

CIC40: Che Foo
Men, women, and children from Che Foo city and the surrounding area lived in a school in the city from December 1941 to September 1943. All were moved to CIC41 (Weihsien).

Weihsien

POW41: Weihsien*
About 1,700 men, women, and children from Peiping, Tientsin, CIC39 (Tsingtao), and CIC40 (Che Foo), including 400 Catholic Fathers and

---

*An asterisk denotes that the camp was liberated in August 1945.

Sisters were housed in the large American Mission Hospital and school compound, 2 miles east of Weihsien.

Rows of student rooms were used by the married couples and children, while the classrooms were used by the single men. Food was prepared in large cauldrons in a central kitchen; the food rations were adequate. The internees ran a children's school, dramatic society, concerts, recitals, and church services by the various denominations.

The Swiss Consul paid regular visits and delivered medical supplies to the camp. Money was pooled in a camp bank for the purchase of extra supplies.

In September 1943 about 300 Americans were exchanged, and 460 Roman Catholic clergy were moved to convents in Peiping. The remainder were liberated in August 1945.

Peiping

CIC42: Peiping Segregation Center*

About 30 men and women, the sick and elderly, lived in the compound of the British Embassy from May 16, 1943, to August 1945, when they were liberated.

Shanghai

CIC43: Haiphong Road Camp

About 325 prominent male political prisoners from Shanghai were housed in the military barracks in the city from November 5, 1942, to June 8, 1945. Just before war's end, the men were transferred to Fengtai (POW207), which the POWs had occupied before they left for Japan.

Some observations of Dr. Sturton, an internee in this camp, provide an interesting glimpse at these "political prisoners":

> On the religious side we had an interesting time. We were allowed to have services most Sundays. Bishop Curtis held celebrations of the Holy Communion before morning roll call, and at eleven o'clock we had a union service at which he, the Rev. W. H. Hudspeth of the British and Foreign Bible Society, and Brigadier Walker of the Salvation Army cooperated. Bishop Ward, American Methodist Bishop, also took part when his rather poor health permitted. On Sunday afternoons Hudspeth used to lead a very useful religious discussion group, and on Tuesday evenings Bishop Curtis gave a Bible talk at which many of us learned a great deal about the Holy Scriptures. It used to be amusing to see how Bishop Curtis's attire "degenerated" as the Sunday hours passed by. At Holy Communion he was properly robed; at the morning service he appeared in a gray suit; but by the afternoon he was wearing an ancient bathing costume or a pair of shorts in hot weather.[1]

The alleged mass murdering of POWs by the Japanese toward the end of the war has always been a controversial topic: Did it happen or not? This is what Dr. Sturton had to say:

> We knew nothing about the first atomic bomb except that the Japanese had complained about a bomb which burst in the air.
> It must have been about this time that the Japanese had too much to drink one night and considered murdering us. So far as we have been able to make out they discussed pouring paraffin into our quarters, setting them on fire, and machine-gunning us as we ran out. Most of us did not know about this at the time, but two of the better-disposed soldiers, including the man who kept the armory key, left the others, came to our side of the wire, and told a recently captured American pilot what was afoot. Through the providence of God nothing happened to us, but the Japanese soldiers had a fight among themselves and one of them was badly injured.[2]

CIC44: Yu Yuen Road No. 1

About 885 men, women, and children from Shanghai and the surrounding area lived in the barracks and a school building in town from February 1943 to April 27, 1945. All were moved to CIC51 (Ningkuo Road).

CIC45: Ash Camp, West No. 2*

About 450 men, women, and children from Shanghai and the surrounding area were housed in wooden military barracks on the Great Western Road—a small family camp—from February 1943 to August 1945, when they were liberated.

CIC46: Columbia Country Club, West No. 3

About 350 men, women, and children from Shanghai and the surrounding area lived on the premises of the country club in town from February 1943 to April 27, 1945. All were moved to CIC51 (Ningkuo Road, East).

CIC47: Chapei*

About 1,050 men, women, and children from Shanghai and the surrounding area lived in the Great China University campus in the suburbs from February 1943 to August 1945. It was a large American family camp with about 100 Dutch families. About 350 Americans were exchanged and the rest of the internees were liberated in this camp.

The following observation by internee Laurence Tipton proves a fascinating insight into aspects of maintaining morale:

Among the highlights of the camp were undoubtedly the four hundred or more Catholic Fathers and the Sisters. They were magnificent. There was no work to which they were not willing to turn their hands. The cheerful manner and the thoroughness with which they did the most menial jobs, their eagerness to assist anyone at any time, their unchanging disposition, their aptitude in mixing with every sort of nationality, and last but not least, their ability to play as hard as they worked, not only endeared them to the whole community but were very important factors in maintaining the morale in the camp—early 1944.[3]

CIC48: Pootung*

About 1,100 men, women, and children (about 700 British, 385 Americans, and 15 Dutch) from Shanghai and the surrounding areas lived in this condemned three-story tobacco warehouse across the Whangpoo from Shanghai's Bund. This was initially a bachelors' camp of 800 men—mostly Americans, with some British, Belgians, Dutch, Irish, and Scots. About 300 women and children came into the camp later.

Recreational and educational activities in this camp were exceptional compared to many other camps. The camp library held 11,000 books. As Edna Lee Booker wrote:

> Fortunately in Pootung camp many of the best university instructors of the Far East were interned with us. These men, having seen the approach of general internment, had realized the need they would be able to meet in relieving the tedium and helping their associates in camp life to improve themselves; and they prepared for the work. The university courses were as follows: languages: English, French, German, Spanish, Russian, Japanese, Chinese, Malay, Greek, Latin, Italian. Mathematics: astronomy, trigonometry, geometry, algebra, engineering. History: Chinese culture, American, European, English. Science: botany, zoology, chemistry, physiology. Business: accounting, commercial law, business methods. General: general psychology, abnormal psychology, Bible, navigation, phonetics, public speaking, sketching, music, commercial geography, physical training, yoga.[4]

CIC49: Lunghwa*

About 1,725 men, women, and children from Shanghai and the surrounding areas were housed in this boarding school outside the city from March 1943 to August 1945, when they were liberated.

CIC50: Lincoln Avenue, West No. 4*

About 320 men, women, and children—the elderly and sick from Shanghai—lived in this block of houses in the suburbs from June 28, 1944, to August 1945, when they were liberated. The camp was specially set aside for old and sick civilians.

CIC51: Ningkuo Road, East*

About 1,200 men, women, and children moved from CIC44 (Yu Yuen Road, West, No. 1) and from CIC46 (Columbia Country Club, West No. 3) to this hospital compound at the harbor area. They lived in this camp from April 27, 1945, to August 1945, when they were liberated.

Hankou

CIC52: Hankou

An unknown number of men, women, and children from Hankou city lived on the premises of a school in town from November 1942 to February 26, 1943, when they moved to CIC47 (Chapei).

Yang Chow

CIC53: Yang Chow A

About 375 men, women, and children from Yang Chow, Nanking, and Shanghai (all British) were housed in this boarding school outside town on the Yangtze River from February 1943 to the end of 1943. They then moved to a camp in Shanghai.

CIC54: Yang Chow B

About 350 men, women, and children from Yang Chow, Nanking, and Shanghai lived in a boarding school outside town from February 1943 to the end of 1943, when they all moved to a center in Shanghai.

CIC55: Yang Chow C*

About 750 men, women, and children from Yang Chow and Nanking lived in a boarding school outside town from March 14, 1943, to August 1945, when they were liberated.

Canton

CIC56: Honam*

About 50 men, women, and children from South China were housed in a school in the suburbs from February 1943 to August 1945, when they were liberated.

Amoy

CIC57: Amoy

About 35 men and women from Amoy lived in a hotel in the suburbs from February 1943 to August 1943. They then moved to a center in Shanghai.

Miscellaneous

CIC58: Convents in various cities
About 700 clergymen lived in semi-internment status.

Hong Kong

CIC59: Stanley*
About 2,500 persons—1,350 men, 850 women, and 300 children—from Hong Kong and Kowloon were housed in a former penal colony near a cove at the southeast end of the island from January 15, 1942, to August 1945, when they were liberated.

There were originally about 2,800 people in the camp, but a group of Americans and a few British were exchanged, and roughly 200 British civilians were allowed to move to Shanghai. In all 127 died in camp.

CIC60: Kowloon*
About 130 men from CIC59 (Stanley) and from Hong Kong lived in a barracks in the suburbs from 1944 to August 1945, when they were liberated.

The Gaols: The Infamous Prisons

No reference to the various camps and internment centers would be complete without mentioning the various "gaols," or jails, controlled by the Kempeitai, the Japanese Military Police, which was an approximate counterpart to the German Gestapo. These gaols housed persons of every type and race who were considered by the Kempeitai to be either spies or disloyal citizens, or were accused of any other real or imagined crime. Many Americans were held in these prisons.

There were two gaols in Shanghai and one in Hong Kong. The following are brief descriptions of these gaols and direct accounts of the experiences of an American and an Englishman.

Stanley Gaol: Hong Kong

Each cell had a granite floor with wooden planking, a bed with a wooden pillow, one metal mug, a pan for washing, and a pan for use as a latrine. The door had a small spy hole.

In a filthy metal bowl a little rice and a few coarse greens were the daily meal. A change of clothes was allowed once a week. All day long one had to sit cross-legged.

The Englishman's experience:

> Bird was told to stand up and put his hands behind his back. Several layers of cloth were wound around his wrists. He was taken to the open doorway and told to stand on a stool. His arms were then jerked up behind him and firmly fastened to the fanlight above the door, so that his toes were just touching the stool. Questions were asked. The questioner thought he was stalling and kicked the stool away in a rage and Bird was left hanging by his arms. This final wrench to his shoulders ended his suffering. As he swung around his head hit the side of the door, and his last memory was of his tongue falling, uncontrolled out of the side of his mouth.[5]

Ward Road Gaol: Shanghai

In June 1942 there were about 8,000 prisoners in this gaol—approximately 100 foreigners, and at no time more than 12 Americans. Mr. Mori, the head warden, had an American mother and consequently never treated the Americans inhumanely.

Bridge House Gaol: Shanghai

Conditions here were terrible. This infamous jail was overcrowded, infested with vermin and filthy. The moral degradation here was sufficient punishment for everyone.

During the day the prisoners were forced to sit in formation, cross-legged on the floor, without any support or rest. A number of Americans were severely maltreated, especially those who the Japanese insisted had valuable information. They were not treated as POWs or internees, but as criminals.

As Quentin Reynolds, an American related:

> The guards made me kneel in front of the desk. That is the routine position you assume for questioning—and I was stripped naked. You kneel on a metal plate with your hands at your sides. If you lean more than a few inches forward you lose your balance and instinctively throw your hands out in front to save you from falling. That is a signal for the guards to beat you. I knelt there, smiling. I had spent so many years on the decks of rolling freighters that keeping my balance was no trick to me, though my knees, of course, were screaming blue murder. Just kneel on your carpeted floor for five minutes with your hands at your sides and you'll see what I mean.[6]

Concluding Information on Civilian Internees

The following statistics are culled from van Velden's *De Japanse Burgerkampen* [The Japanese Civilian Camps], Franeker, the Netherlands, 1977:

Interned	Interned	Died
4,500 men	7,250 British	154
3,350 women	1,200 Americans	78
1,500 children	400 Dutch	20
700 clergy	500 others	
10,050 people*	9,350*	252 (2.7 percent)

*Discrepancy: Listings by nationality not always accurate, which some were afraid to reveal.

NOTES: CHINA AND HONG KONG

1. Dr. Stephen Douglas Sturton, *From Mission Hospital to Concentration Camp*, London, 1948, p. 111.
2. *Ibid.*, pp. 121–122.
3. Laurence Tipton, *Chinese Escapade*, London, 1949, p. 85.
4. Edna Lee Booker, with John S. Potter, *Flight from China*, New York, 1946.
5. Ralph Goodwin, *Passport to Eternity*, London, 1956, pp. 174–175.
6. Quentin Reynolds, *Officially Dead*, New York, 1945, p. 61.

SOURCES: CHINA AND HONG KONG

Abkhazi, Peggy. *A Curious Cafe: A Shanghai Journal.* (CIC). Victoria, BC, 1981.
American National Red Cross. *Prisoner of War Bulletin.* 2 (2) (February 1944).
Baxter, George E. *Personal Experiences During the Siege of Hong Kong.* (CIC). n.p., n.d.
Birch, Alan, and Martin Cole. *Captive Years: The Occupation of Hong Kong 1941–1945.* (CIC). Hong Kong, 1982.
Booker, Edna Lee, and John S. Potter. *Flight from China.* (CIC). New York, 1946.
Bonsaquet, David. *Escape Through China.* (CIC). London, 1943.
Briney, Russell. *Until They Eat Stones.* (CIC). New York, 1944.
Brown, Wenzell. *Hong Kong Aftermath.* (CIC). New York, 1943.
Carew, Tim. *Hostages to Fortune.* (POW). London, 1971.
Cristie, K. "Behind Japanese Barbed Wire: A Canadian Nursing Sister in Hong Kong." (CIC). *Royal Canadian Military Institute Year Book*, 1979.
Clagne, Peter. *Bridge House: Shanghai Chamber of Horrors.* Hong Kong, 1983.
Drage, Charles. *Two-Gun Cohen.* (POW). London, 1954.
Edwards, Jack, and Jenny Walter. *Banzai, You Bastards.* (CIC). Hong Kong, 1988.
Evans, Frank. *Roll Call at Oeyama.* (POW). Wales, 1985.
Field, E. *Twilight in Hong Kong.* (CIC). London, 1960.
Garneau, Grant S. *The Royal Rifles of Canada in Hong Kong.* (POW). Quebec, 1980.
Gilkey, Langdon Brown. *Shantung Compound.* (CIC). New York, 1966.
Gittins, Jean. *Stanley: Behind Barbed Wire.* (CIC). Hong Kong, 1982.
Goodwin, Ralph B. *Passport to Eternity.* (CIC). London, 1953.
Hahn, Emily. *China to Me.* (CIC). New York, 1944.
Hammond, Robert B. *Bond Servants to the Japanese: Missionaries.* (CIC). San Pedro, NM, 1943.

Herlihy, Francis. *Now Welcome Summer.* (CIC). Dublin, 1948.
Kerr, E. Bartlett. *Surrender and Survival.* (POW). New York, 1985.
Luff, John. *The Hidden Years: Hong Kong 1941–1945.* (CIC). Hong Kong, 1967.
Marsman, Jan Hendrik. *I Escaped from Hong Kong.* (CIC). New York, 1942.
Reynolds, Quentin. *Officially Dead.* (CIC). London, 1945.
Ryan, Thomas F. *Jesuits Under Fire in the Siege of Hong Kong.* (CIC). Dublin, 1945.
Short, Stanley W. *My Need, His Care: The Story of God's Faithfulness to Miss Iris Critchell During Three and a Half Years Internment in Hong Kong. Based Upon Her Diary and Written on Her Behalf.* (CIC). London, 1946.
Smith, Mabel Waln. *Springtime in Shanghai.* (CIC). London, 1957.
Sturton, Stephen Douglass. *From Mission Hospital to Concentration Camp.* (CIC). London, 1948.
Tipton, Laurence. *Chinese Escapade.* London, 1949.
van Velden, Dr. D. *De Japanse Burgerkampen* [The Japanese Civilian Camps]. Franeker, the Netherlands, 1977.

International Military Tribunal, Far East:

IMTFE record 14186, exhibits 1893, 1904, 1908.
IMTFE 7176, 7181–82, 7193–94, 13201–07, 15291–472, 26863–68, 40213–14, 40249–50, 40277–78, 40303–04, 40324–25, 40356–61, 40361.
Affidavits and testimonies 27471–73, 27513–33, 35771–72, 4648–49, 13112–84, 13304–11, 40177–83, 40214–17, 40250–51, 40278–79, 40304–05, 40325–26.

FRENCH INDOCHINA

POW Camps

Introduction. According to the Reports Liaison and Research Branch POW Information, dated July 1946, there were eight confirmed and two unconfirmed POW camps in and around Saigon and Hanoi.

The conditions everywhere were deplorable—the POWs worked hard and were forced to beg bread from friendly natives. Both French and Annanite civilians did a great deal to ameliorate the lot of the men by providing them with medicines, clothes, food, and tobacco, all of which had to be smuggled into the camps.

These civilians took tremendous risks to contact the POWs; some even aided their attempts to escape. Of the three attempts, only the third was successful; those who were caught had to dig their own graves and were beheaded.

Allied propaganda about Japanese maltreatment of POWs evoked revenge by the Japanese: 22 Australian POWs were decapitated for reasons that were never explained.

Individual Listings of POW Camps: POW231–POW238

POW231: Saigon Docks
   The camp, which consisted of four huts, each 60 feet by 15 feet, was located on Rue Jean Eudal, directly opposite the docks. There were 1,664 POWs—about 209 Americans, 500 British, 900 Dutch, and 55 Australians. The morale was comparatively good because the POWs were able to make contact with French citizens who kept the men abreast of the world situation.

POW232: Cholong
   Another camp in the Saigon area.

POW233: Battambang

POW234: Phnom Penh
   Prisoners in both POW233 and POW234 were most likely involved with the construction of a highway leading from Battambang to Phnom Penh. About 1,000 Australian POWs were used for this work, together with native "prisoners" who were actually slave laborers.

POW235: Hanoi
POW236: Hanoi Gialam Airfield
POW237: Haiphong
POW238: Sawannaket

Civilian Internment Centers

Introduction. There were about 188 British, American, and Dutch civilians in Indochina, where the Japanese accepted French sovereignty over the territory. In early 1943 the Japanese insisted on interning all non–French civilians, an action that the French admiral and Governor General Decoux protested. Decoux later had to give in, although only partially, by allowing a "token" unobtrusive internment of about 65 men, women, and children in Mytho.

Individual Listings of Civilian Internment Centers: CIC61

CIC61: Mytho
   About 65 people—50 men, 10 women, and 5 children from the country

lived in a block of homes. These captives—30 British, 30 American, and 5 Dutch—were allowed to bring their own furniture and to keep their servants. They were free to leave the compound and to receive visitors. French authorities supervised the internees. The captives lived in this camp from March 1943 to August 1945, when they were liberated.

SOURCES

Blin, Captain L'Art. "Le Camps de la mort leute." *Revue des Troupes Coloniales*, 280 (1946), 17–23.
Brines, Russell. *Until They Eat Stones*. New York, 1944.
Gaultier, Marcel. *Prisons Japonnaises recit veçu*. Monte Carlo, 1950.
Got, Jacques F. *Note concernant ma détention de 28 mois au Japon: 8 decembre 1941–3 avril 1944*. Montligeon, 1947.
Le Bourgeois, Jacques. "Prisonnier des Japonnais." *Revue de Paris* 56 (July 1949), 120–142.
Murakami, Sachiko. "Japan's Thrust into French Indochina 1940–1945." Unpublished Ph.D. thesis, New York, 1981.
Prisoner of War Bulletin 2 (2) (February 1944).
van Velden, D. *De Japanse Burgerkampen* [The Japanese Civilian Camps]. Franeker, the Netherlands, 1977.

International Military Tribunal, Far East:

IMTFE 34466

BURMA-SIAM RAILROAD

POW Camps

Introduction: the railroad. The railroad wound through untracked jungles, across dizzy ravines, astride rivers that became swift and destructive torrents during the monsoon season, through rock- and jungle-choked passes, over rocky cliffs, and through treacherous swamps. On this railroad, hundreds of thousands of POWs and Asian laborers toiled day and night in conditions that, if inflicted on animals at home, would produce an outcry from every citizen. The line, about 260 miles (about 420 km) long, was built in about a year, from October 1943 to October 1944, by approximately 60,000 POWs and about 300,000 Asian conscripted laborers-prisoners.

The government of Siam made surveys during the 1920s and 1930s and consulted many engineering experts, including German technicians, but all had taken one horrified look and said it was impossible to build such a railroad connecting Bangkok (Siam) with Moulmein and extending to Rangoon (Burma). The jungle—the densest in the world, except for the Amazon basin—the climate, and the steep terrain convinced them that it was both physically and economically impossible.

The question of cost did not trouble the Japanese. The railway link was needed to supply Japan with Southeast Asia's timber, oil, rice, and tungsten and to keep the Japanese 15th Army to the west reinforced to deter an Allied counterattack eastward from India.

Travel around the Malay Peninsula was lengthy and treacherous. Allied submarines cost the Japanese many cargo ships.

The construction of the railroad was of a much lower standard than European engineers would have tolerated. Some important bridges had concrete foundations supporting earth filling and precarious structures of timber. Very little mechanical equipment was used, and the formation and laying of track through heavy jungle were carried out by prisoners who were unskilled laborers.

The method of work was for sticks to be placed horizontally to show the level to which the track had to be raised. Groups of prisoners, under the supervision of a guard, then dug out earth from beside the track with crude, hoelike implements; filled up sacking stretchers; and emptied them on the slowly rising mound.

The 16-month timetable the Japanese had in mind would be achieved with this enormous group of laborers. The project was of the same order as the building of the pyramids in Egypt, and the railroad had to be hacked out of the earth by the power of human muscle and very little else, something that makes the railway unique in the annals of history. (There was a similar railroad project in Sumatra but on a far smaller scale—see later in this chapter.) The cost in suffering and blood was astronomical (some worked it out as "one life for every sleeper [railroad tie] laid down") but in monetary terms it was negligible.

Monsoon rains, grossly inadequate shelter, a starvation diet, malaria, cholera, and dysentery contributed to the deplorable conditions under which the men were forced to work.

By October 1942, most of the prisoners were assembled at Ban Pong, Siam, or Thanbyuzayat, Burma, the two ends for the link. The Siam side of the railway link was large and more rugged, and consequently most of the work detail was concentrated on the southern side. At the project's peak, about 40 camps, consisting of at least 1,000 prisoners each, were located at 5- to 10-mile intervals (8 to 17 km) along the route.

When they arrived at the camps, most of the prisoners were weak from malnutrition and disease, and their long journey on foot or in railroad cars or cargo holds depleted their reserves further. They lived in open-sided barracks and worked from dawn to dusk, nine days straight, with the tenth day off.

Malaria was rampant, gangrene resulted in necessary amputations of feet and limbs, and physical abuse and brutality made the situation worse. Guards carried bamboo rods and did not hesitate to strike the prisoners.

One factor that raised the cost in lives was that the Japanese were in a tearing hurry to get the railroad finished. No sooner, however, was the line completed than the Allied forces started bombing it.

Very few Japanese supply trains used the railway, and those trains that did seldom ran the entire length. The route chosen started in the south from Ban Pong and Kanchanaburi, crossed the Mekong River, and then followed the course of the Kwai river (its full name is Menam Kwa Noi, which means Mother of the Waters) to the Burmese border at the Three Pagodas Pass, from which point it would join the line coming to meet it from Moulmein over the watershed. Modern maps do not mark all the places, and many of the names have been changed in the past 50 years. But the river Kwai still follows its course, the Three Pagodas Pass is still there, and it is possible to trace the route adequately on even a small-scale map.

On October 17, 1943, the rails were spiked with a golden nail at Konkoita, marking the meeting point of the two sides. Many of the surviving POWs were retained to cut wood for the steam locomotives and to repair the tracks after Allied bombings. Others were sent to Japan to work.

Introduction: the camps. Railroad projects differed in many respects from other camps. While many prisoners were moved from one camp to another during their years of captivity, railroad camps were different. The environment was a thousand times harsher, the camps were occupied for a very short period (until the stretch of railway passing by the camp was finished), and the barracks were of inferior construction.

Some camps were built and used as transit places for prisoners who were sent from Singapore up the as-yet-unfinished line. A number of camps functioned as "hospital" camps, where the most seriously ill POWs were sent either to recuperate or die.

The camps along the line were mostly of the same pattern: narrow barracks, open-sided, 60-yard-long structures of bamboo poles with roofs of thatch or palm leaves. Two sleeping platforms, two feet high, made of split bamboo, ran the length of the barracks on either side of an earthen-floored walkway. Each barracks held about 200 men, permitting each only a two-foot-wide space.

The barracks were full of bedbugs and lice, and the open latrines were alive with large, gray-white maggots. There were flies everywhere.

Some experiences were common to all POWs, but as the men were

Prison Camps: Burma–Siam Railroad

continually split up and spread along the route of the railway, their experiences varied from camp to camp.

Prisoners who were put to work in base camps coped reasonably well, but those assigned to work "on the line" in remote camps suffered unbelievable hardships. As Hugh V. Clarke wrote:

> There was no one typical prisoner of war experience; being a POW was to become an involuntary subscriber to an extraordinary lottery—remain hungry and bored in Changi (Singapore)—journey to Japan and work as a miner—or end up on the railway.[1]

The following may serve as an example of how rough and primitive the logistics were to get groups of men overland from Singapore to the various camps on the railway:

- June 1942: "First" Force—600 British POWs from Singapore to Ban Pong (POW241, km .005) under Major P. S. Rykes, to prepare the line to be built northward.

- September 1942: "A" Force—3,000 Australians from Burma to Thanbyuzayat (POW278, km 000), under Brigadier Varley, to prepare the rail line to be built southward.

- January 1943: "Dunlop" Force—900 Australians and 600 Dutch to Konyu (POW263, km 166), under Lieutenant Colonel E. E. Dunlop.

- March 1943: "D" Force—2,780 British and 2,220 Australians from Singapore to Ban Pong (POW241, km .005), under Lieutenant Colonel C. A. McEachern.

- April 1943: "F" Force—3,662 Australians and 3,336 British from Singapore to Ban Pong (POW241, km .005), under Lieutenant Colonel S. W. Harris. Over a period of two weeks the men had to cover a 300-km march (±190 miles) in 15 stages of 20 km each (12 miles).

By the time the men were placed in five different camps, 1,805 of the 6,998 men had died. Soon thereafter, another 1,282 men died. The total was 3,662 Australians, of whom 1,058 died (29 percent), and 3,336 British, of whom 2,029 died (61 percent). Thus a total of 3,087 men (44 percent) died as a result of the "death march" up the railroad.

The camps in which the men were placed were Changaraya (POW296, km 115), Konkoita (POW276, km 262), and three subcamps around Sonkurai, or Kaung Kluai (POW256, km 110).

The following is a brief extract of Major Bruce Hunt's story, which originally appeared in the *West Australian* newspaper on November 29, 1945, and was republished in the *Ex-POW Bulletin*:

In April 1943 orders were received that "F" Force was to proceed by rail from Changi camp, Singapore, to a northern destination. These orders further stated that 30% of the 7,000 men were to be *unfit*. Upon inquiries to Maj. Gen. Arimura, it was explained that the journey would not entail any marching and that the force was not required for labor but was destined for "health camps" in a good climate where food would be abundant and the unfit would have a better chance of recovery than at Changi. These orders and the shortage of fit men at Changi caused the inclusion in the force of 2,000 unfit men, while the majority of the remaining 5,000 also had some kind of medical history since the surrender, many of them being recent convalescents from such diseases as diphtheria, dysentery and beriberi. All were already reduced in strength by malnutrition during the previous year and the promise of better food and treatment put everyone in high spirits at departure.

As each party arrived at Ban Pong, it learned to its astonishment that the force was faced with a march of indefinite length, as no transport was available. The route of about 200 miles—320 km—started as a metalled road, but after two stages degenerated into a rough elephant track through hilly jungle.

The ultimate destination of the force was five jungle camps spread over a distance of about 30 miles—38 km—close to the Siam-Burma border. When the men arrived at these camps it was found that the camps had not been completed and all ranks were housed in unroofed huts, exposed to the continual downpour of the monsoon rains.

Cholera broke out at the first camp early in May 1943 at a time when parties were continually passing through on their way to the more forward camps. Appeals to stop all movements were rejected. The marches continued and soon cholera was epidemic in all five camps.

Although cholera killed about 750 of the men of "F" Force, by far the most deadly disease was dysentery, aggravated by malnutrition and generally complicated by malaria, beriberi, or both. By June, two months after leaving Changi, only 700 of the men were out at work and most of these were sick. Survivors of the force were returned to Singapore by the end of December. Of the survivors who eventually reached Singapore, 95% were heavily infected with malaria; 80% were suffering from general debility; 50% required hospital treatment for a long period: dysentery, beriberi, skin diseases, malnutrition. On that "health" trip the force lost 3,087 out of its total of 6,998.[2]

The following are four entries from the diary of a personal friend of this author, Dutch Sergeant F. C. Bernard:

19 April 1943: in Ban Pong—the same midnight start on a 7-day march to Kinsayok—we pass Kanchanaburi, Tarsao, Konyu. In Kanchanaburi we got a cholera-typhoid shot. Here the real jungle camps start. Attacks of marauding Thais on small groups of us, or singles who slowed down. Two Aussies got killed by these people. Indescribable heavy march—bad food–no night bivouacs—poor footwear.

28 April: arrival Kinsayok—first impression is terrible—hundreds of dead and sick people.

Prison Camps: Burma–Siam Railroad

> 2 August: another march—rain, mud, hunger, disease—we pass Rin Tin, Kui Ye, Hindato, Brankasi. In 10 days we reached Kaung Khuai [or Sonkurai]—sleep on the spot—nothing but mud around, sometimes knee deep. Nothing more to eat but dry rice and some small pieces of salted dry fish—drink from puddles. Along the whole pass dead Chinese and Tamil coolies, some in decomposed condition.
>
> 12 August: Kaung Khuai—rotted bamboo barracks, without roofs—decomposed, half-buried bodies everywhere—no kitchen, hospital or latrines—only mud. I am barefooted; my shoes rotted off my feet. No more clothes; I rolled gunisack around me.[3]

The paradoxes are mind-boggling. The Japanese were in a hurry to get the railroad built and in operating condition. Why then would they almost deliberately kill off the workers who would be responsible for the on-time construction?

The following passage by POW Rohan Rivett presents the apparent attitude of the Japanese toward their captives:

> You do not understand us. We will build this railway, if necessary over the bones of the POWs.
> You will never see your homes again. You will work for the Japanese until you die.[4]

Numbering System

The camps along the Burma–Siam railroad are numbered in a similar fashion to the other camps in this volume. Many POWs, however, who worked on the railroad identified their camps often by their "distance" (location), e.g., "Camp km. 210."

Another complication to tie this book's numbering system to the real situation lies in the fact that the line was built starting from one point north, e.g., in Burma—POW278 (Thanbyuzayat, km .000)—and from one point south in Siam—Non Pladuk (POW240, km .000).

In all the literature about this railroad, the "km identification" starts at Non Pladuk (km .000) and ends at Thanbyuzayat (km 415 [414.92]).

To provide the reader and researcher with a better idea of how many kilometers long the "north" groups' part was, and how many kilometers the "south" groups had to lay the line to the meeting point at km 263 (262.87), this author has identified the kilometers going north from km 000 to km 263 (as has been done in the literature). Designations of kilometers going south have been given two sets of numbers: from km 000 to km 152 (which are "new" kilometer numbers) and the continuing ones, from km 263 to km 415, as has been done in the literature.

The following list begins with the starting point of the teams working northward and ends at the point where those teams met the one working southward from Thanbyuzayat.

POW239:		Nakhon Pathom, 25 miles from Bangkok
POW240:	km 000	Non Pladuk
POW241:	km 005	Ban Pong
POW242:	km 013	Rukke
POW243:	km 026	Tauna
POW244:	km 039	Tha Muang—base hospital camp
POW245:	km 041	Tung Tung
POW246:	km 047	Kao Din
POW247:	km 049	Tung Na Talea
POW248:	km 051	Kanchanaburi—large cemetery with 6,957 graves, of which 3,459 are British
POW249:	km 055	Tamarkan—bridge over the river, destroyed several times by attacks; 98 dead, 336 wounded, camp evacuated
POW250:	km 057	Chungkai—1,740 buried here—well-kept cemetery, shaded by huge trees
POW251:	km 069	Wun Lun/Wang Lan—"monkey bend" camp: apes in the trees, two sidings
POW252:	km 079	Tapon/Won Yen
POW253:	km 088	Bankao
POW254:	km 098	Tarkilen/Ta Ki len
POW255:	km 108	Arrow Hill/Wang Sing
POW256:	km 110	Kaung Kluai—Lum Sum waterfalls
POW257:	km 114	Wan Po—"hellfire pass" camp—double viaduct
POW258:	km 125	Wong Yai
POW259:	km 130	Tarsao—midpoint: "bullfrog" camp/base camp
POW260:	km 139	Tonchan/Tonsha Spring—"spring" camp
POW261:	km 147	Tampi/Tampines
POW262:	km 155	Hintok—"pack of cards" bridge
POW263:	km 166	Konyu, with three subcamps
POW264:	km 168	Saiyoku
POW265:	km 172	Kinsayok—limestone, forest, waterfalls
POW266:	km 181	Rin Tin—hill camp
POW267:	km 190	Kuiye Kuei
POW268:	km 198	Hindato—hot springs
POW269:	km 208	Brankassi—smallpox camp—bombed by Allies: 17 dead, 14 wounded
POW270:	km 218	Takamen/Dha Kanun—three camps set apart—narrow valley—cholera: 180 deaths in one month

POW271: km 229   Namajon
POW272: km 237   Tamaja/Tomajo
POW273: km 240   Tamuron Pato
POW274: km 250   Kreung Krai
POW275: km 258   Kun Kanta
POW276: km 262   Konkhuta
           km 263   *Connecting Point*—October 17, 1943

The teams working southward were held in the camps listed in order below. The first kilometer figure for each camp denotes the distance from the northern starting point; the bracketed number is the distance from the southern starting point. The total length of the railroad was 415 kilometers.

POW277: km 000 [415]   Thanbyuzayat—cemetery with 3,035 graves
POW278: km 009 [406]   Wegale
POW279: km 014 [401]   Tettoko
POW280: km 019 [396]   Rabao
POW281: km 024 [391]   Komakoi
POW282: km 030 [385]   Retpu—small hospital camp
POW283: km 040 [375]   Beke Taun
POW284: km 046 [369]   Anankwin
POW285: km 053 [362]   Tambaya
POW286: km 057 [358]   Taungzun
POW287: km 061 [354]   Ronshii
POW288: km 066 [349]   Upper Mesali
POW289: km 072 [343]   Mesali
POW290: km 078 [337]   Aparain
POW291: km 083 [332]   Apalon
POW292: km 095 [320]   Kyandou
POW293: km 100 [315]   Aungganaun 2
POW294: km 104 [311]   Anangganaung
POW295: km 115 [300]   Changaraya
POW296: km 121 [294]   Sunkurai
POW297: km 133 [282]   Nikki/Nieke
POW298: km 142 [273]   Teimonta
           km 152 [263]   *Connecting Point*—October 17, 1943

A total of 60 camps or camp sites were established at one time or another on this railway. Two Japanese regiments totalling 12,000 troops controlled the construction—the Fifth Regiment in the Burma area and the Ninth Regiment in the Siam area.

Individual Listings of POW Camps, Burma: POW299

POW299: Rangoon Prison

This prison in the southwest section of the city, called the "Rangoon Ritz" by its occupants, was converted into a POW camp in 1942. There were approximately 1,200 Allied POWs in this "camp," most of them British and Dutch. In April 1945 about 440 men were evacuated from the jail and marched for three days to a village named Naung Pattaya. Upon their arrival they learned that Burma had been liberated.

Camp vignettes: short extracts. With the enormity of the railroad project and the staggering number of men involved, it is inevitable that numerous sad and disturbing stories came out of these jungle camps. The following are just a few such vignettes.

> Unfortunate was the sale of rupees by the moneyed minority among the prisoners for promissory notes to be met in Australian currency on our repatriation. Current rates—1943—on this black market at Thanbyuzayat varied between two rupees and one rupee for an Australian pound. Just how many of these engagements will be honoured by the parties concerned has remained a keenly debated point in the prison camps.
> It is difficult for an outsider, who has not been faced with starvation and who has never battled month after month for very existence, to weigh ethical pros and cons of this matter.[5]

> A few evenings later, I saw Doc racing barefooted across the grounds toward the back of the kitchen. Realizing something was different, I followed him. The Japanese had killed another water buffalo and had helped the prisoners hang it up on a tree to be butchered. Again they had taken the best parts, and had caught its blood in a tub.
> Doc saw that the prisoners were about to dump the blood on the ground a short distance back from the kitchen, and he raced to stop them. Before anyone could stop him, he grabbed the tub and emptied the contents into one of the kitchen cauldrons.
> "That's rice cauldron you're putting that in," an Australian yelled.
> Doc ignored him.
> "Why are you doing that?" I asked. He was poking wood beneath the kettle, stoking the fire. He didn't look up. "It's protein. Our bodies starve for protein."
> "But you expect us to eat that?"
> "Of course. You will eat what you must to live. In Java cooked blood is a delicacy."
> "Java is a mighty strange country," I said.
> I watched, ready to vomit, as the blood boiled and turned black. Finally, as Doc stirred it around with a pole, it hardened and became grainy. He dipped some of it out with a spoon, blew on it to cool it, then tasted it, smacking his lips. A pleased look appeared on his face. "M-m-m-mm," he said. "Very good! Here. You try it."

Other prisoners were gathering around, some more repulsed than others. The cooked blood was tough enough to chew. If it was good for us, and I had no reason to doubt that it was, I was determined to chew it and ingest it. It tasted a bit like burned rubber with only a bare hint of beef liver. "Not bad," I lied, smacking my lips, trying to hold a straight face. "Excellent," I said, swallowing it.

Doc's face beamed. "See? I tell you so!"

Bird Dog's eyes were like saucers. "You're kidding! Gimme that spoon!"[6]

I acquired a vast reputation for ability to cope with dysentery and I once overheard Pink Lilly pay tribute to my skill of treating men suffering from this disease.

"Pav know anything about dysentery? Good God, man, he's shit hot!"

No doctor could wish for a more appropriate and deeply felt testimonial.[7]

Too Young to Die

What shall I think when I am called to die?
Shall I not find too soon my life has ended?
The years, too quickly, have hastened by
With so little done of all that I've intended
There were so many things I'd meant to try
So many contests I had hoped to win
And lo, the end approaches just as I
Was thinking of preparing to begin.
—by an English youth in Singapore.[8]

There were several gangs about who stole on an organized basis and then had Thai agents who would buy anything they had managed to collect. To these men nothing was sacred. Rings and watches were stolen off dying men in the hospital. Drugs began to disappear, including irreplaceable quinine. It wasn't safe to leave washing hung up outside a hut for more than ten minutes without watching it.[9]

NOTES: BURMA–SIAM RAILROAD

1. Hugh V. Clarke, *Last Stop Nagasaki*, Sydney, 1984, p. xiii.
2. Major Bruce Hunt, "Under the Heel—The Siam-Burma Railway," *Ex-POW Bulletin* (March 1989), pp. 27–32.
3. Frits Bernard, personal diary.
4. Rohan D. Rivett, *Behind Bamboo*, Sydney, 1946, p. 232.
5. *Ibid.*, pp. 208–209.
6. Robert H. Charles, *Last Man Out*, Austin, TX, 1988, pp. 115–116.
7. Stanley S. Pavillard, *Bamboo Doctor*, New York, 1960, pp. 171–172.
8. Ernest Gordon, *Through the Valley of the Kwai*, New York, 1962, p. 145.
9. John Coast, *Railroad of Death*, London, 1946, pp. 77–78.

SOURCES: BURMA-SIAM RAILROAD

Adams, Geoffrey P. *An Illustrated History of the Thailand to Burma Railway.* Adams, 1978.
Audric, John. "Railway of Death," chapter 8 in *Siam Kingdom of the Saffron Robe,* London, 1969.
Bancroft, A., and R. G. Roberts. *The Mikado's Guests.* Perth, 1945.
Bates, H. F. *Vlucht Uit Burma.* Utrecht, 1961.
Beets, Nic. *Niet Meer Aan Denken: Burma-Thailand 1943.* Baarn, the Netherlands, 1980.
Braddon, Russell. *End of a Hate.* London, 1958.
_____. *The Naked Island.* London, 1955.
Bradley, James. *Towards the Setting Sun: An Escape from the Thailand–Burma Railway 1943.* London, 1982.
Burton, Reginald. *The Road to Three Pagodas.* London, 1963.
Caffrey, Kate. *Out in the Midday Sun.* New York, 1973.
Canneco, Dr. J. M. *Bushido: Camps in Java and Siam.* Leiden, 1947.
Carter, Norman. *G-String Jester.* Sydney, 1966.
Charles, Robert. *Last Man Out.* Austin, TX, 1988.
Clarke, Hugh V. *Last Stop Nagasaki.* Sydney, 1984.
_____. *A Life for Every Sleeper.* Sydney, 1986.
_____. *Twilight Liberation.* Sydney, 1985.
Coast, John. *Railroad of Death.* London, 1946.
Collis, Maurice. *Last and First in Burma: 1941–1948.* London, 1956.
Coombs, J. H. H. *Banpong Express: Malayan Campaign and Guest of the Imperial Japanese Army.* Darlington, 1948.
Crawford, H. *The Long Green Tunnel.* London, 1967.
Dunford, J. *Branchline to Burma.* London, 1958.
Eichelberger, Robert L., and Milton MacKay. *Our Jungle Road to Tokyo.* New York, 1950.
Esxritt, Ewart. *Beyond the Three Pagodas Pass.* Oxford, 1988.
Fimerty, John Tim. *All Quiet on the Irrawaddy.* Bognor Regis, England, 1979.
Foster, F. *Comrades in Bondage.* London, 1946.
Futumatsu, Yoshihiko. *Across Three Pagodas Pass: The Story of the Burma-Siam Railway* [in Japanese]. Tokyo, 1985.
Gideonse, Henk. *Vergeten Leger in the Jungle.* Amsterdam, 1989.
Gordon, Ernest. *Through the Valley of the Kwai.* New York, 1962.
Hall, Leslie G. *The Blue Haze: A-Force, Burma-Thai Railway.* Australia, 1985.
Hardie, Dr. Robert. *The Secret Diary of Dr. Robert Hardie 1942–1945.* London, 1983.
Harris, Douglas. *G-Strings and Bangkok Bowlers.* Melbourne, 1978.
Harrison, K. *The Brave Japanese.* London, 1967.
Hastain, Ronald. *White Coolie.* London, 1947.
Hulsbus, Joop. *En de Zon werd Rood: de Hel van de Burma Spoorweg.* Baarn, the Netherlands, 1986.
Ingelse, Tom. *Geschiedenis van een Spoorlijn.* Sweden, 1985.
Kan, Wim. *Burma Dagboek.* Amsterdam, 1986.
Leffelaar, H. L. en E. van Witsen. *Werkers aan de Burma Spoorweg.* Franeker, the Netherlands, 1982.
Lumiere, Cornel. *Kura.* Brisbane, 1966.
MacArthur, Ross. *Diary: Singapore and Burma-Siam Railway.* Unpublished, Imperial War Museum, London.

McClelland, James. *Names of Australians Who Died While POWs on the Burma Death Railway.* Silverdale, 1990.
Owen, Roger. *Death Camp on the River Kwai: The Story of Ernest Gordon.* Exeter, 1981.
Parkin, Ray. *Into the Smother: A Journal of the Burma-Siam Railway.* London, 1963.
Pavillard, Stanley S. *Bamboo Doctor.* New York, 1960.
Paxton, L. *Jap Hell.* Amsterdam, 1960.
Pounder, Thomas. *Death Camps of the River Kwai.* Cornwall, England, 1977.
Peacock, Basil. *Prisoners of the Kwai.* London, 1966.
Poole, Philippa. *Of Love and War.* Sydney, 1984.
Ramsey, Winston G. *'40–'45 Toen en Nu.* London, 1980.
Rivett, Rohan D. *Behind Bamboo.* Sydney, 1946.
Russell, Lord of Liverpool. *The Knights of Bushido.* London, 1958.
Seagrave, Gordon S. *Burma Surgeon.* Chicago, 1943.
Semmeling, L. *Als Dank voor de Bewezen Diensten.* n.p., n.d.
Trager, Frank N. *Burma: Japanese Military Administration, Selected Documents 1941–1945.* Philadelphia, 1971.
Trapper, Charles. *Death Trap: A Living Death on the Siam-Burma Railway.* London, 1961.
Vander Londen, D. A. *Totdat de Atoombom Viel: Java, Burma, Japan.* Utrecht, 1946.
Yoshihara, Tadashi, ed. *Santari tetsudohei no kiroku* (Glorious Records of the Railroad Regiments). Written by Japanese veterans. Tokyo, 1965.

International Military Tribunal, Far East:

IMTFE record p. 27438, 27743, 27662: Good treatment of POWs.
IMTFE exhibit 1983B and record pages 49652 and on: Only occasionally were reports received in Tokyo about atrocities on the railroad; when they were, they were accepted by Tokyo without any comment.
IMTFE 12963–95, 12996–13049, 13051–55, 13057–111, 14629–55, 14658–61: Atrocities
IMTFE 27599–619, 36421–22: POW treatment
IMTFE 5492–96, 5506–07, 5510–12n, 5515–608, 11403–526, 12963–13111, 15500–02: Atrocities during railway construction.
IMTFE 27438–42, 27536–95, 27743–50, 30195–213, 31722–48, 34466, 35772–73, 36421–22.
RvO IC 3850: No-escape pledge
RvO IC 1258: Railroad overview
RvO IC 3181: Making of yeast

BURMA

No POW camps except those involved in the construction of the Burma-Siam Railroad were located in Burma.

Individual Listings of Civilian Internment Centers: CIC62–CIC66

Rangoon

CIC62: Central Gaol
 About 200 men, women, and children from South Burma were intermittently interned in this jail in the city from March 1942 to April 1943, when they were moved to CIC63 (Wireless Station).

Tavoy

CIC63: Wireless Station
 About 300 men, women, and children who were moved from CIC62 (Central Gaol) and those picked up from other areas in Burma lived in a number of houses and barracks outside town from February 1942 to May 1945. No other information is available.

CIC64: Maymiyo—School
CIC65: Signal Lines—Homes
CIC66: Kyaukme—School

Concluding Information on Civilian Internees

170 men	190 British
20 women	10 Americans
10 children	200 persons
200 persons	

SOURCES: BURMA

Corpe, Hilda R. *Prisoner Beyond the Chindwin*. London, 1955.
MacKenzie, Kenneth P. *Operation Rangoon Jail*. London, 1954.
Rodriguez, Helen. *Helen of Burma*. London, 1983.
Stibbe, Philip. *Return via Rangoon*. (POW). London, 1947.

International Military Tribunal, Far East:

IMTFE exhibit 1555, 1557, 1558.

SIAM

The name Siam is used throughout for the nation today known as Thailand since most documents and literature referring to the World War II period used the then-known name of Siam. Since all POW camps in this area were associated with the Burma-Siam railroad, these camps are not discussed here because they were dealt with in the previous section.

Civilian Internment Centers

Introduction. The only independent nation at that time among Southeast Asian colonized countries, Siam surrendered to the Japanese within 24 hours and declared war against England and the United States. The Japanese started the internment of Allied civilians almost immediately after the war started, yet the internees remained under the jurisdiction and supervision of the Siamese authorities.

Individual Listings of Civilian Internment Centers: CIC67–CIC68

Bangkok

CIC67: Tha Phra Chandr
   About 200 people—approximately 155 men, 35 women, and 10 children from all parts of Siam—mostly British, but including some Americans and Dutch—lived in the university compound in the city from January 1942 to April 2, 1945. They then moved to CIC68 (Vajiravudh).
   There was sufficient space for all internees; couples and families had two or more rooms each. There were dining and recreation halls. Free contact between internees and the Swiss and Swedish consulates and the Red Cross was allowed. Visitors from the outside had complete access to the internees.
   Medical treatment was good; the ill were treated in a hospital in Bangkok. A pavilion at the hospital, complete with garden, was made available to the internees for rest and vacation.
   Until June 1943, food was delivered by various hotels in town. Then, the internees decided to cook their meals in their own central kitchen. Food supplies were good.
   On March 5, 1945, some Allied bombs hit the camp; two people were slightly wounded. On April 2, 1945, it was decided to move the internees to Vajiravudh College outside Bangkok.

CIC68: Vajiravudh

About 200 men, women, and children moved from CIC67 (Tha Phra Chandr) to the university outside town. They lived there from April 2, 1945, to August 1945, when they were liberated.

SOURCES: SIAM

American Red Cross. *Prisoner of War Bulletin* 2 (2) (February 1944).
Crosby, Sir Josiah. *Siam, the Crossroads*. London, 1945.
Sparrow, Gerald. *Land of the Moonflower*. London, 1955.
van Velden, D. *De Japanse Burgerkampen* [The Japanese Civilian Camps]. Franeker, the Netherlands, 1977.

International Military Tribunal, Far East:

RvO IC 8042.

PHILIPPINES

POW Camps

Introduction. The surrender of U.S. forces on Bataan and Corregidor brought about the most ruthless mass treatment of POWs in Japanese hands. This treatment was apparently based upon a fixed policy of indifference, debilitation, and humiliation, as stated in military reports in Washington, DC, at the end of 1944.

According to these reports, the Japanese tried to counteract American accounts of the crowding and maltreatment of U.S. POWs by publishing accounts of how Japanese citizens were crowded and underfed while interned before the outbreak of World War II in camps in Java and Singapore.

The Japanese camp commandants and their subordinate officers paid little attention to the POWs and left their welfare to uncouth privates and noncommissioned officers, who gave the POWs orders concerning rules and regulations.

Representatives of the International Red Cross were not permitted to visit the POW camps because before the war it had operated in the Philippines under the control of the American Red Cross. A newly organized Philippine Red Cross was given all the assets of the American Red Cross, but the Japanese would not let the International Red Cross recognize it. As a result the work of the Philippine Red Cross was very limited.

Individual Listings of POW Camps: POW300–POW329

Luzon Island Group

POW300: Bilibid Prison
A prison built by the Spanish in 1805, the camp was used as a "clearinghouse" for details of men. The movements of prisoners were impossible to trace accurately. At one time there were about 8,700 Americans and 3,300 Filipinos—about 12,000 men. At the end of 1944, only about 800 physically incapacitated men were in this camp. They were dramatically liberated by American forces on January 9, 1945, and returned to American control.

POW301: Camp Murphy

POW302: Fort McKinley
About 400 men left Cabanatuan in November 1942 to be placed in Bilibid Prison. The Japanese found the place so overcrowded that they took the POWs to Fort McKinley, where they remained until January 1945, when they were returned to Bilibid because of the advancing U.S. forces.

POW303: Fort Santiago

POW304: Engineer Island
The camp was located at the mouth of the Pasig River. The POWs in this camp worked primarily on the docks.

POW305: Las Piñas (Parañaque)

POW306: Nichols Field
Here POWs were used to move dirt out of the runway with picks and shovels, from daylight to dusk, seven days a week.

POW307: Parañaque

POW308: Port Terminal Building
About 430 POWs were held in the barracks at Port Terminal. The work was very heavy—loading and unloading freight—but the food was better than in any other camp. The men received three meals a day—rice, vegetables, meat, fresh fish, and sugar—in a sufficient quantity to enable

them to perform the heavy duties required of them. The camp was closed on July 17, 1944, and the men were placed in several other camps.

POW309: Zablan Field
POW310: Bayambang

POW311: Cabanatuan No. 1

Two camps were formed at Cabanatuan: No. 1 and No. 2. No. 1 camp was located nine miles (15km) from the city and housed most of the officers from Corregidor. In September 1942, 5,000 were shipped to Japan and 1,000 were sent to Davao. That left about 6,000 in Cabanatuan, 2,000 of whom were too sick to work; all were moved to Cabanatuan No. 3.

POW312: Cabanatuan No. 2

Located four miles [6 km] from Camp No. 1. Used mainly for navy personnel.

POW313: Cabanatuan No. 3

Initially used for the sick. Initially 5,000 men from Corregidor were sent here. When Camp O'Donnell and Cabanatuan No. 1 and 2 were closed, all POWs were placed in Camp 3. It became the largest POW camp in the Philippines.

The attitudes of the men in Cabanatuan, who saw thousands of their comrades die, were inspiring to those who had lost all hope: "Courage is fear wrapped in faith and bound by purpose." "If you've got faith and a purpose with meaning, you can make it."

POW314: Linnay (Bataan)

Following the fall of Bataan and Corregidor, about 200 convalescing prisoners were made to collect scrap metal. Because an excellent relationship was established between the senior American officer and the Japanese commandant, the men were well treated. Said a report prepared by MID in Washington, DC, "Such kindnesses on the part of the Japanese are rare, but have occurred elsewhere."

POW315: Lipa (Batangas)

POW316: Nasugbu

A group of POWs were made to work on the docks without sufficient food or water. After two weeks they were moved to Cabanatuan.

POW317: O'Donnell

The U.S. forces which had been surrendered at Bataan—9,300

Americans and 50,000 Filipinos—were marched and driven to this camp, which was an old Filipino training camp. When the prisoners were moved from this camp to Cabanatuan in July 1942, more than 2,000 Americans and 27,000 Filipinos had died in this camp.

A report prepared by the Office of the Provost Marshal General on November 19, 1945, stated:

> Capt. Mark M. Wohfeld: lacked water. Cooking water taken from a murky creek 2 miles away in empty oil drums. For drinking water 9,000 POWs had to stand in long lines in front of three spigots.
>
> Many men learned that hell is not a place but a condition—and that no matter how bad the condition, everything was relative. To give up and die was painless, while living was terrible. Many men slipped away through inaction—others struggled violently to keep within them the breath of life. To want to live with a mad desire was the sine qua non of survival.[1]

In one six-week period alone—from April 10 to May 5—1,600 Americans and 25,000 Filipinos died from a lack of medicine and food.

POW318: Pasay

From 150 to 400 POWs lived in an elementary school on Park Avenue and worked at Nichols and Nielson airfields. Their treatment was poor; they were underfed and overworked.

POW319: Tarlac

The camp was only in existence for a few months—from May 20, 1942, to August 17, 1942—and was used for high-ranking officers—General Wainwright, four major generals, 10 brigadier generals, and 106 colonels, as well as a number of orderlies. They were treated harshly, since the Japanese seemed to delight in humiliating high-ranking "defeated" Allied officers.

> "Everyone in Japan is willing to endure all sorts of hardships and fighting for the final victory in the war. You must understand, therefore, that it is nothing but natural that you are not allowed an idle life," the officers were told. And they were constantly reminded of it.[2]

POW320: Tuy Air Force Base

Caballo Island

POW321: Fort Hughes
POW322: Fort Mills—Camp No. 7

POW323: Malinta Tunnel Hospital

Most men were litter cases from the battle of Corregidor. They remained here until June 2, 1942, when they were moved to Bilibid Prison. Approximately 100 army and navy nurses were moved to a civilian internment center, Santo Tomas.

POW324: 92nd Garage

In this level area, 500 feet wide and 1,500 feet long with a concrete floor, located between the beach and the cliffs inshore, about 7,000 Americans and 4,000 Filipinos were held. The men were used for large labor details—cleanup, completing the airfield, rebuilding roads, and so forth. On May 24, 1942, all were moved to Bilibid Prison, increasing the population there to 12,000 POWs. "We were at 92nd Garage for two weeks, herded up like a bunch of cattle. We had no bath and lived like groundhogs," wrote former POW Albert Puckett.[3]

El Fraile Island

POW325: Fort Drum

Men captured at Fort Drum were kept there for a short while as punishment for the death of a high-ranking Japanese officer during the battle. A brother of this officer, who was in Manila, ordered "revenge-treatment," even though the surrender had earlier been made official.

Mindanao Island Group

POW326: Davao Penal Colony

In October 1942, 1,000 POWs at Cabanatuan were shipped to Davao via Bilibid Prison. They were joined by another 1,000 men from Malabulay. The POWs were used for menial labor in the rice fields or cleaning Japanese latrines. In August 1944, 1,200 of the men were returned to Manila; about 250 sick men were left at Davao.

The work day started at 5:30 A.M. A large detail made the trip out and back on tiny flat cars, pulled by a diesel locomotive. One day, at about 9 P.M., the train came to take the men back to camp. A heavy tropical rain had started, and the train would not go. The prisoners had to push the train, get on it, and then push it again, until it reached a level stretch and continued to roll on. It was after 10 P.M., 16 hours since the men had left for work. Someone started singing, "God Bless America," wrote POW P. W. Pete:

> Swiftly it swept along, car by car, until a thousand throats shouted it in unison. And when we got to the end of the song we sang it again and

again. Major Herman A. Little, bossman of the whole detail, stood near the engine and shouted at us between phrases, "Louder! Louder!" As the train rolled slowly past the Jap commandant's house, that portly officer stepped out on his porch to see what it was all about. We saw him and sang louder still. Was it to be a riot? Would the guards start shooting? We didn't care, one way or the other. At that moment, we would have taken on the whole Jap army, as indeed we had once before. Finally the ride was over, and we were herded through the wide area. It had been an awful day and a terrible ride, but there were some compensations. For the first time in years, we felt like men again. The Jap sensed our ugly desperation and chose to back away.[4]

POW327: Lasang

About 750 POWs were left on Mindanao Island; they had been transferred to this camp on March 2, 1944. They worked on an airstrip. In late August or early September 1944, the 750 men were loaded aboard a ship, crowded into two holds. On September 7, 1944, the *Shinyo Maru* was torpedoed by the U.S.S. *Paddle*. Only 87 of the 750 men reached shore, where they were helped by Filipino guerrillas to reach the American forces.

POW328: Malabulay

Palawan Island

POW329: Palawan Barracks

In September 1942, a detail of 400 men, mostly marines, were transferred from Cabanatuan to this island. Shortly thereafter eight to 10 POWs escaped. In February 1943, two groups of two men escaped. The first two men were captured, tortured, and killed. The second group of two men was successful.

The work consisted of enlarging the airfield on the island. In July 1943, 150 men were returned to Bilibid. In August, about 70 men from Cabanatuan replaced them. About 350 men were the permanent work detail on the island.

In December 1944, perhaps worried that American forces would soon recapture Palawan, the Japanese started to kill the Americans in a day- and night-long massacre of shooting and bayoneting. Only nine of the 350 men managed to escape the bloody event.

The Bataan death march. Bataan fell on April 8, 1942. The Japanese had originally estimated that 25,000 American and Filipino captives would have to be transported to POW camps at Luzon. In reality the number was three times the estimates: 12,000 Americans and 65,000 Filipinos—77,000 men.

The "march" began at Marivales, proceeded on foot for about 60 miles (96 km), then by boxcar for some 20 miles (32 km), and finally another 10 miles (16 km) on foot to Camp O'Donnell. It was very hot and dusty. There was no food or water.

In *Bataan, The March of Death*, Stanley L. Falk cited several "fatal errors" made on both sides that led to the tragic calamities of the march: the lack of a single U.S. officer in overall command, the Japanese underestimation of the number of Allied soldiers, the misjudgment of the food supply, and the lack of organization in the surrender.

Falk wrote the following:

> The tragic evacuation of the prisoners from Bataan was marked by confusion, inconsistency, and disorganization. There was almost a complete lack of pattern in the way the movement was conducted. Indeed, if there were any plan to mistreat or kill the prisoners, as has sometimes been charged, it was certainly administered in a haphazard and uncoordinated fashion. The lot of a prisoner of war is seldom a happy one, yet many of the captives were relatively well treated. They rode in vehicles or walked at a slow pace, sometimes without guards, were able to eat or drink, and were not molested. Others were beaten, starved, refused water, hurried along by brutal sentries, or otherwise mistreated. Many were killed. No two groups of men had the same specific experience.
>
> The inconsistencies in the Japanese attitude and behavior are best exemplified in the varied actions of the guards.
>
> Except in a few instances, the Japanese officers exercised little or no control over their troops and displayed an appalling indifference and callousness to the suffering of the captives. Given the failure or indifference by the Japanese leadership—General Homma—and that their staff did not plan or intend the harsh treatment accorded the POWs almost irrelevant.

Falk went on to explain the Japanese culture of militarism and the difficulty of living in overcrowded islands and concluded, "An understanding of these factors helps to explain, while it cannot condone, the tragic events of the Death March."[5]

Falk's account brought to light what Lawrence Taylor observed in *A Trial of Generals:* "Some Japanese officers themselves were engaged in a vendetta against the hated American."[6]

The images of the Death March are gruesome and, unfortunately, unforgettable, as the following quotation vividly portrays:

> General Jones recalled the horrors: I shall never forget walking at two or three o'clock in the morning with a fog of death laying on the ground and the taste of death in my mouth, and the groans of the dying and the clanging of canteens of columns of Filipinos with bamboos strung between them taking empty canteens dangling and bumping one another on the way to the river to get polluted water, and the other columns returning from the river and then, in the daylight, seeing the continuous columns

of Filipinos carrying stiff dead Filipinos in a shelter-half slung over a bamboo pole, carrying them over to throw them in the ditch because there were too many to bury, and then a column of Filipinos supporting other Filipinos staggering to the hospital, and the hideous presence of death all about us.[7]

Underground fighter Margaret Utinsky recalled:

We came at last to the road where the March of Death had taken place. We came so soon after the surrender that the dead bodies were everywhere. Bodies lay all around, some beside the road, some in the rice paddies, some in the ditches. I was sick with shock. I couldn't believe my eyes. Every foot of the way brought new horrors. I cannot blot out the awful picture of starved dogs tearing at those poor bodies, running off, growling, carrying a man's hand or a whole arm, tearing at his face.[8]

Corregidor fell on May 6, 1942—one month after Bataan. The survivors of Corregidor were not subjected to the Death March. Before Corregidor fell, the last group of the Bataan Death March had entered Camp O'Donnell on April 24, 1942.

The following poem from Bataan is famous:

We're the battling bastards of Bataan;
No papa, no mama, no Uncle Sam;
No aunts, no uncles, no cousins, nieces;
No pills, no planes, no artillery pieces;
And nobody gives a damn.

Civilian Internment Centers

Introduction. The first Japanese landings in the Philippines occurred on December 8, 1941, one day after the attack on Pearl Harbor, on the island of Bataan, north of Luzon, the main island in the Philippine group. On December 31, 1941, Manila radio announced that the city would be occupied by Japanese forces on the following day. On January 4, the first truckload of American and European "enemy alien" civilians entered the Santo Tomas internment center. As the Japanese forces progressed toward the other islands, the same immediate internment of civilians was implemented.

The history of the various internment centers varies only in details. The story of hardship and privation, of physical suffering, mental anguish, and of needless cruelty and persecution, is the same.

Individual Listings of Civilian Internment Centers: CIC69–CIC78

CIC69: Santo Tomas (Luzon Island)*

About 4,000 men, women, and children from Manila and the surrounding areas lived in the 43-acre Dominican University complex, one mile northeast of the center of Manila. Six principal buildings were used. The main building was a four-story concrete structure with about 1,500 internees. The education building housed 650 persons; the gymnasium, 400; the wooden annex, 360; and the dormitory, 140.

One unique aspect of Santo Tomas was the existence of "shanties" with wooden supports, bamboo floors, sawali sides, and tar-paper roofs. Their design and construction varied widely. In September 1943 609 shanties housed about 1,200 persons.

Some shanty owners embellished their interiors with built-in cabinets, window seats, porches, and other home-made furniture. The area devoted to shanties was divided into districts, each with a supervisor. Names were given to these districts, such as Glamorville, Toonerville, Froggy Bottom, Jerkville, and Over Yonder.

There were numerous "comings-and-goings" to and from other camps. For example, in December 1943, 30 men and 177 women were moved to Los Banos, followed by 530 men, women, and children on April 6 and 7, 1944, and another group of 150 on December 5, 1944.

With that many couples together in one camp, the question of sex was an interesting one—perhaps one for future researchers to analyze:

> Tonight our room monitors read us the following notice issued by our Internee Committee: The commandant has intimated to us in no uncertain terms that the attitude of the Japanese authorities in regard to sexual relations under conditions of internment has *not* been changed [sex was forbidden] and if we are to avoid segregation of the sexes in this camp and retain our privileges, such as the use of shanties at any time, as well as restricted areas after sundown, it is absolutely necessary that these privileges are not abused.[9]

The internees were in camp from January 4, 1942, to February 3, 1945, when they were liberated. The liberation was dramatic, as Ralph DioGuardi recalled:

> Saturday, February 3, 1945: It was about 8:30 PM when Walters and his tank "Battlin Basic" broke through the iron fence and onto the grounds of Santo Tomas. The 3rd platoon of B Co, headed by Lt. Lee,

---

*An asterisk denotes that the camp was liberated in February 1945.

a descendant of one of America's greatest generals, followed, and the liberation was to become a reality. More tanks followed: "Ole Miss," "Block Buste," "Georgia Peach," "San Antone," and "Crusader." The tankers, under the command of Maj. W. P. Meredith and Maj. Barksdale (Lt. Col. Tom Ross, battalion commander, was killed on the road to Manila), were as jubilant as the internees as arm-waving humanity rushed from the main entrance of the university. The tanks halted, unbuttoned, and the men leaped to the ground to greet the overjoyed internees as they shouted, "This is the greatest moment of our lives."

Most of the internees were quickly liberated as the Japanese realized the futility of resisting the might of the tankmen. However, 70 Japanese were hidden in the Education building where they held 276 hostages and threatened to kill them unless granted safe-conduct from the camp.

Lt. Col. Toshio Hayashi, the camp commandant, was adamant in his demands. After a brief exchange of shots, the Americans held their fire. Col. Charles E. Brady, executive officer of the 8th Cavalry Brigade, negotiated with intermediaries, and the hostages were escorted to a point beyond the American lines and released.[10]

CIC70: Los Banos*

About 2,100 men, women, and children from Manila were moved from CIC69 (Santo Tomas) to the grounds of the School of Agriculture, 45 miles south of Manila. They lived in this camp from May 14, 1943, to February 23, 1945, when they were liberated.

CIC71: Old Bilibid*

About 470 men, women, and children from CIC73 (Camp Holmes) were housed in the old jail in Manila. The place was one mass of filth, lice, bed bugs and rats. There were no brooms, no mops, no means except the hands to clean the place. The Japanese guarded the camp so strictly that it took weeks for internees in other camps to become aware of the Bilibid prisoners.

CIC72: Camp John Hay

About 500 men, women, and children from Baguio and northern Luzon were housed in four partly burned and demolished Philippine Scouts barracks. All were crowded into one building. There were no beds. The city was located at the 5,000-foot level, but there were no blankets and no fire for heat. The internees lived in this camp from December 29, 1941, to April 23, 1942, when they were moved to CIC73 (Camp Holmes).

CIC73: Camp Holmes

About 180 men, 180 women, and 125 children from CIC72 (Camp John Hay) were housed in this former Philippine constabulary post, seven miles north of Baguio, from April 23, 1942, to December 28, 1944, when they were moved to CIC71 (Bilibid). In addition, 326 Chinese internees lived in the camp until May 1942, when they were released.

CIC74: Iloilo (Panay Island)
About 50 men, women, and children were taken to Iloilo provincial jail on April 8, 1942, and then to the Iloilo central school on May 18. On June 16, 1943, they were taken to CIC69 (Santo Tomas).

CIC75: Bacolod (Negros Island)
About 148 men, women, and children from Negros Island were housed in this schoolhouse surrounded by eight acres of land and barbed wire, that the Americans had used as an internment camp for Japanese and German civilians before the war. The internees lived in the camp from June 5, 1942, to May 2, 1943, when they were moved to CIC69 (Santo Tomas).

CIC76: Cebu (Cebu Island)
About 148 men, women, and children from Cebu Island were housed in the provincial jail and then in the Junior College compound in town from April 10, 1942, to May 16, 1942.

United States forces had destroyed the city's gas, electricity, and water facilities, which were not repaired for three months. Prisoners had to resort to wells for water, candles or coconut oil for light, and wood or charcoal for cooking fuel. On December 14, 1942, they were moved to CIC69 (Santo Tomas).

CIC77: Tacoblan (Leyte Island)
About 23 men, women, and children from Leyte Island lived in a school compound in the city from March 1942 to December 1942, when they were moved to CIC69 (Santo Tomas).

CIC78: Davao (Mindanao Island)
About 280 men, women, and children from Mindanao Island lived in a school compound in town from April 1942 to December 1943, when they were moved to CIC69 (Santo Tomas).

Fort Santiago: Oriental Inquisitions

In her book *Community Under Stress*, Elizabeth Head Vaughan wrote, "Severed from outside sources of aid, deprived of all assets except those at hand, individuals sought a modicum of personal security in group unification."[11] Although individualism eventually began to reassert itself, the internees felt a sense of security by being part of the camp population.

Except for periodic camp inspections and other harassments by Japanese guards, the individual civilian internee could feel relatively safe within the group structure of the camp. Woe the prisoner, however, who, for whatever reason, was hauled from the camp to a prison for inquisition by the Kempeitai. This happened to Fred Stevens, author of *Santo Tomas Internment Camp*. In the chapter "Fort Santiago—An Oriental Inquisition," Stevens stated that he was taken away from Santo Tomas camp because he was involved in raising money for the internees at the camp who were not fed by the Japanese and needed money to buy food.

His story of seven months' captivity in Fort Santiago, an old historic site of dungeons used to house political prisoners during the Spanish regime of the Philippines and then used by the Japanese Kempeitai, is one of immense abuse and cruelty imposed upon prisoners of many nationalities and races, male and female. For seven months, Stevens was locked up in cell "nine" with 14 others, in a space 12 feet by 15 feet and 10 feet high. The rear wall had a barred window 24 by 20 inches, 7½ feet from the floor. The toilet, or *benjo*, was an oriental squat toilet, and the right rear corner was a water faucet. Stevens stated:

> The whole story is difficult to write. It is a chronicle of these wasted and miserable hours of dirt and filth, of savagery and stupidity, of men who stood the gaff of imprisonment like heroes, and those who weakened and broke under the strain of cruelty and poor food would be a story for a more facile pen than mine.[12]

Facile, or not, Stevens's descriptions of the cruelty inflicted on prisoners of many races—Englishmen, Americans, Filipinos, Spaniards, Japanese—will stand as an example of human suffering under Japanese occupation.

Concluding Information on Civilian Internees

Internees	Internees	Died
4,200 men	6,000 Americans	450
2,300 women	1,500 British	3
1,300 children	150 Dutch	—
7,800	150 others	—
	7,800	453

NOTES: THE PHILIPPINES

1. Manny Lawton, *Some Survived*, Chapel Hill, NC, 1984, pp. 28–29.
2. Colonel William C. Braly, *The Hard Way Home*, Washington, DC, 1947, p. 49.

3. Carol Conrow, "Former POW Albert Puckett Shares Memories," *Ex-POW Bulletin* (February 1991).
4. P. W. Pete, "Nighttrain from Mactan," *Ex-POW Bulletin* (January 1990).
5. Stanley L. Falk, *Bataan: The March of Death*, New York, 1962, pp. 221, 226, 227, 230.
6. Lawrence Taylor, *A Trial of Generals*, South Bend, IN, 1981.
7. Falk, *Bataan*, p. 200.
8. Margaret Utinsky, *Miss "U,"* San Antonio, TX, 1948, p. 18.
9. Tressa R. Cates, RN, *The Drainpipe Diary*, New York, 1957, p. 143.
10. Ralph DioGuardi, "Santo Tomas Testament," *VFW Magazine* (March 1988).
11. Elizabeth Head Vaughan, *Community Under Stress: An Internment Camp Culture (Bacolod)*, Princeton, NJ, 1949.
12. Frederic H. Stevens, *Santo Tomas Internment Camp*, New York, 1946.

SOURCES: THE PHILIPPINES

Abraham, Abie. *Ghost of Bataan Speaks*. (POW). New York, 1971.
Agustin, Conrado G. *Men and Memories in Confinement: Diary Excerpts 1942–1945*. (CIC). Manila, 1973.
Agustin, Yay. *Letter to a War Widow*. (CIC). n.p., n.d.
Aitken, Lowell. "The Los Banos Rescue." (CIC). *Military* (September 1990).
Albertson, Dorothy. *History of the Red Cross in the Philippine Islands*. (POW-CIC). Washington, DC, 1950.
Alvit, Alfonso. *The Conscience of a Nation: A History of the Red Cross in the Philippines*. (POW-CIC). Manila, 1963.
American Red Cross. *Prisoner of War Bulletin* 2 (2) (February 1944) and 2 (4) (April 1944).
Arthur, Anthony. *Deliverance at Los Banos*. (CIC). New York, 1985.
Ashton, Paul. *Bataan Diary*. (POW). n.p., 1984.
ATIS. *Japanese Military Psychology* (Report No. 76, April 1944–October 1945). National Archives, Washington, DC.
Bank, Bertram. *Back from the Living Dead*. (POW). Tuscaloosa, AL, 1945.
Barber, Robert. *Philippine Diary*. (POW). n.p., 1989.
Bell, Francis Eldon. "Bataan Death March." (POW). *American Legion Magazine* (August 1959).
Bergee, Lee K. *Guest of the Emperor*. (POW). High Ridge, MO, 1987.
Braly, Colonel William C. *The Hard Way Home*. (POW). Washington, DC, 1947.
Brines, Russell. *Interviews: Santo Tomas Internment Camp*. (CIC). New York, 1942.
Brougher, Brigadier General William E. *South to Bataan, North to Mukden*. (POW). Athens, 1971.
Brown, Charles T. *Bilibid Prison: The Devil's Cauldron, A Fragment from That Mosaic*. (POW). San Antonio, TX, 1957.
Carr, Lorraine. *To the Philippines with Love*. (CIC). Los Angeles, 1966.
Cates, Teresa R., RN. *The Drainpipe Diary*. (CIC). New York, 1957.
Clark, A. R. "Thirty-seven Months as Prisoners of War: U.S. Army Nurses Interned in the Philippines." (CIC). *American Journal of Nursing* (May 1945), pp. 342–345.

Coleman, J. S. *Bataan and Beyond*. (POW). College Station, TX, 1978.
Colley, George. *Manila, Kuching and Return*. (POW). San Francisco, 1946.
Conrow, Carol. "Former POW Albert Puckett Shares Memories." (POW). *Ex-POW Bulletin* (February 1991).
Cordero, Virgilio. *My Experiences in the War with Japan*. (POW). n.p., n.d.
Cullum, Leo A., and James B. Reuter. *Two Jesuits at Los Banos*. (CIC). Fullerton, 1987.
Dahlstrom, W. "The Release of the Bilibid Prisoners." (CIC). *American Legion Magazine* (April 1963).
DioGuardi, Ralph. "Santo Tomas Testament." *VFW Magazine* (March 1988).
Dopkins, Dale R. *The Janesville 99: The Bataan Death March*. (POW). Janesville, 1981.
Dyess, Lieutenant Colonel William E. *The Dyess Story* (POW). New York, 1944.
Evans, William R. *Soochow and the 4th Marines*. (POW). Rogue River, OR, 1987.
Falk, S. L. *Bataan, the March of Death*. (POW). New York, 1962.
──────. *Liberation of the Philippines*. (POW). New York, 1971.
Feuer, A. B. *Bilibid Diary: The Secret Notebooks of Commander Thomas Hayes*. (POW). Hamden, 1987.
Flanagan, Lieutenant General E. M., Jr. *The Los Banos Raid*. (CIC). n.p., n.d.
Gimenez, Pedro M. *Under the Shadow of the Kempei*. (CIC). Manila, 1946.
Gleeck, Lewis E., Jr. *The Manila Americans*. (CIC). Manila, 1977.
Gloria, Claro C. *All the Way from Bataan to O'Donnell*. (POW). Quezon, 1978.
Gordon, Richard M. "The Death March in Retrospect." (POW). *Ex-POW Bulletin* (September 1989).
Gunnison, Royal Arch. *So Sorry, No Peace*. (CIC). New York, 1944.
Hamilton, Esther Yerger. *Ambassador in Bonds*. (CIC). Philadelphia, 1946.
Hartendorp, A. V. *The Japanese Occupation of the Philippines*. (POW). Manila, 1967.
──────. *The Santo Tomas Story: Edited from the Official History by Frank H. Golay*. (CIC). New York, 1964.
Hersey, J. *Men on Bataan*. (POW). New York, 1942.
Hind, R. R. *Spirits Unbroken*. (CIC). San Francisco, 1946.
Hubbard, Preston John. *Apocalypse Undone*. (POW). Nashville, TN, 1990.
Ind, Allison. *Bataan, the Judgment Seal*. (POW). New York, 1944.
Jarrett, Hazel Jean. "Our Most Unforgettable Thanksgiving." (CIC). *Ex-POW Bulletin* (November 1990).
Joder, Richard F. "Libraries in Japanese Concentration Camps in the Philippine Islands." (POW/CIC). Unpublished master's thesis, Pittsburgh, 1950.
Johnson, Forrest B. *Raid on Cabanatuan*. (POW). Las Vegas, 1988.
Kerr, E. Bartlett. *Surrender and Survival*. (POW). New York, 1985.
Knox, Donald. *Death March*. (POW). New York, 1981.
Labrador, Juan. *A Diary of the Japanese Occupation*. (CIC). Manila, 1979.
Lawton, Manny. *Some Survived*. (POW). Chapel Hill, NC, 1984.
Levering, Robert W. *Horror Trek: A True Story of Bataan, the Death March and Three-and-a-half Years in Japanese Prison Camps*. (POW). Dayton, OH, 1948.
Lucas, Celia. *Prisoners of Santo Tomas—Based on the Diaries of Mrs. Isla Corfield*. (CIC). London, 1975.
Lynip, G. L. *On Good Ground: Missionary Stories from the Philippines*. (CIC). Grand Rapids, MI, 1946.
McCall, J. E. *Santo Tomas Internment Camp*. (CIC). Lincoln, 1945.
McCoy, M. H., et al. *Ten Escape from Tojo*. (POW). New York, 1944.

"Massacre at Palawan." *Yank Magazine* (April 20, 1945).
Mellnik, Brigadier General Steve. *Philippine Diary 1939–1945.* (POW). New York, 1969.
Meyer, Elizabeth Thomas. "Teenage Internee at Santo Tomas" (5 parts). (CIC). *Bulletin of the American Historical Collection* 14:1–4; 15:1; 7–31; 7–33; 38–63; 39–65; 66–99 (1986–87).
Military Personnel Records Center. Modern Military Records NCPMA–CBR 897 (copies of recovered records).
Miller, Colonel E. B. *Bataan Uncensored.* (POW). Long Prairie, MN, 1949.
Mydans, Carl. *More Than Meets the Eye* (POW). New York, 1959.
National Archives. Report on POWs Interned by the Japanese in the Philippines. (POW). Box 2154; 12W3/15/e, 136 pp.
Nelson, Gordon. "The Experiences of a POW." (POW). *Ex-POW Bulletin* (August 1987).
Norquist, Ernest. *Our Paradise: A GI's War Diary.* (POW). Hancock, 1989.
Oliver, William P. *Diary of a Prisoner of the Japanese in the Philippines.* (CIC). Cedar Rapids, IA, 1947.
Onorato, Michael P. *James J. Halsema: The Internment Camp at Baguio.* (CIC). Fullerton, 1987.
Pete, P. W. "Night Train from Mactan." (POW). *Ex-POW Bulletin* (January 1990).
Redmond, Juanita. *I Served on Bataan.* (CIC). New York, 1943.
Russell, Lord of Liverpool. *The Knights of Bushido.* (POW-CIC). London, 1958.
Sneed, Bessie (Mrs. C. Dakin). *Captured by the Japanese.* (CIC). Denver, 1946.
Stevens, Curtis R. "Little Red." (POW). *Ex-POW Bulletin.*
Stevens, Fred. *Santo Tomas Internment Camp.* (CIC). New York, 1946.
Stevenson, Theodore D., MD. "A WWII Episode in the Philippines." (POW). *Ex-POW Bulletin* (March 1990).
Taylor, Lawrence. *A Trial of Generals.* (POW). South Bend, IN, 1981.
Taylor, Vince. *Cabanatuan: True Story of a Secret Death Camp.* (POW). Waco, TX, 1985.
Terry, Carol. *Kept.* (CIC). Philadelphia, 1945.
United States. Santo Tomas Internment Camp: Notices, Orders of the Internee Executive Committee. (CIC). Philippine Research and Information Section, GHQ, AFPAC, APO 500, Manila, 1945.
United States. Japanese Atrocities to POWs. (POW). House Document No. 393, 78th Congress, Second Session, Washington, DC.
van Velden, Dr. D. *De Japanse Burgerkampen* [The Japanese Civilian Camps]. (CIC). Franeker, the Netherlands, 1977.
Vance, John R. *Doomed Garrison: The Philippines: A POW Story.* (POW). Ashland, 1974.
Vaughan, Elizabeth Head. *Community Under Stress: An Internment Camp Culture (Bacolod).* (CIC). Princeton, NJ, 1949.
Volckman, Colonel R. W. *We Remained.* (POW). New York, 1954.
Wainwright, General Jonathan M. *General Wainwright's Story.* (POW). New York, 1946.
Waldron, Ben D., and Emily Burneson. *Corregidor: From Paradise to Hell.* (POW). Freeman, 1988.
Weinstein, Alfred M. *Barbed Wire Surgeon.* (POW). New York, 1948.
Wright, Lieutenant General John M., Jr. *Captured on Corregidor.* (POW). Jefferson, NC, 1988.

International Military Tribunal, Far East:

Panay Incident: 3466–67, 9282–83, 9452, 15678, 17693–95, 21362–66, 21382–87, 28767–81, 30083–84, 33834–35, 33908–10, 34734–38.
Disposal of soldiers and POWs around Leyte: IMTFE exhibit 1464.
Treatment of surrenderers: IMTFE exhibit 1465.
Bataan, Summary: IMTFE 12668; Testimony: IMTFE 12610–39, 12673–724, 12738–75, 12821–27. Statement by General Homma's Chief Takaji Wachi that all was well concerning the Bataan March: IMTFE exhibit 1980E, 1982A.
Camps in the Philippines: IMTFE 27324–34, 27625–54, 27723–42, 27761–85, 27820–21, 32936–38, 33075, 33141–50, 35772–74. See also, 12442–52, 12501–07, 12520–36, 12566, 76, 12592, 12595–96, 12801, 15196–281, 40384–481, and 42662–64.
No-escape pledge, Santo Tomas: RvO IC 3669.
Santo Tomas and Los Banos: RvO IC 6824.
Red Cross parcels for Santo Tomas: Rapport du Comite Internationale de la Croix Rouge, Vol. 1, p. 473 ff.

MALAYA and SINGAPORE

POW Camps

Introduction. After the fall of Singapore and the Malay Peninsula, the Changi Peninsula on the island of Singapore was used by the Japanese as a concentration area for the Allied forces captured at the surrender of Singapore. It was eminently suitable for the purpose. Barbed wire across the portion of the peninsula not already cut off by swamps and river secured the landward side; for the rest, there was the sea.

In general the Japanese acted with restraint. The POWs had their own organization within the area, and the appearances of the Japanese were comparatively rare. Some Indian guards, who had gone over to the Japanese, behaved vindictively, but there were other Indians of unshakable loyalty who made great sacrifices for their European and Australian fellow-prisoners and others who paid with their lives for their refusal to collaborate.

The quarters were fairly good; the food was poor.

The Japanese guards, when they appeared, demanded exaggerated respect. The first prisoner to see them shouted a warning; then all within sight, whatever their rank and whatever the rank of the Japanese, stood rigidly at attention saluting or, if without a hat, bowing to the soldiers of Nippon when they approached. The failure to stand properly at attention or the omission of any detail from this ceremony would bring down on the offender a severe beating. The victim would be lucky if he was beaten only with the fists. A Japanese once explained to a prisoner that for a guard to slap his face was "like a mother lovingly correcting her child." Yet broken jaws and eardrums often resulted from these encounters.

The "Changi Square incident," or "Selarang incident" as it was called, occurred in September 1942, when an order from Tokyo reached all corners of the Japanese Greater Asia Co-Prosperity Sphere that all POWs who were regarded as having been incorporated into the Japanese forces should sign a pledge not to escape and to obey all orders.

This order was universally resisted. The "persuasion" to sign was done by concentrating some 17,000 prisoners in one barracks square—the Selarang barracks, an area of about 10 acres. Under indescribable conditions, the men held out for three days, many already suffering from dysentery and other diseases. Then the senior Allied officer, on the advice of the doctors, ordered the men to sign. He recorded, however, that the signatures had been given only under heavy duress.

Toward the end of 1942, the fittest men were drafted from Changi to work on the Burma-Siam railroad. Changi, largely depopulated, remained by comparison one of the better camps. Later, its prisoners were concentrated in Changi Jail, which, until then, had been the place of internment of civilians.

Individual Listings of POW Camps: POW330–POW331

POW330: Changi Camp

From February 14, 1942, onward, about 35,000 British and 15,000 Australian soldiers were interned in the Changi barracks. It became the central "transit" camp for all Allied POWs transported from areas in the Dutch East Indies via Changi to other camps in Asia and Southeast Asia. The men worked on a nearby airfield (today Changi Airport). On May 31, 1944, the entire camp was moved to Changi Jail, after the civilian internees had been moved to Sime Road Camp.

POW331: Changi Prison

This large municipal jail was built in 1930 and was modeled after New York State's Sing Sing Prison. There was a "permanent" POW population and "transfers"—POWs who came from various areas in the Pacific and were transported to other areas. The treatment was generally good. There were games, entertainment, lectures, and discussion groups, and even a newspaper, the *P.O.W. Wow*.

Civilian Internment Centers

Introduction. Amid the chaos of wrong interpretations of the progress of the Japanese forces, the lack of evacuation procedures, and the absence of proper governmental information, British civilians and soldiers attempted individually and in groups to flee Malaya and Singapore. About 4,000, for example, were able to reach Padang, West Sumatra, and to escape in various ships to Australia. About 600 Allied troops and 100 civilians had to stay behind because of the lack of space on the ships. A number of ships were sunk by the Japanese navy.

On February 17, 1942, civilians were ordered to assemble at certain places in town and were then transported to various assembly centers, where they stayed for about three weeks before they had to march to Changi Prison.

Individual Listings of Civilian Internment Centers: CIC79–CIC84

CIC79: Karikal
About 650 men were housed in a convent outside Singapore.

CIC80: Choo Siat
About 1,350 men lived in police barracks outside the city limits.

CIC81: Karikal 2
About 300 women and children lived in a block of houses outside the city limits.

CIC82: Roxy
About 100 women and children lived in a block of houses near Roxy cinema.

CIC83: Changi Prison
All four centers above were used from February 17, 1942, to March 6, 1942, when all the internees had to march to Changi Prison. About 3,500 men, women, and children from assembly centers CIC79, 80, 81, and 82 and the Malay Peninsula and the Riau Archipelago lived in Changi Prison, a building designed to house 700 inmates. The 670 women and children were placed in a wing separated from the men. Two bamboo barracks were added on the courtyard. The internees lived here from March 6, 1942, to May 1, 1944, when all were moved to CIC84 (Sime Road Camp).

CIC84: Sime Road Camp

All men, women, and children (about 3,500) from CIC83 (Changi Prison) were housed in military barracks outside Singapore city from May 1, 1944, to August 1945, when the camp was liberated.

Concluding Information on Civilian Internees

Internees	Internees	Died
3,175 men	3,900 British	218 died (4.8 percent)
1,020 women	50 American	
330 children	80 Dutch	
4,525 persons	500 others	
	4,530 persons	

Some internees were afraid to reveal their nationality, so these figures are approximate.

SOURCES: MALAYA AND SINGAPORE

Arneil, Stan. *Black Jack: The Life and Times of Brigadier Sir Frederik Galleghan.* (POW). Melbourne, 1983.
———. *One Man's War.* (POW). Sydney, 1981.
Attiwill, Kenneth. *The Singapore Story* (POW). London, 1959.
Bell, Leslie. *Destined Meeting: Changi Jail.* (CIC). London, 1959.
Bloom, Freddy. *Dear Philip: A Diary of Captivity, Changi 1942–1945.* (POW). London, 1980.
Bowden, Tim. *Changi Photographer.* (POW). Sydney, 1984.
Braddon, Russell. *The Naked Island.* (POW). London, 1955.
Brown, C. C. *Mural Ditties and Sime Road Soliloquies.* (CIC). Singapore, 1948.
Caffrey, Kate. *Out in the Midday Sun.* (POW). New York, 1973.
Christie, R. W., and Robert Christie, eds. *A History of the 2/29 Battalion 8th Australian Div. AIF.* (POW). Malvern, 1983.
Cornelius, Mary D. *Changi.* (CIC). Ilfracombe, England, 1953.
Falk, S. L. *Seventy Days to Singapore.* (POW). London, 1975.
Fletcher-Cooke, Sir John. *The Emperor's Guest.* (POW). London, 1982.
Gilmour, O. W. *With Freedom to Singapore.* (POW). London, 1950.
Hamilton, Thomas. *Soldier Surgeon in Malaya.* (POW). Sydney, 1957.
Harrison, K. *The Brave Japanese.* (POW). London, 1967.
Hartley, Peter. *Escape to Captivity.* (POW). London, 1952.
Heriot, Guy. *Changi Interlude: A Third Class Internee.* (CIC). Lewes, England, 1946.
Hofstede, N. W. *De Slaven van Rokuban.* (POW). Franeker, the Netherlands, 1979.
James, David H. *The Rise and Fall of the Japanese Empire.* London, 1951.
Jeffrey, Betty. *White Coolies.* (CIC). London, 1954.
Kennedy, Joseph. "British Civilians and the Japanese War in Malaya and Singapore." (CIC). London, 1987.
Kent, Jim. *Changi Terror.* (POW). Sydney, 1966.
Lambert, Eric. *MacDougall's Farm.* (CIC). London, 1965.
Lumiere, Cornel. *Kura.* (POW). Brisbane, 1966.

McCormac, Charles. *You'll Die in Singapore.* (CIC). London, 1954.
MacGregor, Gordon Scott. *No Other Medicine.* (POW). Falmouth, 1984.
McGregor, John. *Blood on the Rising Sun.* (POW). Perth, 19??.
Mason, W. Wynne. *Official History of New Zealand in the Second World War: Prisoners of War.* (POW). London, 1954.
Montgomery, Brian. *Shenton of Singapore: Governor and Prisoner of War.* (CIC). London, 1984.
Moreton, Miss D. E. *An Irishman in Malaya: John Lowe Woods.* (CIC). Peterhead, Scotland, 1977.
Nelson, David. *The Story of Changi, Singapore.* (POW). Perth, 1976.
Norman, Diana. *Road from Singapore: The Incredible Story of John Dodd Who Survived Changi Jail to Assist Ex-Convicts to Adjust to Society.* (CIC). London, 1970.
O'Connor, Michael P. *The More Fool I.* (CIC). Dublin, 1954.
Pavillard, Stanley S. *Bamboo Doctor.* (POW). New York, 1960.
Poole, Philippa. *Of Love and War: The Letters and Diaries of Capt. Adrian Curlewis and His Family 1939–1945.* (POW). Sydney, 1984.
Probert, H. A. *History of Changi.* (POW). Singapore, 1965.
Reid, Caroline. *Malayan Climax: Experiences of an Australian Girl in Malaya 1940–1942.* Melbourne, 1942.
Skidmore, Jan. *Escape from Singapore.* (POW). New York, 1973.
Sprod, George. *Bamboo Behind My Shoulder: Changi the Lighter Side.* (POW). Kenthurst, 1981.
Thomas, Mary. *In the Shadow of the Rising Sun.* (CIC). Singapore, 1983.
van Velden, D. *De Japanse Burgerkampen* [The Japanese Civilian Camps]. Franeker, the Netherlands, 1977.

International Military Tribunal, Far East:

POW Treatment: IMTFE 5492–96, 5506–07, 5510–12, 5515–608, 5627–65, 5799–801, 27397–411, 30215–46, 40188–95, 40224–28, 40259–60, 5358–610, 5624–846.
Camps: Affidavits-testimonies: IMTFE 27397–411. See also, 5624–53, 5671–76, 5942–93, 12883–962, 13454–76, 40309–11, 40334, 40376–79, 43657–58, 5351, exhibit 152, 27403.

SUMATRA (DUTCH EAST INDIES)

POW Camps

Introduction. When the Allied forces in Java capitulated on March 8, 1942, Dutch troops were stationed all over the island of Sumatra. A number of other Allied forces were also captured on this island.

Some troops and civilians had reached Sumatra from Singapore and found it as difficult to go farther (e.g., to Australia) as did those who wanted to flee from Java. Some of the men and women were survivors of ships sunk in the Banka Strait, where both Japanese air and surface units had maintained a blockade.

Conditions of imprisonment in Sumatra were generally very bad. Food was poor, even when supplemented by judicious thefts from warehouses; the opportunities for local purchases were limited. A fund was generally established from a pool of valuables and spare clothing, and most of whatever could be bought, under black-market conditions, was reserved for the hospital patients.

Individual Listings of POW Camps: POW332–POW342

POW330: Blangkedjeren 9

Located about 108 km (70 miles) from the city of Kota Tjane in North Sumatra, these bamboo barracks housed about 300 Dutch and 200 British POWs who moved to this camp from POW335 (Gloegoer) on March 16, 1944. Work consisted of road widening, clearing of mud slides, and the repair and maintenance of the bridge over the Tripa River.

POW331: Blangkedjeren 23

In April 1944 about 200 men were moved to this camp (from Blangkedjeren 9), located 700 feet high in the middle of the woods. The barracks were the usual open bamboo structures with palm-leaf roofs.

POW332: Blangkedjeren 38

In May 1944 another 130 men moved from Blangkedjeren 9 (POW330) to this camp, 1,250 feet high in the mountains. Without any tools, using their bare hands, the POWs had to remove mud from the roads. In October 1944 all the men were marched to POW342 (Soengai Sengkol), outside Medan city, North Sumatra. The following is from the report of an officer:

> On October 4, 1944 the Japanese camp commandant ordered that the following day a group of at least 100 POWs had to leave on foot for Kota Tjane and to reach that town not later than October 7 at midnight. Distance: 80 miles—131 km. We tried, as fast as possible, to search out the healthiest and strongest of our men for this march.
> On October 5, at 5:00 AM out of our total of 156 in the camp, 106 were ready to march.
> The march was accomplished as follows:

Prison Camps: Sumatra (Dutch East Indies)

- Camp to Blangkedjeren—Oct. 5—15 miles (23 km) 06:00 AM–arrival 13:30 (1:30 PM)
- Blangkedjeren to Koengke—Oct. 5—17 miles (28 km) 19:30 (7:30 PM)–06:30 Oct. 6
- Koengke to Meloewak—Oct. 6—15 miles (23 km) 12:00 noon, Oct. 6–19:30 (7:30 PM)
- Meloewak to Goenoeng Setan—Oct. 7—17 miles (27 km) 06:00–14:30 (2:30 PM)
- Goenoeng Setan to Kota Tjane—Oct. 7—19 miles (30 km) 17:30 (5:30 PM) – 23:00 (11:00 PM).

Total walking hours 40. Including rest and sleep 65 hours. The march was extremely difficult and exhausting—through mountainous terrain. Most of the men had to walk barefoot—having worn out their shoes long ago during 2½ years of internment. The first two stages were marched as a group—after that in an individual format.[1]

POW333: Djambi
POW334: Galang

POW335: Gloegoer I

In May 1942 about 900–1,000 men were housed in seven old labor barracks just outside the city of Medan, East Sumatra, after civilian internees had moved out. The barracks had tiled roofs and unglazed windows along one side; a space 6 feet by 2 feet 6 inches was assigned as a sleeping space, dining space, and recreation and "reception" area. There was no privacy, except "in one's thoughts." In that space the following items were kept: hose pipe, pieces of wood of all shapes and sizes, nails, screws, sheets of tin, gasoline cans, bits of gunnysack, and much more. In early 1943 the men were moved out—one group to the north and a second group to Singapore (their ship was torpedoed).

POW336: Kebon Durian
POW337: Lawesigalagala

Pakanbaroe Railroad

Pakanbaroe city is located on the Kampar River, East Sumatra, somewhat southwest of Singapore. The town itself did not have a POW camp as such—POW338 (Camp 1), was the closest to town—but merely served as the end point of a 220 km (140-mile) long railroad coming from Moearo, to be built by POWs and conscripted native laborers-prisoners.

From Pakanbaroe, the railroad track ran 145 km (90 miles) in a southerly direction. It then turned west. Through the first 65 km (40 miles) the track traversed swampland, jungle-clad hills and broad rivers into Moearo village.

Similar to the Burma-Siam railway, the idea of connecting Pakanbaroe and Moearo by rail was researched before the war by Dutch engineers and abandoned as impractical. The Japanese revived the plan to permit overland transport of much-needed coal from Sawahloento, by existing railway to Moearo, and then via a newly built line to Pakanbaroe, and from there only a short distance over water to Singapore. The Japanese had learned from experience that transportation of coal by rail from Sawahloento to Padang and then by steamer around the northern point of Sumatra was much too risky because Allied submarines were ready to torpedo the ships.

And thus—as with the Burma-Siam—the Japanese decided stubbornly to build a railroad that was impossible to construct. The execution was haphazard, sloppy, and amateurish. No special foundation was laid in the soggy, swampy soil, with the result that embankments often started to sag, especially during the monsoon rains.

Bridges over the three main rivers—Kampar Kiri, Kampar Kanan, and Kuantan—were constructed without taking into account flash floods during heavy rains, which carried jungle debris against the bridges' pillars, so that part of the bridge collapsed into the river.

The prisoners laboring on the railroad were divided into groups, each with a special task: rail carriers, railroad-tie (sleeper) carriers, rail joiners, and a group with heavy hammers to nail the rails to the ties. Others were assigned as brakemen or assistants at the repair workshop of the truck-locomotive (trucks were transformed into makeshift railroad engines). A special detail of tea brewers saw to it that no one became dehydrated in the hot, humid tropical weather.

The barracks were typical of any "built-camp": 100 feet by 25 feet (20 m x 7.5 m), open-sided, with a palm-leaf roof. Sleeping platforms, about 6 feet (2 m) deep, and made of split bamboo, were placed lengthwise on either side of the barracks. An aisle about 4 feet (1.5 m) wide ran the length of each barrack between the two sleeping platforms.

Deep, narrow trenches served as outdoor latrines; some were covered, most were not. There were no regular bathing facilities. The prisoners used adjacent streams, creeks, or jungle pools.

Food was cooked in the camp kitchen in large iron cauldrons. It was the usual horrible diet of soupy rice and tapioca, with some leafy vegetables, such as jungle fern tops. The food supplied represented about 40 percent of the total normal daily requirement of calories.

Medical facilities, equipment, and medicines were absent in all the camps, though POW doctors, trained orderlies, and volunteers did everything humanly possible to help and treat the patients. All the diseases listed in the Burma-Siam railroad project existed in Sumatra, with the exception of cholera.

Prison Camps: Sumatra (Dutch East Indies)

There were no recreational activities. From morning to night the prisoners worked on the railroad, as the Japanese were in a rush to finish the line. On the day of the explosion of the first atomic bomb, the railroad was finished, and its completion was celebrated by hammering gold-plated nails in the ties.

The morale was generally good.

A total of 6,622 POWs were shipped from several areas in the Dutch East Indies to Pakanbaroe, and there were about 30,000 Javanese conscripted laborers/prisoners. The numbers were as follows:

Departure	Arrival	Route	Total POWs
5-14-44	5-17-44	Batavia–Padang–Pakanbaroe	1,937
6-14-44	6-29-44	Palembang–Singapore–Pakanbaroe	385*
?	7-12-44	Java–Singapore–Pakanbaroe	200
?	7-17-44	"	279
6-27-44	7-23-44	"	247
?	7-23-44	"	40
6-25-44	7-27-44	Medan–Singapore–Pakanbaroe	270
?	11-03-44	Land party Atjeh–Pakanbaroe	458
?	8-08-44	Medan–Singapore–Pakanbaroe	94
9-16-44	9-23-44	Batavia–Padang–Pakanbaroe	2,200**
?	?	Gloegoer–Medan–Pakanbaroe	18
?	?	Unknown	494
		Total	6,622
		Total number of POWs who died during construction	706
		Total killed when ships torpedoed	1,698
			2,404
		Those who celebrated liberation:	4,218

Thus about 36.3 percent sacrificed their lives on a railroad that was never used for any purpose.

Of the about 30,000 Javanese laborers-prisoners, about 8,000 died during the various transportations. About 22,000 were put to work on the line. On August 15, 1945, only about 5,000 were found to be still alive. Thus 77 percent perished as of August. How many more died after that is not known.

In Pakanbaroe there is a commemorative monument for those laborers who lost their lives. As far as this author knows, it is the only one of its kind:

> Heroes of labor—Oh flowers of the nation—Carried away by the Japanese rulers—to toil in drudgery and slavery—It was your lot to be humiliated

*Ship torpedoed: 178 died
**Ship torpedoed: 1,520 died

and oppressed—Your bodies became skeletons and your bones were scattered—You rest here with all the others—Your relatives not knowing your resting place—Nameless and without due honor—The country will not forget your merits—You are a hero of toil and labor—Oh God, we surrender them to You and forgive them their trespasses—And have mercy upon them.

POW338: Camp 1

This camp was used for unloading and storing railroad materiel that arrived by ship along the Siak River. It was occupied from May 30, 1944, to October 17, 1945.

POW338: Camp 2

In this base and hospital camp, the accommodations were reasonable and recreation was allowed. It was occupied from May 20, 1944, to November 25, 1945.

The commandant of the hospital camp POW338: Camp 2 was Major Miyazaki Ryohei, who was indicted at the Military Tribunal in Medan, East Sumatra, for extreme torture of POWs and other atrocities. He was sentenced to death.

The following is a translation of a letter from Miyazaki to his defense counsel concerning his request for clemency:

> Medan, 17th June, 1948. To Maj. J.J.A. v.d. Lande—I daresay no POW died because of a personal misconduct throughout my tenure. Every minute and every second I am only awaiting for the warm and merciful mitigation by His Excellency the Governor General, to whom I submitted my petition in due way... by taking my miserable situation into consideration. Your most grateful: Miyazaki Ryohei
>
> Medan Prison.[2]

The appeal was unsuccessful.

The following is a comment from a Dutch POW in his book *Het Pannetje van Oliemans* [Olieman's Mess Kit]:

> We observed that among the prisoners a number had experienced torpedoed hell ships. Some were from the one near Benkoelen on 19 September [should be 18 September] whereby about 1,500 POWs and 3,500 Indonesian laborers died.
>
> The survivors had floated on improvised rafts for a couple of days. What these people had gone through was indescribable and I believe that not many of them were able to survive the horrors of working on the railroad in the year that followed. All these survivors had no possessions at all; they ate with their fingers, or a piece of wood as a spoon. A dried half-gourd was their dish. They had no mosquito nets and next to nothing in clothing. Strikingly in contrast were the "gentlemen" from Java who

had not been torpedoed and had sufficient possessions to share, but the atmosphere along the Pakanbaroe railroad was such that little was done for the torpedoed survivors. They said "Sir" to each other, and that was it.[3]

This description was from Bernard Schoonenberg, another Dutch POW in Pakanbaroe:

> The author's new neighbor discovered that the vegetable gardens in Camp 1 were "in the hands of a clan" who kept tight control over the vegetables. He complained about it at the Dutch camp headquarters and the Japanese commandant, without any results.
> Mad as hell, he said, "Goddamn it, after the war I am going to join the communists. These guys are capitalistic bloodsuckers—they seem to have a monopoly on these gardens. They dictate price and availability. It is not their land! You know what they told me? . . . What are you doing here in our camp? We didn't ask you to come here! They consider us intruders. They look at you with disdain and accuse you of not having enough money to buy their wares. I wish the Japs would interfere in this scheme—distribute the vegetables to all of us. But of course they probably profit from it too. And what is most disgusting, they don't even give anything to the hospital!"[4]

As a 19-year-old, the present author experienced the same conditions described by these two POWs.

POW338: Camp 2A

Located about 10 miles (16 km) from Pakanbaroe near the village of Koebang, the camp was called "mud delight"; it was built in a terrible swampy area. No real work was ever carried out. The camp was occupied from May 25, 1944, to July 14, 1944.

POW338: Camp 3

This camp, located along the Kampar Kanan River near the village of Teratakboeloeh, was occupied from May 20, 1944, to October 6, 1945. Prisoners were used to guard and maintain the bridge over the river, maintain the track, and carry sand for the building of embankments.

POW338: Camp 4

This camp was located about 10 miles (16 km) from Pakanbaroe, almost across from Camp 3. POWs were assigned to lay the track in a southerly direction and to build a shunting yard. The camp was occupied from July 7, 1944, to October 12, 1944.

POW338: Camp 5

Located about 14 miles (23 km) from Pakanbaroe near the village of

Loeboeksakat, this camp was a shunting yard, as well as a sand-digging place. In 1945 the POWs were moved to Camp 11, near Moearo.

POW338: Camp 6

This camp was located 22 miles (36 km) from Pakanbaroe near the village of Soengai Pagar. It was occupied by POWs who moved from Camp 4, as the line progressed in a southerly direction, from October 12, 1944, to December 12, 1944.

POW338: Camp 7

Located 47 miles (75 km) from Pakanbaroe, close to the Kampar Kiri River and near the village of Lipatkain, the camp was occupied by POWs who moved from Camp 4 to Camp 6 and then to Camp 7, to continue laying the line. On Good Friday, March 30, 1945, the bridge over the river collapsed because flotsam that came down on the high, swollen river collected against the piers of the bridge that were constructed too close together.

POW338: Camp 7A

Located on the site where the bridge collapsed, the camp was occupied from April 22, 1945, to June 1, 1945, and housed a small group of POWs who were assigned to repair the bridge.

POW338: Camp 8

This camp was located 70 miles (111 km) from Pakanbaroe near the village of Kota Baroe. It was occupied by POWs who had moved from Camp 7 from January 14, 1945, to June 29, 1945.

POW338: Camp 9

This camp was located 88 miles (142 km) from Pakanbaroe and occupied by POWs from Camp 8.

POW338: Camp 10

Located 100 miles (160 km) from Pakanbaroe near the village of Loeboek-Ambatjan, this camp housed a small group of POWs from Camp 9, who were transferred to this camp to build another section of the railway.

POW338: Camp 11

In March 1945 the Japanese decided to start building the railroad from Moearo northward to Pakanbaroe. Prisoners from Camp 5 were moved to this camp, located at the station-village of Moearo. The camp was occupied from March 17, 1945, to July 12, 1945, when the POWs were moved to Camp 12 as the work progressed.

POW338: Camp 12

Located 124 miles (200 km) from Pakanbaroe on the Kuantan River near the village of Siloewah and about 12 miles (20 km) from Moearo, this camp was occupied from July 12, 1945, to August 10, 1945.

POW338: Camp 13

This camp was about 10 km (6 miles) from the village of Padang Tarap in the narrow valley of the Kuantan River. The work here was done frantically in order to finish the line on August 15, 1945, near the village of Pintoebatoe. The camp was occupied from August 10, 1945, to August 31, 1945.

POW338: Camp 14

This was a small auxiliary camp established to construct a railroad track—regular and narrow gauge—from the Sapar and Karoe coal mines to the main Moearo-Pakanbaroe line. It was occupied from November 3, 1944, to June 28, 1945. In June the POWs were split into two groups; one was transferred to Camp 9 and the other was sent to build Camp 10.

POW339: Chungwa

Located in the city of Palembang, South Sumatra, this camp housed mainly British and Australian POWs.

POW340: Mulo School

Also located in Palembang.

POW341: Soengai Geroe

In March 1944, POWs from POW339 (Chungwa) and CIC340 (Muloschool) were concentrated in this camp. It differed little from other camps: The treatment was brutal and the facilities in which the sick were housed were disgraceful. The excuse of the Japanese was always "general shortage." After liberation, however, the POWs were supplied from warehouses with more clothing and other goods than they could ever use.

POW342: Soengai Sengkol

In October 1944, after the civilian internees had moved out, the POWs from the Blangkedjeren camps—POW330, POW331, and POW332—were moved to this camp, located in the outskirts of the city of Medan in East Sumatra. Their stay lasted only about a month. The men were then transported by truck and train to POW338 (Pakanbaroe) to work on the railroad.

Civilian Internment Centers

Introduction. There is perhaps no better introduction to Sumatran internment centers than a brief listing of the various moves a group of men, women, and children had to make during their time of internment on the island of Sumatra. Similar multiple moves took place in Java.

Men and Women

1	March 28, 1942–June 20, 1942	(85 days)	CIC85
1	June 20, 1942–July 19, 1942	(29 days)	CIC86
2	July 19, 1942–July 22, 1942	(3 days)	CIC87

Men

3	July 22, 1942–August 11, 1943	(385 days)	CIC96
4	August 11, 1943–October 6, 1944	(421 days)	CIC98
5	October 6, 1944–October 30, 1945	(389 days)	CIC131

Women

3	July 22, 1942–Sept. 23, 1943	(428 days)	CIC97
4	Sept. 23, 1943–October 10, 1944	(382 days)	CIC99
5	Oct. 10, 1944–May 10, 1945	(212 days)	CIC129
6	May 10, 1945–Nov. 1, 1945	(174 days)	CIC134

First the men, women, and children made three moves together within 117 days (less than four months). Then the men were separated from the women and children. The men then made three more moves—each after a time span of about one year. The women and the children made four more moves. The first two each occurred after a time span of about one year; the second two came a little more than six months apart.

Individual Listings of Civilian Internment Centers: CIC85–CIC177

North Sumatra

CIC85: Lae Butar
About 80 women and children from the town of Lae Butar lived in various houses in the suburbs from March 28, 1942, to June 20, 1942, when they were moved to CIC86 (Singkel).

CIC86: Singkel
About 95 men, women, and children from Lae Butar and other areas

were housed in the military barracks in town from June 20, 1942, to July 19, 1942, when they were moved to CIC87 (Meulaboh).

CIC87: Meulaboh

The men, women, and children from CIC86 (Singkel) were housed in the school compound from July 19, 1942, to July 22, 1942. The men were then moved to CIC96 (Kuta Alam), and the women and children moved to CIC97 (Kendal).

CIC88: Kualasimpang

About 70 men, women, and children from the town lived in the country club from March 13, 1942, to April 1942. The men were then moved to CIC92 (Bireuen), and the women to CIC89 (Langsa).

CIC89: Langsa

About 250 men, women, and children from CIC88 (Kualasimpang), CIC90 (Lhoseumawe), CIC91 (Takengon), and the east Atjeh area were housed in the jail and school compound from March 12, 1942, to June 1942. Then the men were moved to CIC92 (Bireuen), and the women and children were moved to CIC97 (Kendal).

CIC90: Lhoseumawe

An unknown number of men, women, and children from the area lived in the military barracks in town from March 14, 1942, to April 1942. The men were moved to CIC92 (Bireuen), and the women and children were moved to CIC89 (Langsa).

CIC91: Takengon

An unknown number of men, women, and children from the area were housed in the military barracks in town from May 19, 1942, to April 1942. The men were then moved to CIC92 (Bireuen), and the women and children were moved to CIC89 (Langsa).

CIC92: Bireuen

About 100 men, women, and children from other camps and the area itself occupied the jail in town from March 14, 1942, to June 5, 1942. The men were then moved to CIC96 (Kuta Alam), and the women and children were moved to CIC89 (Langsa). They received harsh treatment from the Japanese troops.

CIC93: Sabang

About 140 men, women, and children from this island on the northern point of Sumatra lived in the school compound and various houses from March 12, 1942, to June 6, 1942. The men were moved to CIC96 (Kuta Alam), and the women and children were moved to CIC97 (Kendal).

Kutaradja

CIC94: Preliminary Camp I

About 40 men from the town lived in the jail and military barracks from March 14, 1942, to June 11, 1942, when they were moved to CIC96 (Kuta Alam).

CIC95: Preliminary Camp II

About 12 women from the town lived in a house from March 14, 1942, to June 11, 1942, when they were moved to CIC97 (Kendal).

CIC96: Kuta Alam

About 240 men and boys from CIC87 (Meulaboh), CIC92 (Bireuen), CIC93 (Sabang), and CIC94 (Preliminary Camp I) lived in the military barracks from June 11, 1942, to August 11, 1943. They then were moved to CIC98 (Lawesigalagala), and 24 men were sent to jail.

CIC97: Kendal (Kutaradja)

About 620 men, women, and children from CIC87 (Meulaboh), CIC89 (Langsa), CIC93 (Sabang), and CIC95 (Preliminary Camp II) were housed in the military barracks in town from June 11, 1942, to September 23, 1943. They then were moved to CIC99 (Lawesigalagala II).

Lawesigalagala

CIC98: Lawesigalagala 1

About 260 men and boys from CIC96 (Kuta Alam) lived in barracks outside the town from August 13, 1943, to October 6, 1944, when they were moved to CIC131 (Siringoringo).

CIC99: Lawesigalagala II

About 600 women and children from CIC97 (Kendal) lived in barracks outside the town from September 24, 1943, to October 10, 1944, when they were moved to CIC129 (Belawan Estate II).

Sibolga (West Sumatra)

CIC100: Sibolga I

About 20 men from town and Nias Island were housed in the jail in town from March 16, 1942, to May 4, 1942, when they were moved to CIC119 (Pematangsiantar I).

CIC101: Sibolga II
About 15 women and children from town and Nias Island lived in the military barracks in town from March 16, 1942, to May 4, 1942, when they were moved to CIC120 (Pematangsiantar II).

Taroetoeng (East Sumatra)

CIC102: Taroetoeng
About 200 men, women, and children from the area were housed separately in a boarding school in town from March 15, 1942, to May 6, 1942. Then the men were moved to CIC119 (Pematangsiantar I) and the women to CIC120 (Pematangsiantar II).

Padangsidempoean (East Sumatra)

CIC103: Padangsidempoean
About 25 men, women, and children from the area lived in a large house in town from April 12, 1942, to May 2, 1942. The men were then moved to CIC119 (Pematangsiantar I) and the women to CIC120 (Pematangsiantar II).

Pangoeroean

CIC104: Pangoeroean
About 30 men, women, and children from the area lived in a house in town from March 20, 1942, to April 4, 1942. The men were then moved to CIC119 (Pematangsiantar I) and the women to CIC120 (Pematangsiantar II).

Balige

CIC105: Balige
About 20 men and about 80 women and children from the area lived in houses in town and in the jail from March 13, 1942, to December 13, 1942. On June 29, 1942, the women and children were moved to CIC106 (Hephata), and on December 13, 1942, the men were moved to CIC116 (Unie Kampong).

CIC106: Hephata
The 80 women and children from CIC105 (Balige) lived in a compound

of the colony of the blind, near the Hutam Salem leper colony, from June 29, 1942, to December 13, 1942, when they were moved to CIC107 (Pulauberajan A, B, C).

Medan (East Sumatra)

CIC107: Pulauberajan A, B, and C

About 1,400 women and children from Medan and the surrounding area and those from CIC122 (Tanjoengbalai) and CIC125 (Bangkatan) lived in barracks and estate labor houses outside town from April 12, 1942, to June 20, 1945, when they were moved to CIC135 (Aik Pamienke II).

CIC108: Pulauberajan D

About 530 women and children from CIC114 (Kampong Baroe), CIC113 (Tanjoengmorawa), and CIC110 (Gloegoer I) lived in houses outside Medan from May 29, 1942, to July 1945. In July 1944 some of them were moved to CIC111 (Gloegoer II), and in July 1945, the rest were moved to CIC134 (Aik Pamienke I).

CIC109: Pulauberajan E

About 1,400 women and children from Medan and from CIC118 (Tebingtinnggi II) lived in the tobacco estate labor barracks outside town from May 29, 1942, to July 1944. The camp flooded during rains. There was no electric light and only 15 bathrooms and toilets. The internees were moved to CIC111 (Gloegoer II).

C110: Gloegoer I

About 530 women and children from the city of Medan and the surrounding areas lived in barracks outside the town from April 14, 1942, to May 29, 1942, when they were moved to CIC108 (Pulauberajan D).

CIC111: Gloegoer II

About 1,370 women and children from CIC108 and CIC109 (Pulauberajan D and E) and CIC115 (St. Josef School) lived in this camp from June 1944 to July 1945. Some were then moved to CIC135 (Aik Pamienke II), and others were moved to CIC134 (Aik Pamienke I).

CIC112: Serdangkwartier

About 800 women and children whose husbands were still working for the Japanese lived in a block of houses in Medan from April 12, 1942, to October 1942. They were then moved to CIC113 (Tanjoengmorawa).

CIC113: Tanjoengmorawa

The 800 women and children from CIC112 (Serdangkwartier) lived in a block of houses in town from October 1942 to June 1943. They then moved to CIC108 (Pulauberajan D) and CIC115 (St. Josef School).

CIC114: Kampong Baroe
About 200 women and children whose husbands were still working for the Japanese lived in a block of houses in town from November 1942 to March 1943. Part of the group was moved to CIC108 (Pulauberajan D), and part was moved to CIC115 (St. Josef School).

CIC115: St. Josef School
Men still working for the Japanese and women and children from CIC113 (Tanjoengmorawa) and from CIC114 (Kampong Baroe) lived here from April 1942 to October 1944. The men were then moved to CIC128 (Belawan Estate I), and the women and children to CIC111 (Gloegoer II).

CIC116: Unie Kampong
About 700 men from eastern Sumatra and from CIC117 (Tebingtinnggi I), CIC121 (Tanjoengbalai), CIC124 (Bindjei), and CIC126 (Kebondjahe) lived in labor barracks near the harbor from April 12, 1942, to July 25, 1943, when they were moved to CIC128 (Belawan Estate I).

Tebingtinnggi

CIC117: Tebingtinnggi I
Men from the town and the surrounding area lived in a house in town from March 26, 1942, to January 1943, when they were moved to CIC116 (Unie Kampong).

CIC118: Tebingtinnggi II
About 120 women and children from the town and surrounding area were housed in the city jail from March 26, 1942, to November 10, 1943. They were then moved to CIC109 (Pulauberajan E).

Pematangsiantar

CIC119: Pematangsiantar I
About 200 men from CIC100 (Sibolga I), CIC102 (Taroetoeng), CIC103 (Padangsidempoean), CIC104 (Pangoeroean), and the surrounding area lived here from March 16, 1942, to April 15, 1943. They were then moved to CIC130 (Sungaisengkol).

CIC120: Pematangsiantar II
About 780 women and children from CIC101 (Sibolga II), CIC102

(Taroetoeng), CIC103 (Padangsidempoean), CIC104 (Pangoeroean), and the surrounding area lived in this hospital compound in town from March 16, 1942, to December 1942. They were then moved to CIC127 (Berastagi).

Tanjoengbalai (East Sumatra)

CIC121: Tanjoengbalai

An unknown number of men from the area were housed in the jail and a house in town from March 23, 1942, to February 8, 1943. They were then moved to CIC116 (Unie Kampong) and CIC130 (Sungaisengkol).

CIC122: Tanjoengbalai I

About 250 women and children from the area lived in a hotel and houses in town from March 23, 1942, to January 1, 1943. Some were moved to CIC107 (Pulauberajan A, B, and C) and others to CIC123 (Tanjoengbalai II).

CIC123: Tanjoengbalai II

About 180 women and children from CIC122 (Tanjoengbalai I) lived in houses outside town from January 1, 1943, to April 25, 1945, when they were moved to CIC134 (Aik Pamienke I).

Bindjei

CIC124: Bindjei

An unknown number of men from the area lived in the hospital in town from March 1942 to October 1944, when they were moved to CIC116 (Unie Kampong) and to CIC132 (Pangoran).

CIC125: Bangkatan

An unknown number of women from the area lived in the hospital in town from March 1942 to January 1943. They were then moved to CIC107 (Pulauberajan A, B, C).

Kebondjahe

CIC126: Kebondjahe

About 126 men from the area were housed in the jail and school in town from April 16, 1942, to May 31, 1942, when they were moved to CIC116 (Unie Kampong).

Berastagi

CIC127: Berastagi

About 750 women and children from the area and from CIC120

(Pematangsiantar II) lived in a boarding school compound outside town from April 16, 1942, to July 15, 1945, when they were moved to CIC136 (Aik Pamienke III). Twenty died.

Belawan (Harbor town of Medan city)

CIC128: Belawan Estate I

About 675 men from CIC116 (Unie Kampong), from CIC115 (St. Josef School), and from the surrounding estates and plantations were housed in the labor barracks from July 25, 1943, to October 5, 1944. Then about 100 men were moved to CIC133 (Aik Pamienke), 30 to CIC132 (Pangoran), and about 545 to CIC131 (Siringoringo). Twenty men died.

CIC129: Belawan Estate II

About 600 women and children from CIC99 (Lawesigalagala II) lived in the labor barracks from October 5, 1944, to May 10, 1945, when they were moved to CIC134 (Aik Pamienke I).

Sungaisengkol

CIC130: Sungaisengkol

About 650 men from the area and from CIC119 (Pematangsiantar I) and CIC121 (Tanjoengbalai) lived in the hospital outside town from March 1943 to October 3, 1944. About 100 men were then moved to CIC133 (Aik Pamienke) and about 550 to CIC131 (Siringoringo).

Rantauprapat

CIC131: Siringoringo*

About 1,500 men and about 500 boys (10 years and older) from CIC128 (Belawan Estate I), CIC130 (Sungaisengkol), CIC98 (Lawesigalagala I), and CIC133 (Aik Pamienke) lived in bamboo–palm leaf roof barracks outside town in the woods of a swampy valley along the Bila River from October 2, 1944, to October 30, 1945, when they were liberated.

From the notes of a boy:

> January 11, 1945: Today is my 14th birthday. Opened a package Mother had given me before I left Berastagi camp—it's a board game. From my neighbors I received a handful of peanuts, a few prunes and some palm sugar. Made a cake from it.[5]

CIC132: Pangoran*

About 160 prominent Americans and British and those who still worked for the Japanese at the various plantations and from CIC124 (Bindjei) and

---

*Camps marked with an asterisk were liberated in September, October, or November 1945.

CIC128 (Belawan Estate I) lived in labor barracks outside the town from October 1944 to October 1945, when they were liberated.

CIC133: Aik Pamienke

About 200 men from CIC128 (Belawan Estate I) and from CIC130 (Sungaisengkol) lived in barracks outside town from October 4, 1944, to April 23, 1945. They were then moved to CIC131 (Siringoringo).

CIC134: Aik Pamienke I*

About 1,000 women and children from CIC123 (Tanjoengbalai II), CIC108 (Pulauberajan D), CIC128 (Belawan Estate II), and CIC111 (Gloegoer II) lived in barracks outside town from April 24, 1945, to November 1, 1945, when they were liberated. Fifteen died during internment.

CIC135: Aik Pamienke II*

About 2,500 women and children from CIC107 (Pulauberajan A, B, C) and CIC111 (Gloegoer II) lived in barracks outside town. They lived here from June 1945 to November 1, 1945, when they were liberated. Seventeen died during internment.

CIC136: Aik Pamienke III*

About 1,500 women and children from CIC127 (Berastagi) lived in barracks outside town from July 1945 to November 1, 1945, when they were liberated. Eight died in the camp.

Pakanbaroe

CIC137: Pakanbaroe I

About 20 men from the area lived in a government guesthouse from April 1942 to June 6, 1942. They were then moved to CIC139 (jail).

CIC138: Pakanbaroe II

About 40 women and children from the area lived in several houses from April 21, 1942, to June 6, 1942, when they were moved to CIC143 (Missie Complex).

Padang (West Sumatra)

CIC139: Jail

About 1,000 men from the area and from CIC137 (Pakanbaroe I), CIC140 (Provoosthuis), CIC141 (Katholieke Sociale Bond), CIC142 (M. V. Building), CIC143 (Missie Complex), CIC146 (Padangpandjang), CIC147 (Fort de Kock), CIC148 (Sawahloento I), CIC150 (Sungaipenuh I), and CIC152 (Rengat I) were housed in the large city jail in town from April 7, 1942, to October 20, 1943, when they were moved to CIC154 (Bangkinang I).

CIC140: Provoosthuis

About 150 men from the countryside were housed in the military jail from April 1942 to February 13, 1943, when they were moved to CIC139 (jail).

CIC141: Katholieke Sociale Bond

British and Dutch men and 41 women and children from the area lived in the Catholic Clubhouse in town from April 7, 1942, to June 1943. The men were moved to CIC139 (jail) and the women to CIC143 (Missie Complex).

CIC142: M. V. Building

About 500 Eurasian men, women, and children lived in a convent in town from August 18, 1943, to September 2, 1943. The men were moved to CIC139 (jail), the women to CIC143 (Missie Complex).

CIC143: Missie Complex

About 2,300 women and children from CIC141 (Katholieke Sociale Bond), CIC142 (M. V. Building), CIC145 (British Camp), CIC147 (Fort de Kock), CIC149 (Sawahloento II), CIC151 (Sungaipenuh II), and CIC153 (Rengat II) lived in the convent and school buildings from April 7, 1942, to October 20, 1943. They were moved to CIC144, the same location as CIC139; the men had been moved to CIC154 (Bangkinang I). Forty-two died in internment.

CIC144: Jail

About 2,340 women and children from CIC143 (Missie Complex) were housed in the city jail, the same site as CIC139, which was used by the men from the area. They lived here from October 20, 1943, to December 15, 1943, when they were moved to CIC155 (Bangkinang II). Nine died in internment.

CIC145: British Camp

About 41 British women and children lived here from April 7, 1942, to June 1943, when they were moved to CIC143 (Missie Complex).

Padangpandjang (West Sumatra)

CIC146: Padangpandjang

An unknown number of men from the area lived in military barracks from April 4, 1942, to May 18, 1942, when they were moved to CIC139 (jail).

Fort de Kock (now Bukittingi) (West Sumatra)

CIC147: Fort de Kock

About 450 men, women, and children from the town and surrounding area lived in the boarding school in town from April 4, 1942, to May 18, 1942. The men were moved to CIC139 (jail), and the women to CIC143 (Missie Complex).

Sawahloento (West Sumatra)

CCIC148: Sawahloento I

An unknown number of men from the town and surrounding area lived in the hospital in town from April 17, 1942, to September 1943. They were then moved to CIC139 (jail).

CIC149: Sawahloento II

About 240 women and children from the town and surrounding area lived in a block of houses from April 17, 1942, to December 7, 1942, when they were moved to CIC143 (Missie Complex).

Sungaipenuh (West Sumatra)

CIC150: Sungaipenuh I

About 50 men from the town and surrounding area were housed in the city jail from April 1942 to August 6, 1942, when they were moved to CIC139 (jail).

CIC151: Sungaipenuh II

About 66 women and children from the town and surrounding area lived in a block of houses from April 1942 to August 6, 1942, when they were moved to CIC143 (Missie Complex).

Rengat (West Sumatra)

CIC152: Rengat I

An unknown number of men from the town and surrounding area lived in the city jail from March 1942 to June 4, 1942, when they were moved to CIC139 (jail).

CIC153: Rengat II

About 36 women and children from the town and surrounding area lived in a large house in town from March 1942 to June 1942, when they were moved to CIC143 (Missie Complex).

Bangkinang (West Sumatra/East Sumatra)

CIC154: Bangkinang I*
About 975 men and boys from CIC139 (jail) lived in barracks built in a rubber forest from October 19, 1943, to September 1945. They were liberated in this camp, but 123 had died.

CIC155: Bangkinang II*
About 2,320 women and children from CIC144 (jail) lived in barracks in the rubber forest from December 16, 1943, to September 1945. The survivors were liberated in this camp; 113 died.

From the diary of a woman:

> 16 October 1944: Today postcards came in from the men's camp next to us. For us nothing. How can I bear all this? I have no more courage left. What a blessing that I have you my little son. You noticed that the cards are distributed and you run to me, yelling, "Did we receive one from daddy?" No, we did not.[6]

Djambi (South Sumatra)

CIC156: Djambi I
About 40 men from the area were housed in the city jail from April 9, 1942, to September 27, 1943. They were then moved to CIC176 (Muntok II) on Banka Island.

CIC157: Djambi II
About 12 women and children from the area lived in a school and then in the city jail from April 9, 1942, to April 24, 1944. They were then moved to CIC166 (Barakkenkamp II).

Benkoelen (South/West Sumatra)

CIC158: Benkoelen I
About 40 men from the area lived in the city jail from April 2, 1942, to September 27, 1943. They were then moved to CIC176 (Muntok II), Banka Island.

CIC159: Benkoelen II
About 125 women and children from the area lived in Old Dutch Fort Marlborough from April 2, 1942, to September 18, 1943, when they were moved to CIC160 (Kepahiang).

CIC160: Kepahiang

About 125 women and children from CIC159 (Benkoelen II) lived in a bamboo movie house from October 18, 1943, to October 3, 1944; nine died. The rest were moved to CIC177 (Muntok III), Banka Island.

Palembang (South Sumatra)

CIC161: Jail

About 450 men from the area, plus shipwrecked men and those from CIC163 (Pladjoe), lived in the city jail from April 1, 1942, to January 16, 1943. They were then moved to CIC162 (Barakkenkamp I).

CIC162: Barakkenkamp I

About 450 men from CIC161 (jail) and subsequently 126 men from the oil refinery, plus 2 cats, 4 dogs, 53 ducks, and 100 chickens lived in an area 330 feet by 150 feet with long windowless barracks of wood and bamboo. There was a barbed-wire fence around the area with high sentry boxes at each corner. The men lived here from January 16, 1943, to September 14, 1943, when they were moved to CIC176 (Muntok II), on Banka Island.

Pladjoe, Oil Town (South Sumatra)

CIC163: Pladjoe

About 150 men from the town lived in the city jail from April 1, 1942, to January 1943, when they were moved to CIC161 (jail).

Palembang (South Sumatra—City and Environs)

CIC164: Bukit Besar

About 150 women and children from Banka Island, CIC175 (Muntok I), among whom were a number of shipwrecked nurses, lived in a block of houses in town from March 3, 1942, to April 1, 1942. They were then moved to CIC165 (Talang Soemoet).

The 31 shipwrecked nurses were on their way back to Australia from Singapore. Their ship, the MS *Vynner Brooke*, was sunk by Japanese planes. The survivors stayed about two weeks in Muntok on Banka Island. There were also a number of British soldiers on board the *Vynner Brooke*. A group of 130 survivors who landed on a stretch of beach on Banka were massacred by the Japanese; one man survived. A group of 23 nurses landed on the same spot on the island and were also massacred; one nurse escaped.

CIC165: Talang Soemoet

About 425 women and children from the area and from CIC164 (Bukit

Besar) lived in a block of houses in the suburbs from April 1, 1942, to September 20, 1943. They were then moved to CIC166 (Barakkenkamp II), which was actually the same site as CIC162 (Barakkenkamp I), and were housed there until September 1943.

CIC166: Barakkenkamp II

About 525 women and children from CIC157 (Djambi II) and CIC165 (Talang Soemoet) lived in barracks outside the town; this was the same site as Barakkenkamp I in which the men were housed. They lived here from September 20, 1943, to November 4, 1944, when they were moved to CIC177 (Muntok III), on Banka Island.

The wells provided only muddy water. One large can of water a day per person was allotted for drinking and washing; the rest was for kitchen use.

Belalau (South Sumatra)

CIC167: Loeboeklinggau I*

About 650 men and boys from CIC176 (Muntok II) on Banka Island lived in a few wooden buildings in a clearing of a rubber plantation, encircled by barbed wire, from March 3, 1945, to October 1945, when the camp was liberated. The only water was from a dirty creek that ran alongside the camp. The buildings were vermin ridden and hot. The undergrowth teemed with edible leaves, vines, and berries. Banana trees were felled, stripped of outer bark, and laid bare, and the heart—a soft, sweet, fibrous white stalk—was diced and boiled. It provided no nourishment, but it was filling. Ninety-six died.

CIC168: Loeboeklinggau II*

About 640 women and children from CIC177 (Muntok II) on Banka Island lived in this camp, which was located two to three kilometers (one to two miles) from the men's camp (CIC167), in similar barracks. They lived here from April 9, 1945, to October 1945, when they were liberated. Ninety-five had died.

Telukbetung (South Sumatra)

CIC169: Telukbetung I

About 50 men from the area lived in a large house and the jail from April 7, 1942, to February 14, 1943. They were then moved to CIC171 (Telukbetung III).

CIC170: Telukbetung II

About 50 women and children from the area lived in a school and a large house from April 7, 1942, to February 19, 1943. They were then moved to CIC171 (Telukbetung III).

CIC171: Telukbetung III

About 100 men, women, and children from CIC169 (Telukbetung I) and CIC170 (Telukbetung II) lived in this family camp in a convent in town from February 14, 1943, to September 27, 1943. Then the families were split up again: The men were moved to CIC176 (Muntok II), on Banka Island, and the women and children were moved to CIC172 (Telukbetung IV).

CIC172: Telukbetung IV

About 50 women and children from CIC171 (Telukbetung III) were housed in the ice factory compound from September 27, 1943, to May 2, 1944. It is not known where they were moved, but it was most likely to Palembang City.

Pangkalpinang (Banka Island)

CIC173: Pangkalpinang I

About 200 men from Banka Island were housed in the city jail from April 9, 1942, to May 30, 1944. They were then moved to CIC176 (Muntok II) on the island.

CIC174: Pangkalpinang II

Four women from the island lived in a house in town from April 9, 1942, to May 30, 1944, when they were moved to CIC177 (Muntok III), on the island.

Muntok (Banka Island)

CIC175: Muntok I

About 1,000 or so shipwrecked men, women, and children, including some military personnel, lived in the jail and movie theater in town for three weeks from February 15, 1942, to March 2, 1942. They were then moved to CIC161 (Palembang Gevangenis, jail), and CIC164 (Bukit Besar), both on the island of Sumatra.

CIC176: Muntok II

About 600 men from CIC156 (Djambi I), CIC158 (Benkoelen I), and CIC171 (Telukbetung III)—all on the island of Sumatra—lived in the city jail—a pile of stone and bricks built by the Dutch in the 1800s to house life-term Indonesians. Subsequently 300 men were added from CIC171

(Telukbetung III). In June 1944, there were about 910 men, with 200 in the hospital. The food became so bad that rats went from a value of two Dutch guilders each to five guilders in a short time, and mice went to two and a half guilders. The men lived here from September 5, 1943, to April 9, 1945, when they were moved back to Sumatra Island, CIC167 (Loeboeklinggau I). Of their total, 259 died.

CIC177: Muntok III

About 720 women and children from CIC166 (Barakkenkamp II), CIC174 (Pangkalpinang II), and CIC160 (Kepahiang) lived in seven wooden barracks set on a hill from October 7, 1944, to April 1945; 76 died. The rest were moved to CIC168 (Loeboeklinggau II).

Concluding Information on Civilian Internees

Interned	Interned	Died
4,000 men	12,000 Dutch	1,100 Dutch
4,500 women	700 British	190 British
4,700 children	10 Americans	10 others
13,200 persons	500 others	1,300 persons (about 10 percent)
	13,210 persons	

Of the 93 camps that were at one time or another used, set up, established, or built in Sumatra, only 9 camps existed at the time of liberation. At no time were civilian internees subjected to massive overseas transports, except the short-distance ones from Sumatra to Banka.

NOTES: SUMATRA

1. RvO IC 4268.
2. *London FEPOW Post Bulletin*, No. 88/5 (September-October 1988).
3. C. van Heekeren, et al., *Het Pannetje van Oliemans* [Olieman's Mess Tin], Freneker, the Netherlands, 1975, p. 185.
4. Bernard Schoonenberg, *De Poorten der Hell* [The Gates of Hell], Bussum, the Netherlands, 1978, pp. 224–225.
5. D. J. Dragt, et al., *Si Rengo Rengo*, Amsterdam, 1982, p. 9.
6. RvO IC 6829.

SOURCES: SUMATRA

Althorp, A. A. *The British Sumatra Battalion*. (POW). East Sussex, England, 1988.
Brandt, Willem. *De Gele Terruer* [The Yellow Terror]. (CIC). The Hague, 1947.

_____. *Het Geheim* [The Secret] (CIC). The Hague, 1960.
_____. *Zwarte Moesson* [Black Monsoon]. Baarn, the Netherlands, 1967.
Bullwinkel, Sister V. Statement VFX 61330, p. 2, 2/14th AGH War Diary, part 2, Written Records 1939–1945, 11/2/14. (CIC). Australian War Memorial, Canberra.
Burghardt-de Boer, H. L. *Als Een Dauwdrop Is Het Leven* [Life Is Like a Dew-Drop]. (CIC). Franeker, the Netherlands, 1983.
Colijn, Helen. *De Kracht van een Lied* [The Power of a Song]. (CIC). Franeker, the Netherlands, 1989.
de Jongh, Wil. *Olie en Zweet, een Traan, een Lach* [Oil and Sweat, a Tear, a Smile]. (CIC). The Hague, 1980.
De-Vreede, Mischa. *Een Hachelijk Bestaan* [A Precarious Existence]. (CIC). Amsterdam, 1974.
Den-Ouden-Hille, M. H. *Ik Wou Dat Ik Een Vlinder Was* [I Wish I Were a Butterfly]. (CIC). Franeker, the Netherlands, 1983.
Eaton-Lee, J. J. "Three Years as a White Coolie." (CIC). *Grey and Scarlet*, 3 (1981), 11.
Eijke-van Velzen, Truus van. *Vrouwen op Sumatra Achter Japans Prikkeldraad—Dagboek* [Women in Sumatra Behind Japanese Barbed Wire—Diary]. (CIC). Utrecht, 1984.
Hartley, Peter. *Escape to Captivity*. (POW). London, 1952.
Hovinga, Henk. *Dodenspoorweg door het Oerwoud* [Death Railway Through the Jungle]. (POW). Franeker, the Netherlands, 1976.
Jacobs, An. *Ontwortelden* [The Uprooted Ones]. (CIC). The Hague, 1947.
Jacobs, G. F. *Prelude to the Monsoon*. (POW). Capetown, 1965.
Jeffrey, Betty. *White Coolies*. (CIC). Sydney, 1954.
Kenny, Catherine. *Captives: Australian Army Nurses in Japanese Prison Camps*. (CIC). St. Lucia, 1986.
Kuyl, Arie. *Opgeborgen bij de Evenaar: het leven in vier Kampen op Sumatra* [Locked Up Around the Equator: Life in Four Camps in Sumatra]. (CIC). 'sGravenpolder, the Netherlands, 1984.
Leffelaar, H. L. *De japanse Regering Betaalt aan Toonder: Een Oorlog die niet Verdween* [Japan Pays to the Receipt Holder: A War Which Did Not Disappear]. (CIC). Alphen aan den Rijn, the Netherlands, 1980.
McDougall, William H., Jr. *By Eastern Windows: The Story of a Battle of Soul and Minds*. (CIC). New York, 1949.
McLellan, Jean M. Personal Diary, January 3, 1942, to September 1945. Personal collection of Mrs. J. M. Harwood (McLellan). (CIC). Queensland.
Meyer, Hans. *Fremde so me Uber Sumatra* [Strangers Came to Sumatra]. (CIC). Zurich, 1949.
Morris, J. Newman. "The Story of the Red Cross and POWs in Japanese Hands." Mitchell Library, Sydney-Melbourne, 1944.
Neilen, M. *Japanse Kampen* [Japanese Camps]. (CIC). Sittard, the Netherlands, n.d.
Nelson, Hank. *POW: Prisoners of War—Australians Under Nippon*. Sydney, 1985.
Neumann, H., and E. van Witsen. *The Sumatra Railway*. Middellie, 1989.
Piekaar, A. J. *Atjeh en de Oorlog met Japan* [Atjeh and the War with Japan]. (CIC). The Hague, 1949.
Recovery of 24 Members of the AANS from the Japanese. Department of the Army Minute Paper, 11 October 1945, MP 742, 336/1/1289. Australian Archives, Melbourne.

Rijkhoek, D. *De Gele Mierenplaag: De Interneringskampen op Noord Sumatra* [The Yellow Plague: Internment Camps in North Sumatra]. (CIC). Amsterdam, 1946.
Salin, Leon. *Prisoners at Kota Tjane.* (CIC). Cornell, 1986.
Schoonenberg, Bernard. *De Poorten der Hel* [The Gates of Hell]. (POW). Bussum, the Netherlands, 1978.
Simons, Sister J. E. *While History Passed.* (CIC). Melbourne, 1954.
Smyth, Sir John. *The Will to Live: The Story of Dame Margot Turner.* (CIC). London, 1970.
van de Velde, J. J. *Brieven uit Sumatra* [Letters from Sumatra]. (CIC). Franeker, the Netherlands, 1982.
van Dijk, Fokke N. J. *Noord Sumatra in Oorlogstijd* [North Sumatra in Wartime (diaries)]. (CIC). Makkum, the Netherlands, 1989.
Van Heekeren, C., et al. *Het Pannetje van Oliemans* [Olieman's Mess Tin]. (POW). Franeker, the Netherlands, 1975.
van Velden, Dr. D. *De Japanse Burgerkampen* [Japanese Civilian Camps]. (CIC). Franeker, the Netherlands, 1977.
Warner, Lavinia, and John Sandilands. *Women Beyond the Wire: A Story of Women Prisoners of the Japanese.* (CIC). London, 1982.

International Military Tribunal, Far East:

Sumatra Camps—Affidavits and testimonies: 27431–34, 27532, 27655–79, 30195–246, 32935, 33061–65, 33123–33, 33195–98; see also, 13297–303, 13554–604, 13733–820, 40265–65, 40292–93, 40313–14, 40337–38, and 40382.

Netherlands Institute War Documentation:

Peace announcement Pakanbaroe: RvO IC 6866.
Report on CIC130 Sungai Sengkol camp: RvO IC 4265.
Reports on CIC155 Bangkinang II: RvO IC 6816, 6829, 9015.
Convictions of war criminals: RvO IC 4272, 7455.
General rules for Sumatra civilian centers: RvO IC 6822.
Statement by Major General Shozo Yamamoto about the quantities of food distributed by the 25th Army: RvO IC 9901.
Red Cross parcels to Sumatra camps: RvO IC 3664, 3667.
Reports on CIC99 (Lawesigalagala): RvO IC 9718 and IMTFE 13733.
Reports on CIC116 (Unie Kampong): RvO IC 4264.
Reports on CIC119 (Pematangsiantar I): RvO IC 4270.
Report on personal experiences at CIC97 (Kendal): RvO IC 742.
Report on dysentery in North Sumatra: RvO IC 4272.
March from Blangkedjeren to Kota Tjane: RvO IC 4268.
Documents on POW Camps and Civilian Internment Centers: RvO IC 26, 32, 368, 445, 464, 465, 589–591, 592–597, 598–602, 689, 742, 774, 859, 1215, 1216, 1217, 1218, 1219–1221, 1222, 1223, 1226, 1227, 1316, 1333, 1362, 1458, 1527, 1528, 1529, 1891, 1948, 1971, 1974, 2412, 3475, 3518, 3663, 3664–3670, 4264, 4265, 4270, 4274, 4292, 4460, 5083, 5274, 5280, 5375, 5514, 5956, 6122, 6241, 6440, 6457, 6662, 6816, 7684, 8155, 6822, 6829, 9015, 9703, 9704, 9709–9711, 9715–16, 9718, 9731–32, 9749, 9756, 9757, 9787, 9788, 9791–804, 9812.

JAVA (DUTCH EAST INDIES)

POW Camps

Introduction. . When the Dutch and Allied forces in Java capitulated on March 8, 1942, several hundred members of the British, Australian, New Zealand, and American forces found themselves unable to leave the island of Java. One party of Australian air force men made their way to Java's south coast and began building a boat to take them to Australia, but after six weeks the Javanese police made them surrender to the Japanese. Another air force party at Tjilatjap, a south-coast port, made valiant efforts to get away. The Dutch refused to allow them to take over a corvette that was abandoned by its crew, fully fueled and provisioned; instead, the corvette was sunk to block the entrance to the harbor that the Japanese never attempted to use. Then, in an aged launch, towing two lifeboats, 62 men began their journey. After a few miles the launch broke down and one of the lifeboats was damaged while being beached. This was the end of the escape attempts.

Soon, Dutch and Allied forces were put in POW camps, of which the two most important were the "Bicycle" camp, or Xe Battalion Camp, as it was officially known, and the XVe Battalion Camp in Bandoeng, West Java.

Individual Listings of POW Camps: POW343–POW357

POW343: Artillery Barracks

POW344: Tjimahi
Prisoners were concentrated in the Dutch barracks in a small town close to the city of Bandoeng in West Java, known as a military town before the war. This was one of the "transit" camps from which POWs were shipped to camps in other cities. To many men waiting to be put on transport, it was a boring, day-to-day existence of making ropes in a factory.

POW345: Exhibition Building
A temporary assembly camp in the city of Bandoeng.

POW346: XVe Infantry Battalion Barracks
This was a large compound of the prewar Dutch XVe Battalion infantry,

used for POWs from March 1942 until mid–1942. The 4,000 to 5,000 men assembled in this camp were transported to a number of other camps.

POW347: First Infantry Depot

This camp was much like POW346 and was located in the city of Bandoeng, West Java. It was most likely used for Allied officers. Prisoners from Makassar Camp in Makassar, South Celebes, arrived here in October 1944; these 800 men were added to the 700 Dutch already there. In these old Dutch military barracks, there were only five small water taps for 1,500 men. In April 1945 the men were moved to POW350 (Land's Opvoedings Gesticht) in Bandoeng.

POW348: 134th Depot Battalion

POW349: Soekamiskin

An old prison in the city of Bandoeng.

POW350: Land's Opvoedings Gesticht (LOG)

To this 200-yard-square compound, surrounded by a 20-foot-high wall, containing the buildings of the Dutch State Correctional Institute-School, about 1,500 men from POW347 (First Infantry Depot) were moved in April 1945. Another 1,800 men came in from Batavia. There were only 22 squatting-type toilets for the more than 3,000 men. The barracks had two tiers of wooden platforms, providing three layers of sleeping space: "dog kennel," the bottom; "chicken coop," the middle; and "bird's nest," the top tier. It was a very muddy compound; in 40 days, 800 officers moved over 700 tons of stone to cover the muddy areas.

POW351: Tjilatjap

Located on the south coast of West Java, this city, with its natural harbor, was used by the Dutch and Allied forces as the "last stronghold" against the advancing Japanese troops. On March 8, 1942, however, the Dutch surrendered. In the meantime about 4,000 Allied forces had assembled in the town. Several ships were anchored in the harbor ready to escape to Australia. Only one succeeded, however; the others were unable even to raise anchor.

After the surrender the troops were interned in some old Dutch barracks, from which they were transported to other camps a few months later.

The overcrowding, insufficient food, and lack of medical treatment were no better or worse than in other camps.

POW352: Adek

This old building in the city of Batavia, West Java, was later occupied by women and children internees.

POW353: Xth Battalion

Before the war, this was one of the main Dutch military compounds in the city of Batavia, West Java. Because of its size the POWs nicknamed it the "Bicycle Camp." The compound was 900 feet by 700 feet and enclosed by a high brick wall; its coordinates were 6°12'S and 106°50'E (today the site of the Borobudur Intercontinental Hotel). The camp was first occupied on March 26, 1942. On April 13, about 354 survivors of the USS *Houston* arrived in the camp.

Arrivals and departures of POWs maintained an average POW population of about 4,000 men—largely Dutch and British, with some Americans (from the Texas 131st Field Artillery Regiment) and Australians. With occasional exceptions, the treatment in the Bicycle Camp was better than the POW camps elsewhere in the Pacific. This better treatment could be attributed to the fact that this camp was used mostly as a "transit" point; that is, before POWs from other camps in the Dutch East Indies were sent to Japan or the Burma-Siam railroad, they were sent here to be "fattened."

The rule of Lieutenant Sonei, commandant of the camp from September 20, 1942, to March 15, 1944, was, however, one of such brutality that, even with the better food, no POW who was in this camp would ever forget him. In fact, no Japanese commandant was loathed more, by both POWs and civilian internees, than was Sonei. In March 1944 he was transferred to become commandant of one of the largest civilian camps in the Indies, CIC189 (Tjideng). After the war, he was sentenced to death by the local Batavia Military Tribunal.

As POW Roy Bulcock wrote:

> Sonei! Despot of the barbed-wire kingdom. A bantam cock crowing on his dung-hill. A tin God of a sadist religion! He's a dictator with the power of life and death over his subjects—a megalomaniac to whom cruelty is a drug and a tonic.
>
> There is something feminine about his appearance, but it is the feline treachery of a tigress about to strike. I'd rather trust a tigress any time. He has that cruel look about his eyes and mouth that indicates a love of causing pain, so much so that he won't let his guards beat up a prisoner— he always does the job himself.[1]

Said POW George T. Cooper:

> A swine. Spoke and understood English. Hated the Dutch, whom he called gutless, selfish and dishonest. Did not admire the English. The "bashing" type—frantic rages—brutal to his own men.[2]

POW354: Glodok Gaol

A prison in Batavia.

POW355: Struiwijk
Another prison in Batavia.

POW356: Darmo
A camp in Soerabaja, East Java.

POW357: Jaarmarkt
A camp in Soerabaja, East Java.

Civilian Internment Centers

Introduction. Java was, and always has been, the most densely populated island of the Indonesian archipelago, with regard to both the indigenous population and the Dutch people. With such a large number of civilians to intern—hundreds of thousands of Dutch and Eurasians—the Japanese had a formidable task ahead of them. By excluding most Eurasians from internment, the Japanese somewhat reduced the logistical problems of finding appropriate camps, or housing.

When possible, they initially used schools, convents, and other buildings that were once used by the Dutch, or had bamboo barracks built. Later, after most POWs had left Java, the Japanese utilized the military barracks used by the POWs. Another popular method of internment was to cordon off neighborhood blocks, where the Dutch used to live, and simply to dump thousands of men, women, and children in these so-called safety zones and let them do whatever they could to fend for themselves.

As the war progressed, the men and boys aged 10 and older were separated from the women and placed in different internment centers and camps.

As with the POWs, the civilians were subjected to numerous moves. Weak and ill and with young children to provide for, the women offered a pitiful picture trying to go from place to place, loaded with all their little possessions.

Daphne Jackson and her daughter Jane, for example, were subjected to four moves, staying in five camps from October 1942 to war's end. As Mrs. Jackson wrote:

> At about two-thirty we moved out of the prison—a most pitiable collection of humanity, covered with ulcers on arms and legs on which the flies settled, and laden with bits of luggage, tins, buckets, and bags, for by this time we had learned to hang on like grim death to any nail, tin or bit of string.[3]

Individual Listings of Civilian Internment Centers: CIC178–CIC291

West Java

Serang

CIC178: Serang
About 60 men, women, and children from the area were housed in the city jail from March 2, 1942, to July 10, 1942. About 25 women and children were moved to CIC205 (Kota Paris III), and the men were moved to CIC199 (Ursulinen).

Batavia (now Jakarta)

CIC179: Glodok I
About 500 men, workers and employees of the city council and the police were housed in the city jail from March 6, 1942, to March 25, 1942, when they were moved to CIC181 (Struiswijk I).

CIC180: Glodok II*
Eurasians from Central and West Java were housed in the same city jail as CIC179 (Glodok I) from January 1945 to September 1945, when they were liberated.

CIC181: Struiswijk I
About 3,500 men from the city were housed in the large city jail from March 10, 1942, to February 1944. They were then moved to CIC213 (Tjikoedapateuh).

CIC182: Struiswijk II
An unknown number of American and British women and children were housed in the city jail (part of CIC181) from April to June 1942. They were freed and then reinterned from October 1942 to December 1943 and moved to CIC193 (Tanahtinggi).

CIC183: Struiswijk III*
About 1,450 women and children from CIC188 (Kramat III), CIC214 (Tjihapit I), and CIC201 (Gedongbadak II) lived in the city jail. After the men were moved out in February 1944, the women and children were moved in on November 1, 1944, and stayed until October 1945, when they were liberated. Thirty died in internment.

*Camps marked with an asterisk were liberated in August, September, or October 1945.

CIC184: Adek I

About 3,000 men from the city lived in the labor barracks in the suburbs from June 1942 to February 1944. They then moved to CIC213 (Tjikoedapateuh).

CIC185: Adek II*

About 2,200 women and children from CIC187 (Kramat II), CIC195 (Tangerang II), and CIC214 (Tjihapit I) lived in the same labor barracks as CIC184. After the men were moved away in February 1944, the women and children were moved in in November 1944; they stayed until October 1945, when they were liberated.

At this time the women and children had been incarcerated for two or more years. Certain items taken for granted in regular society became unbelievable luxuries when they were suddenly acquired. As Lome Blankwaardt-van der Jagt wrote in her diary:

> We went with our children—Violet [who had just been interned in May 1945] had twins—to the communal showers. Violet had soap, real soap. I did not know what I saw. She soaped my back and we soaped the children. What a feast! This was such a luxury after being two years without it. We laughed and ignored the dark looks of some women. We laughed and laughed and forgot about the long wait for freedom.[4]

CIC186: Kramat I

About 2,500 women and children from the city and from CIC230 (Cheribon II) lived in a block of houses from October 1, 1942, to September 1943, when they were moved to CIC189 (Tjideng).

CIC187: Kramat II

About 3,400 men, women, and children—those still working for the Japanese, non–Dutch citizens, the handicapped and the mentally ill, and those from CIC203 (Kota Paris I) and from CIC204 (Kota Paris II)—lived in the same block of houses where a group of women and children had stayed until September 1943. This group stayed from September 1943 to September 1944. The men were then moved to CIC191 (Grogol II), and the women moved to CIC189 (Tjideng) and CIC188 (Kramat III).

CIC188: Kramat III*

Another group of women and children—from CIC187 (Kramat II) and CIC214 (Tjihapit I)—and a group of Eurasians and nuns lived in the same block as CIC186 and CIC187 (Kramat I and II); 28 died. This current group stayed from September 1944 to October 1945.

CIC189: Tjideng*

In many respects, this was the most infamous camp and perhaps the largest group of women and children ever assembled in Japanese camps. In various stages, up to 10,500 women and children were moved from CIC186 (Kramat I), CIC187 (Kramat II), CIC190 (Grogol I), CIC192 (Grogol III), CIC195 (Tangerang II), CIC201 (Gedongbadak II), and CIC202 (Gedongbadak III) to many blocks of houses in the Tjideng district. They lived in this camp from October 1, 1942, to October 1945, when they were liberated.

In March 1944 the infamous Lieutenant Sonei was transferred from the POW camp in Batavia to become commandant of this camp. Mrs. Lea Morris wrote the following about Sonei in a long-since-defunct Dutch newsletter, *Nederland en Overzee*:

> Camp commandant Sonei stopped the wagon loaded with bread and being pulled by a few of the strongest women in camp. Instead of having the bread distributed, Sonei ordered some of the women to dig a deep hole and throw the bread in it. He then poured kerosene over it. The bread became thus totally inedible. When the women protested vehemently, he punished them by refusing to let them return to their houses. The group of women remained outside in the rain, all day long.

CIC190: Grogol I

About 1,200 women and children from the area lived in a compound and facilities of the city's insane asylum from July 4, 1943, to August 27, 1944, when they were moved to CIC189 (Tjideng).

CIC191: Grogol II

An unknown number of men and boys over 10 years old, from CIC187 (Kramat II) and CIC189 (Tjideng), both of which would now be occupied only by women and children, were moved to the same place as CIC190, from which the women had moved in August 1944. This camp was occupied from September 1944 to November 1944, when the men were moved to CIC224 (Baros II).

CIC192: Grogol III

When the men and boys were moved out of CIC191, about 1,050 women, children and handicapped persons moved in from CIC214 (Tjihapit I) and CIC189 (Tjideng). They lived here from November 30, 1944, to April 18, 1945, when they all were moved again to CIC189 (Tjideng).

CIC193: Tanahtinggi

About 1,500 American, Jewish, and Iraqi women and children from all over Java and those from CIC290 (Batoe), CIC217 (Lengkong), CIC245 (Broederschool), and CIC283 (Werfstraat) were housed in the youth jail facility in town from October 9, 1943, to March 1944.

The jail facility was a single-story, star-shaped prison with cells on two sides of high, tiled corridors. The toilet facilities were a long trench in the floor. There was practically no medical aid; the seriously ill were sent to a hospital in town.

CIC194: Tangerang I

About 1,350 men and boys from CIC291 (Kesilir) lived in the youth educational compound outside town from September 11, 1943, to March 1944, when they moved to CIC226 (IVe, IXe Battalion).

CIC195: Tangerang II

After the men were moved out of CIC194 (Tangerang I), about 1,600 women and children were moved in from CIC193 (Tanahtinggi), CIC189 (Tjideng), CIC283 (Werfsraat), and CIC286 (Darmo). They lived here from March 1944 to April 26, 1945, when they were moved to CIC189 (Tjideng) and CIC185 (Adek II). Twenty-eight died in internment.

From the diary of a woman:

> September 1944: I am Protestant and I am a Jewish woman—if I were a man, I would be a Jew—that's all what my little girl can say to me. This reform school compound is truly like a jail with all its iron bars, cells and rooms with multi-tiered bunks and the "public" bathroom and toilets. We all long for home. There are a few schools—so to speak—for the children. There's no furniture and the kids sit on the floor. For a lack of a blackboard the walls are used to explain the lessons. My little girl is in first grade.
>
> "Mama, why are you on earth? I know you haven't been naughty . . . Oh, I know it: you curse once and a while and you have to take care of me."[5]

CIC196: Kampong Makassar*

About 3,600 women and children, some from CIC189 (Tjideng) and from CIC202 (Gedongbadak III), CIC205 (Kota Paris III), and CIC214 (Tjihapit I) lived in barracks outside the town from January 1, 1945, to October 1945. Forty died; the rest were liberated in this camp.

This camp was one of the few work camps for women. They tilled the soil used for growing vegetable gardens, fruit trees, and the like.

Mrs. J. A. A. Luyck-Sleyfer, a member of the First Chamber (the Upper House or Senate in Holland) after the war and author of *Het Verbluffende Kamp* [The Bewildering Camp], wrote:

> It is not surprising that the women showed more strength of mind than the men in our camps, because conditions dictated that family bonds, sense of community, and responsibility were even more important in camp than in normal life.
> Stimulated by the presence of so many children, our feelings of adjustment and flexibility increased a hundred-fold.[6]

CIC197: Vincentius*

This central hospital for the camps in Batavia (a convent in town) housed about 350 staff personnel and about 1,200 sick men and women from March 1945 to October 1945, when it was liberated. When the hospital was in operation, the death rate was about 12 a day.

CIC198: Mater Dolorosa*

About 1,000 sick men (423 of whom died) from all areas of Java were housed in this convent in town from May 7, 1945, to October 1945, when the camp was liberated.

Buitenzorg (now called Bogor)

CIC199: Ursulinen

An unknown number of men from the town and the area lived in this convent in town from July 1942 to November 1942, when they were moved to CIC200 (Gedongbadak I).

CIC200: Gedongbadak I

About 1,200 men from the area and from CIC199 (Ursulinen) lived in houses plus a barrack from September 1942 to February 1944. They were then moved to CIC226 (IVe, IXe Battalion).

CIC201: Gedongbadak II

About 1,000 women and children were moved to CIC200 (Gedongbadak I) on March 3, 1944, after the men moved out. They came from CIC235 (Todanstraat), CIC233 (Goedang Garam), and CIC203 (Kota Paris I). On October 12, 1944, they moved to CIC189 (Tjideng).

CIC202: Gedongbadak III

After a group of women and children was moved out in October 1944, another group of about 1,000 women and children was moved in on November 3, 1944, from CIC216 (Karees). In March 1945 they were moved to CIC189 (Tjideng) and CIC196 (Kampong Makassar).

CIC203: Kota Paris I

About 250 men, women, and children—those still working for the

Japanese—lived in a block of houses outside town from April 20, 1943, to May 3, 1944. The men were moved to an unknown destination, and the women and children were moved to CIC201 (Gedongbadak II) and CIC187 (Kramat II).

CIC204: Kota Paris II

When the internees held at CIC203 (Kota Paris I) were moved out, another group of about 250 women and children moved in. This group lived here from May 9, 1944, to November 2, 1944, when they were moved to CIC187 (Kramat II).

CIC205: Kota Paris III

In November 1944, after the second group of internees had left this camp, another group of about 250 women and children was moved in from CIC216 (Karees), together with some elderly and sick persons. On March 19, 1945, they were moved to CIC196 (Kampong Makassar).

Bandoeng (Bandung)

CIC206: Sukamiskin

An unknown number of Dutch governmental authorities from the Bandoeng area and those moved from CIC231 (Gevangenis) and CIC237 (Gevangenis II) lived in this camp from March 1942 to February 1944. They were then moved to CIC226 (IVe, IXe Battalion).

CIC207: Lands Opvoedings Gesticht (LOG)

An unknown number of men from the city and surrounding area lived in a reform school in the suburbs from July 18, 1942, to February 1944. They were then moved to CIC225 (Baros III) and CIC226 (IVe, IXe Battalion).

CIC208: Stella Maris

About 1,000 men and boys from the city lived in a convent in town from August 1942 to February 1944. About 500 were moved to CIC225 (Baros III), and 500 were moved to CIC213 (Tjikoedapateuh—XVe Battalion).

From the diary of a university professor in the camp:

> 14 November 1942: Lectured about British India. If possible I'll do something like this every Saturday.
> 4 January 1943: Given a lecture on England's social history.
> 16 January 1943: I'm considered a walking encyclopedia—every moment boys stop me to ask questions.
> 27 February 1943: I am teaching regularly now. We are congregating behind the barracks in a quiet corner.

3 June 1943: Final high school exams. Two boys received their algebra diploma. It has been decided to give basically verbal exams, with two professors present.
20 July 1943: A meeting was held by all teachers: vocational and non-vocational. Although not all courses can be given, we are preparing a program. The thing is running. Government civil servants in the camp are willing to witness the exams and give those who passed a diploma that will be accredited after the war.[7]

CIC209: Pasir Andir
About 550 men from the area lived in stables outside town from August 1942 to November 1942, when they were moved to CIC210 (the Palace Hotel).

CIC210: Palace Hotel
About 850 men from the area and from CIC209 (Pasir Andir) lived in this hotel in town from November 1942 to October 1943, when they were moved to CIC225 (Baros III).

CIC211: Zeelandia
About 800 men from the city lived in a school in town from August 1942 to October 1943, when they were moved to CIC225 (Baros III).

CIC212: Dick de Hoog
About 800 men from the city lived in a school in town from November 1942 to February 1943, when they were moved to CIC225 (Baros III).

CIC213: Tjikoedapateuh (XVe Battalion)*
About 10,000 men and boys from all over the Dutch East Indies— CIC184 (Adek I), CIC181 (Struiswijk I), CIC208 (Stella Maris), CIC215 (Tjihapit II), CIC218 (Bloemenkamp B and C), CIC229 (Cheribon I), CIC247 (Sompok Lama), CIC249 (Halmaheira II), CIC268 (Banjoebiroe 10-I), CIC282 (Boeboetan II), and CIC285 (Werfstraat III)—lived in the military barracks in town. In May 1945 some prominent men were moved to CIC225 (Baros III), and about 2,000 men were moved to CIC221 (Tjitjalengka Workcamp). The rest lived in the camp from January or February 1944 to October 1945, when they were liberated.

CIC214: Tjihapit I*
About 14,000 women and children from the city of Bandoeng lived in blocks of houses in town. In November-December 1944 all but 60 were moved to various other camps: CIC183 (Struiswijk III), CIC185 (Adek II), CIC188 (Kramat III), CIC192 (Grogol III), CIC196 (Kampong

Makassar), and CIC242 (Ziekenzorg II). Those who remained were liberated in this camp.

CIC215: Tjihapit II
About 1,000 men and boys lived in a block of houses next to CIC214 (Tjihapit I). On May 6, 1945, they were moved to CIC213 (Tjikoedapateuh).

CIC216: Karees
About 6,000 women and children from West Java and the western part of Central Java lived in a block of houses in the suburbs from December 2, 1942, to December 28, 1944. They were then moved, beginning in November 1944, to CIC202 (Gedongbadak III), CIC205 (Kota Paris III), and CIC256 (Ambarawa (1)6).

CIC217: Lengkong
About 100 British and American women from the city lived in the school in town from June 1943 to October 1943, when they were moved to CIC193 (Tanahtinggi).

CIC218: Bloemenkamp B and C
Families whose husbands were still working for the Japanese lived in houses in the suburbs from August 1943 to November 1944. The men were then moved to CIC213 (Tjikoedapateuh) and the women to CIC214 (Tjihapit I).

CIC219: Bloemenkamp
About 1,200 women and children from CIC223 (Baros I) lived in blocks of houses next to CIC214 (Tjihapit I) from July 20, 1944, to November 1944, when they were moved to CIC257 (Ambarawa 7I).

CIC220: Rama
About 900 older men and the sick with families lived in houses in the suburbs from December 1942 to June 3, 1944. They were then moved to CIC214 (Tjihapit I).

CIC221: Tjitjalengka*
About 4,000 men and boys moved from various camps, including CIC213 (Tjikoedapateuh) and CIC226 (IVe, IXe Battalion), to this work camp outside town. The men and boys were put to work building a small railroad from May 1945 to August 1945. They were liberated in this camp.

Tjimahi City

CIC222: Treinkampement
About 1,200 women and children from the city and surrounding area

lived in military barracks and houses from November 20, 1942, to December 20, 1942. They were then moved to CIC223 (Baros I).

CIC223: Baros I
About 1,200 women and children were moved from CIC222 (Treinkampement) to military houses and barracks (Tjimahi was one of Java's cities with the largest number of Dutch military camps). They lived here from December 20, 1942, to July 20, 1944, when they were moved to CIC219 (Bloemenkamp).

CIC224: Baros II*
About 1,700 men and boys were moved into this camp (the same site as CIC223) from CIC191 (Grogol II) after the women and children were moved out. They lived here from July 1944 to October 1945, when the camp was liberated.

CIC225: Baros III*
An unknown number of men and boys from various other camps—CIC207 (LOG), CIC208 (Stella Maris), CIC210 (Palace Hotel), CIC211 (Zeelandia), CIC212 (Dick de Hoog), and CIC213 (Tjikoedapateuh)—lived in military barracks in town from October 1943 to October 1945, when they were liberated.

CIC226: IVe, IXe Battalion*
About 10,000 men and boys from camps all over the Dutch East Indies—CIC194 (Tangerang I), CIC200 (Gedongbadak I), CIC206 (Sukamiskin), CIC207 (LOG), CIC232 (Muloschool), CIC240 (Vredenburgh), CIC263 (Djoe Eng), CIC274 (Benteng I), CIC276 (Gevangenis), CIC277 (Sentono Pande), and CIC288 (Marinekampement)—were moved to the military barracks and houses in town in February 1944. Some were moved to other camps—about 1,250 elderly and the sick to CIC258 (Ambarawa 7II) and CIC198 (Mater Dolorosa), and about 2,000 to CIC221 (Tjitjalengka Work Camp); 744 died. The remainder lived in the camp until October 1945, when they were liberated.

CIC227: Hospital*
An unknown number of sick men from CIC225 (Baros III) and CIC226 (IVe, IXe Battalion) were housed in this hospital in town from July 1944 to October 1945, when they were liberated.

Soekaboemi (Sukabumi)

CIC228: Rosalie*
About 150 sick men and women lived in a house in the suburbs from January 1943 to October 1945, when they were liberated.

Cheribon

CIC229: Cheribon I
An unknown number of men from the city and the area were housed in the jail in town from March 1942 to February 1944. They were then moved to CIC213 (Tjikoedapateuh).

CIC230: Cheribon II
An unknown number of women and children from the city and the area were housed in the same jail as CIC229 (Cheribon I), but in a different block. They lived here from June 1942 to June 1943, when they were moved to CIC186 (Kramat I).

Central Java

Pekalongan

CIC231: Gevangenis (Jail)
An unknown number of men from the city and from CIC234 (Gevangenis) and CIC236 (Gevangenis I) were housed in this jail from March 1942 to September 1943. In December 1942 some were moved to CIC232 (Muloschool), and in September 1943, the rest were moved to CIC206 (Sukamiskin).

CIC232: Muloschool
About 120 men from CIC231 (Gevangenis) lived in the school in town from December 1942 to September 3, 1943. They were then moved to CIC274 (Benteng I) and CIC226 (IVe, IXe Battalion).

CIC233: Goedang Garam
An unknown number of women and children from the city and the area lived in the salt warehouse in town from October 31, 1943, to March 3, 1944. They were then moved to CIC201 (Gedongbadak II).

Tegal

CIC234: Gevangenis (Jail)
An unknown number of men from the city and the area were housed in the city jail from March 1942 to June 7, 1942, when they moved to CIC231 (Gevangenis).

CIC235: Todanstraat
An unknown number of women and children from in and around the

city lived in a block of houses in town from October 7, 1943, to March 3, 1944. They were then moved to CIC201 (Gedongbadak II).

Poerwokerto (Purwokerto)

CIC236: Gevangenis I (Jail)
An unknown number of Dutch governmental officials from the area were housed in the city jail from March 1942 to September 1942, when they were moved to CIC231 (Gevangenis).

CIC237: Gevangenis II
An unknown number of high-ranking Dutch governmental officials from CIC206 (Sukamiskin) were housed in the same city jail as CIC236 (Gevangenis I) from August 1943 to July 1944. They were then moved to CIC225 (Baros III).

CIC238: Broederschool
About 4,000 men from the area lived in the Catholic school compound from April 1942 to October 1943, when they were moved to CIC274 (Benteng I).

Djokajakarta (Jocjakarta)

CIC239: Gevangenis
An unknown number of Dutch officials from the city and the area were housed in the city jail from April 23, 1942, to June 23, 1942, when they were moved to CIC240 (Vredenburgh).

CIC240: Vredenburgh
Governmental officials from CIC239 (Gevangenis) and Dutch businessmen from the city lived in the old Dutch fort from June 23, 1942, to February 1944. On September 23, 1942, the Dutch officials were moved to CIC281 (Boeboetan I) and the others to CIC226 (IVe, IXe Battalion).

Soerakarta (Surakarta)

CIC241: Ziekenzorg I
An unknown number of men from the city lived in the hospital in town from March 25, 1942, to September 1943, when they were moved to CIC274 (Benteng I).

CIC242: Ziekenzorg II
About 4,200 women and children were moved from CIC289 (Wijk),

CIC214 (Tjihapit I), and CIC257 (Ambarawa 7I) to the hospital and barracks. They lived here from December 2, 1943, to June 1945, when they were moved to CIC272 (Moentilan), CIC258 (Ambarawa 7II), and CIC250 (Halmaheira III).

Semarang

CIC243: Djatingaleh
An unknown number of men from the city and from the Jepara and Kedoe districts were housed in the city jail from April 22, 1942, to August 9, 1942. Then some were moved to CIC281 (Boeboetan I) and some to CIC291 (Kesilir).

CIC244: Kalibanteng
An unknown number of men from the area were housed in the city jail from July 3, 1942, to August 9, 1942, when they were moved to CIC291 (Kesilir).

CIC245: Broederschool
An unknown number of British and American women and children from the area lived in the school compound in town from September 1942 to December 23, 1943. They were then moved to CIC193 (Tanahtinggi).

CIC246: Lampersari-Sompok*
About 8,000 women and children from all areas of Central Java and from other camps—CIC254 (Karangpanas), CIC253 (Gedangan), CIC251 (Bangkong I), CIC 247 (Sompok Lama), and CIC248 (Halmaheira I)—lived in a block of houses in a suburb from November 1942 to October 1945. They were liberated from this camp.

CIC247: Sompok Lama
An unknown number of men and their families—those still working for the Japanese—lived in houses in a suburb from December 1942 to December 28, 1944. The men were moved to CIC213 (Tjikoedapateuh), and the women and children to CIC246 (Lampersari-Sompok).

CIC248: Halmaheira I
An unknown number of men and their families—those still working for the Japanese—lived in houses in a suburb from December 1942 to June 1, 1943. The men were then moved to CIC249 (Halamheira II), and the women and children to CIC246 (Lampersari-Sompok).

CIC249: Halmaheira II
An unknown number of men and boys from Semarang and from

CIC248 (Halmaheira I) lived in houses in a suburb from June 1, 1943, to January 22, 1944, when they were moved to CIC213 (Tjikoedapateuh).

CIC250: Halmaheira III*
About 3,700 women and children from CIC242 (Ziekenzorg II) and CIC253 (Gedangan) lived in a block of houses in a suburb from February 3, 1944, to October 1945, when they were liberated.

CIC251: Bangkong I
About 1,200 women and children from the city and from CIC286 (Darmo) lived in this convent and boarding school in town from June 11, 1943, to September 13, 1944. They were then moved to CIC253 (Gedangan), CIC250 (Halmaheira III), and CIC246 (Lampersari-Sompok).

CIC252: Bangkong II*
About 1,400 older men and boys and the sick from CIC226 (IVe, IXe Battalion) and CIC253 (Gedangan) lived in the same convent and boarding school (CIC251) out of which the women and children had been moved in September 1944. They lived here from September 13, 1944, to October 1945, when they were liberated.

CIC253: Gedangan
About 3,700 women and children from CIC251 (Bangkong I) and CIC286 (Darmo) lived in the convent in town from October 21, 1943, to May 6, 1945. In September 1944 some 40 boys and older men were moved to CIC252 (Bangkong II). Others were moved to CIC250 (Halmaheira III), CIC246 (Lampersari-Sompok), CIC259 (Ambarawa 8I) and CIC261 (Ambarawa 9I).

CIC254: Karangpanas
About 2,600 women and children from CIC286 (Darmo) and CIC289 (Wijk) lived in this orphanage and barracks from February 1944 to November 28, 1944; 100 died. In June 1944, 500 women and children were moved to CIC256 (Ambarawa [1]6). In September 1944, some boys and older men were moved to CIC252 (Bangkong II) and CIC246 (Lampersari-Sompok).

Ambarawa (Central Java)

CIC255: Tangsi Perlindungan
About 400 women and children from the city lived in houses outside town from October 27, 1942, to December 30, 1942. They were then moved to CIC256 (Ambarawa [1]6).

CIC256: Ambarawa (1)6*

About 4,000 women and children from various other camps—CIC255 (Tangsi Perlindungan), CIC264 (Soemowono), CIC259 (Ambarawa 8I), CIC261 (Ambarawa 9I), CIC272 (Moentilan), CIC254 (Karangpanas), CIC216 (Karees)—lived intermittently in these barracks of bamboo and palm-leaf thatch outside town from December 18, 1942, to October 1945. In May 1945, about 800 women and children were moved to CIC262 (Ambarawa 9II), a work camp; 116 died. Others remained and were liberated from this camp.

CIC257: Ambarawa 7I

About 2,000 women and children from the area and from CIC264 (Soemowono) and CIC219 (Bloemenkamp) lived in this old hospital compound in town from December 22, 1942, to December 31, 1944, together with some older men. Many of the internees were moved to CIC242 (Ziekenzorg II) and CIC272 (Moentilan); some of the older men and boys stayed in camp. Twelve died.

CIC258: Ambarawa 7II*

About 4,000 boys, older men, and the sick from CIC260 (Ambarawa 8II), CIC242 (Ziekenzorg II), and CIC226 (IVe, IXe Battalion) lived in this hospital compound in town from January 1, 1945; 640 died. Those who survived stayed until October 1945, when they were liberated.

From the diary of a boy:

> Thursday, 1 February 1945: Dear mother, Washed my clothes today. I hate mending my clothes. The thread breaks constantly because I pull too hard. And the thread always gets entangled—how, I don't know. It took me almost two hours to sew a patch in my shirt. I wash clothes once every three days. Last night I made some pancakes from the breakfast porridge. Fried them without oil. They were hard like seaman's biscuits.
>
> Tuesday, 20 March 1945: Haven't written for a while. I was sick—malaria again—shivering and shivering. I feel much better now. Will probably go back to my kitchen job. We get maize porridge every morning now—tastes damn good.
>
> In the beginning, when I was here in camp without you, I was always thinking of you. When I woke up in the morning, my first thoughts were for you. But no more. One gets such doggone homesick feelings and so, I think as little as possible about you. You don't mind, do you?[8]

CIC259: Ambarawa 8I

About 900 women and children from the area and from CIC253 (Gedangan) lived in this school outside town from June 19, 1943, to September 19, 1944; 10 died. The women and children were moved to CIC256 (Ambarawa [1]6) and CIC269 (Banjoebiroe 10II). Some of the men and boys who were also in this camp stayed but were later moved to CIC260 (Ambarawa 8II).

CIC260: Ambarawa 8II

About 1,000 older men and boys and the sick from CIC259 (Ambarawa 8I) and from other areas lived in this school compound from September 19, 1944, to May 1, 1945, when they were moved to CIC258 (Ambarawa 7II) and CIC265 (Bandungan work camp).

CIC261: Ambarawa 9I

About 1,300 women and children were moved from CIC253 (Gedangan) and from other unknown camps to the school compound outside town on October 29, 1943; 18 died. Those who survived stayed until May 10, 1945, when they were moved to CIC256 (Ambarawa [1]6), CIC269 (Banjoebiroe 10II), and CIC270 (Banjoebiroe 11).

CIC262: Ambarawa 9II*

About 800 women and children moved from CIC256 (Ambarawa [1]6) to this school outside, which was run as a work camp. They lived here from May 1945 to October 1945, when the camp was liberated. As one woman wrote:

> The menu causes problems. No more bread for breakfast, but "katjang idjoe"—a small green pea—with a palm sugar syrup. You get used to it, but the boys don't like it. The main meal consists of red rice—it doesn't look appetizing, but it contains all the necessary vitamins. This rice-eating causes problems.[9]

Those captives who before the war had adapted to the indigenous (peasant) foods of the countries they lived in had a much greater chance of surviving the incarceration.

The *katjang idjoe* the woman referred to is the mung bean, used to generate bean sprouts—one of the most nutritious beans in Southeast Asia. The "red rice" is peasant rice, rice from which the bran has not been removed. It is extremely nutritious. The "rice-eating problem" of the lady and her two sons would not have occurred if they had not relied too much on Western food before the war.

In 1944, the writer of the "food" story—1 meter, 70 centimeters tall (5 feet, 7 inches), weighed 48 kilograms (105 pounds). The 15-year-old son weighed 38 kilograms (83.7 pounds), and the 10-year old son weighed 26 kilograms (57 pounds), and the 4-year-old son weighed 14 kilograms (30.8 pounds).

CIC263: Djoe Eng

An unknown number of men from the area lived in a house in town from September 1943 to February 1944, when they were moved to CIC226 (IVe, IXe Battalion).

CIC264: Soemowono

About 550 women and children from Soerakarta lived in the military bivouac from December 27, 1942, to March 15, 1944. They then moved to CIC256 (Ambarawa [1]6) and CIC257 (Ambarawa 7I).

Bandoengan (Bandungan)

CIC265: Bandoengan*

About 250 boys moved from CIC258 (Ambarawa 7II) and CIC260 (Ambarawa 8II) to houses outside town—a work camp. They lived here from September 29, 1944, to October 1945, when the camp was liberated.

Kalitjeret

CIC266: Kalitjeret*

About 200 boys from CIC258 (Ambarawa 7II) and CIC260 (Ambarawa 8II) lived in houses outside town. They were held in this work camp from March 1945 to August 1945, when the camp was liberated.

Gedongdjati

CIC267: Gedongdjati*

About 200 boys from CIC258 (Ambarawa 7II) and CIC260 (Ambarawa 8II) lived in houses outside town—a work camp from September 1944 to August 1945, when they were liberated.

East Java

Banjoebiroe

CIC268: Banjoebiroe 10I

About 1,650 men from CIC291 (Kesilir) were housed in the city jail from August 1943 to February 5, 1944. They were then moved to CIC213 (Tjikoedapateuh).

CIC269: Banjoebiroe 10II*

About 5,500 women and children from CIC289 (Wijk), CIC279 (Kawarasan I), CIC280 (Kawarasan II), CIC278 (Galoehan), CIC273

(Redjosari), CIC259 (Ambarawa 8I), and CIC261 (Ambarawa 9I) were housed in the city jail from February 13, 1944; 163 died. Those who survived lived here until October 1945, when they were liberated.

CIC270: Banjoebiroe 11*
About 4,500 women and children from CIC261 (Ambarawa 9I) and CIC272 (Moentilan) lived in the military barracks from December 27, 1942; 100 died. Those who survived stayed until October 1945, when the camp was liberated.

CIC271: Banjoebiroe 12*
About 1,200 women and children from CIC272 (Moentilan) lived in this school compound outside town from August 3, 1945, to October 1945, when they were liberated.

Moentilan

CIC272: Moentilan
About 4,200 women and children from CIC257 (Ambarawa 7I), CIC286 (Darmo), and CIC242 (Ziekenzorg) lived in this boarding school in town from September 26, 1943, to August 21, 1945, when they were moved again even though liberation was imminent. They were moved to CIC256 (Ambarawa [1]6), CIC269 (Banjoebirow 10 II), CIC270 (Banjoebiroe 11), and CIC271 (Banjoebiroe 12).

Madioen

CIC273: Redjosari
About 50 women and children from the city of Madioen lived in a house in a suburb from September 1943 to February 1944, when they were moved to CIC269 (Banjoebiroe 10II).

Ngawi

CIC274: Benteng I
Men from Central and East Java and from CIC284 (Werfstraat II), CIC281 (Boeboetan I), CIC232 (Muloschool), CIC238 (Broederschool), and CIC241 (Ziekenzorg I) lived in the old Dutch fort outside town from February 27, 1943, to February 1944. They were then moved to CIC226 (IVe, IXe Battalion).

CIC275: Benteng II*
An unknown number of Eurasian men lived in the old Dutch fort that

was also the site of CIC274 from January 1945 to September 1945, when they were liberated.

Kediri

CIC276: Gevangenis
An unknown number of men from the city and surrounding area were housed in the city jail from November 1942 to February 1944, when they were moved to CIC226 (IVe, IXe Battalion).

CIC277: Sentono Pande
An unknown number of men from the Kediri district lived in houses outside town from July 1943 to February 1944. They were then moved to CIC226 (IVe, IXe Battalion).

CIC278: Galoehan
About 300 women and children from Kediri lived in houses in a suburb from September 1943 to March 17, 1944. They were then moved to CIC269 (Banjoebiroe 10II).

Blitar

CIC279: Kawarasan I
About 200 women and children from the area lived in houses in a suburb from May 1943 to March 17, 1944, when they were moved to CIC269 (Banjoebiroe 10II).

CIC280: Kawarasan II
About 300 women and children from the Wlingi district lived in houses in a suburb from September 1943 to March 17, 1944, when they were moved to CIC269 (Banjoebiroe 10II).

Soerabaja

CIC281: Boeboetan I
Dutch governmental officials from CIC240 (Vredenburgh), CIC243 (Djatingaleh), and CIC337 (Mataram I) were housed in the city jail from April 22, 1942, to February 27, 1943, when they were moved to CIC274 (Benteng I).

CIC282: Boeboetan II
An unknown number of non–Dutch men were housed in the city jail from October 1943 to February 1944. They were then moved to CIC213 (Tjikoedapateuh).

CIC283: Werfstraat

An unknown number of American and British women and children and about 250 Jewish and Iraqi women and children from Soerabaja city were housed in the city jail from March 1942 to March 1944. Some were moved to CIC193 (Tanahtinggi), and some to CIC195 (Tangerang II).

CIC284: Werfstraat II

An unknown number of American and British men from Soerabaja were housed in the city jail that was also the site of CIC283, in another part next to the women, from October 1942 to March 1943. They were then moved to CIC274 (Benteng I).

CIC285: Werfstraat III

About 2,000 Dutch men from Soerabaja were housed in still another part of the jail that held CIC283 and CIC284 from April 1943 to February 1944. They were then moved to CIC213 (Tjikoedapateuh).

CIC286: Darmo

About 6,000 women and children from the city and surrounding area lived in houses in the suburbs from January 1943 to March 1944. They were then moved to CIC272 (Moentilan), CIC251 (Bangkong I), CIC254 (Karangpanas), and CIC253 (Gedangan).

CIC287: Camphuislaan*

An unknown number of sick women and their families lived in houses in the suburbs from January 1945 to October 1945, when they were liberated.

CIC288: Marinekampement

About 1,000 men and boys from eastern Java lived in navy barracks outside town from January 1943 to February 1944. They were then moved to CIC226 (IVe, IXe Battalion).

CIC289: Wijk

About 7,000 women and children from the city and other parts of eastern Java lived in a block of houses from November 1942 to August 1944. They were then moved to CIC242 (Ziekenzorg II), CIC254 (Karangpanas), and CIC269 (Banjoebiroe 10II).

CIC290: Batoe

An unknown number of American and British women and children from eastern Java lived in a hospital compound outside town from March 1942 to December 1943, when they were moved to CIC193 (Tanahtinggi).

CIC291: Kesilir

About 3,000 men from eastern Java and from CIC243 (Djatingaleh) and CIC244 (Kalibanteng) lived in barracks and houses in an agricultural community from July 1942; 44 died. Those who survived stayed until September 24, 1943, when they were moved to CIC268 (Banjoebirow 10I) and CIC194 (Tangerang I).

From the diary of a young man:

> 12 July 1942: In Malang they have been rounding up boys over 17 for three days now, and they have shipped them to Kesilir. Each house in town is searched thoroughly—the Japs look under beds, in cupboards.
> 24 July 1942: In Soerabaja notices were delivered to the homes where Dutch men and boys live, with the order to report to Boeboetan. Loaded with mattresses and suitcases they sing out loud and shout, "We'll soon be home again."[10]

This camp was set up primarily as an agricultural colony for 70,000 Dutch and other Allied civilians with the goal of making them self-sufficient. Document RvO IC 2112, addressed to the assigned camp leader J. G. Wackwitz, contains the following message:

> What great pleasure it will give us to see our trust in you rewarded by your increasing efforts to perform this heavy task. We sincerely hope that you will be successful saving your people from unemployment. Be always healthy and happy. Signed: the Japanese.

In Document RvO IC 2419 Mr. Wackwitz points out the impossibility of instituting such a massive plan of an agricultural colony in an area not suitable for an agricultural farm and with workers who had never been involved in farming. The Japanese nevertheless sent 3,000 men to the camp.

Concluding Information on Civilian Internees

29,000 men	80,000 Dutch	
25,000 women	700 British	
29,000 children	100 American	
±83,000 internees	1,800 others	
	±82,600 internees	±11,000 who died (13.2 percent)

Of the 114 camps that the Japanese established, set up, had built, or used in Java, only 30 remained at the time of liberation, August–October 1945.

NOTES: JAVA

1. Roy Bulcock, *Of Death But Once*, Melbourne, 1947, p. 156.
2. George T. Cooper with Dennis Holman, *Ordeal in the Sun*, London, 1963.
3. Daphne Jackson, *Java Nightmare*, Padstow, England, 1979, p. 67.
4. Philip Cockrill, *The War in Malaya and Indonesia: Diary of Lome Blankwaart*, n.p., n.d., p. 47.
5. RvO IC 9005.
6. Ko Luykcx, *Het Verbluffende Camp* [The Bewildering Camp], The Hague, 1945, p. 29.
7. RvO IC 9009.
8. RvO IC 9002.
9. J. H. Helfferich-Koch, *Een Dal in Ambarawa* [A Valley in Ambarawa], The Hague, 1981, p. 22.
10. RvO IC 6886.

SOURCES: JAVA

Boissevain, Gon, and Lennie van Empel. *Vrouwenkamp op Java: A Diary* [Women's Camp in Java: A Diary]. (CIC). Amsterdam, 1981.
Boogaard, W. van den. *Het Geheim van Kebon Barat* [The Secret of Kebon Barat]. (CIC). The Hague, 1947.
Boomkamp, I. *Vrouwenkamp op Java*. (CIC). Amsterdam, 1946.
Brouwers, Jeroen. *Bezonken Rood* [Sunken Red]. (CIC). Amsterdam, 1981.
Bulcock, Roy. *Of Death But Once*. (POW). Melbourne, 1947.
Bulem, Mayra. *Wees Niet Bang voor Je Eigen Herinneringen* [Don't Be Afraid of Your Own Memories]. (CIC). Den Helder, the Netherlands, 1981.
Canneco, Dr. J. M. *Bushido: Camps in Java and Siam*. (POW). Leiden, 1947.
Chagall, Lydia. *Zes Jaren en Zes Maanden: Herinneringen van een Kind aan Vijf Kampen* [Memories of a Child; Five Internment Camps]. (CIC). Bussum, the Netherlands, 1981.
Chattel, C. J. H. du. *Storm over Java* [Storm over Java]. (CIC). Assen, the Netherlands, 1946.
Cockrill, Philip. *The War in Malaya and Indonesia*. (CIC/POW). England, 1988.
Cohen Stuart-Franken, M. *Van Indie tot Indonesie: Voor, In en Na het Kamp* [From the Indies to Indonesia: Before, In and After the Camps]. (CIC). Amsterdam, 1947.
Cooper, George T., with Dennis Holman. *Ordeal in the Sun*. (POW). London, 1963.
De Jongh, Wil. *Olie en Zweet, een Traan, een Lach* [Oil and Sweat, a Tear, a Smile]. (CIC). The Hague, 1980.
De Wit, Oscar. *Met Koele Obsessie* [With Cool Obsession]. (CIC). Amsterdam, 1979.
Doorn, Iens van. *Geluk is als een Vogel* [Luck Is Like a Bird]. (CIC). Franeker, the Netherlands, 1981.
Droste, Chr. B. *Tot Betere Dagen* [Until Better Days]. (CIC). n.p., 1946.
Dunlop, E. E. *The War Diaries of Weary Dunlop*. (POW). Melbourne, 1986.
Fabrisius, Johan. *Nacht over Java* [Night over Java]. (CIC). The Hague, 1977.

———. *Mammie, ik ga dood* [Mother, I'm Dying]. (CIC). The Hague, 1976.
Gomes, Paula. *Sudah, laat maar* [Well, Let It Be]. (CIC). Amsterdam, 1975.
Hakkert, Ann. *Glimlach van Tenno Heika* [Smile from Tenno Heika]. (CIC). The Hague, 1970.
Hellferich-Koch, Han. *Een Dal in Ambarawa* [A Valley in Ambarawa]. (CIC). Amstel a/d Rijn, 1981.
Hofstede, N. W. *De Slaven van Roku Ban* [The Slaves of Roku Ban]. (POW). Franeker, The Netherlands, 1979.
Hooykaas-van Leeuwen, J. H. *Vrouwenkamp op Java* [Women's Camp in Java]. (CIC). Amsterdam, 1946.
Idenburg-van de Poll, M. *De Vlag moet blijven staan* [The Flag Shall Remain]. (CIC). The Hague, 1947.
Jackson, Daphne. *Java Nightmare*. (CIC). Padstow, England, 1979.
Keesing, Elizabeth. *Op de Muur* [On the Wall]. (CIC). Amsterdam, 1981.
Keizer-Heuzeveldt, H. E. *En de lach keerde terug* [And the Smile Returned]. (CIC). Franeker, The Netherlands, 1982.
Kramer, Diet. *Thuisvaart* [Homecoming]. (CIC). Amsterdam, n.d.
Luyckx, Ko. *Het Verbluffende Kamp* [The Bewildering Camp]. (CIC). The Hague, 1946.
MacGilavry, Annemarie. *Je kunt niet altijd huilen* [You Cannot Always Cry]. (CIC). Baarn, the Netherlands, 1975.
———. *Want ik heb uw vader gekend* [Because I've Known Your Father]. (CIC). Bussum, the Netherlands, 1978.
Manders, Jo. *Vrouwen achter prikkeldraad* [Women Behind Barbed Wire]. (CIC). Batavia, 1947.
Nieuwenhuis, Rob. *Een beetje oorlog* [A Little Bit of War]. (CIC). Amsterdam, 1979.
Ofeigssen-Takes, Annie. *Wel en Wee in Vrouwenkampen op Java* [Weal and Woe]. (CIC). Epe, the Netherlands, 1955.
Reede, Theo Wilton. *Een draad van angst: rouwenkampen op Java* [A Thread of Fear: Women's Camps in Java]. (CIC). The Hague, 1984.
Renes-Boldingh, M. A. M. *Ik kom terug, zegt Loes* [I Shall Return, Says Loes]. (CIC). Meppel, the Netherlands, 1947.
Rinzema, Wim. *Did was uw Tjideng* [This Was Your Tjideng]. (CIC). The Hague, 1989.
Schoonenberg, Bernard. *De Poorten der Hel* [The Gates of Hell]. (POW). Bussum, the Netherlands, 1978.
Smit, H. *Van katjong tot rijksambyenaar* [From Rebel to Civil Servant]. (CIC). The Hague, 1982.
Thompson, Eliza. *Setengah Mati* [Half Dead]. (CIC). Amsterdam, 1965.
Tuckerman, Ingeborg. *Tjideng, Zwart op Wit* [Tjideng, Black on White]. (CIC). Amsterdam, n.d.
van der Post, Laurens. *The Night of the New Moon*. (POW). London, 1970 (American title: *The Prisoner and the Bomb*, New York, 1971).
van Engelenburg, Dick. *Jongenskamp Baros en Tjimahi* [Boys' Camp Baros and Tjimahi]. (CIC). Amsterdam, 1990.
van Sprang, Alfred. *Dodenkamp Ambarawa* [Deathcamp Ambarawa]. (CIC). Amsterdam, 1946.
Vander Londen, D. A. *Totdat de Atoombom viel: Java, Thailand, Japan* [Until the Atomic Bomb Fell: Java, Thailand, and Japan]. (POW). Utrecht, 1946.

Vermeer-van Berkum, Carla. *Kon ik maar weer een gewoon meisje zijn* [Could I Be Just a Girl Again]. (CIC). Amsterdam, 1980.
Vonk, Corry en Wim Kan. *Honderd dagen uit en thuis* [A Hundred Days Out and Back]. (CIC). Bussum, the Netherlands, 1946.
Wackwitz, J. G. *Kesilir, July '42–Sept. '43* [Kesilir Camp]. (CIC). The Hague, 1988.
Warmer, Joh. A. G., et al. *Kampschetsen uit Kesilir, Banjoebiroe, Tjikoedahpateuh* [Camp Vignettes from Kesilir, Banjoebiroe and Tjikoedahpateuh Camps]. (CIC). Rijswijk, the Netherlands, 1984.

International Military Tribunal, Far East:

Camp affidavits and testimonies: IMTFE 30183–88, 30195–213, 30215–38, also 13291–97, 13476–91, 13537, 13629, 13644–47, 13700, 40220–22, 40255–57, 40283–84, 40307, 40329–32, 40372–75, 13654, exhibit 1703, 1720S, 1724A, 1747A, 1752A, 1751, document 5680, 1755.

Netherlands Institute War Documentation: RvO IC

CIC189 Tjideng: 9004, 939
CIC195 Tangerang II: 9005
CIC208 Stella Maris: 9009
CIC214 Tjihapit: 5269
CIC250 Halmaheira III: 6823
CIC258 Ambarawa 7II: 9002, 6826
CIC270 Banjoebiroe II: 9008
CIC265 Bandoengan: 9013
CIC291 Kesilir: 6886
CIC189 Tjideng: 3307, 2365, 5279—Actions of commandant Sonei against the women and children.

All RvO IC documents related to Java camps: 47, 76, 80, 277, 367, 508, 541, 551, 569, 571, 579, 597, 613–14, 619, 641, 656, 667–68, 696, 720, 797, 858, 860, 862, 77, 904, 905, 939, 942–44, 975, 983–84, 939, 986, 1020, 1127, 1140, 1142, 1144, 1146, 1149–54, 1240, 1245, 1249–50, 1368, 1423, 1484, 1497, 1636, 1666, 1849, 1851, 1855, 1993, 2086, 2112, 2114, 2121, 2149, 2167, 2171, 2180, 2406, 2419, 2619, 2624–25, 2628, 2753, 2768, 2793, 2812, 3207, 3439, 3452, 3474, 3476, 3544, 3588, 3590–94, 3598, 3601–04, 3607–19, 3633, 3662, 3674–86, 3751, 3862–63, 3860, 4067, 4077, 4119, 4122, 4166, 4338, 4363, 4388, 4444, 4472, 4519, 4538, 4550, 4668, 5079, 5110, 5260, 5264, 5285, 5527, 5578, 5787, 6081, 6105, 6153–59, 6161, 6276, 6395, 6413, 6422, 6506, 6696, 6823, 6814, 6826, 6856, 6883, 7195, 7249, 9700–02, 9708, 9717–29, 9736, 9748, 9751–55, 9758, 9760–80, 9782–86, 9789, 9790, 9796, 9798, 9799, 9804, 9809, 9814–15, 9002–05, 9008–09, 9013.

BORNEO

POW Camps

Introduction. The Borneo POW camps were perhaps the ghastliest of all prisoner camps in the Dutch East Indies. Future researchers may want to analyze why the Japanese were so brutal in these parts of the Pacific.

It was here that the Sandakan Death March occurred, and here that the Japanese massacred civilians and military personnel who were hiding in the jungles of Borneo after the surrender of the Dutch but not engaging in guerrilla activities.

Individual Listings of POW Camps: POW358–POW359

North and West Borneo

POW358: Kuching

This camp was located in a barren area, eroded brown wasteland crossed by washed-out gullies with row after row of withered palm-leaf huts.

To let a POW tell the story:

> Over 1,200 begrimed, sweating prisoners, with torn boots and blistered feet, faltered over the last yards of dusty track spewing out, as it were, to the depths of Hell.... In this hutted camp hundreds were to fret and despair there, eventually to gasp out, uncaringly, their dying breath, the fleshless corpses, with banana leaves as shrouds, to be buried on a nearby slope nicknamed "Boot Hill."
>
> In this camp of ours there was little colour, no jacaranda, no frangipani, no hibiscus, for all was drab.
>
> We cleared tangled jungle. We truncated hillocks—basketed the soil to level out hollows, elsewhere thus forming new quays and runways. We mucked out for our captors, we mucked out for ourselves. We squabbled over our meagre rations of rice and the stew concocted from tropical greenery; we filched from the natives' gardens and we bartered threadbare clothes with the Dayaks for cooking oil, salt, sugar, rice and cassave root. We learned to steal, to scrimp and to conserve calories. We learned to dream but not to believe and some to accept death with fatalism. And I learnt to survive.
>
> By July 1945 slave labour, coupled with lack of food, clothing and medication was taking its dreadful toll. Daily, five matchwood boxes with detachable wooden covers were taken to Boot Hill with banana leaf swathed corpses—reeking of blood and pus—to return the same day ready to receive five more emaciated bodies.[1]

About 2,000 men total were transported from Singapore to Kuching, North Borneo. In August 1945 only 750 men were still alive, of whom 650 were seriously ill. Only 30 men were strong enough for use in a work party.

POW359: Sandakan

There were three transports of POWs from Singapore to Sandakan, a place just outside Kuching, North Borneo.

- July 1942: "B" Force—1,500 Australians to Sandakan No. 1 camp.

- March 1943: 700 British POWs to Sandakan No. 2, next to No. 1 camp.

- April 1943: "E" Force—500 Australian POWs to Sandakan No. 3 camp, next to No. 2 camp.

This made a total of 2,700 men, of whom about 200 were sent to Kuching and 100 to Labuan. Of the 2,400 men left in the Sandakan camps—and who later were part of the Sandakan Death March—only six men were eventually liberated. The three camp populations had literally been exterminated.

Prior to these marches, which began in February 1945, the men were used to build an airfield three miles away from their camp. The stories of these POWs speak for themselves:

> The Japs must have wanted that aerodrome badly from the way they made us toil at it. Everyone, officers included were forced to work—if a patient was so much as able to stand up without help, he would be forced to go out and work. The Isolation Hut was a ghastly place to visit. I went there some times to visit a stricken friend, and it was appalling to see men lying there, mere shadows of their former selves, with sunken eyes, and excreta pouring from them, defying all of the efforts of the orderlies to keep them comfortable. And night by night more sufferers succumbed to the plague, and each day more wooden boxes were carried out.
>
> Singing was the only relaxation we had, and we made the most of it. In camp at night was the time when we mostly indulged in it, when we were sitting around the little fires lighted in holes in the ground for the purpose of warming up our left-over portions of rice. Someone would start a tune, his hut companions would pick it up, and in a few minutes the whole camp would be singing "Waltzing Matilda"; "I've Got Sixpence"; "She'll Be Coming Round the Mountain When She Comes." Those songs still bring back the echo of my comrades' voices, and if I shut my eyes I can see again the flickering fires with the tired men sitting around them, and overhead perhaps the Southern Cross.[2]

In the testimonies of the IMTFE, it was recorded that a special group of old Japanese soldiers was brought to the camp, not to get more work out of the POWs, but specifically to maltreat them. This group was "The Bashers":

> One day, eight men were dragged from their work for no reason at all and beaten with pick handles, bamboo canes and other items, for about twenty minutes. The only result of this senseless brutality was that on the following day there were eight men less working on the airfield. This was not an isolated occurrence—it happened frequently and when it did, the result would be that a number of prisoners would be taken back each night, either carried on stretchers, unconscious, or with a broken arm or leg or in badly beaten up condition, for the men were already so weak.[3]

In June two groups of POWs, totaling eight men, escaped from Sandakan camp and were able to reach American-led Filipino guerrilla groups on the southern islands of the Philippine archipelago. One group consisted of Jock McLaren, Jim Kennedy, and Rex Butler. In the other group were Walter Wallace, Ray Steel, Miles Gillon, Charlie Wagner, and Rex Blow.

After this escape, the Japanese concluded that the Allies were now definitely aware of the presence of the camp and the way the POWs were treated. Thus, when the American forces came closer and closer to North Borneo in early 1945, the Japanese forced the POWs into hellish marches inland to the slopes of Mount Kinabalu to prevent their liberation. About 1,000 men left Sandakan for Ranau in different groups between January and May 1945.

The following is an account of how only six men of the 1,000 survived this death march:

> Returning from the Far East in 1945 with other POWs from Java, I met an English planter from Serawak who had been home on leave when the Japs struck and who had joined the Army. He had subsequently been sent out and landed by submarine near Sandakan, shortly before that ghastly march. He went on to say that he just had time to organize a small commando unit, mainly of Dayaks whom he knew from his planter days. When the march started, they followed alongside in the jungle, hoping to get near enough to pull some of our men from the column and have them looked after until the Allies re-occupied Serawak. Those of us who have had experience in jungle trekking will know only too well the difficulties involved.
>
> The commandos were for some time unable to get near enough to contact the marchers, without putting the whole scheme in jeopardy, so they radioed the approaching Allied forces and arranged for an air strike just ahead of the column. This caused the desired panic amongst the Japs and it was during this short-lived flap that they were able to go in and pull out six men—the only ones to survive the holocaust.
>
> These survivors told him that for some weeks the Japs had their rations

increased whilst those of the prisoners had been drastically reduced. This was clearly following the Tokyo instructions for the elimination of prisoners, which can now be seen in the Imperial War Museum.[4]

Civilian Internment Centers

Introduction. The island of Borneo served as an imaginary dividing line between territorial command and control by the Japanese army or navy. British North Borneo and Dutch West Borneo were under the army, while South and East Borneo were the responsibility of the navy. Before Christmas 1941 Japanese forces landed in Miri, Kuching, Brunei. Civilians were immediately interned.

Individual Listings of Civilian Internment Centers: CIC292–CIC301

North and West Borneo

CIC292: Gouvernementshuis
About 30 men from Sandakan lived in a house in town from January 20, 1942, to March 12, 1942, when they were moved to CIC294 (Berhala Island).

CIC293: Woning
About ten women and children from Sandakan lived in a house in the city from January 20, 1942, to May 12, 1942, when they were moved to CIC294 (Berhala Island).

CIC294: Berhala Island
About 75 men, women, and children from CIC292 (Gouvernementshuis) and CIC293 (Woning) and from the surrounding districts lived in barracks on the island of Berhala from May 12, 1942, to January 1, 1943, when they were moved to CIC298 (Batu Lintang).

CIC295: Jesselton
About 50 men, women, and children from the town of Jesselton and surrounding area lived in a house in the city from May 15, 1942, to September 17, 1942, when they were moved to CIC298 (Batu Lintang).

CIC296: Zaid Rock Road
About 35 men from the city of Kuching and surrounding area lived in a house in town from January 8, 1942, to May 16, 1942. They were then moved to CIC297 (Pandungan).

CIC297: Pandungan

About 35 men were moved from CIC296 (Zaid Rock Road) to a house in town, where they lived from May 16, 1942, to July 14, 1942. They were then moved to CIC298 (Batu Lintang).

CIC298: Batu Lintang*

About 530 men, women, and children in separate groups on different dates were moved here from CIC294 (Berhala Island), CIC295 (Jesselton), CIC297 (Pandungan), CIC299 (Pontianak), CIC300 (Singkawang), and CIC301 (Sambas). They lived in the camp from July 13, 1942, to September 1945, when they were liberated.

The camp was located about three miles outside Kuching—22 miles up the Serawak River. There were eight separate compounds. One of them housed a few thousand British, Dutch, and Australian POWs. In the women's compound were about 242 women and children: 120 Dutch and 20 British Roman Catholic nuns, 73 other women, and 29 children. Later another 12 women, six children, and two nuns came into camp.

Batu Lintang was made famous by Agnes Newton Keith's book *Three Came Home* and the subsequent movie based on it. The following are some of her observations:

> Women who had performed impossible physical tasks, and who looked it. Faces were strained, lined, agonizingly controlled. Hands were stained and blunted and calloused. Feet were bare, broken toenailed, grimey with sores and septic toes. Clothes were torn, patched, faded and scanty.
>
> The cost of captivity: the utter waste of those years; the children we did not have; the entire absence of beauty, either physical in our surroundings or emotional in our living; the arrival at disillusionment in ourselves and others and in the conscious mess of human suffering which has become part of us forever. These things, even more than physical pain.[5]

CIC299: Pontianak

An unknown number of men, women, and children from the city of Pontianak, West Borneo, and the surrounding area lived in the convent in town from February 1942 to July 15, 1942, when they were moved to CIC298 (Batu Lintang).

CIC300: Singkawang

An unknown number of men from the city of Singkawang, West Borneo, were housed in the city from February 1942 to July 12, 1942. They were then moved to CIC298 (Batu Lintang).

CIC301: Sambas

About 35 men and women were moved separately from the town of

Sambas, West Borneo, to the city jail. They lived in the jail from May 13, 1942, to July 12, 1942, when they were moved to CIC298 (Batu Lintang).

South and East Borneo

CIC302: Bandjermasin I

About 70 men and boys from South and East Borneo lived in military barracks in town (Bandjermasin, South Borneo) from April 1942 to January 29, 1945; 15 died. The survivors were moved to CIC304 (Kandangan I).

CIC303: Bandjermasin II

About 70 women and children from South and East Borneo lived in the military barracks from April 1942 to February 10, 1945. Seven died; the survivors were moved to CIC305 (Kandangan II).

From the diary of a nurse:

> We had a totally different leadership and communal system than the larger camps in Java. We did not have an assigned group to work in our vegetable garden, for example. *Everybody* had to work: in the garden, wood splitting, taking care of the sick and the children. All this was done by each of us in turn—and we cooked our own food. Individualism and group concern blended into one effective way of dealing with each other.[6]

CIC304: Kandangan I

In South Borneo, 54 men and boys who had been moved from CIC302 (Bandjermasin I) lived in military barracks from January 1, 1945, to August 3, 1945, when they were moved to CIC306 (Puruktjau).

CIC305: Kandangan II*

About 160 women and children who were moved from CIC303 (Bandjermasin II) lived in the military barracks from February 11, 1945, to September 1945, when they were liberated.

CIC306: Puruktjau*

In South Borneo, about 54 men and boys were moved from CIC304 (Kandangan I) to the barracks outside town, where they lived from August 14, 1945, to September 1945, when the camp was liberated.

CIC307: Samarinda

About seven women from the town of Samarinda, East Borneo, lived in a house in town from June 25, 1943, to December 5, 1943, when they were moved to CIC303 (Bandjermasin II).

CIC308: Kazerne I

About 20 men from Tarakan, an oil town in East Borneo, lived in the military barracks in town from February 12, 1942, to November 29, 1943. They were then moved to CIC302 (Bandjermasin I).

CIC309: Kazerne II

About 17 women from Tarakan lived in another part of the barracks that also housed CIC308 from February 16, 1942, to February 24, 1942, when they were moved to CIC310 (Radiostraat).

CIC310: Radiostraat

About 80 women and children were moved from CIC309 (Kazerne II) and from areas in East Borneo to military houses in town, where they lived from February 24, 1942, to October 13, 1943, when they were moved to CIC311 (Lingkas).

CIC311: Lingkas

About 80 women and children were moved from CIC310 (Radiostraat) to military houses. They lived in these houses from October 13, 1943, to November 29, 1943, when they were moved to CIC305 (Kandangan II).

Concluding Information on Civilian Internees in Borneo

329 men	225 British
330 women	500 Dutch
120 children	10 American
779 internees	35 others
	770 internees; 60 died (7.8 percent)

Of the 21 camps established at one time or another, only three were operative at the time of liberation.

NOTES: BORNEO

1. Wiltshire, "My Life in War Time," *Far East POW Forum* (London), (May-June 1983).
2. Walter Wallace, *Escape from Hell*, London, 1957, pp. 23, 27, 28.
3. IMTFE 13354.
4. R. E. Hope-Falkner, "More Memories of Sandakan," *Far East POW Forum* (London) (June 1981).

5. Agnes Newton Keith, *Three Came Home*, New York, 1947.
6. RvO IC 6825.

SOURCES: BORNEO

Archer, J. B. *Lintang Camp: Official Documents and Papers Collected from the Records of the Internment Camp at Lintang, Kuching, Serawak*. Kuching, 1946.
Colley, George. *Manila–Kuching and Return*. (POW). San Francisco, 1946.
de Wit, P. J. "Terugblik op Kuching kamp." *Annals of the St. Joseph Congregation*. (CIC). (May 1948).
Far East POW Forum (London): June 1981, May-June 1983, and February 1984.
Forbes, G. K., et al. *Borneo Burlesque*. (CIC). Sydney, 1947.
Harrison, Tom. *World Within: A Borneo Story*. (POW). London, 1959.
Keith, Agnes Newton. *Three Came Home*. (CIC). New York, 1947.
O'Connor, Michael P. *The More Fool I*. (CIC). Dublin, 1954.
Richardson, Hal. *One-Man War: The Jock McLaren Story*. (POW). Sydney, 1957.
Russell, Lord of Liverpool. *The Knights of Bushido*. (CIC–POW). London, 1958.
Wallace, Walter. *Escape from Hell*. (POW). London, 1957.
Zusters penitenten Recollectinen: Gevangenschap op Borneo [Imprisonment in Borneo]. (CIC). n.p., 1946.

International Military Tribunal, Far East:

IMTFE 1688A: A number of men, women, and children from Serawak and Brunei escaped to Longnawan in Central Dutch Borneo as soon as the Japanese landed. In April 1942 a number of Dutch soldiers and two American missionaries, one with a wife and baby, joined the group. When the Japanese forces discovered them, the escapees surrendered without any struggles. All were murdered.
IMTFE 13354: Beating of POWs, 27599–619: POW treatment.
IMTFE: 12043–44, 12047–53, 13312–16, 13344, 13420–49, 13492–95, 13499–504, 13505–28, 40168–72, 40203–06, 40236–39, 40267–69, 40294–95, 40316 18, 40340–46: Atrocities.
IMTFE, record p. 13360 ff: Sandakan Death March.
IMTFE, exhibit 1658: Murder of POWs in Kuching.
IMTFE 27565, 27822–33, 30195–213, 30215–20, also 1319, 5418–19, 13193–200, 13212–16, 13344, 13504, 13537, 13573, 13629, 13644–47, 13700, 13750, 13784, 13820, 13913–34: POWs in Borneo.

Netherlands Institute War Documentation:

RvO IC 799, 2416: Plans to transport prisoners inland in case of Allied invasion.
RvO IC 4305: A group of men and women and a Dutch army lieutenant retreated to the town of Putussibau in the heart of Dutch Borneo. They refused to surrender to the Japanese, and Dayak headhunters murdered them all.
RvO IC 4651: All Europeans—85 of them—connected with the destruction of the oil facilities in Balikpapan, East Borneo, were killed by the Japanese.
RvO IC 290, 570, 2055, 2170, 2809, 2890, 3388, 3620, 3631, 3632, 3634, 3637, 3638, 4081, 4305, 4306, 4331, 4651, Borneo.

OTHER ISLANDS and TERRITORIES

POW Camps

Introduction. On the same level as Borneo, the camps in the outer islands of the Dutch East Indies were ghastly, and the treatment of POWs was brutal. In the Ambon Islands a Korean interpreter shouted into a hospital full of desperately ill prisoners, "Why don't you hurry up and die?"

In Makasser, South Celebes, where survivors of HMS *Exeter* and USS *Houston* were imprisoned, there was a mass beating of 300 POWs for one man's offense: bringing food into camp that he picked up while on a working party.

Individual Listings of POW Camps: POW360–POW378

Celebes Island

POW360: Makasser

This compound, with rain trees and coconut groves, a soccer field on one end and the jungle on the other, was about 300 yards from the ocean. There were dirt roads along the perimeter and down the center of the compound, with blocks of barracks between the roads.

The camp held survivors and crews of ships that had taken part in the Battle of the Java Sea—the USS *Houston*, USS *Pope*, and USS *Perch* and the Allied ships HMS *Encounter*, HMS *Exeter*, HMS *Stronghold*, and HMS *Prince of Wales*. The total number of POWs was 2,915: 1,800 Dutch, 945 Australians, and 170 Americans.

In October 1942 1,000 men were shipped on the *Asama Maru* to Japan. In January 1943 a group of 200 men were moved to the Pomalaa camp on the west side of the island's eastern leg. In October 1943 about 200 men—28 British, 6 American, and 166 Dutch—left with the *Rio de Janeiro Maru* for Japan.

The conditions in this camp were the same as everywhere else and conformed to the Japanese pattern of neglect and brutality. The torture and beatings went on unceasingly. The prime instigator was Yoshida, or "Yosh," as he was called, who was never absent from the torture sessions and was, more often than not, an active participant.

George Cooper, senior officer of the camp, wrote this about the Makasser camp:

> Yosh controlled everything. Headquarters had no control over him, nor did they wish to. He ran the camp on a policy of fear with collective and indiscriminate reprisals for the slightest infraction of rules on any and everybody, whether innocent or guilty, healthy or sick. He was the evil of sadism, brutality, dishonesty—he was cunning, and inhuman.[1]

Recreational activities—reading, playing cards, baseball, football, and boxing—and religious services were allowed. In the preface of his book, Cooper wrote:

> The disappointment of missing that meal [to be especially prepared for the survivors of *Perch* by the mess crew of the Dutch hospitalship *Op ten Noort*] was indescribable. We nearly wept and were very angry. No amount of pleading and arguing could turn our guards, and from that moment we hated them. It was a burning hate, sometimes bursting out in flames, most of the time only smouldering, but always there in our hearts and the gnawing voids in our stomachs.
> In return the guards treated us with malice, sheer sadistic malice, every day from the dawn muster in the morning watch till late at night.
> From here on it is the story of that malice, of its intensity, its violence, of the diabolical things it inspired, and of how we reacted individually or as a group.[2]

POW361: Pomalaa

In January 1943, 200 men were moved to the Pomalaa area. The camp was located on the west side of the eastern leg of the Celebes, one mile south of the village of Pomalaa, on the edge of the jungle in a mosquito-infested swamp area. The POWs were used to reclaim salt from a marsh by digging in slime and mud from 7 A.M. to 5 P.M., with two hours off at midday.

In the eight months the men were at Pomalaa (January 17, 1943 to September 16, 1943), 16 died, and most of them were afflicted with malaria, beriberi, pellagra, blindness, ulcers, scabies, septic bed sores, gastric troubles, heat exhaustion, dengue fever, prickly heat, and general debility. At the end of August only 19 men were fit to work, 28 were able to walk no more than a short distance, 68 were incapable of walking at all, and 16 were dangerously ill. The other 53 were barely hanging on to life.

POW362: Menado Military Barracks
POW363: Poso
POW364: Rapang

Lesser Sunda Islands

POW365: Atamboea (Timor Island)
POW366: Dilli (Timor Island)

POW367: Flores (Flores Island)
From a report by three Dutch soldiers, dated April 18, 1946:

> When the healthy POWs arrived at the so-called camp on May 10, 1943, at 5:00 P.M., it was nothing but a coconut grove located 3 km east of the town of Maoemere. There were only two native houses which were immediately occupied by the guards. The POWs were forced to sleep in the open air without any means to hang their mosquito nets.
> This situation continued to exist for two weeks until the first barracks were constructed—which could only be done after the daily work in the harbor was completed.
> Supply of medicines was terrible. In several cases cerebral malaria and death could not be prevented. There was no medicine for dysentery or beriberi. We made yeast, soybean cakes, and extract from the Cassia florida leaves, and the bark of the Lawsonia inermis to supplement our protein.[3]

The Moluccas

POW368: Amahei (Ambon Island)
On April 29, 1943, about 1,000 Dutch POWs arrived at Ambon Island with the *Kuritama Maru*. They built their own camp and worked on the construction of an airfield. There was no recreation or religious services. They stayed almost six months. In October 1943 they moved to Haroekoe I, on Haroekoe Island.

POW369: Haroekoe I
The 970 men from Amahei supplemented the 2,070 British POWs already present—a total of 3,040 men. Under extremely harsh conditions and brutal treatment, the men were again put to work building an airfield—breaking down coral with hammers and chisels.
In November 1943, 700 sick men were transported back to Java with the *Suez Maru*. The rest continued to work until April 1944, when 960 men were transported back to Ambon Island; 1,000 stayed behind to repair the finished airstrip that was damaged by Allied bombardments. Between mid-April 1943 and April 1944, 380 men had died.

POW370: Liang (Ambon Island)
The 960 men who arrived in Liang supplemented the approximately 1,000 British and Australian POWs already working on an airfield on Ambon

Island. There were three transports of sick men from Ambon back to Java in 1944, at which time the camp was closed. Of the 450 men who stayed behind in other areas of Ambon, about 200 died.

Dr. R. Springer, a Dutch medical officer, wrote the following, quoted in Lord Russell's book:

> We still believed in humanity even from the Nips, but that proved to be silly. Even now, while writing this report [November 1945] and reading my notes, I get the impression that the Nips were out for willful murder. When we told them our fear for the future regarding the danger of spreading an epidemic of dysentery, and that we expected many death cases, we often got the answer, "Nice when dead!"[4]

The tally of those who died and those who survived speaks for itself regarding the inhumane treatment of the POWs:

Camp	Population	Died on the Islands	Died During Transport	Total Deaths	%
Amahei	1,012	47	247	294	29
Haroekoe	2,070	382	1,331	1,838	59.1
Liang	1,037	125			
Total	4,119	554	1,578	2,132	51.8

New Guinea

POW371: Manokwari
POW372: Prafi River Camp
POW373: Windehsi
POW374: Wiringgi

New Britain

POW375: Bita Paka
POW376: Kokupo

POW377: Rabaul
   In 1942 some 160 British POWs were captured in Rabaul; only 18 survived. By March 1944 there were 59 Allied POWs, only 17 of whom were alive at liberation in 1945.

Palau Islands

POW378: Yamato Camp (Babel Thuap Island)
   On May 5, 1943, the *Thames Maru* left Singapore for the Palau Islands,

with 522 Indian POWs and an unknown number of Indonesian prisoners. At the time of liberation in August 1945, 433 Indian POWs were found alive of the original 550. Later 18 were added; 117 (or 21 percent) had died. The nature of the work was airfield construction, loading and unloading ships, digging trenches, and breaking stones.

Civilian Internment Centers

Introduction. Except on the large islands of Celebes and New Guinea, by the end of 1942, there were virtually no "white" Allied civilians on the islands in the eastern part of the Dutch Archipelago. All civilians were moved as fast as possible to either Celebes or Java. The movements of these civilians from the smaller islands to the large ones constituted the only massive overseas transports of civilian internees.

Individual Listings of Civilian Internment Centers: CIC312–CIC358

Celebes Island

CIC312: Goaweg I
About 250 men from the South Celebes and from CIC335 (Denpasar), CIC336 (Singaradja), CIC339 (Bima), and CIC340 (Waingapu I) lived in the military barracks in the city of Makasser from February 9, 1942, to September 28, 1942. They then moved to CIC316 (Parepare).

CIC313: Goaweg II
In the same camp, next to the men, lived about 200 women and children from Makasser from February 9, 1942, to May 1, 1942, when they were moved to CIC314 (Malino).

CIC314: Malino
About 1,200 women and children from CIC313 (Goaweg II), CIC341 (Waingapu), CIC342 (Ende I), CIC343 (Ende II), and CIC344 (Ndona) lived in a block of houses in a suburb east of Makasser from April 1942 to May 5, 1943. They were then moved to CIC315 (Kampili).

CIC315: Kampili*
About 1,670 women and children from CIC314 (Malino), CIC330 (Bethanykerk), CIC345 (Soé), and CIC346 (Atambua) lived in barracks and

*Camps marked with an asterisk were liberated in August or September 1945.

a sanatorium near Makasser from March 22, 1943, to September 1945. Thirty-seven died; the remainder were liberated in September 1945.

From the diary of a woman internee:

> 17 August, 1945: It is peace! I repeated this one word a hundred times last night when I had difficulties falling asleep. There is still wonderment. How is it possible: suddenly peace! I was in the garden yesterday, when my son came running to me. "Mother, come right now. The camp commandant has an important announcement to make. It's true—there's a note on the bulletin board." Chills ran up my spine... "An important announcement, you say? Oh, my child perhaps it is a truce." On the way to the open space in the camp we could hardly express ourselves for fear of disappointment.
>
> We stood there with great expectation, our hearts beating wildly. Then they came: our camp leader and the Japanese commandant. A stillness settled in. And the so long expected words were spoken: the war is over. An intense happiness came over us. But not a boisterous yelling and screaming. The moment was too great, too important for that. It was also too overwhelming—so suddenly: peace. A magic word. Never has life seemed so good to savor and look at.[5]

CIC316: Parepare

About 650 men and boys from South Celebes and from CIC329 (Adventskerk), CIC345 (Soé), and CIC346 (Atambua) lived in the military barracks in town from September 8, 1942, to October 22, 1944, when they were moved to CIC317 (Bodjo).

CIC317: Bodjo

About 650 men and boys were moved from CIC316 (Parepare) to the stables outside town on October 22, 1944; 25 died. The survivors lived there until May 30, 1945, when they were moved to CIC318 (Bolong).

CIC318: Bolong*

About 625 men and boys moved from CIC317 (Bodjo) to the barracks outside town, where they lived from May 30, 1945, to August 28, 1945, when the camp was liberated.

CIC319: St. Jozef, Manado (North Celebes)

About 160 men and boys from North Celebes lived in the boarding school in town from January 13, 1942, to March 14, 1942, when they were moved to CIC320 (Teling).

CIC320: Teling, Manado (North Celebes)*

About 160 men and boys moved from CIC319 (St. Jozef) to the military barracks in town on March 14, 1942; 70 died. In this period, some men were moved to CIC321 (Gevangenis, the jail). The remainder stayed until September 1945, when the camp was liberated.

CIC321: Gevangenis, Manado (North Celebes)
Some of the men from CIC320 (Teling) lived in the city jail from September 1944 to July 10, 1945. No further movements are known.

CIC322: St. Walterus, Tomohon
About 400 women and children from North Celebes lived in a convent in town from January 15, 1942, to February 25, 1942, when they were moved to CIC323 (Kaaten).

CIC323: Kaaten, Tomohon
About 400 women and children were moved from CIC322 (St. Walterus) to a school outside town on February 25, 1942; 10 died. The remainder stayed there until March 28, 1944, when they were moved to CIC324 (Airmadidi).

CIC324: Airmadidi, Tomohon*
About 390 women and children were moved from CIC323 (Kaaten) to barracks outside town on March 28, 1944; 18 died. The survivors stayed until September 1945, when this camp was liberated.

Ambon

CIC325: Boskamp
About 300 men, women, and children from the island lived in barracks outside the town from February 1, 1942, to February 28, 1942. Seven died; the survivors were moved to CIC326 (Stovil).

CIC326: Stovil
About 300 men, women, and children from CIC325 (Boskamp) and about 250 from CIC331 (Manokwari) and from other islands were moved to this school compound on the coast on February 28, 1942; 20 died. The survivors lived there until December 28, 1942, when the men were moved to CIC327 (Tantui I) and the women were moved to CIC328 (Tantui II).

CIC327: Tantui I
About 140 men were moved from CIC326 (Stovil) to the barracks on the coast, where they lived from November 27, 1942, to February 15, 1943. They were then moved to CIC329 (Adventskerk).

CIC328: Tantui II
About 360 women and children moved from CIC326 (Stovil) to the

barracks on the coast on December 28, 1942; 22 died. The survivors stayed until February 15, 1943, when they were moved to CIC330 (Bethanykerk).

The following is from a report by a woman internee:

> January 15, 1943: Oh my God, we fear a thousand fears—just outside our compound the Japs placed an anti-aircraft gun with hundreds of [rounds of] ammunition stacked next to it.
> February 15, 1943: Yes, here it comes—ten to fifteen Allied planes attack Ambon. We all cheer. Then, one of them attacks the gun emplacement and drops a bomb. Our campleader yells for us to wade into the sea. Many of us do so but others go into the barrack and hide under their mattress. Another bomb drops just next to our barrack—one wall collapses. Then, the third bomb hits our barrack. The Aussies next door break loose of their POW camp and run to help. So do our own men from the camp next to us. More bombs rain down and from the sea I can see the carnage—like a battleground with dead and wounded everywhere. Our barrack is burning down—and the sky is black with smoke. Women and children scream and run wild not knowing where to hide.
> Then it's all over—9 Aussies and 5 of our men lost their lives—18 women and children were killed. Many were seriously wounded and about 100 received minor injuries. Later in the day we were moved to the Bethany Church [CIC330], and the men to Advents Church [CIC329].[6]

CIC329: Adventskerk

On February 15, 1943, about 340 women and children were moved from CIC328 (Tantui II) after the Allied air attack; 20 died. The survivors lived there until March 17, 1943, when they were moved to CIC315 (Kampili).

CIC330: Bethanykerk

On February 15, 1943, about 130 men were moved from CIC327 (Tantui I) after the Allied air attack. They lived there until March 17, 1943, when they were moved to CIC316 (Parepare).

Dutch New Guinea

CIC331: Manokwari

An unknown number of men, women, and children from the north coast lived in a guest house in town from May 1942 to June 1942. They were then moved to CIC326 (Stovil).

CIC332: Prafirivier

About 500 men, women, and children from all over the island lived in barracks outside the town. About 300 died. No other information is available; probably the survivors were moved to Celebes Island or to Java.

CIC333: Hatam

About 500 women and children from the island lived in barracks outside the town. About 400 died. No other information is available.

CIC334: Hollandia

About 200 clergy and nuns from CIC350 (Alexishaven) in Australian New Guinea lived in this camp. About 100 died. No other information is available.

Bali

CIC335: Denpasar

An unknown number of men from Denpasar town and the area were housed in the city jail from February 28, 1942, to July 1942. They were then moved to CIC312 (Goaweg I).

CIC336: Singaradja

An unknown number of men from the town of Singaradja were housed in the city jail from February 28, 1942, to July 1942, when they were moved to CIC312 (Goaweg I).

Lombok Island

CIC337: Mataram I

An unknown number of men from the island and from Soembawa Island lived in the city jail from May 9, 1942, to July 1942, when they were moved to CIC281 (Boeboetan I).

CIC338: Mataram II

An unknown number of women and children from the island and from West Soembawa Island lived in houses in town from May 9, 1942, to September 1942. They were moved to Soerabaja, East Java, and then were released.

Sumbawa Island

CIC339: Bima

An unknown number of men, women, and children from the island were housed in the city jail from May 1942 to July 1942. They were then moved to CIC312 (Goaweg I).

Sumba Island

CIC340: Waingapu I

About 30 men from the island lived in the city jail from May 18, 1942, to July 14, 1942, when they were moved to CIC312 (Goaweg I).

CIC341: Waingapu II

About 55 women and children from the island lived in a guest house in town from May 20, 1942, to July 14, 1942, when they were moved to CIC314 (Malino).

Flores

CIC342: Ende I

An unknown number of men from the island were housed in the city jail from May 15, 1942, to July 15, 1942, when they were moved to CIC314 (Malino).

CIC343: Ende II

An unknown number of women from the island lived in houses in town from May 15, 1942, to July 15, 1942, when they were moved to CIC314 (Malino).

CIC344: Ndona

About 156 clergy and nuns from the island lived in a convent from May 15, 1942, to July 15, 1942, when they were moved to CIC314 (Malino).

Timor

CIC345: Soé

About 120 men, women, and children from the Dutch part of the island (the other half was Portuguese) lived in two houses outside town from February 24, 1942, to September 3, 1942. The men were then moved to CIC316 (Parepare), and the women were moved to CIC315 (Kampili).

CIC346: Atambua

About 40 clergy and nuns lived in a convent in town from February 1942 to August 30, 1942. The men were then moved to CIC316 (Parepare), and the women were moved to CIC315 (Kampili).

CIC347: Dili I

An unknown number of men from Portuguese Timor and Alor Island were housed in the city jail from February 1942 to June 1942, when they were moved to CIC345 (Soé).

CIC348: Dili II

An unknown number of women and children from Portuguese Timor

*Camps marked with an asterisk were liberated in September 1945.

and Alor Island lived in houses in town from February 1942 to June 1942, when they moved to CIC345 (Soé).

CIC349: Liquica*
An unknown number of Portuguese men, women, and children from Portuguese Timor were held in houses outside town from February 1942 to September 1945, when they were liberated.

Australian New Guinea

CIC350: Alexishaven
About 200 clergy and nuns from Alexishaven and Kariru lived in a convent from March 1942 to February 1944, when they were moved to CIC334 (Hollandia).

Bismarck Archipelago

CIC351: Kazerne (Rabaul)
An unknown number of men, women, and children from the islands, Solomon Islands, and New Guinea lived in military barracks in town from February 1942 to the end of 1943. The clergy were moved to CIC352 (Vunapope), and the others were killed.

CIC352: Vunapope
About 380 men, women, and children from the islands lived in a convent from January 25, 1942, to June 6, 1944; 30 died. The survivors were moved to CIC353 (Ramale).

CIC353: Ramale*
About 350 men, women, and children were moved from CIC352 (Vunapope) to barracks outside the town, where they lived from June 6, 1944, to September 1945, when the camp was liberated.

Other Pacific Islands

CIC354: Naaru
Of the seven men from Naaru Island who lived in this camp from February 1942 to January 26, 1943, five were killed; two clergy moved to Truk.

CIC355: Ocean Island
All seven men from the island who lived in this camp were killed in February 1942.

CIC356: Betio on Tarawa, the Gilbert Islands
All 22 men who were captured were killed.

CIC357: Guam

About 160 men, women, and children from the island lived in houses in town from December 10, 1941, to January 1, 1942. They then moved to Japan: CIC21 (Hyogo 1), CIC22 (Hyogo 2), CIC23 (Hyogo 3), and CIC24 (Hyogo 4).

CIC358: Wake

About 1,220 men, women, and children from the island lived in military barracks from December 23, 1941, to October 1943. There were a number of transports: about 800 men were shipped to POW222 (Woosung) in Shanghai, about 280 persons were moved to Japan, and 100 were killed.

Concluding Information on Civilian Internees

Celebes Island

815 men	2,625 Dutch
1,120 women	240 others
935 children	2,865 internees
2,870 internees; 182 died (6.3 percent)	

All Other Islands

±4,400 men, women and children
±1,020 (23.2 percent) died or were killed, the highest percentage of any civilian internments.

NOTES: ALL OTHER ISLANDS

1. George T. Cooper with Dennis Holman, *Ordeal in the Sun*, London, 1963.
2. *Ibid.*
3. RvO IC 5271.
4. Lord Russell of Liverpool, *The Knights of Bushido*, London, 1958, p. 156.
5. RvO IC 5719.
6. RvO IC 9001.

SOURCES: CELEBES ISLAND

Bruckel-Beiten, Mary. *Nederlandse Vrouwen in een Japans Interneringskamp, met 51 tekeningen* [Dutch Women in an Internment Camp, with 51 Drawings]. (CIC). Alphen aan den Rijn, the Netherlands, 1972.

Congregatie der Fraters O.L. Vrouwe Moeder van Barmhartigheid. *Verleden en Heden: de Fraters van Manado en Tomohon.* Makasser, July 1946.
Cooper, George T., with Dennis Holman. *Ordeal in the Sun.* London, 1963.
Kenyon, Albert. *Leonard Goes East.* (CIC). London, 1952.
Russell, Lord of Liverpool. *The Knights of Bushido.* London, 1958.
Valkenburg, Rik. *Het Appel is Afgelopen* [Reveille Is Finished]. (CIC). Dordrecht, the Netherlands, 1977.
Zusters Missionarissen. *Kampleven onder tropenzon* [Camp Life Under the Tropical Sun]. (CIC). Den Bosch, 1946.

International Military Tribunal, Far East:

IMTFE, exhibit 1810, 1811, 1811A, 1812: Camps Celebes.

Netherlands Institute War Documentation:

RvO IC 688, 1251, 6841: CIC316 Parepare Camp.
RvO IC 9024: CIC324 Airmadidi Camp.
RvO IC 9030: CIC312 Goaweg
RvO IC 6794: CIC322 St. Walterus
RvO IC 63: 249, 276, 361, 446, 716, 728, 896, 985, 987, 1251, 1912, 1990, 2060, 2693, 3348, 3629, 3694, 3717, 4120, 6794, 6841, 9805, 9806, 9007, 9025, 5719.

SOURCES: OTHER ISLANDS

Benson, James. *Prisoners Base and Home Again.* (CIC—Rabaul). London, 1957.
Binnerts, C. *Alles is in orde heren: een dagboek van het eiland Flores* [Everything Is in Order, Gentlemen: A Diary from Flores]. (POW—Flores Island). Amsterdam, 1947.
Bor, A. W. *Retour Amahei* (POW—Ambon Island). Privately printed, the Netherlands, 1962.
Bulcock, Roy. *Of Death But Once.* (POW). Melbourne, 1947.
Chauvel, Richard. *The Rising Sun in the Spice Islands.* (POW—Ambon Island). Clayton, VIC, 1985.
Conelissen, P. F., and P. A. A. Steyl. *Missiewerk onder de Japanse Bezetting* [Missionwork Under Japanese Occupation]. (CIC—Flores Island). St. Willibrord, 1949.
Devereux, James P. S. *The Story of Wake Island.* (POW—Wake). New York, 1947.
Harrison, Courtney T. *Ambon: Island of Mist.* (POW—Ambon Island). North Geelong, Australia, 1988.
Kenny, Catherine. *Captives: Australian Nurses in Japanese Prison Camps.* (CIC—Rabaul). St. Lucia, 1986.
Korteweg, Captain. *De 1000 van Amahei.* (POW—Ambon Island). Amsterdam, 1946.
Nason, Joseph G., and Robert Lawrence. *Horio, You Next Die.* (POW—Rabaul). Carlsbad, 1987.

O'Reilly, Patrick, and Jean Marie. *Jaunes, noir et blanc: trois annees de guerre aux Iles Salomon* [Black and White: Three Years of War in the Solomons]. (CIC). Paris, 1949.

Sleeman, Colin. *Trial of Gozawa Sadaichi and Nine Others.* (POW—Palau Islands). London, 1948.

Veenstra, J. H. W., et al. *Als Krijgsgevangene naar de Molukken en Flores* [As a POW in the Moluccas and Flores]. (POW—Ambon and Flores Islands). The Hague, 1982.

International Military Tribunal, Far East:

IMTFE 1817: 300 Australian POWs murdered at the Laha Airport.

IMTFE 14104–30, 40188, 40208, 40257–58, 40284–86, 40332–33, 40375: Camps in New Britain.

IMTFE 14066–103, 40188, 40222–24, 40258–59, 40286–87, 40308–09, 40333–34, 40375–76: New Guinea Camps.

IMTFE 27176, 27354–85, 33515–22, also 14911–15047, 40201–02, 40231, 40293, 40314, 40382–83: Affidavits and testimonies, Pacific Islands Camps.

IMTFE 1817, 13821, exhibit 1788, 1783, 1789, 1790, 1783A, 1788, 1789A, 1817, 14911 and on: Information POWs–Internees, Other Islands.

RvO IC 5271: Flores island

RvO IC Haroekoe and Liang Camps.

Appendix A:
The 1929 Geneva Convention Relating to the Treatment of Prisoners of War

The following excerpts are the portions of the 1929 Geneva Convention that directly relate to the manner in which prisoners of war are to be treated by their captors. The conditions to which POWs were subjected by Japan and Germany during World War II prompted an expanded and more forcefully worded set of conventions to be written in 1949.

GENERAL

Article 2

Prisoners of war are in the power of the hostile power, but not in the individuals' or corps' who have captured them.

They must at all times be humanely treated and protected, particularly against acts of violence, insults and public curiosity.

Measures of reprisals against them are prohibited.

Article 7

Prisoners of war shall be evacuated within the shortest possible period after their capture, to depots located in a region far enough from the zone of combat for them to be out of danger.

Only prisoners who, because of wounds or sickness, would run greater risks by being evacuated than by remaining where they are may be temporarily kept in a dangerous zone.

Prisoners shall not be needlessly exposed to danger while awaiting their evacuation from the combat zone.

Evacuation of prisoners on foot may normally be effected only by stages of 20 kilometers a day, unless the necessity of reaching water and food depots requires longer stages.

CAMPS

Article 9

Prisoners of war may be interned in a town, fortress or other place, and bound not to go beyond certain fixed limits. They must also be interned in enclosed camps; they may not be confined or imprisoned except as an indispensable measure of safety or sanitation, and only when the circumstances which necessitate the measure continue to exist.

Prisoners captured in unhealthful regions or where the climate is injurious for persons coming from temperate regions, shall be transported, as soon as possible, to a more favorable climate.

Belligerents shall, so far as possible, avoid assembling in a single camp prisoners of different races or nationalities.

No prisoner may, at any time, be sent into a region where he might be exposed to the fire of the combat zone, nor used to give protection from bombardment to certain points or certain regions by his presence.

Article 11

The food ration of prisoners of war shall be equal in quantity and quality to that of the troops of the base camp.

Furthermore, prisoners shall receive facilities for preparing themselves, additional food which they might have.

A sufficiency of potable water shall be furnished them. The use of tobacco shall be permitted. Prisoners may be employed in the kitchens.

All collective disciplinary measures affecting the food are prohibited.

Article 12

Clothing, linen and footwear shall be furnished prisoners of war by the detaining Power. Replacing or repairing of these effects must be assured regularly. In addition, laborers must receive work clothes wherever the nature of the work requires it.

Canteens shall be installed in all camps where prisoners may obtain, at the local market price, food products and ordinary objects. Profits made by the canteens for camp administrations shall be used for the benefit of the prisoners.

Article 13

Belligerents shall be bound to take all sanitary measures necessary to assure the cleanliness and healthfulness of camps and to prevent epidemics.

Prisoners of war shall have at their disposal, day and night, installations conforming to sanitary rules and constantly maintained in a state of cleanliness.

Furthermore, and without prejudice to baths and showers with which the camp shall be as well provided as possible, prisoners shall be furnished a sufficient quantity of water for the care of their own bodily cleanliness.

It shall be possible for them to take physical exercise and enjoy the open air.

Article 18

Officers who are prisoners of war are bound to salute only officers of a higher or equal rank of that Power.

LABOR

Article 30

The length of the day's work of prisoners of war, including therein the trip going and returning, shall not be excessive and must not, in any case, exceed that allowed for the civil workers in the region employed at the same work. Every prisoner shall be allowed a rest of twenty-four consecutive hours every week, preferably Sunday.

Article 31

Labor furnished by prisoners of war shall have no direct relation with war operations. It is especially prohibited to use prisoners for manufacturing and transporting arms or munitions of any kind, or for transporting material intended for combat units.

In case of violation of the provisions of the preceding paragraph, prisoners, after executing or beginning to execute the order, shall be free to have their protests presented through the mediation of the agent whose functions are set forth in Articles 43 and 44, in the absence of an agent, through the mediation of representatives of the protecting Power.

Article 32

It is forbidden to use prisoners of war at unhealthful or dangerous work. Any aggravation of the conditions of labor by disciplinary measures is forbidden.

EXTERNAL RELATIONS

Article 40

Censorship of correspondence must be effected within the shortest possible time. Furthermore, inspections of parcels post must be effected under proper conditions to guarantee the preservation of the products which they may contain and, if possible, in the presence of the addressee or an agent duly recognized by him.

Prohibition of correspondence promulgated by the belligerents for military or political reasons must be transient in character and as short as possible.

Article 42

Prisoners of war shall have the right to inform the military authorities in whose power they are of their requests with regard to the conditions of captivity to which they are subjected.

They shall have the right to address themselves to representatives of the protecting Powers to indicate to them the points on which they have complaints to formulate with regard to the conditions of captivity. These requests or complaints must be transmitted immediately. Even if they are recognized to be unfounded, they may not occasion any punishment.

DISCIPLINARY PUNISHMENT

Article 45

Prisoners of war shall be subject to the laws, regulations, and orders in force in the armies of the detaining Power.

An act of insubordination shall justify the adoption towards them of the measures provided by such laws, orders and regulations.

The provisions of the present chapter, however, are reserved.

Article 46

Punishments other than those provided for the same acts for soldiers of the national armies may not be imposed upon prisoners of war by the military authorities and courts of the detaining Power.

Rank being identical, officers, non-commissioned officers or soldiers who are prisoners of war undergoing a disciplinary punishment shall not be subject to less favorable treatment than that provided in the armies of the detaining Power with regard to the same punishment.

Any corporal punishment, any imprisonment in quarters without daylight and, in general, any form of cruelty, is forbidden.

Article 47

Acts constituting an offense against discipline, and particularly attempted escape, shall be verified immediately; for all prisoners of war, commissioned or not, preventive arrest shall be reduced to the absolute minimum.

Judicial proceedings against prisoners of war shall be conducted as rapidly as the circumstances permit; preventive imprisonment shall be limited as much as possible.

In all cases, the duration of preventive imprisonment shall be deducted from the disciplinary or judicial punishment inflicted, provided that this deduction is allowed for national soldiers.

Article 51

Attempted escape, even if it is a repetition of the offense, shall not be considered as an aggravating circumstance in case the prisoner of war should be given over to the courts on account of crimes or offenses against persons or property committed in the course of that attempt.

After an attempted or accomplished escape, the comrades of the person escaping who assisted in the escape may incur only disciplinary punishment on this account.

Article 54

Arrest is the most severe disciplinary punishment which may be imposed on a prisoner of war.

The duration of a single punishment may not exceed thirty days.

This maximum of thirty days may not, further, be exceeded in the case of several acts for which the prisoner has to undergo discipline at the time when it is ordered for him, whether or not these acts are connected.

When, during or after the end of a period of arrest, a prisoner shall have a new disciplinary punishment imposed upon him, a space of at least three days shall separate each of the periods of arrest, if one of them is ten days or more.

Article 56

In no case may prisoners of war be transferred to penitentiary establishments (prisons, penitentiaries, convict prisons, etc.) there to undergo disciplinary punishment.

The quarters in which they undergo disciplinary punishment shall conform to sanitary requirements.

Prisoners punished shall be enabled to keep themselves in a state of cleanliness. These prisoners shall every day be allowed to exercise or to stay in the open air at least two hours.

JUDICIAL PUNISHMENT

Article 60

At the opening of a judicial proceeding against a prisoner of war, the detaining Power shall advise the representative of the protecting Power thereof as soon as possible, and always before the date is set for the opening of the trial.

Article 65

Sentences pronounced against prisoners of war shall be communicated to the protecting Power immediately.

Article 66

If the death penalty is pronounced against a prisoner of war, a communication setting forth in detail the nature and the circumstances of the offense shall be sent as soon as possible to the representative of the protecting Power, for transmission to the Power in whose armies the prisoner served.

The sentence shall not be executed before the expiration of a period of at least three months after this communication.

INFORMATION

Article 77

Upon the outbreak of hostilities, each of the belligerent Powers, as well as the neutral Powers which have received belligerents shall institute an official information bureau for prisoners of war who are within their territory. Within the shortest possible period, each of the belligerent Powers shall inform its information bureau of every capture of prisoners affected by its armies, giving it all the information regarding identity which it has, allowing it quickly to advise the families concerned, and informing it of the official addresses to which families may write to prisoners.

The information bureau shall immediately forward all this information to the interested Powers, through the intervention, on one hand, of the protecting Powers and, on the other hand, of the central agency provided for in Article 79.

U.S. Department of State, *Multilateral Agreements—1918–1930*, pp. 938–957.

Appendix B: Japanese Army Regulations for Handling Prisoners of War

Army Instruction No. 22, February 1904, with Revisions—in force during World War II

GENERAL RULES

Article 1

The term prisoner(s) of war as used in these regulations shall refer to combatants of enemy nationality or to those who by treaty or custom are entitled the treatment as prisoners of war.

Article 2

Prisoners of war shall be treated with a spirit of goodwill and shall never be subjected to cruelties or humiliation.

Article 3

Prisoners of war shall be given suitable treatment in accordance with their position and rank. However, those who fail to reply with sincerity and truth to questions regarding name and rank, and violations of other rules, shall not be included in this.

Article 4

Prisoners of war shall be required to conform to the discipline and regulations of the Imperial Army. Beyond this their persons shall not be subjected to unwarranted restriction.

Article 5

Insofar as military discipline and moral standards are not affected, prisoners of war shall have freedom of religion and shall be permitted to attend worship in accordance with respective sects.

Article 6

In case of disobedience it shall be permissible to hold a prisoner of war in confinement or detention or to subject him to other necessary disciplinary action. In case a prisoner of war attempts to escape, he may be stopped by armed force and if necessary killed or wounded.

Article 7

When a prisoner of war not under oath is captured in attempted escape, he shall be subjected to disciplinary action. When such a prisoner of war, after successful escape, is again made prisoner of war, no punishment shall be inflicted for the previous escape.

Article 8

The methods of disciplining prisoners of war shall besides following the foregoing articles, be in accordance with the provisions of the army regulation for minor punishments. Criminal acts of prisoners of war shall be tried by army court-martial.

CAPTURE AND TRANSPORTATION TO THE REAR OF PRISONERS OF WAR

Article 9

When a person to be treated as a prisoner of war is captured, his personal belongings shall be immediately inspected, and weapons, ammunition and other articles which may be put to military use shall be confiscated. Other belongings shall either be held in deposit or shall be left in his possession as circumstances require.

Article 10

When, among the prisoners of war mentioned in the foregoing article, there are officers who should be treated with special honor, an army commander or independent divisional commander may permit them to carry their own swords. In such cases the names of the prisoners of war together with the reasons shall be reported to Imperial General Headquarters, from whence due notice shall be transmitted to the Ministry of War. The weapons which had been carried shall be held in deposit in the prisoners of war camp.

Article 11

Commanders of armies and of independent divisions shall, upon negotiations with the enemy forces after combat, be permitted to return or exchange captured sick and wounded prisoners of war who swear on oath not to take part in combat during the remainder of the same war. In such case, names, total number and reasons shall be reported to Imperial General Headquarters from whence the Ministry of War shall be duly notified.

Article 12

Each unit capturing prisoners shall duly interrogate said prisoners, prepare a roster containing the name, age, rank, home address, home unit and place and date of wounding; a prisoner of war diary; and inventories of articles confiscated or held in deposit in accordance with the provisions of Article 9.

When, as provided for in the foregoing article, the return, exchange or release on oath of prisoners of war are effected, the fact shall be noted on the prisoner of war roster.

Article 13

Prisoners of war shall be divided into officers and warrant officers and under and shall be transported under guard to the nearest line of communications command or transport and communications organization. When this is done, the articles held in deposit, prisoner of war rosters, prisoner of war diaries and inventories shall be forwarded together with the captured personnel.

Article 14

Army units, line of communications commands or transport and communication organizations may, upon conference on the handing over of PW's by a naval commanding officer, receive into custody those prisoners of war together with deposited articles, rosters, diaries, and inventories.

Article 15

Commanders of armies or independent divisions shall promptly report to Imperial General Headquarters the number of prisoners of war they desire to send to the rear. Imperial General Headquarters shall inform the Ministry of War thereof.

Article 16

When the Ministry of War is in receipt of the information mentioned in the foregoing Article 15, it shall report to the Imperial General Headquarters the post or other location where the reception of prisoners of war shall be effected. Imperial General Headquarters shall inform the Ministry of War regarding the expected date of arrival at the designated point. The same procedure shall be followed when the Ministry of War has been informed regarding the reception of prisoners taken by the army.

Article 17

Line of communications commands and transport and communications organizations which in accordance with Articles 13 and 14 have accepted prisoners of war shall transport said prisoners of war under guard to the location(s) mentioned in the foregoing article and shall there transfer said prisoners together with deposited articles, PW rosters, PW diaries and inventories to the custody of the officer of the War Ministry charged with reception.

Article 18

When no Imperial General Headquarters is established, "Imperial General Headquarters" in this chapter shall be taken to read "General Staff Headquarters."

ACCOMMODATIONS AND CONTROL OF PRISONERS OF WAR

Article 19

Rescinded.

Article 20

For prisoners of war accommodations, army establishments, temples or other buildings which suffice to prevent escape and are not detrimental to the health and honor of the prisoners shall be utilized.

Appendix B 357

Article 21

The army commander or garrison area commander under whose jurisdiction comes the administration of Prisoner of War camps (hereinafter to be referred to as the High Administrator of PW camps) shall determine "regulations concerning PW camp duties" and shall make a report thereof to the Minister of War and duly inform the Director General of the PW Information Bureau.

Article 22 (Rescinded)
Article 23 (Rescinded)
Article 24 (Rescinded)
Article 25 (Rescinded)

Article 26

Insofar as mail sent and received by prisoners of war, by international treaty, are exempted from postage dues, the High Commissioner of PW camps shall confer with the Post Office in the vicinity of the PW accommodations and shall determine a suitable procedure for the handling of postal matters.

Article 27

Rules and regulations concerning control within PW camps shall be determined by the High Commissioner.

MISCELLANEOUS RULES

Article 28

Those enemy sick and wounded who, after medical treatment at dressing stations or hospitals, are considered incapable of military service shall, after due promise not to service in the same war, be returned to their homes. However, those who have important relations with the conduct of the war are not included in this.

Article 29

Articles belonging to the prisoners of war and held in deposit by Imperial Government offices shall be restored to their possession at the time of their release.

Article 30

In case of the death of a prisoner of war, the money and possessions of the deceased shall be sent to the Prisoner of War Information Bureau by the unit, organization, hospital or dressing station concerned. When the belongings are of a perishable nature, such shall be sold and the proceeds of the sale shall be forwarded instead.

Article 31

The last will and testament of the deceased prisoner of war shall be handled in the same way as that of Japanese military personnel by the unit, organization, hospital or dressing station concerned, and shall be duly forwarded to the Prisoner of War Information Bureau.

Article 32 (Rescinded)

Article 33

Direct welfare activities for the benefit of prisoners of war by organizations legally established for charitable purposes may be permitted on submittal of a written pledge to the effect that no infractions or violations of the rules and regulations concerning prisoners will be made.

Appendix C: United States Armed Forces Code of Conduct

Article 1

I am an American fighting man. I serve in the forces which guard my country and our way of life. I am prepared to give my life in their defense.

Article 2

I will never surrender of my own free will. If in command, I will never surrender my men while they still have the means to resist.

Article 3

If I am captured I will continue to resist by all means available. I will make any effort to escape and aid others to escape. I will accept neither parole nor special favors from the enemy.

Article 4

If I become a prisoner of war, I will keep faith with my fellow prisoners. I will give no information or take part in any action which might be harmful to my comrades. If I am senior, I will take command. If not, I will obey the lawful orders of those appointed over me and will back them up in every way.

Article 5

When questioned, should I become a prisoner of war, I am required to give name, rank and service number, and date of birth. I will evade answering further questions to the utmost of my ability. I will make no oral or written statements disloyal to my country and its allies or harmful to their cause.

Article 6

I will never forget that I am an American fighting man, responsible for my actions, and dedicated to the principles which made my country free. I will trust in my God and in the United States of America.

Appendix D: Prisoner of War Resistance: U. S. Army Field Manual No. 21-78

INTRODUCTION

The field manual provides guidance to United States Army personnel in applying techniques of resistance to interrogation, indoctrination, and exploitation and in responding to POW management procedures should they become POWs.

The material in the manual was obtained from debriefings of former POWs, autobiographical material related to POWs' experiences, personal conversations and discussions with POWs, and correspondence and discussions with professional personnel involved in the study of POWs, including follow-ups and authoritative scholarly comments and works.

Ideas were also accepted from commercial sources generally recognized as authoritative by the United States Army and civilian personnel who are professionally involved in the subject matter.

CONTENTS

The manual contains 9 chapters—The Battlefield, Excerpts of the Geneva Convention, Captivity, Challenges of Captivity, Captor Approaches and Your Defenses, Exploitation, Resistance, Communication.

The 10 Appendixes cover such topics as References, Reading Material, Films, and POW Training Programs, Department of Defense Directive, Elements of Basic POW Resistance Training, Policy, Administrative Orders, Standing Operating Procedures, Release, and Signal Operations Instructions.

The manual is published by Paladin Press, Boulder, Colorado.

Appendix E: Glossary of Terms Used by POWs

Adge: Adjutant.
agents: Ways of getting things.
air raid red: Japanese guards in hut.
air raid yellow: Japanese guards approaching.
backup: Second helping.
backup king: A man who is always chasing second helpings.
bad house: Cell, prison.
bamboo-and-atap: Japanese aircraft.
bamboo rattler: A man who disturbs neighbors by his movements on the *bali* (bed).
banga: A bag and poles for carrying dirt.
banjo: Latrine.
bash artist: A guard who always beats up POWs.
beat it up: Make whoopee.
benjo-ka: Going to the toilet.
beokee: A very sick man.
beokee house: A hospital.
Bible basher: A priest.
big fellows: Liberators or other four-engine planes.

bimbo: A batman.
birdie: A secret radio.
bird seed: A secret radio.
bioki: Sick.
bite: Ask for, borrow.
blazer rade: A razor blade.
blue: A row of trouble.
blue, the: A show, fight, battle.
blue Danube: POW stew with mung means.
blue orchids: Army slang for air force.
boof head: One with a big head.
boong: Asian or colored person.
boong brandy: Native spirits.
boongs with boots on: Japanese.
boxing presento: A Japanese term for a beating.
brothel of a place: A poor place.
browned off: Fed up, weary.
bug, the: Fever.
buggero: A Japanese swear word.
bullshartist: Great talker, garrulous person.
bumpf: Paper of any kind.

363

campu: Camp.
canary: Hidden radio.
cart, in the: In trouble, facing trouble.
cat house: Brothel.
chat: To delouse.
chat happy: Weary of delousing clothes.
chee chee: Interpreter.
cheese eater: Dutchman.
cheesed off: Browned off.
chicken feed: Weed served in stew.
clomper: Wooden clog.
coconut oiler: Japanese aircraft.
coffee king: A POW with a large business who employs other POWs.
conyero: A Japanese swear word.
crabs, draw the: Attract bombers.
damme damme: No good.
death house: Hospital with a high mortality rate.
dicky-bird: A secret radio.
do, to: To punish.
dog's disease: Malaria.
doings: News, secret radio bulletins.
doover: News, secret radio bulletins.
doovah: A rice cake or extra radio news.
dope: Radio news.
ear basher: One who talks too much.
ear bashing: A long harangue.
face fungus: A beard.
Fanny Adams: Nothing, nil.
flap: Anxiety, confusion.
flog: Sell, exchange for food.
fly spot: An officer's pip.

form: News, situation, position.
for the high jump: Sentenced to death.
funk hole: Slit-trench.
gash: Extra, second helping.
gink: Term of abuse.
go bush: Take to the jungle.
go through: Leave.
go through on: Take something away, steal.
good guts: News, information, secret radio news.
gooderama: Good.
griff: News, radio news.
growter: Putting something over.
hag's bush: Tobacco.
hank: Roll, section of native tobacco.
heat: Light for a smoke.
hen fruit: Eggs.
hot cock: Nonsense, boasting, vain talk.
ignition: A light for a cigarette.
jen: News, information.
jiggy jig: Sexual intercourse.
jungle leaves: Any leaf added to stew.
kipper: Englishman.
kongsie: Personal group.
kurra: Stop, what, come here, I say, now then.
ladders up: I'm all right.
lao: Native wine or toddy.
latrine buzz: Any wildly improbable rumor.
latts: Latrines.
leggie: More.
means, the: The material for making a cigarette.
monty: A certainty, a safe thing.
mooblah: A pancake made from rice flour.

mulga: The surrounding jungle.
mutta mutta birds: Allied aircraft.
natter: To converse, chatter.
nightingale: Radio news, secret radio.
no good house: Prison.
offal eater: Dutchman.
oil: News, information.
olds and bolds: Officers in cushiony jobs.
on the nose: Ill smelling, unsavory.
ooloo: Jungle, scrub.
organize: Obtain, steal, scrounge, acquire.
over the fence: Outside the camp.
pap: Soft, mushy boiled rice.
peter: Cell, prison.
pips, to pull the: To make use of superior rank.
pissaphone: Bamboo urinal.
pom-pom: Motorboat.
presento: Have, give.
racketeer: One engaged in doing business inside or outside the camp.
rackets: Ways of making money without working.
raw prawn: Something far-fetched, absurd.
rock: Shake, surprise, amaze.
sand: Guts, courage.
scram: Food.
shakes: Malarial shivers.
slap happy: Anybody foolish or stupid.
snakes and ladders: Officer's hut.
speedo: Hurry, be quick.
spin: Excitement, a flurry.
spin a dit: Chat.
spin in: To crash.
spinebasher: Someone who is always on his back, is always resting.
spliced: Drunk.
spud barber: A potato peeler.
squeeze: Japanese graft.
squitters: Dysentery, diarrhea.
stemtug: Bug.
sweejibah: Cookhouse.
sweet bucks: Sweet potatoes.
sweet cop: An easy job.
swen: News, radio news.
tanko: Parade, count, check on numbers.
tin can: Destroyer, corvette.
tin fish: Torpedo.
toban: A batman.
tojo-presentos: Japanese cigarettes.
tomitts: Dysentery, diarrhea.
tong: Bath, wash.
trader: Anyone who goes out of camp to trade or sell.
troppo: Mad, sunstruck, weakminded, affected by captivity.
trots: Diarrhea.
tunga: A carrying litter for earth, wood, etc.
turn it up: Give it up, don't do it.
up the ladder: Someone who thinks only of himself.
wet: Foolish, idiotic, stupid.
white death: Melon in stew.
white Jap: Someone who acts like a Japanese.
white Nip: Someone who acts like a Japanese.
wog it: Act or live like an Asiatic laborer.
yasmea: Holiday, rest period.

SOURCES

Various books, documents, and other literature, especially Rohan D. Rivett, *Behind Bamboo*, London, 1947.

Appendix F: Special Literary Sources

BOOKS ENCOMPASSING A WIDE RANGE OF SUBJECTS

Kerr, E. Bartlett. *Surrender and Survival: The Experience of American POWs in the Pacific 1941–1945.* New York, 1985. China, Guam, Wake, Java, Japan, other islands, Philippines, Formosa, Manchuria, Burma, Siam, Singapore, Korea.

Russell, Lord of Liverpool. *The Knights of Bushido.* London, 1958. War crimes and atrocities: Manchuria, China, Burma, hellships, death marches, POW camps, civilian internment camps, the Kempeitai.

van Velden, Dr. D. *De Japanse Burgerkampen* [The Japanese Civilian Internment Camps During World War II]. Franeker, the Netherlands, 1963, 1977, 1985. Japan, China, Manchuria, Korea, French Indochina, Siam, Burma, the Philippines, all the islands of the Dutch East Indies (now Indonesia), and the Pacific Islands occupied by the Japanese.

BIBLIOGRAPHIES AND DOCUMENTS

Baylin, Gwyn M. *Bibliographic Guide to the Two World Wars.* London, 1977.

Benda, Harry J., James K. Irikura, and Koichi Kiri, eds. *Japanese Military Administration in Indonesia: Selected Documents.* New Haven, CT, 1965.

Bloomberg, Marty, and Hans H. Weber. *World War II and Its Origins: A Selected Annotated Bibliography.* Littleton, 1975.

Borton, H., et al. *A Selected List of Books and Articles on Japan.* Cambridge, 1954.

Brugmans, Dr. I. J., et al. *Nederlands Indie Onder Japanse Bezetting:*

Documents 1942–1945 [The Dutch East Indies Under Japanese Occupation: Documents]. Franeker, the Netherlands, 1960.

Dull, Paul S., and Michael Takaaki Uemura. *The Tokyo Trials: A Functional Index to the Proceedings of the IMTFE.* Ann Arbor, MI, 1957.

Edwards, John B. *Bibliography on Prisoner of War Labor.* Washington, DC, 1947.

Enser, A. G. S. *A Subject Bibliography of the Second World War: Books in English 1939–1974.* London, 1977.

Funk, Arthur L. *The Second World War: A Selected Bibliography of Books in English Since 1975.* Claremont, CA, 1985.

Gibbs, John M. *On Prisoner of War Camps in Japan and Japanese Controlled Areas: Reports of Interned Americans.* Mimeographed report. POW Information Bureau, Washington, DC, July 31, 1946.

Imperial War Museum. *Subject Index of Booklists.* London, 1976.

Kodansha Encyclopedia of Japan. New York, 1983.

Kondo, Shinji. *Japanese Military History: A Guide to the Literature.* New York, 1984.

Lebra, Joyce C., et al. *Japan's Greater East Asia Co-Prosperity Sphere in World War II: Selected Readings and Documents.* Oxford, 1975.

Lewis, John R. *Uncertain Judgment: A Bibliography of War Crime Trials.* Santa Barbara, CA, 1979.

Morley, James Williams. "Checklist of Seized Japanese Records in the National Archives." *Far Eastern Quarterly* 9 (1950), 306–333.

Netzorg, Morton J. *The Philippines in World War II and to Independence: An Annotated Bibliography.* Ithaca, NY, 1977.

Onorato, Michael P. *Philippine Bibliography: 1899–1945.* Santa Barbara, CA, 1968.

Sharp, John Charles. *A Collection of Papers from Japanese Sources Relating to POW and Internment Camps in the Far East.* Birmingham, 1952.

Shulman, Frank Joseph. *Doctoral Dissertation on Asia: Annotated Bibliographical Journal of Current International Research.* Ann Arbor, MI, 1978.

Tutorow, Norman E. *War Crimes, War Criminals and War Crime Trials: An Annotated Bibliography and Source Book.* New York, 1986.

United States Army Center of Military History. *Bibliography on U.S. Prisoners of War, 1776–1973.* Washington, DC, 1973.

Ziegler, Janet. *World War II: Books in English 1945–1965.* Stamford, CA, 1971.

Appendix G: Additional Sources of Information

THE NETHERLANDS

Leger Voorlichtingdienst, Spui 32, Den Haag (Armed Forces Information Center).
Algemeen Rijksarchief, Prins Willem Alexanderhof 20, 2595BE Den Haag (National Archives).
Rijksinstituut voor Oorlogsdocumentatie, Indonesie Afdeling, Herengracht 474, 1017CA Amsterdam (War Documentation Center).
Taal, Land en Volkenkunde, Reuvenplaats 2, 2311BE Leiden (Institute of Culture).
Ministerie van Defensie, Centraal Archievendepot, 2e v.d. Kunststraat 19, 2521BD Den Haag (Department of Defense).

ENGLAND

Ministry of Defence, Naval Historical Branch, Empress State Building, London, SWY 1TR.
Public Record Office, Kew, Richmond, Surrey, TW9 4DU.
War Graves Commission, 2 Marlow Road, Maidenhead, Berkshire, SL6 7DX.
General Register Office, St. Catherines House, 10 Kingsway, London, WC2B 6JP.
Army Records Centre, Bourne Avenue, Hayes, Middlesex UB3 1RF.
Far Eastern POWClub, 193 Ashendon, Deacon Way, Walworth, London, SE17 1UA.
Imperial War Museum, Lambeth Road, London, SE1 6HZ.
The Daily Telegraph, 135 Fleet Street, London, EC4.

Index

"A" Force 239
Abkhazi, Peggy 233
Abraham, Abie 262
Achi Yamakita 194
Adachi, Sumio 51
Adams, B.D. 103
Adams, Geoffrey 212, 246
Adek 297
Adek I 301, 306
Adek II 301, 303, 306
Admiralty Islands 18, 19
Advents Church 338
Adventskerk 336, 337, 338
Affairs Bureau 36
Africa 16
Agustin, Conrado G. 262
Agustin, Yay 262
Aichi 209
Aik Pamienke 285, 286
Aik Pamienke I 282, 284, 285, 286
Aik Pamienke II 282, 286
Aik Pamienke III 285, 286
Aioshi 200
Airmadidi, Tomohon 337
Aitken, Lowell 262
Akasaka 194
Akenobe 197
Akita 194
Albertson, Dorothy 262
alcoholism 93
Alexander the Great 33
Alexishaven 339, 341
Alleman, R.J. 103
Allen, Louis 28, 50
Allied War Crimes Trials 144
Allport, G.W. 78
Alor Island 340, 341
Althorp, A.A. 293
Alvit, Alfonso 262
Amagasaki Subcamp 200
Amagi Maru 154, 167
Amahei, Ambon Island 333
Amazon basin 237

Ambarawa 9, 25
Ambarawa, Central Java 312
Ambarawa (1) 6 307, 312, 313, 314, 315, 316
Ambarawa 7I 307, 311, 313, 315, 316
Ambarawa 7II 308, 311, 313, 314, 315, 322
Ambarawa 8I 312, 313, 314, 316
Ambarawa 8II 313, 314, 315
Ambarawa 9I 312, 313, 314, 316
Ambarawa 9II 313, 314
Ambon 7, 143, 161, 334, 337, 338
Ambon camp 8
Ambon Island 7, 10, 160, 161, 165, 331, 333, 343
amebiasis 87, 97
American Association POW Committee 224
American Ex-POWs, Inc. 83, 100, 137, 141, 162, 166
American Mission Hospital 227
American National Red Cross 233
American Prisoner of War Information Bureau 154, 157, 199, 202
American Psychiatric Association 90
American Red Cross 41, 42, 187, 216, 221, 250, 262
American Red Cross *Prisoner of War Bulletin* 196, 199
American Revolution 149
Amoy 226, 230
Anami, Korechika 176
Anangganaung 243
Anankwin 243
Andaman Islands 18
Andersonville 3, 4, 33, 135, 136, 137, 138, 139
Andersonville's Prisoner of War Museum 4
Ando, N. 118
Anloff, G.J. 163
Aoki, Kazuo 176
Aokuma 203

371

Aomori 190, 194
Apalon 243
Aparain 243
Appleman, John Alan 123
Araki, Sadao 113
Arao 204
Archer, J.B. 330
Archibald, H.C. 104
Argall, Phyllis 28
Argentina 35
Argentina Maru 154, 167
Argyle, C.J. 28
Argyle Street 222
Arima, Kaoru 177, 240
Arisan Maru 155, 158, 167
Army Center of Military History, Washington, DC 221
Arneil, Stan 268
Arnold, A. 104
Arnold, Al 104
Arrow Hill/Wang Sing 242
Arthur, Anthony 262
Artillery Barracks 296
Asahigawa 190
Asaka Maru 167, 208, 331
Asama Maru 49
Ash Camp, West No. 2 228
Ashibetsu 189
Ashihara, Yoshinobu 28
Ashikago 194
Ashton, Paul 262
Asia 1, 19, 20, 25, 38, 53, 171, 266
Atamboea (Timor Island) 333
Atambua 335, 336, 340
Atami 194
ATIS 262
Attiwill, Kenneth 268
Attu 207
Atwater, Dorence 136
Audric, John 246
Aungganaun 2 243
Auschwitz 1
Australia 1, 16, 17, 19, 73, 114, 125, 180, 267, 270, 290, 296, 339
Australian Archives, Melbourne 170, 294
Australian New Guinea 341
Australian War Memorial, Canberra 170
avitaminosis 85, 87, 94, 96
Awa Maru 13

Babel Thuap Island, Yamato Camp 166, 334
Bacharach, A. 104

Bacolod (Negros Island) 54, 55, 57, 58, 59, 60, 61, 62, 63, 64, 260
Baguio 259
Bailey, James E. 102
Bailey, Ronald 50
Baird, J.T. 104
Baker, S. 104
Bali 7, 339
Balige 281
Balikpapan, East Borneo 330
Ballard, J.C. 28
Ban Pong 237, 238, 239, 240, 242
Bancroft, A. 246
Bandjermasin, South Borneo 328
Bandjermasin I 328, 329
Bandjermasin II 328
Bandoeng, West Java 9, 10, 13, 172, 175, 209, 297, 305, 306
Bandoengan 315, 322
Bandungan work camp 314
Bangka Islands 7
Bangkatan 282, 284
Bangkinang, West Sumatra/East Sumatra 289
Bangkinang I 286, 287, 289
Bangkinang II 287, 289, 295
Bangkok (Siam) 46, 237, 242, 249
Bangkong I 311, 312, 318
Bangkong II 312
Banjoebiroe 315
Banjoebiroe II 322
Banjoebiroe 10-I 306, 315, 319
Banjoebiroe 10 II 313, 314, 315, 317, 318
Banjoebiroe 11 314, 316
Banjoebiroe 12 316
Bank, Bertram 262
Banka 293
Banka Island 289, 290, 291, 292
Banka Strait 270
Bankao 242
Bankingang II 289
Barakkenkamp I 290, 291
Barakkenkamp II 289, 291, 293
Barber, Robert 262
Barker, A.J. 50
Barksdale, Maj. 259
Baron Hideo Kodama 10
Baros I 307, 308
Baros II 302, 308
Baros III 305, 306, 308, 310
Bartlett-Kerr, E. 51
Barton, Clara 136
Bashee Group 155
Bataan 1, 18, 38, 69, 70, 83, 87, 132, 250, 255, 256, 257, 265
Bataan Relief Organization 83

Bataan Veterans' Organization 83
Batavia 8, 9, 10, 13, 47, 150, 153, 158, 160, 164, 167, 172, 175, 273, 297, 298, 299, 300, 302, 304
Batavia, Tjideng camp 9
Batavia Military Tribunal 298
Bates, H.F. 180, 186, 246
Batoe 303, 318
Battambang 235
Battle of the Java Sea 7, 210, 331
Batu Lintang 326, 327, 328
Baxter, George E. 233
Bayambang 252
Beaumont, Joan 50, 79
bedbugs 72
Beebe, G.W. 104
Beets, Nic 212, 246
Beke Taun 243
Belalau, South Sumatra 291
Belawan 285
Belawan Estate I 283, 285, 286
Belawan Estate II 280, 285, 286
Belgian Bulge 83
Belgium 16
Bell, D.R. 106
Bell, Francis Eldon 262
Bell, Leslie 268
Bell, P.G. 104
Belsen 1
Benchimol, A.B. 110
Benedict, Ruth 28
Benjamin, M. 110
Benjo Maru 156, 167
Benkoelen 274, 289
Benkoelen I 289, 292
Benkoelen II 289, 290
Benkulen, West Sumatra 158
Bensheim, H. 104
Benson, James 343
Benteng I 308, 309, 310, 316, 317, 318
Benteng II 316
Beppu 203, 204
Beppu Camp 216
Berastagi 284, 286
Bergamini, David 28
Bergee, Lee K. 262
Berger, Lee K. 212
Berhala 26
Berhala Island 326, 327
beri-beri 85, 87, 94, 95
Bern, Switzerland 35
Bernard, F.C. 240
Bernard, Frits 245
Bernard, H. 114
Bethany Church 338
Bethanykerk 335, 338
Betio 341

Bettelheim, Bruno 104
Bibai-Machi 190
Bila River 285
Bilibid 9, 69, 70, 251, 254, 255, 259, 260
Bima 335, 339
Binder, M. 154
Bindjei 284, 285
Binnerts, C. 343
Biological Warfare Research, Fort Detrick, Maryland 221
Birch, Alan 233
Bireuen 279, 280
Birkhimer, L.J. 104
Bismarck Archipelago 8, 19, 341
Bita Paka 334
Bittle, George 91
Blackwater, C.F. 212
Blaha, F. 104
Blair, Clay 160, 164
Blair, Joan 160, 164
Blake, D.J. 104
Blanchard, E.B. 104
Blangkedjeren 271, 277, 295
Blangkedjeren 9 270
Blangkedjeren 23 270
Blangkedjeren 38 270
Blankenhorn, M.A. 104
Blanny, General 27
Blewett, George F. 123
Blin, L'Art 236
Blitar 317
Bloemenkamp 307, 308, 313
Bloemenkamp B and C 306, 307
Bloom, Freddy 58, 61, 104, 268
Blow, Rex 180, 325
Bobbitt, Robert G. 91
Bodjo 336
Boeboetan 319
Boeboetan I 310, 311, 316, 317, 339
Boeboetan II 306, 317
Boeton 7
Boissevain, Gon 320
Bolong 336
Bondy, C. 104
Bonsaquet, David 233
Booker, Edna Lee 229, 233
Boomkamp, I. 320
Booth, Martin 212
Bor, A.W. 343
Borneo 45, 143, 177, 180, 323, 326, 329, 330, 331
Borneo, North 145
Borneo, South 145
Borobudur Intercontinental Hotel 298
Boskamp 337
Bougainville Islands 7

Bowden, Tim 268
Bowen Road Military Hospital 223
Boyington, Pappy 194
Brackman, Arnold C. 116, 123, 130
Braddon, Russell 5, 55, 246, 268
Bradley, James 180, 186, 246
Brady, Charles E. 259
Braly, William C. 3, 6, 28, 153, 154, 157, 163, 164, 212, 215, 216, 221, 261, 262
Branchey, L. 104
Brandt, Willem 79, 293
Brankasi 241
Brankassi 242
Brazil Maru 156, 157, 163, 167
Brende, J.O. 104
Bridge House Gaol: Shanghai 232
Brill, N.O. 105
Brines, Russell 28, 233, 236, 262
Britain 16
British and American Business Men's Club 220
British and Foreign Bible Society 227
British Camp 287
British Embassy 227
British North Borneo 326
British Third Army 18
Broederschool 303, 310, 311, 316
Brougher, William E. 79, 221, 262
Broughton, Douglas C. 218
Broughton, Douglas G.B. 221
Brouwers, Jeroen 320
Brown, C.C. 79, 268
Brown, Charles 69, 79, 102, 105, 262
Brown, Courtney 28
Brown, D. Denny 105
Brown, Maude Gallman 168
Brown, Wenzell 233
Bruckel-Beiten, Mary 342
Brugmans, I.J. 50, 153
Brunei 326
Brussels 102
Buchenwald 1
Buitenzorg 304
Bukit Besar 290, 291, 292
Bulcock, Roy 5, 28, 37, 49, 172, 185, 298, 320, 343
Bulem, Mayra 320
Bullwinkel, Sister V. 294
Bureau for Control and Administration of Prisoners of War (Japan) 9, 174, 186
Burgess, R.C. 105
Burghardt-de Boer, H.L. 294
Burki, Charles 69, 79
Burlingame, Dorothy 78
Burma 1, 2, 8, 9, 10, 17, 18, 21, 37, 40, 45, 62, 82, 127, 143, 145, 150, 160, 161, 162, 167, 173, 179, 182, 184, 239, 241, 243, 244, 247, 248
Burma-Siam 128, 144
Burma-Siam railroad 3, 9, 32, 56, 59, 73, 117, 127, 128, 144, 184, 236, 241, 247, 249, 266, 272, 298
Burstein, L. 105
Burton, Reginald 246
Burwell, Frank 162
Butai, Akatsuki 174
Butler, Rex 180, 325
Butow, Robert J.C. 28

Caballo Island 253
Cabanatuan 8, 9, 144, 251, 252, 253, 255
Cabanatuan-Bilibid 161
Cabanatuan No. 1 252
Cabanatuan No. 2 252
Cabanatuan No. 3 252
Caffrey, Kate 56, 73, 246, 268
Cairo Declaration 113
California 19, 95
California State University, Northridge 221
Cam Ranh Bay 17
Camp 1 274
Camp 2 274
Camp 2A 275
Camp 3 275
Camp 4 275
Camp 5 275
Camp 6 276
Camp 7 276
Camp 7A 276
Camp 8 276
Camp 9 276
Camp 10 276
Camp 11 276
Camp 12 277
Camp 13 277
Camp 14 277
Camp Holmes 259
Camp John Hay 259
Camp Murphy 251
Camp No. 11 203
Camp No. 23 201
Camp O'Donnell 8, 252, 256, 257
Camp Sumter, Georgia 3
Camp Sutter 135
Camphuislaan 318
Canada 16, 42, 114
Canadian Inventor 161
Canadian University 209
Canberra, Australia 125, 170

Canneco, J.M. 246, 320
Canton 230
Canton Group 222
Carew, Tim 161, 212, 233
Carnahan, Clarence 92, 102
Carr, Lorraine 262
Carroll, B.J. 105
Carter, Norman 246
Cates, Teresa R. 262
Cebu Island, Zamboanga 167, 260
Cedarbaum, J.M. 105
Celebes 143, 144, 177, 332, 335
Celebes, North 145
Celebes, South 145
Celebes Island 331, 335, 338, 342
Central Gaol 248
Central Java 7, 9, 172, 307, 309, 311, 312, 316
Ceylon 19
Chagall, Lydia 320
Chaiotoukai 225
Changaraya 239, 243
Changi, Singapore 10, 40, 45, 46, 56, 58, 74, 239, 240, 266
Changi Airport 266
Changi Camp 240, 266
Changi Jail 69, 266
Changi Peninsula 265
Changi Prison 266, 267, 268
Changi Square incident 266
Chapei 173, 228, 230
Chapman, F. Spencer 180, 186
Charles, Robert 245, 246
Chattel, C.J.H. du. 320
Chauvel, Richard 343
Che Foo 226
Chen, Joseph C.Y. 221
Cheribon 309
Cheribon I 306, 309
Cheribon II 301, 309
Chessman, H.R. 69
Cheung Kong 222
Cheung Pang 222
Cheung Ping 222
Chiba 194
Chin Hua 224
China 16, 21, 40, 44, 46, 49, 64, 73, 82, 113, 114, 143, 144, 145, 155, 173, 176, 180, 182, 184, 225, 233
Chingwantao 225
Cho, Sung Yoon 123
Chodoff, P. 105
Cholong 235
Choo Siat 267
Chosen, Manchuria 38
Christensen, Arthur G. 192
Christie, R.W. 268

Christie, Robert 268
Chugenji 194
Chungkai 242
Chungwa 277
Chunking Regime 185, 225
Churchill, Winston 20, 33, 48, 70, 71
cirrhosis 97
Civic Center 224
Civil War 3, 4, 5, 33, 135, 136
Clagne, Peter 233
Clark, A.R. 262
Clark, C.A. 105
Clark airfield 9
Clarke, Hugh V. 32, 48, 105, 142, 143, 146, 212, 239, 245, 246
Coast, John 73, 78, 129, 130, 245, 246
Cockrill, Philip 320
Cohen, B.M. 105
Cohen, Elie A. 50, 79
Cohen Stuart-Franken, M. 320
Cole, Martin 233
Coleman, J.S. 162, 263
Colijn, Helen 294
Colley, George 263, 330
Collinson, A.C. 222
Collis, Maurice 246
Colonel Ota 63
Columbia Country Club, West No. 3 228, 230
Committee on Veterans' Affairs of the United States House of Representatives 88
Conelissen, P.F. 343
Congregatie der Fraters O.L. Vrouwe Moeder van Barmhartigheid 343
Conrow, Carol 262, 263
Conte, H.R. 105
Coombs, J.H.H. 246
Cooper, C.T. 164
Cooper, George T. 298, 320, 332, 343
Cooper, M.Z. 105
Co-Prosperity Sphere 18, 21
Coral Maru 156, 167
Coral Sea 19
Cordero, Virgilio 263
Cornelius, Mary D. 268
Cornfield, R.B. 107
Corpe, Hilda 62, 248
Corregidor 8, 18, 132, 250, 252, 254, 257
Costello, John 28
Cramer, M.C. 114
Crawford, H. 180, 186, 246
Crawford, J.N. 105

Creel, George 123
Crimes Trials 1
Cristie, K. 233
Crosby, Sir Josiah 250
Cruikshank, E.K. 105
Cuetter, A.C. 106
Cullum, Leo A. 263

"D" Force 239
Dachau 1
Dahlstrom, W. 263
Dai Nichi Maru 156, 167
Dairen 220
Danang 17
Darmo 299, 303, 312, 316, 318
Daughters of the Confederacy 136
Davao, Mindanao Island 72, 252, 254, 260
Davao Island (the Philippines) 167
Davao Penal Colony 9, 10, 180, 254
Davis, G.C. 109
Day of Beating 8
Deacon, Richard 28
Declaration of Potsdam 115
Decoux, Governor General 235
de Grey, Shin 80
de Hoog, Dick 306, 308
de Jongh, Wil 294, 320
Deller, John J., Jr. 105
Denenchofu I 206
Denenchofu II 206, 207
Den-Ouden-Hille, M.H. 294
Denpasar 335, 339
Denver, Colorado 83
Denver Service Center 137
Department of Veterans Affairs 85
de Ruyter, Gwendolyn 79
de Terente, Violette 78
de Veen, W. 105
Devereux, James 18, 212, 343
De-Vreede, Mischa 294
De Wit, Oscar 320
de Wit, P.J. 330
Dickman, Harold R. 101
Dili I 340
Dili II 340
Dilli, Timor Island 333
DioGuardi, Ralph 258, 262, 263
Director General of the PW Information Bureau (Japan) 357
Djambi, South Sumatra 7, 271, 279
Djambi I 289, 292
Djambi II 289, 291
Djatingaleh 311, 317, 319
Djoe Eng 308, 315
Djokjakarta (Central Java) 172, 310

Dobbs, D. 105
Dobervitch, Michael 180
Doihara, Kenji 113, 177
Domei, Japan 28
Domei Agency 181
Dominican University 258
Doorn, Iens van 320
Dopkins, Dale R. 263
Doughty, Bryan I. 83
Dower, John 20, 27, 28, 29, 142, 146, 221
Downer, Sidney F. 79
Drage, Charles 233
Dragt, D.J. 293
Droste, Chr. B. 320
Duffy, George 159
Dull, Paul S. 50, 51, 120, 123, 368
Duncan, J.L. 103
Dunford, J. 246
Dunlop, E.E. 212, 239, 320
"Dunlop" Force 239
Dutch Archipelago 335
Dutch Borneo 330
Dutch East Indies 1, 7, 8, 10, 17, 18, 24, 25, 40, 44, 47, 49, 50, 61, 73, 127, 142, 144, 150, 153, 171, 173, 179, 182, 266, 269, 273, 296, 298, 306, 323, 331
Dutch East Indies, Haroekoe, Cream Island 154
Dutch New Guinea 338
Dutch State Correctional Institute School 297
Dutch West Borneo 326
Dutch XVe Battalion infantry 296
Dyess, Ed 10, 180
Dyess, William E. 186, 263
dysthymic disorder 85

East Asia 17, 18, 24
East Borneo 7, 9, 13, 184, 326, 328, 329, 339
East Borneo, Java 177
East Java 10, 160, 161, 165, 172, 175, 299, 315, 316, 339
East Malaya 7
East Sumatra 8, 158, 271, 274, 277, 281, 282
Easterlin, Lewis F. 5
Easterlin, William 5
Eaton-Lee, J.J. 294
Edman, Irwin 62, 78
Edo 15
Edwards, Jack 233
Edwards, John B. 368
Eichelberger, Robert L. 212, 246

Eijke-van Velzen, Truus van 294
Eitinger, E. 103
Eitinger, L. 105
El Fraile Island 254
Elliott, Mabel 78
Embree, John 29, 78
Encyclopaedia Britannica 34
Ende I 335, 340
Ende II 335, 340
Engineer Island 251
England 24, 73, 114, 149, 369
England Maru 156, 167
Enoshina 208
Enoura Maru 156, 157, 163, 167
Enser, A.G.S. 368
Erickson, Edward 162
Esxritt, Ewart 246
Evans, Frank 212, 233
Evans, William R. 150, 212, 263
Exclusion Act of 1924 19
Exhibition Building 296
Ex-POW Bulletin 101, 103, 105, 163, 239
Ex-POWs, Inc. 102, 103

"F" Force 239
Fabrisius, Johan 320
Falcon, S. 105
Falk, Richard A. 123
Falk, Stanley L. 256, 262, 263, 268
Far East 184, 229, 236, 248, 250, 265, 295, 322, 325, 330, 344
Feighner, J.P. 106
Feis, Herbert 29
Fengtai 223, 227
Fengtai Camp, China 190
Fernando, T.B. 106
Feuer, A.B. 263
Field, E. 233
Fields, G.L. 196
Figley, Charles 91, 101
Fiji 19
Fimerty, John Tim 246
Firey, Jane J. 99, 103
"First" Force 239
First Infantry Depot 297
Fischer, A.L. 58
Fisher, M. 106
Flanagan, E.M., Jr. 263
flashback phenomena 90
Fletcher, William H. 29
Fletcher-Cooke, John 150, 156, 168, 212, 268
Flores 10, 40, 333, 343, 344
Flory, William E.B. 50, 190
Folkow, B. 106

Forbes, G.K. 330
Ford, Carey 78
Foreign Analysis Division, Bureau of Overseas Intelligence, Office of War Information, Record Group 208 50
Foreign Minister Arita 17
Foreign Morale Analysis Division, Bureau of Overseas Intelligence, Office of War Information, Record Group No. 208 29
Former Prisoner of War Benefits Act 84
Formosa 8, 10, 40, 41, 150, 153, 154, 155, 156, 157, 158, 163, 166, 173, 184, 204, 215, 216, 219, 222
Fort de Kock 286, 287, 288
Fort Detrick, Maryland, Biological Warfare Research 221
Fort Drum 254
Fort Hughes 253
Fort McKinley 251
Fort Mills 253
Fort Santiago 251, 260, 261
Fortier, Malcolm Vaughn 79
Foster, F. 246
Fowler, Halstead 78, 79
France 16, 17, 114
Francis, George 193, 212
Franciscan Monastery 194
Franeker, Netherlands 49, 232
Frankl, Victor 106
French Indochina 17, 40, 173, 184, 234
Freud, Anna 78
Friedman, Matthew J. 91, 101, 106
Friedman, S.B. 106
Friend, Theodore 29
Fuji 194
Fuji Maru 157
Fujizuka, Tasao 178
Fukai Maru 157, 167
Fuku Maru 157, 167
Fukuji Mari 157, 168
Fukuoka 202, 203
Fukushima 208
Funatsu 197
Funk, Arthur L. 368
Furashi 200
Furumaki 194
Fusan, Korea 218, 223
Fusan, Manchuria 157
Fuse 200
Futababi 209, 210, 211
Futase 202
Futatsui City 194
Futumatsu, Yoshihiko 246

Galang 271
Galoehan 315, 317
gaols 231
Gardner, Mona 19, 22, 28, 29
Garneau, Grant S. 233
Gaultier, Marcel 236
Gayn, Mark 212
Gedangan 311, 312, 313, 314, 318
Gedongbadak I 304, 308
Gedongbadak II 300, 302, 304, 305, 309, 310
Gedongbadak III 302, 303, 304, 307
Gedongdjati 315
Geneva Convention 32, 34, 35, 36, 37, 48, 361
Georgia 3
Georgia Department of the Grand Army of the Republic 136
Germany 17, 18
Gestapo 120, 231
Gevangenis, Manado 337
Gevangenis Jail 305, 308, 309, 310, 317, 337
Gevangenis I, Jail 309, 310
Gevangenis II 305, 310
Gibberd, F.B. 106
Gibbs, John M. 199, 368
Gibson, Michael 29
Gideonse, Henk 246
Gifu–Nagara Hotel 200
Gilbert Island 8, 341
Gilkey, Langdon Brown 233
Gill, G.V. 98, 106
Gillespie, R.D. 106
Gillman, J. 106
Gillman, T. 106
Gillon, Miles 180, 325
Gilmour, O.W. 268
Gimenez, Pedro M. 263
Gittins, Jean 233
Gleeck, Lewis E., Jr. 263
Glodok Gaol 298
Glodok I 300
Glodok II 300
Gloegoer 273
Gloegoer I 271, 282
Gloegoer II 282, 283, 286
Gloria, Claro C. 263
Glueck, Sheldon 123
Goaweg I 335, 339
Goaweg II 335
Goedang Garam 304, 309
Goenoeng Setan 271
Goethe, John 29
Goldblith, Samuel 166
Goldstein, F.J. 109
Gomes, Paula 321

gonadal deficiency 94
Goodman, Julien M. 158, 204, 212
Goodwin, Ralph 233
Gordon, Ernest 60, 245, 246
Gordon, Richard M. 263
Gostas, T.W. 106
Got, Jacques F. 236
Gothier, Mack L. 87, 101, 106
Gould, S.E. 106
Gouvernementshuis 326
Gozawa, Sadaichi 123
Grad, B. 106
Graef, Calvin 155
Great Britain 1, 17, 22, 42, 48, 113, 185
Great China University 228
Great Western Road 228
Greater East Asia Co-Prosperity Sphere, The 18, 31, 185
Greenstein, R. 107
Grew, Joseph C. 29, 201
Griffin, S.G. 106
Grogol I 302
Grogol II 301, 302, 308
Grogol III 302, 306
Gronvik, O. 106
Guam 7, 17, 132, 142, 143, 206, 209, 210, 342
Guam Island 154
Gunnison, Royal Arch 263
gynecomastia 94

Hachow 222
Hague Convention 34
Hahn, Emily 233
Hainan Island 159, 164, 222
Haiphong 235
Haiphong Road Camp 226, 227
Hakkert, Ann 321
Hakodate Divisional Camp 190
Hakodate Main Camp 188, 190
Hakone 194
Hakusan Maru 155, 157, 168
Halamheira II 311
Hall, David O.W. 50
Hall, Leslie G. 246
Hall, R. 106
Halloran, Ray "Hap" 194
Halmaheira I 311, 312
Halmaheira II 306
Halmaheira III 311, 312, 322
Hamilton, Esther Yerger, 263
Hamilton, Thomas 268
Hammond, Robert B. 233
Hanifin, J.M. 106
Hankou 230

Hanoi 234, 235
Hanoi Gialam Airfield 235
Hanson, Jessie Bell 74, 78
Hanson, John F. 123
Harada, Kumakishi 177
Harbin 219, 220
Hardie, Robert 246
Hargreaves, G.M. 102
Harina, Camp No. 29 200
Haroekoe 154, 333, 344
Haroekoe I 333
Harris, Douglas 246
Harris, S.W. 239
Harris, Sheldon 221
Harrison, Courtney T. 343
Harrison, Earl H. 78
Harrison, Kenneth 82, 101, 212, 246, 268
Harrison, Tom 330
Hartendorp, A.V. 263
Hartley, M.G. 79
Hartley, Peter 268, 294
Haru Maru 157, 168
Harukiku Maru 158, 168
Harvey, A.M. 106
Harvey, Eleanor T.M. 79
Hase, Shinsaburo 178
Hashimoto, Kingoro 113
Hashimura Togo 19
Hastain, Ronald 75, 78, 127, 130, 155, 212, 246
Hata, Shunroku 113
Hatam 339
Hatch, Gardner 50, 185
Hauri, P. 106
Havens, Thomas P.H. 29
Hawkins, Jack 180
Hayashi, Toshio 259
Hayashi Village 194
Heito 215
Heito, Camp No. 3 215
Helion, Jean 78
Hellferich-Koch, J.H. 320, 321
Henderson, F.W. 107
Henry, J.P. 98, 107
hepatitis 89
Hephata 281
Herberg, H. 109
Heriot, Guy 268
Herlihy, Francis 82, 101, 234
Hersey, J. 263
Hewlett, Thomas H. 203, 212
Hewton, T. 123
Hibbs, O.R. 107
Hibbs, Ralph E. 98
Hideki Tojo 18
Higashi-Misone, Subcamp No. 10 201

Higasikumi, General 176
Higgitt, A.C. 107
High Administrative of PW camps (Japan) 357
Hilfman, M.M. 212
Hillinger, Charles 6
Himeji 200
Hind, R. Renton 185, 263
Hindato 241, 242
Hintok 242
Hiranuma, Kiichiro 113
Hiraoka, Subcamp No. 3 194
Hirohata Divisional Camp 199, 200
Hiroshima 13
Hirota, Koki 113
Hitachi, Ibargi-ken 192
Hitachi Motoyama 194
HMS *Encounter* 331
HMS *Exeter* 331
HMS *Petrel* 224
HMS *Prince of Wales* 331
HMS *Stronghold* 331
HMS *Tradewind* 158
HMS *Truculent* 158
Hocking, F. 107
Hoda, chief of the Armed Forces Bureau 36
Hofstede, N.W. 212, 268, 321
Hofuku Maru 157
Hogben, G.L. 107
Hoihow 222
Hokkaido 187, 188, 211, 223
Holdoff, B. 111
Hollandia 339, 341
Holman, Dennis 164, 320, 342, 343
Holton, D.C. 29
Homma, Lieutenant General 36, 37, 256
Honam 230
Hong, Chang-Zern 95, 102, 107
Hong Chi Salt Godown, Kinhua 224
Hong Kong 7, 18, 45, 46, 47, 92, 145, 154, 155, 158, 160, 166, 173, 174, 180, 184, 189, 221, 222, 223, 231, 233
Hong Kong News 64
Honshu Island 223
Hoogenband, C. van den 29
Hooykaas-van Leeuwen, J.H. 321
Hope-Falkner, R.E. 329
Hornung, Elvera 98, 103
Horwitz, Solis 123
Hoshino, Naoki 114
Hosoya, C. 118, 122, 123
Hospital 308
Hoten 173, 219, 220
Hoten Main Camp 218

Hoten Temporary 218
Hoten "Work" Camp No. 1 219
Hoten "Work" Camp No. 2 219
Hoten "Work" Camp No. 3 219
Hovinga, Henk 294
Howard, Chris Pereze 212
Hoyt, Edwin P. 29
Huang, Y.H. 110
Huangsikan 225
Hubbard, Preston John 4, 6, 263
Hudspeth, W.H. 227
Hulsbus, Joop 246
Humiliation Day 19
Hunt, Bruce 239, 245
Hutam Salem 282
Hyogo 210
Hyogo No. 1 209, 210, 342
Hyogo No. 2 209, 210, 211, 342
Hyogo No. 3 210, 342
Hyogo No. 4 210, 342

Iba 198
Ibargi-ken 192
Idenburg-van de Poll, M. 321
Ienega, Saburo 29
Iizuka 202, 204
Ike, Nobutaka 29
Iloilo (Panay Island) 260
Imamura, Hitoshi 177
Imoshima Island, Subcamp No. 2 201
Imperial Army 353
Imperial General Headquarters 355, 356
Imperial Government 357
Imperial Rescript 22
Imperial War Museum 326, 368
Imura, Minoru 177
Ind, Allison 263
Indies, the 73, 82
Indochina 17, 127, 145
Ingelse, Tom 246
inquinal hernia 87
International Medical Conference, Brussels 102
International Military Tribunal for the Far East 5, 28, 48, 49, 50, 52, 113, 115, 119, 120, 122, 123, 124, 129, 185, 186, 216, 221, 234, 236, 247, 248, 265, 269, 295, 322, 325, 329, 330, 343, 344,
Iriye, Akira 29
Irwin, Wallace 19
Isa, Seizaburo 189
Ishigase 209
Ishigooka, Kozo 189
Ishii, Ryosuke 29

Ishizawa, Y. 24
Itagaki, Seishiro 114, 116, 177
IVe, IXe Battalion 303, 305, 307, 308, 309, 310, 312, 313, 315, 316, 317, 318
Iwamura, Seiichi 178
Iwo Jima 8
IXe, IXe Battalion 304

Jaarmarkt 299
Jackson, Daphne 64, 65, 299, 320, 321
Jacobi, Johan 78
Jacobs, An 294
Jacobs, Eugene C. 79, 107
Jacobs, G.F. 294
James, David H. 268
Jansen, Marius B. 29
Japan Sea 197, 198
Japanese Army Regulations for Handling Prisoners of War 353
Japanese Civilian Camps 232
Japanese Greater Asia Co-Prosperity Sphere 266
Japanese War Ministry 39
Jaranilla, D. 114
Jarrett, Hazel Jean 263
Java 8, 9, 10, 18, 27, 40, 45, 47, 64, 118, 128, 130, 143, 145, 150, 165, 172, 174, 175, 177, 184, 186, 244, 270, 273, 274, 278, 296, 299, 303, 304, 318, 319, 320, 322, 325, 328, 333, 334, 335, 338
Jay, John L. 70
Jeffrey, Betty 5, 75, 78, 268, 294
Jepara 311
Jervey, L.P. 107
Jesselton 326, 327
Jessfield Road Police Station 224
Joder, Richard F. 263
Johnson, Forrest B. 263
Johnson, Sheila K. 29
Jones, F.C. 29
Jones, General 256
Jones, Thomas C. 107
Junji, Kinoshita 123
Junyo Maru 159, 168

Kaaten, Tomohon 337
Kabahashi 220
Kachidoki Maru 159, 164, 168
Kagawa Christian Fellowship Home 194
Kaitak airfield 223
Kalibanteng 311, 319

Index

Kalitjeret 315
Kamakura Maru 49, 160, 168
Kamean Islands 165
kami 15
Kamioka 200
Kamiso Subcamp 190
Kamitan Kozan, Sendai No. 11 195
Kampar Kanan 272
Kampar Kanan River 275
Kampar Kiri River 271, 272, 276
Kampili 335, 338, 340
Kampong Baroe 282, 283
Kampong Makassar 303, 304, 305, 306, 307
Kan, chief of the Ordinance Bureau 36
Kan, Wim 246
Kanagawa 207
Kanagawa Kneko 195
Kanagawa Prefecture 116
Kanagawa Tokyo 2 194
Kanase, Shiro 178
Kanazawa 195
Kanchanaburi 238, 240, 242
Kandangan I 328
Kandangan II 328
Kanori, Sergeant Major 196
Kao Din 242
Karangpanas 311, 312, 313, 318
Karees 304, 305, 307, 313
Karenko, Formosa 10, 40, 215
Karikal 267
Karikal 2 267
Kariru 341
Karoe coal 277
Kashii Camp No. 1 202
Kashiide, Isamu 194
Katholieke Sociale Bond 286, 287
Kato, Masuo 29
Katz, C.J. 107
Katz, J. 107
Kaung Kluai 239, 241
Kaung Kluai—Lum Sum waterfalls 242
Kawarasan I 315, 317
Kawarasan II 315, 317
Kawasaki, Hisao 189
Kawasaki Camp—Kobe 200
Kawasaki Dispatch Camp No. 5 195
Kawasaki No. 1 195
Kawasaki Subcamp No. 2 195
Kaya, Okinori 114
Kazerne (Rabaul) 341
Kazerne I 329
Kazerne II 329
Keane, T.M. 107
Kebon Durian 271
Kebondjahe 283, 284
Kediri 317
Kedoe 311
Keehn, R. 107
Keeler, M.H. 107
Keelung 216
Keesing, Elizabeth 321
Keijo 218
Keischico 207
Keith, Agnes Newton 26, 29, 75, 78, 327, 330
Keizer-Heuzeveldt, H.E. 321
Kelnhofer, Guy 82, 85, 86, 98, 101, 131, 134
Kelnhofer, Maria 98, 99, 103
Kempeitai 4, 46, 76, 120, 122, 231, 261
Kendal 279, 280, 295
Kenichi Sonei 13
Kennedy, Jim 180, 325
Kennedy, Joseph 268
Kenny, Catherine 61, 107, 294, 343
Kent, Jim 268
Kenworthy, Aubrey 123
Kenyon, Albert 343
Kepahiang 289, 290, 293
Kerr, Bartlett E. 49, 107, 143, 144, 146, 154, 155, 156, 158, 161, 162, 163, 164, 165, 166, 167, 216, 221, 234, 263
Kesilir 303, 311, 315, 319, 322
Key, Barbara F. 91, 101
Keystal, H. 107
Kiangsu Middle School 224
Kiangwan 223, 224, 225
Kido, Koichi 114
Kieta, Bougainville Islands 7
Kilung, Formosa 155, 157
Kim, Jai-Hyup 29
Kimura, Heitaro 36, 114
King Kong Maru 160, 161, 168
Kingaseki 216
Kinhua 224
Kinney, L. 107, 108
Kinsayok 240, 242
Kirchman, Charles 123
Kita Cotygara 195
Kitaniban 208
Kitchner, I. 107
Klein, Hilel 107
Knight, R.B. 108
Knox, Donald 263
Kobe 195, 196, 209, 210
Kobe, Camp No. 31 200
Kobe, Divisional Camp 200
Kobe POW Hospital 195
Kochi 201

Kodama, Baron Hideo 10
Kodama, Yoshio 29
Koebang 275
Koengke 271
Koestler, Arthur 78
Koiso, Kuniaki 114, 176
Kokubu, Shinsichiro 177
Kokupo 334
Kolb, L.C. 108
Komakoi 243
Kondo, Shinji 368
Konkhuta 243
Konkoita 238, 239
Konyu 239, 240, 242
Kopanda, R.T. 110
Korea 38, 73, 116, 143, 144, 166, 173, 184, 218, 223
Korean Peninsula 20
Korner, Ija 58, 78
Korteweg, Captain 154, 160, 161, 165, 343
Kosaka 195
Koshian Hotel 200
Koshuyu 218
Kota Baru, East Malaya 7, 276
Kota Paris I 301, 304, 305
Kota Paris II 301, 305
Kota Paris III 300, 303, 305, 307
Kota Tjane 270, 271, 295
Kowloon Camp 223, 231
Koyagi Shima 202
Kraft, G.H. 108
Kral, V.A. 102, 108
Kramat I 301, 302, 309
Kramat II 301, 302, 305
Kramat III 301, 306
Kramer, Diet 321
Kramer, M. 107, 108
Kreung Krai 243
Krokos 33
Krol, V.A. 106, 108
Krystal, H. 108
Kualasimpang 279
Kuantan 272
Kuantan River 277
Kuching 323, 326, 327
Kuching, North Borneo 8, 46
Kui Ye 241
Kuiye Kuei 242
Kumamoto 204
Kun Kanta 243
Kuno, Yoshi Saburo 29
Kure 201
Kurihashi, chief of the Intelligence Bureau 36
Kurimata Maru 168, 333
Kuroda, Shigenori 177

Kurume 204
Kuta Alam 279, 280
Kutaradja 280
Kuyl, Arie 294
Kwai River 238
Kwantung 16
Kwantung Army 16
Kyandou 243
Kyaukme—School 248
Kyokko Maru 160, 168
Kyota—branches Hakata, Kaira 200
Kyoto 15
Kyushu, Japan 10, 202, 203
KZ Syndrome 88

Labrador, Juan 263
Lae Butar 278
Lael, Richard L. 123
Laha Airport 344
Lahey, Q.J. 108
Lai Chi Kok 223
Lake Buva 198
Lake Ogawahara 190
Lambert, Eric 268
Lampersari-Sompok 311, 312
Lande, J.J.A. v.d. 274
Lands Opvoedings Gesticht 297, 305
Langsa 279, 280
Las Piñas 251
Lasang 255
Lavie, P. 108
Lawesigalagala 271, 280, 295
Lawesigalagala I 280, 285
Lawesigalagala II 280, 285
Lawrence, Robert 343
Lawton, Manny 108, 155, 164, 165, 261, 263
Lay, John 84
Le Bourgeois, Jacques 236
Lebra, Joyce C. 29, 368
Lebra, Takie Sugiyama 30
Lee, Henry G. 80
Leffelaar, H.L. 246, 294
Leighton, A.H. 78
Lengkong 303, 307
LeQuesne, P.M. 108
Lesser Sunda Islands 333
Letarte, F. 108
Levenson, H. 108
Levering, Robert W. 263
Levie, Howard S. 52
Lewis, John R. 123, 368
Lhoseumawe 279
Liang (Ambon Island) 333
Liang Camps 344
Lifton, R.J. 108

Lin Cha Lu 224
Lincoln Avenue, West No. 4 229
Lindbergh, Charles 30
Lingayen Gulf, Philippines 156
Lingkas 329
Linnay (Bataan) 252
Linton, Ralph 78
Lipa (Batangas) 252
Lipatkain 276
Lipe, Frances Worthington 184
Lipton, Merrill 90, 101
Liquica 341
Lisbon Maru 164, 168, 223
Little, Herman A. 255
Livermore VA Medical Center 95
Loeboek-Ambatjan 276
Loeboeklinggau I 291
Loeboeklinggau I 293
Loeboeklinggau II 291, 293
Loeboeksakat 276
LOG 308
Loma Linda VA Hospital 92
Lombok Island 339
Lome Blankwaardt-van der Jagt 301
Lonnum, A. 106, 108
Lorry, Hillis 30
Los Angeles Times 20
Los Banos 47, 258, 259, 265
Lucas, Celia 263
Luff, John 234
Lumiere, Cornel 246, 268
Lumry, Gayle K. 91, 101
Lunghing 225
Lunghwa 173, 225, 229
Luyck-Sleyfer, J.A.A. 303
Luyckx, Ko 320, 321
Luzon 9, 161, 251, 255, 257, 258, 259
Lynch, Major 188
Lynip, G.L. 263

M.V. Building 286, 287
Ma Tan Chaung 223
MacArthur, Douglas 115, 180
MacArthur, Ross 246
MacBain, Alastair 78
McCall, J. 79, 80, 263
McClelland, James 247
McClure, J.N. 109
McCormac, Charles 269
McCoy, Alfred W. 30
McCoy, M.H. 79, 180, 186, 263
MacDonald, D.A. 104
McDougall, E.S. 114
McDougall, William H. 54, 59, 60, 294
McEachern, C.A. 239
MacGilavry, Annemarie 321
MacGregor, Gordon Scott 269
McGregor, John 4, 6, 269
McGregor, Rob 160
MacKay, Milton 246
McKeever, Philip 159
MacKenzie, Kenneth P. 248
McLaren, Jock 180, 325
McLellan, Jean M. 294
McNamara, J.O. 108
McQueen, E.G. 103
Madioen 316
Maibara 200 Maisure 200
Makassar 10, 161, 164, 172, 177, 210, 211, 297, 331, 332, 335, 336
Maki, John M. 30
Malabulay 255
Malacca Strait 158
Malang 9, 175, 319
Malaria 238
Malay 18, 128, 174, 179, 229, 237, 265, 267
Malaya 8, 9, 17, 21, 38, 44, 45, 55, 69, 73, 82, 127, 142, 143, 145, 173, 180, 182, 184, 186, 265, 267
Malino 335, 340
Malinta Tunnel Hospital 254
Mallal, Bashir A. 123
Mallory, P.F. 108
Malone, P. 106
Malseed, R.T. 109
Maltby, Major General 222
Manado, St. Jozef 336
Manchuko 16, 219
Manchuria 1, 9, 16, 38, 40, 73, 90, 116, 143, 144, 150, 157, 163, 173, 176, 182, 184, 204, 209, 216, 218, 219
Manders, Jo 321
Manes, Donald L. 50
Mangshih 225
Manila 7, 38, 42, 55, 117, 118, 154, 155, 156, 157, 158, 161, 162, 163, 166, 177, 254, 257, 258, 259
Manokwari 334, 337, 338
Maoemere 333
Marie, Jean 344
Marinekampement 308, 318
Marivales 255
Maros Maru 161, 168
Marshall Island 8
Marsman, Jan Hendrik 186, 234
Martaban Bay 163
Maslow, A.H. 79

Mason, J. 109
Mason, J.W. 109
Mason, W. Wynne 269
Mataram I 317, 339
Mataram II 339
Mater Dolorosa 304, 308
Matsui, Iwane 114
Matsumura, chief of the Army Press Bureau 36
Matsuoka, Yosuke 114
Matsusima 192
Matsuzaki, Akira 178
Mattbey, Paul 153
Matti Matti Maru 161, 168
Maydon, Captain 158, 159
Mayebassi Maru 160, 161, 168
Mayer, S.L. 30
Maymiyo—School 248
Medan, East Sumatra 8, 158, 270, 271, 273, 274, 277, 282, 285
MedSearch Committee 84
Meerlo, J. 109
Mei, Ju Ao 114
Meiji Restoration of 1867 15
Mekong River 238
Melbourne 170, 294
Mellman, T.A. 109
Mellnik, Steve 109, 186, 264
Meloewak 271
Menado, North Celebes 7
Menado Military Barracks 332
Meredith, W.P. 259
Merkel, W.C. 109
Merrill, Francis 78
Mesali 243
Meulaboh 279
Meulaboh Bireuen 280
Meyer, Elizabeth Thomas 264
Meyer, Hans 294
Michael, Maurice 33, 48, 51
Miki, Chief of the Surgeon General's Bureau 36
Mikio, Lieutenant General 37
Milanes, F.J. 109
Military Affairs Bureau (Japan) 36, 48
Military Personnel Records Center 264
Military Tribunal in Medan, East Sumatra 274
Miller, E.B. 162, 264
Miller, Minos D. 194, 212
Mimura, Gunichi 177, 178
Minami, Jiro 114
Minato-ku 200
Mindanao 180, 254, 255
Minear, Richard H. 118, 123

Minister of War (Japan) 357
Ministry of Army Notification No. 22 36
Ministry of Defense, Bureau of Military Affairs (Japan) 173
Ministry of Foreign Affairs (Japan) 45
Ministry of Internal Affairs (Japan) 173
Ministry of Overseas Territories (Japan) 173
Ministry of the Army (Japan) 36, 37
Ministry of War (Japan) 45, 355, 356
Miri 326
Mishima, Yukio 30
Missie Complex 286, 287, 288
Mito 195
Mitsu, Branch Camp No. 5 201
Mitsubishi Mining Company 197
Mitsuishi 190
Mitsuo Fuchida 18
Miyazaki, Kiyoshi 25
Miyazaki Ryohei 274
Miyazu 198
Miyoshi 210
Miyoshi I 206, 208, 210
Miyoshi II 210, 211
Mizonkuchi 195
Moearo 271, 272, 276, 277
Moearo-Pakanbaroe line 277
Moentilan 311, 313, 313, 316, 318
Moji 203
Moji Hospital 204
Moji No. 2 204
Moji No. 4 204
Moluccas 7, 8, 10, 160, 161, 165, 333
Montevideo Maru 161, 168
Montgomery, Brian 269
Moran, C. 109
Moreton, D.E. 269
Morgan, H.J. 109
Morioka 195
Morita, K. 109
Morley, James Williams 30, 368
Morris, Harold C. 101
Morris, Ivan 30
Morris, J. Newman 294
Morris, Lea 302
Morrison, S.E.
Mosley, Leonard 30
Moss, Lawrence R. 102
Mototerako 206, 208, 208
Motoyama, Subcamp No. 8 201
Moulein-Rangoon, Burma 162
Moulmein 10, 127, 160, 161, 167, 237, 238
Mount Juragaki 192
Mount Kinabalu 325

Index

Mowery, E. 52
MS Vynner Brooke 290
Mukaishima, Japan 40
Mukden, Manchuria 173, 219, 220
Muloschool 277, 308, 309, 316
Muntok (Banka Island) 292
Muntok I 290, 292
Muntok II 289, 290, 291, 292
Muntok III 290, 291, 292, 293
Murakami, Sachiko 195, 236
Muroran 190
Murphy, Supreme Court Justice 118
Murray, Major 188
Muto, Akira 36, 114
Muwazo, E.M.K. 111
Mydans, Carl 264
Myers, Hugh N. 50
Myers, Ramon H. 30
Myoshi 201
Mytho 235

Naaru 341
Nacama No. 21 204
Nagano, Osami 114
Nagano, Yosiuchi 177
Nagasaki, Senryu No. 24 204
Nagasaki 13, 166, 205, 211
Nagasaki No. 2 204
Nagasaki No. 4 204
Nagasaki No. 14 204
Nagasaki University 221
Nagato Maru 9, 161, 168
Nagoya 209
Nagoya, Subcamp No. 10 200
Nagoya Main Camp 200
Nakamura, Hajime 30, 36, 111
Nakamura, Toshihisa 177, 178
Nakao, Unesaku 189
Nakhon Pathom 242
Namajon 243
Nanada, Ichiro 178
Nanazawa 208
Nanking 230
Narashino Airport 195
Nardini, John E. 92, 102, 109
Narumi, Nagoya Subcamp No. 2 200
Nason, Joseph G. 343
Nasugbu 252
National Archives 141
National Ex-Prisoners of War Association 133
National Park Service 136, 137
National Prisoner of War Museum 137

National Research Council 141
Natoru Maru 162, 168
Naung Pattaya 244
Naval POW Camp 224
Ndona 335, 340
Nealis, Perry M. 102
Nefzger, M.D. 109
Negishi 207
Neilen, M. 294
Nelson, David 269
Nelson, Gordon 264
Nelson, Hank 294
Nelson, Rachel E. 99, 103
Nerac, Eleanore 79
Netherlands 49
Netherlands Institute of War Documentation 28, 144
Netzorg, Morton J. 368
Neumann, H. 294
neuropathy, peripheral 85, 87, 95
New Britain 19, 82, 143, 161, 162, 207, 334, 344
New Caledonia 19
New Guinea 7, 8, 118, 166, 334, 335, 339, 341, 344
New Zealand 1, 17, 114
Newman, P.H. 58, 79
Newman, Samuel A. 50, 80
Newsberg, Alan 80
Newsweek 27, 28
Newton Keith, Agnes 327, 330
Ngawi 316
Nias Island 280, 281
Nichols airfield 9, 251, 253
Niederland, W.G. 108, 109
Nielson airfield 9, 253
Nieuwenhuis, Rob 321
Nihonjiron 17
Niigata 193
Niihama, Branch Camp No. 2 201
Niizuma, Kinsaburo 189
Nikki/Nieke 243
Nimoto, Captain 192
92nd Garage 254
Ningkuo Road 228, 230
Nisho, Hidemi 177
Nissyo Maru 162, 168
Nitimei Maru 10, 163, 168
Nitobe, Inazo Ota 30
Nitta Maru 162, 168
Nixon, Thomas 133, 134
Noell, Livingstone, P., Jr. 179
Nogeyama Park 195
Nomura, Naokuni 176
Non Pladuk 242
Nooetzu Camp 195

Norman, Diana 269
Norquist, Ernest 109, 264
North Borneo 1, 7, 8, 26, 45, 46, 75, 76, 180, 184, 187, 323, 325, 326
North Celebes 7, 336, 337
North Point Camp 223
North Sumatra 270, 278, 295
Northcroft, E.H. 114
Noto Maru 163, 168
Notogawa 198
Noyes, R., Jr. 109
Numata, Takazo 177
Nuremberg 113, 119

Obourn, Robert L. 90, 95, 101, 102
Ocean Island 341
O'Connor, Michael 76, 78, 269, 330
Odate 195
Odawara 207
O'Donnell 144
Oeyama, Osaka 198
Ofeigsen-Takes, Annie 73, 80, 321
Ofuna 195
Ohama, Subcamp No. 9 201
Ohashi 195
Ohkochi, Denshichi 177
Oka, Takasuni 114
Okawa, Shumei 114
Okayama 210
Okazaki 209
Okazaki, Seisaburo 177
Old Bilibid 259
Old City Hall 195
Old Dutch Fort Marlborough 289
Oliver, William P. 264
Omine, Subcamp No. 6 201
Omori 194
Omori Main Camp 194
Omuta, Camp 17 203
Onada, Branch Camp No. 8 201
Onada, Branch Camp No. 9 201
134th Depot Battalion 297
O'Neill, J.C. 104
Onodo, Hiroo 30
Onorato, Michael P. 264, 368
Onuma, Y. 115, 118
Op ten Noort 8, 210, 332
O'Reilly, Patrick 344
Oryoku Maru 156, 157, 163, 168, 202
Osaka 9, 196, 197, 198, 200
Osaka Mainichi 21
Osaka No. 1 Headquarters Camp 200
Oshima, Hiroshi 114
Ota, Colonel 63
Otaru 190

Outram Road Gaol 4
Owen, Roger 247
Oyama, Chief of the Legal Affairs Bureau 36

Pacific Islands 1
Pacific War 20
Padang 47, 272, 273
Padang, West Sumatra 8, 158, 267, 286
Padang Tarap 277
Padangpandjang 286, 287
Padangsidempoean 281, 283, 284
Pakanbaroe 159, 271, 272, 273, 275, 276, 277, 286, 295
Pakanbaroe I 286
Pakanbaroe II 286
Pakanbaroe Railroad 271, 275
Pakkai 222
Paksha Kong 222
Pal, R.B. 114
Pal, Radhabinod 123
Palace Hotel 306, 308
Palau Islands 166, 334
Palauberajan D 282, 283 Palauberajan E 282, 283
Palawan 255
Palawan airfield 9
Palawan Barracks 255
Palawan Island 118, 255
Palembang 7, 273
Palembang, South Sumatra 277, 290
Palembang City 292
Palembang Gevangenis 292
Pan American Airways 142
Panay Incident 265
Pandungan 326, 327
Pangkalpinang, Banka Island 292
Pangkalpinang I 292
Pangkalpinang II 292, 293
Pangoeroean 281, 283, 284
Pangoran 284, 285, 285
Parañaque 251
Parepare 335, 336, 338, 340
Parfitt, Iris 69, 80
Park, S. 110
Park Avenue 253
Park Central Camp 195
Park Central Stadium 195
Parkin, Ray 247
Parkinson's disease 96
Pasay 253
Pasig River 251
Pasir Andir 306
Patrick, Lord 114
Paul, H. 109

Pavillard, Stanley 59, 72, 245, 247, 269
Paxton, L. 247
Peacock, Basil 247
Pearl Harbor 7, 23, 117, 150, 151, 205, 257
Peattie, Mark R. 30
Peiping, Tientsin 226, 227
Peiping Segregation Center 227
Pekalongan 309
Peking 13, 225
pellagra 85, 87, 94, 96
Pelletier, Lawrence L. 109
Pematangsiantar I 281, 283, 285, 295
Pematangsiantar II 281, 283, 285
Penang, West Malaya 7, 10
Peoples, Shavey 73
Percival, Arthur Ernest 18
Perry, Matthew 15
Pete, P.W. 254, 262, 264
Peterson, Richard W. 61
Philippine Department, U.S. Army, Machine Records Unit 144
Philippine Red Cross 250
Philippines 2, 7, 8, 9, 13, 17, 18, 21, 36, 38, 40, 45, 54, 60, 61, 63, 72, 73, 82, 83, 89, 90, 114, 143, 144, 145, 150, 154, 156, 157, 164, 167, 173, 174, 180, 182, 183, 184, 193, 250, 257
Phnom Penh 235
Piccigallo, Philip 124
Piekaar, A.J. 294
Pingfan 220
Pitts, F.N. 109
Pladjoe 290
Pladjoe, Oil Town 290
Poe, R.O. 109
Poerwokerto 310
Pokong 222
Pollard, E.G.F. 189
polyneuritis 85
Pomalaa 331, 332
Pontianak, West Borneo 7, 327
Poole, Philippa 247, 269
Pootung 173, 229
Pootung, China 3
Port Otaru 211
Port Terminal Building 251
Portuguese Timor 340, 341
Poso 332
Post, R.M. 110
Post-Traumatic Stress Disorder 89, 90, 91
Postman, Leo 78
Potsdam 13
Potsdam Declaration 113

Pounder, Thomas 247
POW MedSearch 88
Poweleit, Alvin C. 95, 102
Powell, J.W. 27, 124, 221
Powell, Robert 162
Power Station 224
Prafi River Camp 334
Prafirivier 338
Preliminary Camp I 280
Preliminary Camp II 280
Prescott, Peter S. 27, 28
Prichard, Rosemary 79
Prisoner of War Information Bureau (Japan) 35, 358
Prisoner of War Medal 131
Prisoner of War Resistance: U.S. Army Field Manual No. 21-78 361
Prisoners of War Bulletin (American Red Cross) 42, 49, 78, 200
Pritchard, R. 124
Probert, H.A. 269
Provoosthuis 286, 287
Puckett, Albert 254
Pulauberajan 282
Pulauberajan A, B, and C 282, 284, 286
Pulauberajan D 286
Puruktjau 328
Pusan, Korea 166
Putussibau 330
PWIB 36

Rabao 243
Rabaul, New Britain 82, 161, 206, 334, 341, 343
Rabaul, New Guinea 7, 118
Radiostraat 329
Rama 307
Ramale 341
Ramsey, Winston G. 247
Ranau 325
Rangoon (Burma) 8, 62, 167, 237, 248
Rangoon Prison 244
"Rangoon Ritz" 244
Ransom, John 3
Rapang 332
Ravaris, C.L. 110
Rawlings, Leo 69, 80
Red Cross 9, 41, 44, 48, 51, 174, 187, 189, 196, 197, 205, 208, 212, 215, 218, 222, 224, 226, 249, 250, 265, 295
Redford, Larry H. 124
Redjosari 316
Redmond, D.E., Jr. 110

Redmond, Juanita 264
Reed, Emil P. 87, 101
Reede, Theo Wilton 321
Reel, Adolf Frank 117, 118, 123, 124
Reid, A. 80
Reid, Caroline 269
Reid, Dr. 98
Reid, J.A.G. 105
Reid, Pat 33, 48, 51
Reid-Collins, Lieutenant Colonel 47
Reif, A. 110
Reischauer, Edwin O. 30
Renes-Boldingh, M.A.M. 321
Rengat, West Sumatra 288
Rengat I 286, 288
Rengat II 287, 288
Repatriation of Allied Prisoners of War and Internees (RAPWI), The 44
Reports Liaison and Research Branch POW Information 234
Retpu 243
Reuter, James B. 263
Reynolds, Quentin 186, 232, 233
Riau Archipelago 267
Richards, J.G. 110
Richardson, Hal 186, 330
Rijkhoek, D. 295
Rijksinstituut voor Oorlogsdocumentatie; Amsterdam, Indonesian Collection 6868 28, 50, 52, 130, 153, 157, 158, 185, 247, 250, 265, 293, 295, 319, 320, 322, 330, 342, 343
Rin Tin 241, 242
Rinko 193
Rinzema, Wim 321
Rio de Janeiro Maru 164, 168, 331
Ripley, H.S. 112
Rivett, Rohan D. 74, 160, 241, 245, 247, 366
Roberson, Robie 73
Roberts, R.G. 246
Robinett, George 165
Robinson, John J. 103
Rodriguez, Helen 248
Rohan River 241
Roku Roshi 198
Rokyo Maru 164, 168
Röling, B.V.A. 114, 115, 117, 122, 124
romushas 9, 10
Ronshii 243
Roosevelt, Theodore 18, 19, 20
Rosenzweig, Saul 79
Ross, Tom 259
Roxy 267
Rue Jean Eudal 235
Ruff, George E. 110

Rukke 242
Rundell, James Jay 102
Russell, F.P. 110
Russell, John F. 92, 101
Russell, Lord of Liverpool 50, 160, 161, 162, 165, 166, 216, 247, 264, 330, 342, 343
Russo-Japanese War of 1904–05 16
Ruter, C.F. 117, 122, 124
Ryan, Thomas F. 234
Rykes, P.S. 239
Ryukyu Maru 164, 168

Sabang 279, 280
Saigon 17, 45, 176, 177, 234, 235
Saigon Docks 235
St. Franciscus I 210, 211
St. Franciscus II 211
St. Josef School 282, 283, 285
St. Jozef, Manado (North Celebes) 336
St. Walterus, Tomohon 337
Saitawa 208, 209
Saito, Masatoshi 174
Saito, Yaheita 153, 162, 177
Saiyoku 242
Sakai, Saburo 30
Sakai Prison 201
Sakurajima 196
Sakurajima Ichioka School 196
Salin, Leon 295
Salvation Army 227
Samal Naval Base 222
Samarinda, East Borneo 328
Sambas, West Borneo 327, 328
Samoa 19
Samshuipo 221, 222, 223
San Fernando, the Philippines 157
Sandakan 1, 180, 325, 326
Sandakan Death March 323
Sandilands, John 295
Santa Anita 25
Santo Tomas internment camp 2, 25, 65, 67, 183, 254, 257, 258, 259, 260, 261, 264, 265
Sapar 277
Saphir, O. 110
Sappo Penitentiary 190
Sasebo 205
Sato, Kenryo 36, 114
Saunders, Lieutenant 72, 73
Sawahloento 272, 288
Sawahloento I 286, 288
Sawahloento II 287, 288
Sawannaket 235
Schaffer, William 90

Index

Schlesinger, P. 110
Schmieder, R.E. 110
Schofner, Austin 180
Scholten, P. 221
Schoonenberg, Bernard 110, 130, 275, 293, 295, 321
Schroeder, Phyllis 98, 103
Schwartz, Otto C. 103
Scolossberg, A. 110
Scott, G.I. 110
scurvy 96
Seagrave, Gordon S. 247
Searle, Ronald 69, 80
Second Washington Conference 10
Segal, H.A. 110
Seibo 207
Sekiguchi 195, 206, 207
Selarang 266
Selarang incident 266
Semarang 9, 311
Semmeling, L. 247
Sendai 208
Sendai Camp 190
Senryu 205
sensorineural deafness 94
Sentono Pande 308, 317
Seoul, Korea 38
Serang 300
Serawak 325
Serawak River 327
Serdangkwartier 282
Seto Inland Sea 150
Seyle, H. 110
Shadish, William R. 85, 101
Shaffer, Laurance 79
Shanghai 9, 13, 46, 160, 162, 164, 173, 224, 225, 227, 228, 229, 230, 232, 342
Shanghai Group 224
Shanghai's Bund 229
Shangkiakai 225
Shantung Group 225
Sharp, John Charles 368
Sheehan, D.V. 110
Sheffield, Robert 149
Shen, W.W. 110
Sheridan, R.E. 79
Shibata, Yaichiro 178
Shibaura 195
Shigemitsu, Mamoru 30, 114, 176
Shimada, Shigetaro 114, 176
Shimodate 195
Shimomago Hitachi 195
Shimomura, Sadamu 176
Shimonseki 201
Shimorejogakuen II 211
Shimura, Funio 177

Shinagawa Main Camp 195
Shinei 220
Shingu 200
Shinhlushan 222
Shinjuku Camp No. 1 195
Shinsei Maru 160, 164, 168
Shinto 15, 16
Shinyo Maru 164, 168, 255
Shirakawa 215, 216
Shiratori, Toshio 114
Shiro Ishii 220
Shiroyama 206, 209, 211
Shizuoka 195
Short, Stanley W. 234
Shozo Yamamoto 295
Shulman, Frank Joseph 368
Siak River 274
Siam 18, 40, 46, 73, 143, 145, 173, 179, 184, 237, 243, 249
Siam-Burma 240
Siam-Burma railroad 75
Siam—Non Pladuk 241
Sibolga, West Sumatra 280
Sibolga I 280, 281, 283
Sibolga II 281, 283
Signal Lines—Homes 248
Silberman, Bernard S. 30
Simard, P. 108
Sime Road 46
Sime Road Camp 69, 266, 267, 268
Simmonds, J.P. 106
Simons, Jessie Elizabeth 83, 101, 295
Simons, R. 110
Sindangan Point 165
Sing Sing Prison 266
Singapore 7, 8, 9, 10, 17, 18, 32, 38, 40, 44, 56, 58, 61, 74, 127, 128, 142, 150, 154, 155, 156, 157, 158, 159, 160, 161, 163, 164, 165, 166, 167, 173, 174, 177, 182, 184, 238, 240, 265, 267, 268, 269, 271, 273, 290
Singapore Maru 165, 168
Singaradja 335, 339 Singer, Kurt 30
Singkawang, West Borneo 327
Singkel 278, 279
Siringoringo 285, 286
Sissons, D.C.S. 124
Skelton, William P. 95, 102, 110
Skidmore, Ian 180, 187, 269
Skvorzov, A.V. 80
Sleeman, Colin 166, 344
Smethurst, Richard J. 30
Smit, H. 321
Smith, Mabel Waln 3, 5, 234
Smith, William A. 79
Smyth, Sir John 295
Sneddon, I.B. 105

Sneed, Bessie 61, 79, 264
Soé 336, 340, 341
Soebang, Java 118
Soekaboemi 308
Soekamiskin 297
Soembawa Island 339
Soemowono 313, 315
Soengai Geroe 277
Soengai Pagar 276
Soengai Sengkol 270, 277
Soerabaja, Dutch East Indies 154, 172, 175, 317, 318, 319
Soerabaja, East Java 160, 161, 165, 172, 299, 339
Soerakarta 310, 315
Solomon Islands 19, 341
Sommers, Stanley G. 61, 84, 88, 101
Sompok Lama 306, 311
Sonkurai 239, 241
Sorokin, P.A. 65, 79
South Borneo 8, 184, 326, 328
South Burma 8, 248
South Celebes 8, 10, 161, 164, 177, 210, 297, 331, 335, 336
South China 230
South French Indo China 24
South Sumatra 7, 289, 290, 291
Southeast Asia 1, 19, 31, 53, 127, 171, 175, 215, 237, 266, 314
Sparrow, Gerald 250
Spies, T.D. 110
Spillane, J.D. 110
spondylosis 94
Sprague, H.B. 111
Springer, R. 334
Sprod, George 80, 269
Spurlock, Paul E. 124
Srichaikul, T. 111
SS *President Harrison* 224
Staal, M. van der 30
Stahl, Alfred 70, 80
Stanley 231
Stanley Camp 223
Stanley Gaol: Hong Kong 231
Steel, Ray 180, 325
Steele, Benjamin Charles 69
Stella Maris 305, 306, 308, 322
Stenger, Charles 51, 111
Stevens, Curtis R. 264
Stevens, Fred 74, 79, 261, 262, 264
Stevenson, Theodore D. 264
Steyl, P.A.A. 343
Stibbe, Philip 248
Stollerman, G.H. 103
Stonington, Connecticut 149
Storry, Richard 30

Story, Luther H. 136
Stovil 337, 338
Strachan, H. 111
Strassman, Harvey D. 102, 111
Strom, A. 103, 111
Struiswijk I 300, 306
Struiswijk II 300
Struiswijk III 300, 306
Struiwijk 299
Sturton, Stephen Douglas 227, 228, 233, 234
Subano, Sergeant Major 190
Subcamp No. 12 205
Suez Maru 165, 168, 333
Sugamo Jail 205
Sugiyama, Field Marshal 176
Sukamiskin 305, 308, 309, 310
Sumatra 8, 37, 40, 45, 47, 61, 128, 130, 145, 174, 177, 184, 237, 269, 270, 272, 278, 279, 292, 293, 295
Sumba Island 339
Sumbawa Island 339
Sumidagawa 195
Sumirejogakuen I 206, 208, 209
Sumirejogakuen II 206, 208
Sumitomo Concern 209
Sumitomo Industries 209
Sumiyoshi-ku 201
Summers, Stephen 52
Sungai Sengkol 295
Sungaipenuh, West Sumatra 288
Sungaipenuh I 286, 288
Sungaipenuh II 287, 288
Sungaisengkol 283, 284, 285, 286
Sunkurai 243
Suzuki, Kantaro 176
Suzuki, Kunji 37
Suzuki, Teiichi 114
Suzuki Aio No Moto Factory 195
Suzurandai 201
Swatow 225
Sweeting, A.J. 170
Swiss Consul 227
Swiss Consulate 226
Swiss Legation 208, 209
Szepingkai 220

Ta Hsi Lu No. 65 224
Tacoblan (Leyte Island) 260
Tada, Takeo 177, 178
Taga Maru 165, 168
Taichu 216
Taiden 218
Taihoku 216
Taiohoku Camp No. 2 216

Index 391

Takaaki, Michael 120
Takadanobaba 195
Takahashi, K. 111
Takamen/Dha Kanun 242
Takao, Formosa 156, 157, 158, 166
Takao Harbor, Formosa 163
Takasu, Shiru 177, 178
Takengon 279
Takeuchi, Tatsuji 30
Takhahashi, Ibo 177
Takikawa 188, 189
Talang Soemoet 290, 291
Talukbetung I 292
Talukbetung III 292
Tamaja/Tomajo 243
Tamano, Branch Camp No. 3 201
Tamarkan 242
Tamasata 215
Tambaya 243
Tambelan Islands 7
Tampi/Tampines 242
Tamuron Pato 243
Tanabe, Moritake 177
Tanagawa 201
Tanahtinggi 300, 302, 303, 307, 311, 318
Tanaka, Chikagu 30, 36
Tanforan 25
Tangerang I 303, 308, 319
Tangerang II 301, 302, 303, 318, 322
Tango Maru 165, 168
Tangsi Perlindungan 312, 313
Tanjoengbalai 282, 283, 284, 285
Tanjoengbalai I 284
Tanjoengbalai II 284, 286
Tanjoengmorawa 282, 283
Tantui I 337, 338
Tantui II 337, 338
Tapon/Won Yen 242
Tarakan, East Borneo 7, 13, 329
Tarawa 341
Tarkilen/Ta Ki len 242
Tarlac 253
Taroetoeng, East Sumatra 281, 283, 284
Tarsao 240, 242
Tasikmalaja, West Java 172
Tatamiyasho 209
Tatsatu Maru 49
Tauna 242
Taungzun 243
Tavoy 248
Taylor, Lawrence 124, 256, 262, 264
Taylor, Vince 264

Tazang Motor Road 224
Tebingtinnggi I 283
Tebingtinnggi II 282, 283
Tegal 309
Teia Maru 49
Teimonta 243
Teling 336
Telukbetung, South Sumatra 291
Telukbetung I 291
Telukbetung II 291, 292
Telukbetung III 291, 293
Telukbetung IV 292
Ten Points, The 18
Tengchung 225
Teniya Park Stadium 190
Tenno 26
Tenryu River 192
Teratakboeloeh 275
Terauchi, Hisaichi 45, 174, 176, 185
ter Poorten, H. 153
Terry, Carol 79, 264
Tettoko 243
Texas 131st Field Artillery Regiment 298
Tha Muang 242
Tha Phra Chandr 249, 250
Thames Maru 166, 168, 334
Thanbyuzayat, Burma 8, 237, 239, 241, 242, 243, 244
Theorell, T. 111
Thomas, Mary 56, 64, 74, 269
Thomas, P.K. 111
Thompson, Eliza 321
Thompson, William J. 137
Three Pagoda Pass 127, 238
Thygeses, P. 111
Tientsin 225, 226
Tietz, E.I. 111
Timor Island 164, 333, 340
Tindo, Lieutenant 188
Tinduk Mine 222
Tipton, Laurence 228, 233, 234
Tjideng 9, 10, 13, 298, 301, 302, 303, 304, 322
Tjihapit 10, 13, 322
Tjihapit I 300, 301, 302, 303, 306, 307, 311
Tjihapit II 306, 307
Tjikoedapateuh 300, 301, 305, 306, 307, 308, 309, 311, 312, 315, 317, 318
Tjilatjap 175, 181, 296, 297
Tjimahi 172, 296, 307, 308
Tjitjalengka 307
Tjitjalengka Work Camp 306, 308

Tobata 202
Tochan/Tonsha Spring 242
Todanstraat 304, 309
Togo, Shigenori 114, 176
Tojo 36, 37, 48, 114, 115, 176
Tokyo 8, 9, 15, 18, 35, 36, 37, 38, 113, 114, 115, 116, 117, 118, 125, 174, 186, 192, 194, 205, 206, 209, 221, 223, 326
Tokyo Bay 194
Tokyo War Crimes Trial 1, 113, 150
Tokyo War Ministry 22
Toland, John 4, 6, 30
Tomakomai 190
Tominago, chief of the Personnel Bureau 36
Tomohoku Maru 166, 168
Tomohon 337
Toshimi, Yoshiaki 221
Toshina, Fusutaro 178
Totsuka 207, 208
Tottori Maru 9, 166, 168
Toyama 195
Toyama Maru 166, 168
Toyofuku Maru 157
Toyoka 201
Tradewind 159
Trager, Frank N. 247
Trapper, Charles 247
Treinkampement 307, 308
Tripa River 270
Trowell, H.C. 111
Truk 341
Tsingtao 226
Tsingtao CIC 226
Tsukada, Osamu 177
Tsuneishi, Kei-ichi 221
Tsuruga 198
Tsurumi, Kazuko 30
Tsurumi, Shumsuke 30
Tsurumi Subcamp No. 5 195
Tuckerman, Ingeborg 79, 321
Tuddenham, R.D. 104
Tulischus, Otto D. 30
Tullipan, Ray 80
Tung Na Talea 242
Tung Tung 242
Turnbull, Stephen R. 30
Tutorow, Norman E. 119, 124, 368
Tuy Air Force Base 253

U.S.S. *Paddle* 255
Ube, Subcamp No. 7 201
Uemura, Michael Takaaki 368
Umeda Bonshu 196

Umeda Maru 166, 168
Umemura, Michael Takaaki 123
Umezu, Yoshijiro 114, 176
Unie Kampong 281, 283, 284, 285, 295
United Nations 142
United Nations Commission for the Investigation of War Crimes 9
United States 1, 4, 7, 16, 17, 18, 19, 22, 23, 24, 25, 35, 42, 51, 52, 73, 83, 113, 114, 118, 131, 136, 145, 155, 160, 185, 201, 264
United States Armed Forces Code of Conduct 359
United States Army 162
United States Army Air Corps 162
United States Army Air Force 179
United States Army Center of Military History 368
United States Department of Defense 141
United States Department of State 35, 351
United States Merchant Marine 141
United States Naval Historical Center, Navy Yard, Washington, DC 170
United States War Department 187
Uozumi, Second Lieutenant 190
Uraga 195
Urawa 208
Urawa Saitama 206
Ursano, Robert Joseph 102
Ursulinen 300, 304
USS *Bonefish* 165
USS *Grouper* 160
USS *Houston* 298, 331
USS *Missouri* 13
USS *Paddle* 165
USS *Pampanito* 159
USS *Perch* 331
USS *Pope* 331
USS *Sealion* 164
USS *Snook* 155
USS *Tang* 166
USS *Wake* 224
Utashinai 189
Utinsky, Margaret 123, 257, 262
Utsonomiya 195
Uyemura, General 37
Uywake 195

VA Medical Center in Long Beach, California 95
Vajiravudh 249, 250

Index

Valkenburg, Rik 343
Vance, John R. 264
van den Boogaard, W. 320
van der Kolk, B.A. 111
Vander Londen, D.A. 247, 321
van der Post, Laurens 116, 123, 321
van Dijk, Fokke N.J. 295
van Empel, Lennie 320
van Engelenburg, Dick 321
van Heekeren, C. 293, 295
van Hoogstraten, J.E. 24
van Kleffens, E.N. 24
van Mook, H.J. 24
van Sprang, Alfred 321
van Starkenborg Stachouwer, Tjarda 153
van Velden, D. 49, 50, 51, 52, 145, 146, 211, 218, 221, 232, 234, 236, 250, 264, 269, 295
van Witsen, E. 170, 246, 294
Varley, H. Paul 30
Vaughan, Elizabeth Head 51, 54, 56, 57, 59, 60, 61, 62, 64, 67, 260, 262, 264
Vedder, E.B. 111
Veenstra, J.H.W. 344
Vermeer-van Berkum, Carla 322
Verzlaff, Ulrich 103
Veterans Administration 85, 86, 88, 91, 105, 108, 111
Veterans Administration Medical Centers 91
Victor, M. 111
Vincentius 304
Vitale, J.J. 111
Volckman, R.W. 264
Vonk, Corry en Wim Kan 322
Vredenburgh 308, 310, 317
Vunapope 341

Wackwitz, J.G. 319, 322
Wagner, Charlie 180, 325
Wagner, Dorothy 78, 79
Waingapu 335
Waingapu I 335, 339
Waingapu II 340
Wainwright, Jonathan M. 204, 221, 253, 264
Wakasa Bay 198
Wakasen 195
Wakayama 201
Wake Island 7, 8, 17, 18, 82, 118, 132, 142, 143, 162, 190, 202, 206, 342, 343
Waldron, Ben D. 170, 264
Walker, J.I. 111, 227

Wallace, Walter 180, 187, 325, 329, 330
Wallebout Bay, New York 149
Walter, Jenny 233
Wan Po 242
War Crimes Investigators 116
War Ministry (Japan) 9
War Prisoner Control Bureau 36, 37
Ward, Bishop 227
Ward, Robert S. 30
Ward Road Gaol: Shanghai 232
Warmer, Joh. A.G. 322
Warner, Lavinia 295
Webb, William 114
Wegale 243
Weihsien 173, 226, 227
Weills Maru 167, 168
Weinstein, Alfred M. 264
Weishian, China 47
Weiss, S. 111
Werfstraat 303, 318
Werfstraat II 316, 318
Werfstraat III 306, 318
Wertheim, W.F. 144, 146
West Borneo 7, 8, 184, 323, 326, 327, 328
West Java 7, 9, 10, 13, 158, 160, 164, 167, 172, 175, 209, 297, 298, 300, 307
West Java, XVe Battalion Camp in Bandoeng 296
West Malaya 7, 10
West New Guinea 8
West Sumatra 8, 158, 267, 280, 286, 288
Whangpoo 229
White, Norman S. 89, 90, 101
White River Junction, Vermont 91
Wijk 310, 312, 315, 318
Wijngaard, Maria 80
Wiley, James 136
Wilke, G. 111
Wilkins, R.W. 111
Wilson, J.D. 112
Wilson, W.P. 105
Wilson, William Scott 30
Wiltshire 329
Windehsi 334
Winnovich, Karen 119
Wiringgi 334
Wirz, Henry 135
Wohfeld, Mark M. 253
Wolf, S. 112
Wolff, C.T. 112
Woman's Relief Corps 136
Wong Yai 242
Woning 326

Woodward, Theodore 88, 101
Woodworth, Robert S. 60, 79
Woosung 223, 224, 225, 342
Woosung Forts 225
Wozniak, Larry W. 198
Wright, John M., Jr. 170, 264
Wun Lun/Wang Lan 242

Xe Battalion Camp 296
Xth Battalion 298
XVe Battalion Camp Bandoeng, West Java 296
XVe Infantry Battalion Barracks 296

Yacht Club I 207
Yacht Club II 207
Yahagi, Major General 177
Yamada, Lieutenant 196
Yamakita 207
Yamamoto, Moichiro 177
Yamamoto, Tsunetomo 30
Yamashita, General 117, 118
Yamashita Camp No. 1 195
Yamato 15, 23
Yamato Camp (Babel Thuap Island) 334
Yamatoist Japanese 20
Yang Chow, Nanking 230
Yang Chow A 230
Yang Chow B 230
Yang Chow C 230
Yangtze River 230
Yashu Maru 167, 168
Yaumati Jail 223
Yawata, Camp No. 3 205

Yinagata Maru 160, 161, 167, 168
Yodagawa Bunsho 201
Yokkaichi 201
Yokohama 207, 208, 211
Yokohama No. 5 195
Yomai, Mitsumasa 176
Yonago 201
Yoshida 331
Yoshida Maru 156, 167, 168
Yoshihara, Tadashi 247
Yoshizawa, Kenkichi 24
Yost, J. 112
Young, Eunice F. 5
Yu Yuen Road, West No. 1 228, 230
Yumoto, John M. 30
Yunan Group 225
Yura 201

Zablan Field 252
Zaid Rock Road 327
Zaide, John 124
Zaide, Sonia 124
Zamboanga 167
Zamboanga, Mindanao Island, Philippines 164
Zaryanov, I.M. 114
Zeelandia 306, 308
Zentsuji, Subcamp No. 3 201
Zentsuji Headquarters Camp 201
Zich, Arthur 30
Ziegler, Janet 368
Ziekenzorg 316
Ziekenzorg I 310, 316
Ziekenzorg II 310, 312, 313, 318
Zikawei 224
Zusters Missionarissen 343